BITTER PILLS

ALSO BY STEPHEN FRIED

THING OF BEAUTY
The Tragedy of Supermodel Gia

BITTER PILLS

Inside the Hazardous
World of Legal Drugs

STEPHEN FRIED

Bantam Books

NEW YORK TORONTO LONDON SYDNEY AUCKLAND

BITTER PILLS

A Bantam Book

PUBLISHING HISTORY

Bantam hardcover edition / April 1998
Bantam trade paperback edition / May 1999

BOOK DESIGN BY DANA TREGLIA.

ISBN-13: 978-0-553-37852-8

Published simultaneously in the United States and Canada

Bantam Books are published by Bantam Books, a division of Random
House, Inc. Its trademark, consisting of the words "Bantam Books" and
the portrayal of a rooster, is Registered in the U.S. Patent and
Trademark Office and in other countries. Marca Registrada. Bantam
Books, 1540 Broadway, New York, New York 10036.

PRINTED IN THE UNITED STATES OF AMERICA

BVG 10 9 8 7 6 5 4 3

To my wife,
DIANE AYRES

BITTER PILLS is a work of investigative and personal journalism. Although it raises some frightening questions about legal drugs—I know they scare me—the book is meant to help reform the system and inform your choices when using medications, not to scare you out of taking them at all.

Suddenly halting the use of a safe drug can be more deadly than taking a so-called "dangerous" drug. Please do not do it. Read the book, talk to your doctors, and if they don't seem to understand why you want to know more about your own medical care, get new doctors. Get to know your pharmacists and nurses, consider a consultation with a clinical pharmacologist. And when asked what drugs you take, make sure you include all nonprescription medicines. Improperly used, they can kill you, too.

But always remember that we as medical consumers are part of the problem. Drug companies and doctors often make decisions based on the assumption that we are too dumb to understand the medications we're given. Don't prove them right.

CONTENTS

"Fortunately, a surgeon who uses the wrong side
of the scalpel cuts his own fingers and not the patient.
If the same applied to drugs, they would have been
investigated very carefully a long time ago."

DR. RUDOLPH BUCHHEIM,
the father of pharmacology, 1847

"Here was the medicine, the patients died
And no one asked: Who thrived?
So have we with hellish electuaries
In these valleys, these mountains,
Raged worse than any plague.
I have myself given the poison to thousands.
They withered, I must live to see
The impudent murderers praised."

**FROM *FAUST* BY
JOHANN WOLFGANG VON GOETHE (1831);**
*as recited by Widikund Lenz—the German physician who
first linked thalidomide to birth defects—at the
Kyoto International Conference against
Drug-Induced Sufferings, April 1979*

PROLOGUE

I t began with a pill. One pill.

My wife's gynecologist gave her samples of a new antibiotic to treat a urinary tract infection so minor, she didn't even know she had it. The doctor told her to take this new wonder drug twice a day for three days.

Your doctor gives you a pill, you take it. When I left for work the next morning, I said good-bye to Diane as she swallowed the first pale yellow oval tablet with breakfast.

Six hours later I was bringing her, delirious, to the emergency room. Our lives haven't been the same since.

Diane called me at work several hours after she took that pill and said she felt strange. I knew something was *really* not right, because my wife comes from a long line of "it's just a flesh wound" stoics who underreact to all physical discomfort. She said she was disoriented and hallucinating. Her mouth was dry, and she felt tingling in her left arm and hand. She was having trouble talking.

After we spoke, she found herself wandering around in her small home office, and when she located her desk, she couldn't figure out how to turn off the computer she writes on every day. When she went to lie down, she started shaking uncontrollably and then saw white. She was sure she was dying.

Then she heard the phone ring. It was me, calling to see if she was feeling any better. Luckily, she was able to reach over, pick up the receiver and mumble to me about what was going on. I called her gynecologist, who told me to take her to the hospital. When the cab got me home from the office, I found Diane lost in her closet. She stammered that she wanted to get dressed to go out but couldn't find her white shirt. I looked down and saw that it was an inch from her hand.

Married people can afford to panic only one at a time, so I pretended I was not scared as I helped her on with the shirt and took her to the hospital closest to where we live in Philadelphia, which happens to be Pennsylvania Hospital, the oldest hospital in America and one of the very best. As Diane spoke—haltingly, elliptically—to the ER doctors, more symptoms emerged. Her jaw was terribly sore from clenching against what we assumed had been a seizure. Her pupils were fixed and dilated, like blobs of black ink. She said she felt as though something were "melting" just behind her green eyes.

It was late Friday afternoon at the ER, just before the weekend rush, so we got a good, slightly private, curtained-off area. An emergency medicine specialist and several neurology residents tag-teamed in and out of our space. Each one asked a slightly different version of the same questions. I worried that we weren't being clear because there didn't seem to be any accumulation of knowledge taking place. They all had tests they wanted Diane to perform.

"Spell the word 'world' backwards," one asked. She did it and was then asked to name the U.S. presidents in reverse chronological order.

"Can you spell 'world' backwards?" the next one asked. Then he requested that she touch her finger to her nose.

"I'd like you to try to spell—" the next one began.

"—yeah, yeah," Diane said, " 'world' backwards." But she was bobbing in and out of full lucidity. Only seconds after cracking a joke, her mind would be sluggish again, and she would barely respond when I stroked her cheek or her shoulder-length brown hair.

After nearly five years of marriage, this was the first medical emergency we ever had to face. The only thing that kept me from really losing it was a woman in the next cubicle who already *had* lost it. Dragged in by the police in the middle of a major psychotic episode, she screamed continually in English and Chinese about everything from her husband's homosexuality to her close personal friendship with the president of the United States. Her screams pierced the crackly trauma calls from ambulances all over the area, which were being broadcast on a loudspeaker system for the ER staff to monitor. The combined noise was oddly stabilizing, a constant reminder that things could be considerably worse.

After several hours of neurological exams, the word came back—from a place called the Poison Control Center—that all of Diane's symptoms had been previously reported as reactions to the antibiotic she took. The drug is called Floxin. She had, as we now say, been "Floxed."

My wife took a pill. It made her sicker than she was before.

World backwards. Tell me about it.

The ER doctors, however, were not through with us. They still wanted to run more tests. Even though Diane's symptoms, such as "acute delirium," were consistent with a reaction to the Floxin, they could also be caused by a brain tumor, a stroke or a big horrible infection with larger neurological implications, like spinal meningitis. They wanted to do a CT scan.

I got to sit in the CT control room and watch the machinery visually slice and dice. There is nothing quite so frightening as watching your loved one's brain being scanned for tumors, especially when you're not exactly sure what a normal brain looks like. But it is also very moving to peer directly into your wife's mind. What spouse hasn't at one time or another wished to be able to do that?

Back in the ER after a clean scan, we were then told the prevailing wisdom about all adverse drug reactions: that the effects would subside when the medication left her system. And we were sent home—with a supply of the milder, cheaper antibiotic she probably should have taken in the first place for her urinary tract infection (UTI)—to wait for that to happen. On our way out, we walked past the main ER desk. On the wall behind it was a light box for reading X-rays, which was still illuminating pictures from the inside of Diane's brain. To the left of the viewer was a shiny metal towel dispenser. It was adorned with Floxin advertising magnets that had been left by some enterprising drug sales rep.

At that moment I thought the Floxinalia would actually make a nice detail for our emergency room horror story, the recitation of which would commence as soon as Diane was fine, ostensibly in a couple of days. But her symptoms did not disappear as promised. Some waned, but new ones developed. Besides the "melting" and the fixed pupils, she had really aggressive, buzzy insomnia, visual distortions that made the world seem six-dimensional and aphasia: she would get halfway through a sentence and just couldn't get the rest of the words out. For a woman with a high school trophy for "best negative debater" sitting on a shelf behind her desk, this was probably the scariest symptom of all.

Over the next two weeks, she endured an electroencephalogram (EEG), which tests electrical function in the brain; a magnetic resonance imaging (MRI) of her head, which offers more structural detail than the

CT scan; and a spinal tap, to check the cerebrospinal fluid for infections, as well as some blood work. All these tests just to rule out any other possible explanation for her continuing symptoms than an adverse reaction to the drug—the same drug that was supposed to be long gone from her system. While the tests themselves were creepy, what they were testing *for* was absolutely horrifying. I found myself weighing which awful result would be most acceptable, watching the life we had planned to have pass before my eyes.

The tests all came back on a Thursday, one of the most harrowing days of our lives. As we were read the results over the phone by our internist, I found myself mentally checking off all the nightmares that had been eliminated by the process—"brain tumor, no; stroke, no; AIDS, no." But Diane still wasn't well. The doctors concluded that the drug reaction had triggered some genetic predisposition to neurological illness. Since her body hadn't been able to correct the situation naturally, she would need to take a combination of heavy-duty drugs, each with its own possible side effects, to do it. If, in fact, it could be done at all.

But at least that urinary tract infection had cleared up.

It has now been five years since Diane got Floxed. In that time, we have learned more than we thought we'd ever want to know about what has been called "the *other* drug problem." The one with *legal* drugs.

Since that day in the emergency room, I have been on a quest. An investigative journalist and exasperated husband, I am trying to find out if my wife was the victim of a pharmacological foul-up or just a statistically acceptable casualty of "friendly fire" in the war on disease. I am also trying to find meaning in our experience, a married couple searching for each other through a medical emergency that never seems to end, the siren never completely quieted.

Along the way, I have met the people behind the studies, the statistics, the press releases and the lawsuits: heroes, scoundrels, geniuses and idiots, victims and victimizers, the amorphous "less than one percent" of the population who have the adverse reactions you read about in the fine print on your drug labels and even the people who massage the numbers to get them under one percent. I have seen close up what happens at that moment when science officially becomes commerce, when exciting new drugs are handed over from the lab nerds to the marketing types. I have watched everyone in the pharmaceutical food chain describe everyone but themselves as unhealthily arrogant. I have seen the world's top drug cop, the head of the U.S. Food and Drug Administration (FDA), excoriated as a "thug," a "bully" and even a "killer" by an industry-friendly legislator. And I have listened to the head of one of America's largest drugstore chains turn to me and growl, "These drug companies always hide under the cloak of 'We're these great research and development houses and without us there would be no medications.' I think they're full of shit."

The Europeans have a very elegant word for a certain type of drug safety research. The word is *pharmacovigilance,* and it refers to research that is supposed to be done *after* a drug has been approved and we're taking it. Because the people who do this work are the sole link between the pharmaceutical world and the real world and are often the bearers of unwelcome news, they sometimes seem like pharmacovigilantes. Over these years, I have been doing my own form of pharmacovigilantism. I use my press credentials to move effortlessly between the camps warring for control of your medicine cabinet.

My quest began with tracking down everything I could find about Floxin. But I realized that the only way to understand what had happened to Diane was to see beyond one pill and journey to the heart of the legal-drug culture: the international pharmaceutical industry, the government drug police in countries large and small, the physicians, the researchers, the pharmacists, the nurses, the consumer advocates—and the patients who unwittingly place their blind faith in this system. In college there was a book we had to read for political science class called *The Dance of Legislation,* about how a bill becomes law. Since Diane's drug reaction, I have been investigating politic*ized* science and watching "the dance of medication"—how a *pill* becomes law.

Much to my surprise, I found that the world of legal drugs is actually far more fascinating than its illicit counterpart, where we journalists generally focus our attention. It can also be more dangerous. While pharmaceutical science has made some medical miracles almost routine, the sheer size of the legal-drug world means that its problem areas are bigger than the entire illegal-drug problem.

For example, far more people die each year from adverse reactions to prescription and over-the-counter medications than succumb to *all illegal drug use.* Illicit drugs kill anywhere from 5,000 to 10,000 Americans a year. The estimates for U.S. deaths from *legal* drugs have ranged from 45,000 to over 200,000 per year, which represents 2 to 9 percent of the 2.3 million people who die annually, thereby qualifying as at least the sixth leading cause of death in America, and possibly as high as the third—behind only heart disease and cancer. Of course, many people take many medications without experiencing such problems, which are referred to as "adverse drug reactions" in the United States, "medication misadventures" in the U.K. and "drug-induced sufferings" in Japan. But according to studies in the *Journal of the American Medical Association (JAMA)*, as many as 11 percent of all hospital admissions are the result of adverse drug reactions, or ADRs, as they are often called. More than one-quarter of all inpatients have adverse reactions to the drugs they are given *in the hospital*—many the result of preventable medication errors—which makes ADRs the leading cause of in-hospital injury.

In America more people die each year from reactions to the drugs they get in the hospital than are killed in automobile accidents. (Some 10 percent of all auto accidents involve drivers impaired by medications.) Outpatients are victimized in greater numbers in another way by drug reactions: they stop taking their pills after being spooked by annoying side effects, neglect to tell their doctors, and are then hurt or killed by the untreated illness.

Before Diane got Floxed, I thought of medicines as pretty much idiot-proof. You take them assuming that the worst that can happen is that they won't work. It turns out the *worst* that can happen is that you drop dead. The next worse is that your body is permanently damaged. Less worse, but still not very good, is that you suffer for hours, days or weeks with something your doctor may or may not recognize as a drug reaction—anything from a skin rash to heart failure to a sudden inability to have an orgasm. The symptom may or may not go away by itself, but until it does, your doctor may mistake it for another illness and give you more drugs for that, leading to a cascade of prescribing. And your drug experience may affect how the next medication you take works in your body—or how well your body is able to fight infection in the future.

Adverse drug reactions are clearly a huge international health problem. A few enlightened pharmacologists also see them as an enormous learning opportunity, a "gift" that accidentally offers a chance to deepen understanding of drugs and the human body. For me, they have been both. Understanding drug reactions has been a way to explore what is wrong with the entire international pharmaceutical business—a $250 billion enterprise ($700 billion if you count all the other products sold by drug companies) that has managed to repel scrutiny more effectively than almost any other major industry, while remaining the world's most profitable business through many changes in economic climate.

Asking questions about what government regulators were doing about the drug reaction problem also became my way of infiltrating the

FDA, an agency so misunderstood that it is easy to overlook its omnipresence in our lives. The FDA is responsible for regulating *25 percent* of America's entire gross national product and its policies are the benchmark for world regulation of drugs and medical devices.

The work done by understaffed national agencies like the FDA has never been more important, because in all too many cases, the new economics of health care have transformed drugs from one possible treatment into the *only* possible treatment—or at least the only reimbursable treatment. In the past five years, drug sales in U.S. pharmacies and outpatient clinics have risen more than 50 percent and the total number of prescriptions dispensed, more than 2 billion a year, has risen over 25 percent. The vast majority of those increases are attributable to managed care's growing use of drugs to avoid hospitalization.

Drugs have become not only the tail that wags the dog but the tail that feeds the dog, trains the dog and makes the dog do tricks. And the growing power of the pharmaceutical industry is being controlled by a shrinking base of owners. Not only are the huge "drug houses" merging with each other and streamlining, but they are buying the firms that decide which drugs will be made available to patients in HMOs and other managed health care organizations. The companies also control the flow of information about medicines. The drug industry now funds, directly or indirectly, almost all the research done on drug products and almost all the drug education doctors get after medical school. Most of the destigmatizing public-awareness advertising campaigns about illnesses are paid for by the companies whose drugs are used to treat or in some cases *define* those illnesses. And more than ever, drug companies are end-running physicians' authority by advertising directly to consumers, which is why your magazines and newspapers are overflowing with pharmaceutical ads, your favorite TV shows are interrupted by pleas to "ask your doctor" about drugs and your doctor is quietly wincing every time he or she is "asked."

It's a situation that can easily turn unhealthy and too often does. Companies can't always be counted on to do "the right thing" when they're faced with a tough choice between profit and public safety. Experts in the field are growing worried about where the in-house "conscience" of these companies will be found, especially when firms with sterling reputations merge with their less high-minded competitors.

While drug therapies grow stronger and more profitable every day, the system that is supposed to assure the safety of those drugs is getting relatively weaker, an economic and bureaucratic liability easily targeted for downsizing. Even as computers and easier international communication make *more* drug safety efforts possible, the chasm between what *can* be done and what *is* being done to keep us safe grows constantly larger.

Ten years ago, the bottom-line business practices of the pharmaceutical companies were considered by many to be the dark underside of health care. Today, all of health care is being run like a drug company.

It's no wonder that, more than ever, patients and their doctors feel—well, pillaged.

How unhealthy is the legal-drug culture? I put that question to two of the world's leading minds in drug research during a big clinical pharmacology cocktail party. The two disagreed on the extent of the risks to everyday medicine-takers: one thought patients were too scared, while the other thought we might not be scared enough. But they shared a general perspective on the state of the pharmaceutical art.

"The amazing thing about this world," one said, sipping his drink, "is that everybody in it is really trying to do the right thing. If you look hard, you won't find many real villains. Yet the whole thing is still so messed up."

This is a book about how it got so messed up. It is what I wish I had known about drugs before my wife took that one pill.

In 1979 an international conference that some consider the Woodstock of drug safety was held in Kyoto, Japan. Its goal was to make some sense of a legal drug disaster that most people have never heard of, even though it affected as many patients as thalidomide. It was an outbreak of an irreversible neurological condition, sometimes leading to blindness and degeneration of the spinal cord, that was caused by an over-the-counter medication for intestinal disorders and diarrhea so widely used that some people sprinkled it over their breakfast cereal as a preventive measure. There were some 10,000 cases in Japan, and smaller numbers in twenty-five other countries where the drug was sold. It took nearly fifteen years to finger the drug as the culprit. And even though the epidemic in Japan stopped almost immediately after the drug was banned, one of its three manufacturers continues to insist the condition was caused by a virus.

During the course of this five-day conference, a call went out for a New International Pharmaceutical Order. Almost twenty years later, with all our advances in medical treatment, we are still waiting for that New Order. While pharmaceutical science has obviously made great strides since 1979, it is amazing and horrifying how many of the complaints about pharmacovigilance brought up at the conference are just as valid today. Some are actually *more* valid, because recent economic pressures have dramatically narrowed what was once a comfortably broad margin of error in all matters medical. Back then, fewer illnesses were treated *only* with drugs and fewer strong drugs were available over the counter, allowing people to haphazardly self-medicate.

If something isn't done, the price we will pay could be far more than the health of the patients who get the drug reactions listed on the impenetrable, mind-numbing package inserts that come with our medicines. A growing number of experts are worried how the casual, often irrational use of antibiotics will affect our ability to treat infectious disease. They believe our refusal to take drugs seriously will eventually unleash untamable viruses that could kill huge numbers of people—perhaps the planet's entire population. Their fears were recently confirmed with the discovery of a new strain of staph, one of the first infections ever conquered by medicine, that is impervious to even our strongest intravenous anti-infectives. It was caused, researchers believe, by stupid, unwarranted use of antibiotics.

That's how you spell world backwards, doctor.

PART 1

CHAPTER 1

All Floxed Up

We had planned to spend those first two "Floxed" weeks preparing for a trip to New Mexico, where we were going to celebrate our fifth wedding anniversary at a friend's cabin in the mountains outside of Santa Fe. Neither of us had come out and said so, but a certain window of opportunity had recently opened for us. I had just turned in the final galleys of my first book, ending two years of near-total immersion in the life of a model who had died (like the people in so many of my magazine stories) as a result of illegal drug use. We were thinking about focusing ourselves completely on Diane's next book: she had already finished two novels and was about to begin her third when she had to put it aside to edit me.

Or we were going to try to have a baby. Or both.

Instead, the window of opportunity was shut. Diane became a watched pot. Much of our time was spent anticipating how her new drugs would counter the effects of the first drug and make this all go away.

Everybody waits and worries differently. Some people brood, some people drink, some people pray, some people watch TV. I investigate. It makes me feel that I'm doing something useful. And it creates the illusion that I've earned the right to interact with certain professionals—like, say, doctors—as something closer to a peer than a client. So while we waited, I dug in.

I called the company that makes Floxin to request any information they could send me. Then I logged on to the computer: keywords *Floxin* and *antibiotic*. It is unnerving to do a newspaper database search on a drug that has knocked your loved one's life off course and find that the only articles ever written about it appeared in the business section. But the only editorial mentions of Floxin in America's major daily newspapers were in pharmaceutical industry reports. The articles discussed how the introduction of the drug was expected to boost stock prices for the New Jersey–based pharmaceutical and toiletries behemoth Johnson & Johnson, a $14 billion firm best known for, besides its drugs, shampoos and baby products. The stories went on to explain how J&J's profits in the first quarter of 1991, when Floxin hit the American market, had jumped 13 percent. In the third quarter of 1992, which ended just weeks before my wife was Floxed, earnings were up another 17 percent.

Besides the sales figures and stock prices, I learned a little bit about Floxin as a drug. I found out that it is one of a family of fairly new antibiotics called fluoroquinolones, or just plain quinolones, all of which have a *flox* or *ox* in their generic names. Floxin is ofloxacin. Quinolones are primarily prescribed for infections of the skin and the urinary and respiratory tracts and for sexually transmitted diseases. At that moment the star of the quinolone family was ciprofloxacin; marketed as Cipro, it was by far the largest seller and one of the best-selling drugs in the world. The family also included Noroxin (norfloxacin), Penetrex (enoxacin) and Maxaquin (lomefloxacin).

I also discovered that in June 1992, just five months before Diane was Floxed, the quinolone family had lost a relative. Omniflox (temafloxacin) was withdrawn worldwide after only four months on the market in the United States (but over a year in Europe, Asia and South America) because of hundreds of severe adverse reactions. It was only the ninth drug in modern FDA history to be withdrawn, and the members of the product liability bar were already tripping over one another to become lead counsel in the class action suit against Omniflox's manufacturer, Chicago-based Abbott Laboratories.

The handful of news stories about the Omniflox fiasco were both horrifying and strangely calming. They begged the question of how the FDA approval process worked: If a drug was that dangerous, how could it get approved in the first place? Could Floxin be the next Omniflox? *Should* Floxin be the next Omniflox? But the stories also reminded us that Diane's drug reaction could have been a lot worse. Several of the Omniflox patients had taken the drug, suffered multiple organ failure and died.

I called the FDA to find out what it had available on Floxin and Omniflox and was told I had to file a written Freedom of Information (FOI) request to get anything. In the United States much of the paperwork submitted on a drug becomes "public" under the Freedom of

Information Act when the product gets approved. That is how journalists, lawyers and competing drug companies get much of their information about drug products. Few of the other countries with advanced drug regulatory systems bother to make such materials available to the public at all, so the whole world benefits from the American Freedom of Information Act. Making the specific requests, however, is something of an art form, so I went through several false starts before finally writing one the FOI office would honor. And then they said we'd have to wait awhile.

As we waited, Diane continued to suffer, her symptoms so ubiquitous in our daily lives that I was developing a shorthand checklist of those problems that seemed quantifiable so I could make medical updates as quick and painless as possible. I usually started with the vision problems, which I was having a hard time visualizing myself, and worked my way back across her head. "Any visuals?" I would begin, as we sat together on the brown couch in our den, watching TV and each other. "How about melting?"

I quickly came to understand the complex psychology behind the seemingly simple act of asking how someone is. If you ask too often—as I tend to do—your concern can be undermined by the constant reminder of illness. But avoiding the issue sometimes means you can't connect at all. And I was desperate to connect.

Or maybe I was just desperate. And extremely angry. The problem was, I couldn't decide whom to hate. I tried hating the gynecologist, the drug company, the medical-industrial complex, even the whole world. I tried hating myself—for not protecting my wife, and for not knowing how to cure her. But the only hatred I could really justify was directed at the pill itself. Sometimes I would pick up the package the pill had been in and stare at it. The samples came two to a box, so the second one was still there, encased in clear plastic with its silver foil backing intact. "FLOXIN 300 mg" was stamped on it in dark red letters. I handled it gingerly, as if it might blow up in my hand the way it had exploded in Diane's head.

This pill could save someone's life, I thought, but it is my enemy.

I wanted to know my enemy, to begin to see it not just as a small inert clot of chemicals but as something *alive,* something that had traveled through Diane's body like the miniaturized submarine in *Fantastic Voy-*

age, its crew members performing their tasks until something went terribly wrong. But I had only a vague idea of how to get the information I needed to sketch the drug's character.

The next source I consulted was the *Physicians' Desk Reference,* the thick-enough-to-be-a-weapon navy blue book that American doctors use to look up information on medications. The *PDR,* I was surprised to learn, is not a critical or objective guide at all. It's simply a collection of the previous year's FDA-approved package inserts—the company-issued fact sheets—arranged alphabetically not by drug but by drug *manufacturer.* (Package inserts include what the FDA refers to as "labeling information," so they are often referred to as "labels" even though they aren't directly affixed to the bottle. As is common in the pharmaceutical world, I use "package insert" and "label" interchangeably.) The entries aren't even standardized: each company seems to have its own signature style. There are no prices, no comparisons of drug safety. So many frightening side effects are listed so dispassionately that except for an occasional boldfaced or boxed warning, it's nearly impossible to determine which ones are really important or worrisome. And since manufacturers pay the *PDR*'s publisher to have their drugs included, many older, less profitable drugs aren't even listed.

Diane had a dog-eared *PDR* in her library—she is the kind of person who buys the books in the bibliographies of *Scientific American* articles and does all manner of technical research to inform her fiction writing. But her *PDR* was too old to include Floxin. That's why she hadn't been able to look it up, as she normally would have, before taking it. The samples, as is typically the case, had been given to her without any instructions or warnings at all.

Physicians get a new *PDR* free every year, like a pharmaceutical phone book. Patients like us have to go out and buy a new one, for fifty-eight dollars. So I did. This was the first time in my life that I had ever bothered to read the fine print about a drug. We looked up all of Diane's new medications—which she had swallowed with considerably more courage than I could have mustered under the circumstances—and several other antibiotics. Then we looked up Floxin.

The entry began with an explanation of what Floxin did and what its chemical structure was. Then there appeared Contraindications, followed by Warnings, Precautions and, finally, Adverse Reactions. The contraindications appeared to be commandment-like advice for doctors—"thou shalt not prescribe this drug if . . ." Warnings looked like problems that had come up often enough to worry about, and Precautions were what the doctor was supposed to advise patients to do in order to prevent these problems. As far as we could tell, the Adverse Reactions section was just a laundry list of things that had happened to some patient somewhere.

The only contraindication listed was that people with a history of hypersensitivity to Floxin or other quinolones shouldn't take it. This didn't seem like terribly useful advice, since there were only four or five quinolones available, and only two of them had been available in the United States for more than two years. Many antibiotics we saw listed in the *PDR* cited, say, hypersensitivity to penicillin as a contraindication. That seemed like a more useful predictor of possible problems.

Nonetheless, the stakes for those hypersensitive to Floxin appeared quite high. Every anti-infective from penicillin on down had some dangerous reactions listed, especially at high doses. But according to one of the warnings, Floxin and other quinolones had reportedly caused "serious and occasionally fatal hypersensitivity reactions, *some following the first dose* [my emphasis] . . . some reactions were accompanied by cardiovascular collapse, loss of consciousness, tingling."

Then came the paragraph I have read a thousand times—because I'm sure someone at the drug company thinks it would have sufficiently warned someone like Diane. It discusses what are called central nervous system or CNS effects.

"Convulsions, increased intracranial pressure and toxic psychosis have been reported in patients receiving quinolones, including ofloxacin," it says. "Quinolones may also cause central nervous system stimulation, which may lead to tremors, restlessness, lightheadedness, confusion and hallucinations. . . . No evidence of an effect of ofloxacin on the electrical activity of the brain has been demonstrated. . . . However, until more information becomes available, ofloxacin . . . should be used with caution in patients with known or suspected CNS disorders, such as severe cerebral arteriosclerosis or epilepsy, or other factors . . . that predispose to seizures."

If I had read this beforehand, would I have known that my wife shouldn't have taken Floxin? Absolutely not.

In the aftermath of being Floxed, Diane discovered that her maternal grandmother had experienced seizures. Did that make her a patient with "a known or suspected CNS disorder," a patient who needed to be warned against Floxin? I even knew that Diane had received a concussion, with temporary amnesia, in an auto accident when she was a kid. But even if she had included that in a medical history (the way one would mention sensitivity to penicillin), would any clinician have been reasonably expected to cross-reference that fact with this warning and know that my wife shouldn't take Floxin?

After the Warnings were the Precautions, which weren't of much interest to me. (It was a bit late for that, and most of the precautions concerned children and pregnant women anyway.) So I skipped ahead to the Adverse Reactions. These were divided into two categories: reactions that the company agreed were "likely to be drug related" and those the company said it was listing "regardless of relationship to the drug." For example, the label said that 11 percent of patients had drug-related effects (ranging from a lot of headaches, nausea and insomnia to a handful of serious central nervous system reactions). But of the 7 percent of patients reporting insomnia, less than half of them were considered drug related.

I wondered who had made *this* judgment and who had the burden of proof as to whether a drug reaction was really "drug related."

Down among the litany of problems found in "less than one percent" of patients—and included on the label "regardless of relationship to the drug"—were the ones that interested me: seizures, hallucinations, cognitive changes and several other CNS reactions. Diane looked at these and found them strangely comforting. They meant that she wasn't alone, and they meant that nobody could accuse her of making this all up, of being a "hysterical woman."

Until I was married, I never quite understood the difference between the ways men and women are treated by doctors. Five years earlier, I might have considered Diane's fears of being labeled a hysteric to be somewhat . . . hysterical. Now that I've seen what she and other women regularly go through in the largely male-dominated medical system, their fears seem perfectly justified.

As I researched Floxin, I was telling my wife's story to anyone who would listen. Almost everyone responded with a tale about an unexpected drug reaction they or someone close to them had had. They were telling me these stories to make me feel better—"See, I had convulsions from a cold pill, but I'm fine now." But all I kept hearing was a chorus of people who had quietly endured what often sounded like pretty serious drug reactions. None of them seemed to have any lasting resentment toward the medication they had taken. Many had never even told their doctors what had happened to them. It was always an "allergic reaction" or an "unforeseen interaction," incidents for which they thought nobody could or should be blamed, incidents best forgotten.

Only one person could muster the same kind of anger and frustration that I felt: my Pop-pop, my father's eighty-two-year-old father. Pop-pop, who looked like a Jewish version of Cab Calloway, was in the midst of one of his periodic stays in the nursing home built by the community where I was raised in Harrisburg. Unlike my Nana, his wife, who had been living there for years following a stroke, Pop-pop was only there "temporarily," he insisted. The way he clung to that distinction made me think of Monopoly and one of the first cosmic subtleties we learned as kids: how two players could be on the same space, but one was "in jail" and the other "just visiting." During the course of this third "just visit" in two years, Pop-pop had been given a pill for a bladder infection. The result, he told me—in the gruff, gravelly voice I had learned to love as a kid during family Friday night dinners—was "Goddammit, now I can't pee. Why they gave me this damn drug in the first place, I have no idea."

It was another in a series of medicine mishaps Pop-pop had experienced since he went from being my Nana's primary caregiver and cheerleader to being a patient himself—and a very cranky one. Some of his drug problems had to do with his doctors failing to communicate. One didn't know what the other had already prescribed, which left the family pharmacist trying to tell Pop-pop what to do, which was never easy. But many of the problems he brought on himself.

Among his maladies was emphysema, for which he often overmedicated himself with prescription and over-the-counter inhalers. He carried them and all his pills around in a Baggie. Once, when he was still living at home, Diane and I came to give him a ride to a family dinner. He sat at the kitchen table talking to us, using his inhaler more in fifteen minutes than he probably was supposed to all day. When it was time to go, I pulled my car up into his garage so he wouldn't have to walk very far, and he got in. But as I started to pull out, he accidentally pushed the button on the remote garage door opener he kept in his jacket pocket. He was so confused from the inhalers that he couldn't figure out how to push it again to stop the garage door, which was quickly coming down onto my car. I had to jump out and grab the door, Superman-style, to keep it from crushing my hood.

While Pop-pop had barely understood what was happening that day in his driveway, he knew when he couldn't pee that he was having an adverse reaction to "that goddamned drug." He insisted they switch him to another medication, but only weeks later, the nursing home staff gave him the same drug again by mistake, with the same result. He was incensed at "these bastards, these idiots." And he quickly became the family member who most understood why I was so interested in exploring what had happened to Diane.

It was not uncommon for him to take an interest in my work, especially if it dovetailed with something he was reading about in *The Wall Street Journal* that might provide him with a stock investment idea. But it is also true that, in my family's section of Harrisburg, people tend to be inordinately interested in the drug business anyway. A local clan controlled the Rite Aid drugstore chain—which went public in the late 1960s and is now one of America's largest—and many people there made and lost fortunes in Rite Aid stock. I recall lots of happy faces at the R n' L Delicatessen when Rite Aid stock split. But I never heard anyone talk about whether the drugs they sold at Rite Aid were safe.

The Floxin promotional material I requested finally showed up in the mail. It came in a bloodred folder with a huge X on it, and the slogan: "A powerful new antimicrobial makes its mark." (The terms *antimicrobial, anti-infective* and *antibiotic* tend to be used interchangeably for drugs that kill infectious organisms. True antibiotics are based on naturally occurring substances; quinolones, which are produced synthetically, are technically antimicrobials. I use *antibiotic* as a generic term for all anti-infective drugs.)

The Floxin press releases explained that the drug was the first oral anti-infective product for either of the two Johnson & Johnson subsidiaries that were comarketing it. McNeil Pharmaceuticals, the suburban Philadelphia company best known for Tylenol, was handling the intravenous version. New Jersey–based Ortho Pharmaceutical, which specialized in women's health care products and the acne/wrinkle cream Retin-A (tretinoin), was selling Floxin in pill form.

Diane had actually just finished taking another Ortho drug several weeks before her adverse reaction to Floxin. She had been put on a one-month cycle of birth control pills as a nonsurgical treatment for a common ovarian cyst. She later noted to me that the packaging for Ortho-Novum (estrogen/progestin), the leading brand of birth control pills, is where most of her peers first learned about—and first learned to overlook—the possibility of drug reactions.

It was during the office visit to confirm that the cyst was gone (it was) that her gynecologist diagnosed a UTI as well as slightly elevated blood pressure, which the Pill can sometimes cause. That's when Diane was given her Floxin samples, which I could now see were perfectly color-coded with the rest of the promotional packet.

Predictably, the press releases sang the praises of Floxin, which was "the first new antibiotic specifically indicated for treating prostate infections in 19 years . . . the first quinolone available in equivalent IV and oral doses." The big selling point seemed to be that the pill form had "the potency of injectable medications." Its strength could mean a shorter course of therapy with fewer pills a day than usual, and shorter hospital stays.

The drug was "well-tolerated . . . [with] an excellent safety profile" and had already "successfully treated 65 million patients worldwide." However, Floxin hadn't been sold overseas by Ortho or J&J. It had been invented by a Japanese company called Daiichi, which had been marketing it in Japan, and later in Europe, since 1984 under the name Tarivid. Ortho had apparently entered into a licensing agreement with Daiichi to sell the drug in the United States after getting the necessary approvals.

This was a new concept to me. My image of the pharmaceutical industry was that of firms laboring for years to produce perfect drugs in which they would have great pride of ownership and, ideally, great hope for profit. Most of the major international pharmaceutical companies had initially been built on one such drug. In Philadelphia we have one of the greatest little twentieth-century art museums in the world—the home of the amazing Barnes Collection—and it was all paid for from the profits of a single drug from the 1920s. The drug, Argyrol, was a horrible-tasting silver compound used to treat infections before real antibiotics were discovered. A more lasting product from the same era was insulin, which became the cornerstone of Eli Lilly and Company. But, as I was learning from reading about drugs in the business section of the newspaper, the comarketing, cross-marketing and international licensing of Floxin is a more accurate image of how the pharmaceutical industry now functions.

Although someone occasionally discovers a breakthrough medication, companies mostly create drugs that might be decent investments, might be worth owning a piece of. If they are simply slight variations of drugs that are already on the market—but still patentable as new products—they are derisively referred to as "me-too" drugs. While me-too drugs can be enormously profitable and somewhat useful therapeutically, they do not create much scientific or medical excitement because they glut markets and waste finite resources that might be used to solve new problems, rather than compete in markets created by solved problems.

Was Floxin a me-too? I wondered. Had my wife's life been turned upside down by a drug that didn't even dare to be great?

During my panicked weeks of networking, one friend I spoke to about Diane's situation was a local TV journalist. He, like those 65 million other people, had used Floxin himself without incident—and thought he might still have a few pills left in his medicine cabinet. He mentioned Diane's plight to a Philadelphia lawyer who specialized in medical product liability cases and occasionally appeared on his show.

The lawyer was astonished by what he heard. It wasn't just that it sounded like the kind of hard-luck tale from which big-money lawsuits sometimes grow. The lawyer also knew personally that my wife's problem with Floxin was not an isolated case. A female attorney who worked for him had had an alarmingly similar experience. The label said such side effects were experienced by "less than one percent" of the patients taking Floxin. Two women who worked less than a mile from each other being stricken by the same lightning didn't sound like a "less than one percent" risk to him. He promised to put me in touch with her.

Speaking to litigator Stacy Phillips* was an immense relief. Now I knew that Diane wasn't the only person in America who considered herself Floxed. But the experience was also pretty chilling, because Stacy still wasn't feeling great, nearly a *year* after taking Floxin.

In her case, it was two pills.

Stacy was thirty and had two kids. Not long after the birth of her second son, on Christmas Eve 1991, she began having pain that she suspected was a recurrence of a pelvic infection. She wanted to catch it right away this time, so she went to her doctor and asked for a prescription for Keflex (cephalosporin), the antibiotic she had used to treat it before.

"He said, 'Well, Keflex can clear it up, but I have something that's supposed to be as good or better,' " she recalled. "He prescribed Floxin and some Motrin [ibuprofen] for the pain, and I went to the pharmacy and got them." She took one Floxin that morning, and another before going to sleep.

She woke up hours later with her husband screaming at her. "This was the single most terrifying experience of my life," she said. "My husband thought I was going to die. I was having a severe seizure—I was

---

* I've changed this name for reasons of privacy, but nothing else about Stacy's story has been altered in any way.

convulsing, my eyes rolled back, I was drooling, and I bit my tongue almost all the way through.

"When I finally came to, I couldn't remember anything. I didn't know who he was. He got me to stand up and walk into the boys' room. I was staring into the crib, and *I didn't know who my baby was.* My husband kept talking to me and eventually my memory started coming back. I called the doctor the next morning, and he had me go in for an MRI and EEG. The EEG was abnormal—it showed a seizure disorder, and the doctor said I probably had some preexisting seizure disorder."

Stacy's descriptions of how she had felt since her drug reaction were eerily similar to things Diane was telling me as her weeks in treatment began turning into months. Listening to her made my wife's experiences more palpable to me. I could ask Stacy questions I wouldn't ask Diane, and I knew she had no incentive to sugarcoat any of her answers or minimize her suffering. Diane had a different life than most people even before being Floxed—after doing some nonfiction writing and research for magazines and public television, she had committed herself to writing fiction from a home office. Although her alternative lifestyle was part of the reason I loved and married her, I never had a perfectly clear picture of what her days were like. So I was starved for these kinds of insights.

"I felt for months and months that there was just a cloud in my head," Stacy said.

In the emergency room, I recalled, Diane had described a cloud passing before her eyes.

"I just always felt like I was on horribly strong cold medicine," she continued. "I was just about to switch jobs when this happened, but I got to the point where I couldn't work for a period of time. I finally did come back, but I have to work twice as hard to do the same amount. I have cognitive problems, a lot of trouble remembering. Luckily, being a lawyer, a lot of the work is paperwork, stuff you don't have to think about too much.

"You said your wife is a writer? I can't *imagine* having to do something creative."

Actually, I told her, Diane was still having some trouble writing fiction, although she was meticulous about keeping her journal. Having lost so much control of her own reality, the last thing she wanted to write was fantasy.

"And when I'm driving, I sometimes get panicked," Stacy said. "I see light in a funny way—the way light flashes between trees and things. And when I see this, I get this feeling that makes me feel like I might get a seizure. So I have to pull over."

I asked her if she could describe the feeling.

"It's right between my eyes," she said, "but it's hard to describe."

Diane has lived in the city so long that she hasn't driven in years—that's my job—but she had tried to tell me about this problem seeing light. Her brain seemed to be having difficulty processing broad differences in brightness.

I told Stacy that Diane often spoke of a feeling that there was something melting inside her head—a certain internal, oozy warmth, like a nosebleed, only behind her eyes.

"Oh my god, *melting,* that's exactly it," Stacy said. "See, she's a writer, she knew the right word. That's what it's like—when I think I'm going to have a seizure. The melting."

But do you ever have a seizure? I asked.

"No, actually. I just get afraid I will. Mostly I just get headaches. But I'm almost at the point where I'm afraid that my fear of having another seizure is part of the problem. I'm just very anxious. I haven't really talked to many people about this, especially at work, because you don't want anybody to know you have cognitive problems. There's such a stigma, to say a drug has damaged you."

Diane, thank God, hadn't had any thinking problems: we had both been paying very careful attention to that. But she knew all about the stigma. Most of the time, we were afraid to tell anybody anything—even our own families.

Stacy's parents, it turned out, were both physicians. They had been actively encouraged to prescribe Floxin. "They tell me that the people selling Floxin are *big* marketers," she said. "They come to the doctors' offices, giving frequent flyer awards and gift certificates. My parents just went to a big dinner they had. They went to check it out, find out more about the drug. They were told there was a very slim chance of a reaction like mine. Less than one percent, you know. Although if it's one in a hundred, that's pretty bad.

"They seem to be pushing this drug so it would be as widely prescribed as Keflex—all these little drug reps out there telling people the drugs are interchangeable. But I don't think it should be so widely prescribed. I think it should be more of a last resort."

Since Stacy was the only other Floxed person I knew, I was especially interested to hear how she and her doctor had decided to treat her symptoms. She explained that the doctor who gave her the Floxin had immediately wanted to put her on an anticonvulsant—an antiseizure medication that helps control electrical activity in the brain—because her EEG was now abnormal. But Stacy felt so medically violated that she couldn't bring herself to take another pill.

Since then, she said, "The doctor just didn't want to have anything to do with me. I asked him if he wanted me to come in, and he said it wasn't necessary. I'm not sure what to do. . . . I'm just afraid, afraid to take any more medication. And I'm afraid I'll go to a doctor and be told I shouldn't drive—because I *have* to drive for work. I don't know what I'd do if I was told I couldn't drive again."

I understood completely how Stacy's fear had led to a reasoning gridlock that kept her from getting any care at all. It was one of my greatest worries that the same thing would happen to Diane. Had I been Floxed, I probably would have fled mainstream medicine altogether, following the lead of the millions of people who throw up their hands in disgust and allow a chiropractor, or the clerk at the health food store, to become their primary care physician. In fact, I had done so twice before: once for stomach problems I had during college, another time for my chronic bad back. And I'm clearly the more conventional half of this marriage.

Diane's father was a small-town dentist, and nobody is more distrustful of medical care than the kids of medical people. She also simply didn't like to be told what to do, making her a prime candidate for what doctors call noncompliance—not taking your medicines. Still, Diane never balked at taking the replacement antibiotic she was given in the ER. And she was diligent about the anticonvulsant and the mood-stabilizing agent that her doctors—the gynecologist had passed her along to an internist, a neurologist and a psychiatrist—agreed that she needed.

I doubted that her medicinal bravery was necessarily a good sign. More likely, it meant that she was so scared, so desperate for relief, that she was willing to take any risk, willing even to pretend that there *wasn't* any risk, on the chance that she might feel better. Instilling fear and desperation are, I suppose, a backhanded way of assuring she took the pills. But they are also what allows doctors to give drugs thoughtlessly, and patients to take them recklessly.

We liked Diane's doctors, who seemed genuinely concerned and, perhaps more important, genuinely inquisitive about her situation and willing to admit what they didn't know. I was especially impressed with the way they were able to add the psychiatrist to the treatment team without ever making us worry that they considered Diane's symptoms to be "in her head," as opposed to "in her brain." That is a terribly important distinction when it comes to drug reactions, which can easily be blamed on the patient's personality rather than the pill.

But I found that the doctors were generally more interested in what was happening with Diane now than in what *had* happened. Our pharmacists at the local CVS pharmacy—Ann McParlin and Kristen Burt, our new best friends—were the ones who expressed the most continuing interest in the drug reaction itself, and the whole issue of what it said about the safety of the drug. I didn't really understand why there would be such a difference in perspective on drugs between physicians and pharmacists. After all, medications are the most common way doctors treat an illness. At least 60 percent of all doctor visits end with a pre-scription—or a "script," as they say in the business. And an increasing number of scripts are being called in without doctors' visits.

Yet the worldviews of our physicians and pharmacists seemed far apart. Unlike the kindly practitioners at the old See-Right and Emerald drugstores where I grew up, who seemed like little more than mouth-pieces for our physicians, these younger pharmacists were more actively involved in patient care and were unafraid to openly question a doctor's orders. Their attitude suggested that there was a new, more interactive, more aggressive way of approaching the use of medicines. Pharmacists understood it, and many doctors just *didn't get it.*

While doctors seemed to underplay drug side effects, perhaps believ-ing that suggestible patients would develop any symptom they were warned of, the pharmacists were much more concerned and candid about the possibility of "problems" with medicines. I was interested that our physicians had barely heard about the problems with that quinolone antibiotic Omniflox—even though it had been publicly withdrawn only seven months earlier, all doctors had been informed by mail about the extreme action, the death toll from the drug was mounting and the manufacturer had sales reps in their offices virtually every week hawking other products.

The pharmacists knew all about Omniflox. And their reactions to Diane's case mirrored my own growing suspicions.

"Jeez," one of them said, "I wonder if there's something wrong with Floxin, too."

.   .   .

If I really wanted to understand what had happened to Diane on that dreadful October Friday, I needed to find someone who both knew pills and treated patients. A lawyer had given me the names of several doctors across the country he had used as expert witnesses in drug cases. The first one, in Texas, was somewhat helpful but dry and detached. The second was Dr. David Flockhart, a clinical pharmacologist at Georgetown University Hospital in Washington. His enormous curiosity and commitment came through as loud and clear over the phone as his Scottish accent.

Flockhart is a practicing physician who also does research and teaches pharmacology. He explained that one of the main areas of research in his department is pharmacogenetics. Experts in this fledgling field try to understand the genetic roots of drug metabolism to figure out why certain types of people might have problems with drugs that are "safe" by FDA standards—thereby predicting and avoiding certain adverse drug reactions and drug interactions. Only 10 percent of drug reactions are truly *allergies,* in which the body actually decides that a medication—say, penicillin—is a foreign substance and mounts an immunological attack against it. (If this happens immediately upon taking the drug, it can produce a condition called anaphylactic shock, which can quickly become life-threatening.) The rest of the ADRs are technically intolerances, overdoses or poisonings, which are caused by a single drug or an interaction between two or more drugs.

Flockhart's job was to gather clues until he could tease out the mechanism that led to a drug reaction; it's the clinical pharmacology version of detective work. For example, a genetic inability to properly metabolize a drug can be the culprit, resulting in an "overdose" from what is normally a safe amount. The same thing can happen for more preventable nongenetic reasons: when, for example, a doctor doesn't adjust dosages for body weight, gender or ethnic differences in metabolism. Flockhart said physicians in the office setting often take a "one dose fits all" approach and don't bother to adjust drug dosages for body weight as is done in the hospital—even though the instructions for such adjustments are right on the label. Adjusting for gender and ethnic differences in drug responses is harder, because little is known about these areas. The research needed to determine such distinctions, he explained, has only very recently begun to be funded.

Flockhart himself is doing some of that work. One of his research passions is mapping the various pathways that drugs follow as they are metabolized in the liver, the tributaries in what is called the cytochrome

P450 system. Then he tries to identify genetic markers for irregularities in the pathways. He, and others around the world who study this system, believe that one day a simple blood screen will be able to predict and prevent many drug reactions.

When it comes to central nervous system reactions—to Floxin or to anything else—Flockhart was, unfortunately, mostly telling me what wasn't known or *knowable* yet. Brain chemistry is the body's last frontier. Almost 95 percent of what is known about the brain has been learned in the past fifteen years, and many basic mechanisms remain a mystery. But Flockhart did know that quinolones have been reported to cause neurological and psychiatric problems. All antibiotics can cause seizures at very high doses, but quinolones appear to be more neurotoxic than other classes of anti-infectives even at standard doses.

Drugs can become neurotoxic, he explained, when they reach high enough concentrations to cross the "blood-brain barrier," which normally protects delicate brain and nervous system tissues from the day-to-day fluctuations in the bloodstream. (That's why infections that reach the brain or spinal fluid are so feared.) Quinolones reach very high concentrations in the blood very quickly: that's part of their appeal as antibiotics, but it's also the reason they appear to leap the blood-brain barrier. Once in the brain, the drugs are believed to attach to binding sites called GABA receptors. Those receptors influence what is referred to as the "seizure threshold"—the point beyond which the brain's built-in surge protector can't prevent an electrical overload, or seizure. Flockhart explained that some people are unaware that they have a genetic predisposition to seizures, or a "seizure focus" perhaps created by a past head injury. It is also possible, however, that the drug blocks the metabolism or disposal of some other substance in the brain, and as a result, the levels of *that* substance go too high, causing the seizure and the other CNS problems that go along with being Floxed.

Either way, Flockhart wanted to know more about Floxin and the patients who had been affected. While offering to check the scientific literature himself, he gave me the overall impression that pursuing this subject was terribly important. More than just Diane's health was at stake. "My suspicion," he said on the phone, "is that this drug is okay for most people and dangerous for some people. And we need to let the people in danger know that."

The way to go about doing this, he said, was to get hold of *all* the clinical data on the drug. The best-case scenario would be that my snooping around would pique the FDA's interest—or attract the attention of medical consumer advocates who are good at piquing the FDA's interest. That could lead to the agency convening something called an advisory committee meeting, to look into the type of adverse reaction Diane had.

The FDA advisory committee is the Supreme Court of legal drugs. Each division of the agency has a standing tribunal of experts who rule on controversial issues concerning approvals and relabelings. The Anti-Infective Drugs Advisory Committee could force Floxin's manufacturer to specifically study who was at risk and why. Then the firm would have to alert doctors about which patients should not be given the drug— unless it was the *only* choice in a life-threatening situation and the bene-fits outweighed the specific risks. Such an action would likely change physicians' perception of the quinolones. One of the essential issues in drug prescribing is figuring out what is called the "risk/benefit ratio" for each medicine for each individual patient. All drugs have risks. The question is whether doctors and patients actually pay attention to them.

In fact, Flockhart was still trying to figure out why Diane's doctor had used something as powerful as Floxin as the first line of defense against a minor urinary tract infection anyway. He believed that "most people would have used a smaller gun."

But he wasn't exactly surprised. He knew that antibiotics, even though they are the second most commonly used class of drugs in the world, are improperly prescribed 40 to 50 percent of the time. Either they aren't necessary at all, or the wrong drug, wrong dose or wrong duration is prescribed.

Apparently everyone in medicine knows this except the patients.

Soon Flockhart and I were faxing things back and forth and playing endless games of telephone tag on each other's voice mail and answering machines. Besides providing information, he helped me focus my panic, always reminding me about the difference between a cover-up and some-thing that wasn't yet known.

I was having a hard time making this distinction. I still couldn't be-lieve something Flockhart had very casually mentioned to me one day. He said that the FDA and the drug companies don't know how most of the drugs we take actually work. For FDA approval, the companies simply need to prove that their products *do* work somewhat better than a placebo, a sugar pill. It is helpful to be able to offer an informed guess as to *why* they work, but it isn't required. For example, the Floxin package insert said the drug was "thought to exert a bactericidal effect on susceptible micro-organisms by inhibiting DNA gyrase."

Flockhart was also kind enough to take the time to teach me some of the basics. One day he couldn't explain over the phone the difference between Floxin, the other quinolones still on the market, and the dreaded, recently recalled Omniflox. To me, a flox was a flox, and why *shouldn't* I assume the worst? So he drew me a picture of the basic compound all the quinolones were built on—nalidixic acid, which is also the basis of many antimalarial drugs—and then sketched out the various chemical structures. He slipped the drawing into his fax machine, and I had a new visual aid.

Speaking to Flockhart, I picked up some of the lingo of the legal-drug world. The pharmaceutical companies are referred to collectively, and sometimes a little ominously, as "industry." Pharmaceutical company sales representatives are called "detail men," and what they do is referred to as "detailing." Medicines are "meds," physicians are "docs." Clinical pharmacology is "clin-pharm," used as either a noun or an adjective. Clinical pharmacologists are interested in drug safety and drug "efficacy," the blanket term for whether a medicine actually works. Any pharmaceutical acronym that is even vaguely pronounceable is used as a word. There are literally hundreds of such acronyms at CDER—pronounced "cedar"—which is the FDA's Center for Drug Evaluation and Research. One of my personal favorites is the agency's Division of Drug Marketing, Advertising and Communications (DDMAC), which is referred to as "Dee Dee Mac," like a character from a great old soul song.

While searching for more information about Diane's specific reaction and how best to treat it, Flockhart and I also came across some general material about quinolones. It turned out that their strength—the size of the "gun"—had been a concern since they first came on the market in the 1980s. Nobody doubted that the drugs were strong and effective against certain difficult-to-treat infections. In the often mundane world of pharmacology, quinolones even had something of a trendy buzz attached to them: a "novel group of antibiotics . . . extensively used in Europe" was the description in one of the standard drug handbooks that I picked up at my local medical bookstore.

After their release they were almost immediately considered anti-infectives with a great potential for overuse. "Because of the tremendous investment and time it takes to bring new antimicrobials on the market," noted a 1990 article about quinolones in the British *Journal of Antimicrobial Chemotherapy,* "the pressure from the pharmaceutical companies upon the physicians [to use quinolones] increases, with a real danger of overpromotion and overprescription." The article went on to urge that "these drugs should not be used for the treatment of trivial infections.

On the contrary, they should be restricted for treatment of difficult-to-treat infections, including those infections where, previously, only [intravenous] therapy was available."

This advice hardly jibed with the Ortho-McNeil press release, which recommended Floxin for "broad use against common infections."

I was curious to know how much more dangerous Floxin was than some of the other antibiotics Diane's doctor could have tried. And how much more effective was it—enough to justify that risk? Flockhart warned me that these were the kinds of questions that rarely if ever got studied. And when there were such studies, they were usually funded by drug companies and often released only if the company happened to manufacture the drug that came out on top. We could find only one paper, in an obscure journal, that actually compared adverse effects caused by antibiotics prescribed for a similar problem—in this case, lower respiratory tract infections. The author noted that even though Floxin was effective and in some cases slightly superior to other antibiotics, the drug produced many more side effects: 16 percent of patients taking Floxin had adverse drug reactions, compared with 10 percent of those taking amoxicillin or erythromycin and 8 percent of those being treated with other antibiotics.

We also dug up a study done by Daiichi, the Japanese company that developed ofloxacin. It further fueled my suspicion that patients taking Floxin weren't being warned strongly enough about the specific dangers of central nervous system adverse effects. The company doctor who published the study hailed the drug's effectiveness and reported the incidence of adverse drug reactions at a mere 2.6 percent. But he also confirmed that, unlike other antibiotics, adverse reactions "peculiar to new quinolones are probably of neuropsychiatric origin." While occurring in only 0.6 percent of the patients involved, neuropsychiatric effects accounted for 18 percent of *all* the adverse reactions reported.

What did all these numbers mean? The journal articles certainly suggested that what had happened to Diane was the tip of an iceberg. But which iceberg? Was it the dangers of Floxin for thirty-six-year-old women? Was it the dangers of antibiotic overuse? Was it the dangers of an international system of drug regulation that didn't work properly? Or was it merely the dangers of a journalist-husband overreacting to a drug safety problem, because his wife just happened to be beaten by the odds and experienced the "less than one percent" reaction that society has already agreed is the risk it is willing to take?

·   ·   ·

Diane's treatment and my research were becoming two independent entities. Neither one was getting fabulous results, but both were slowly progressing. Months after the original episode, she still suffered from visual distortions and that peculiar "melting" sensation. I knew when she was feeling the "melting," because she got a certain look on her face—a look I can only compare to the combination of discomfort and involuntary relief I imagine you'd get from peeing your own pants. It didn't happen a lot, and when we were together, we'd spend hours at a time in a subdued version of what we used to think of as normal. But then some symptom we had just managed to forget about would crop up. We'd be yakking, and she would suddenly become aphasic (which is like forgetting what you were about to say, multiplied by 100). Her moods were torturously unstable, so another medication was added to treat them.

The medications helped her sleep, but they also made it harder for her to wake up. I was always an earlier riser than Diane. It was our custom for me to get up first, make coffee and bring her a cup in bed. She would sit up, take a few sips and join me for breakfast, where we would tussle over who got to read the "ladies' section" of the newspaper first. Now, when she heard me come in saying "special coffee delivery," she often just half opened her eyes, mumbled a thank you, pointed to where she wanted me to put down the cup and rolled back over.

I had begun to tell people that Diane was feeling "better." But I was using the term very literally, to mean "improved" rather than "well." And I was starting to wonder if it was time to adjust to what she was experiencing: to decide that, for us, her diminished condition would now be part of our definition of "normal." But when you don't know exactly what's wrong, how long is temporary? How soon is permanent?

CHAPTER 2

Less Than

One Percent

One morning late in December—three full months after Diane was Floxed—I received several small brown envelopes in the mail from the U.S. Department of Health and Human Services. Inside were dozens of four-by-six-inch clear plastic cards covered with microscopic blue lettering. They were copies of the FDA's files on Floxin, on microfiche. The accompanying letter apologized for the agency's reliance on such an outdated technology and suggested that many public libraries still had their old microfiche readers.

I was startled to say the least. My technophobic mother was using a computer for her holiday recipes, yet the FDA hadn't computerized its applications for new drugs?

The main public library in Philadelphia—the palatial building just down the parkway from the Art Museum—isn't far from my office, so I started going over there in the afternoons and sifting through the microfiche on one of the old gray-metal readers in the periodical room. The contraptions had ancient photocopying machines attached to them, and for a quarter you could make a fuzzy copy of a fuzzy page.

The FDA files contained close to a thousand of those fuzzy pages. The first six hundred were the agency's review of the New Drug Application (NDA), the permanent record of the studies that were the basis of the drug's approval, including the human studies, the "clinical trials," which are divided into Phases I, II and III. It's all there in brain-curdling detail, except for the occasional line that has been deleted—just crossed out, really—because it might give away something the company considers a trade secret. The finished NDA review combines an abridged version of the truckload of information submitted by the drug company with a running commentary from the FDA medical officer assigned to ride herd on the application. The medical officer's observations are footnoted at the bottom of each page like a teacher's comments, so you can watch some of the scientific give-and-take between the company and the FDA.

The first page that caught my eye was number forty, detailing the results of a Phase I study of safety and pharmacokinetics in thirty-two healthy male geriatric subjects in Senneville, Quebec. (Pharmacokinetics involves how a drug is absorbed, as opposed to pharmaco*dynamics,* which involves the actions a drug causes *after* being absorbed.) Study number E84-070 was a "randomized, double-blind, placebo-controlled" study, which meant the group was randomly divided, with half put on the drug and half on a sugar pill, with no one, including the doctors, knowing which was which until the "blind" was broken at the conclusion.

I found myself less interested in the test results, however, than in their analysis. The drug company had told the FDA there were "no clinically significant changes" in vital signs or in any neurological, ophthalmologic, heart, blood or urine tests. The company also told the FDA that the differences in the "subject incidence of adverse experiences" between the two groups was "not significant."

But the medical officer noted—in boldface underlined type, to drive home the point—that included among these "insignificant" adverse experiences was one subject who had to discontinue taking Floxin because of dizziness, tinnitus (ringing in the ear), nausea, vomiting and faintness. The subject had taken only one ofloxacin pill—at a dose of 100 milligrams higher than the one Diane had taken, but a dose the company does sell—and experienced both a hearing loss in one ear and an ongoing loss of balance that persisted *even at the six-month checkup.*

In fact, the medical officer noted, the Floxin subjects had "3.4 times more adverse reactions than the placebo group." Yet the drug company said the difference between the groups was "not significant."

Except for writing that little underlined commentary, I saw nothing to indicate that the medical officer took any other action to address the gap between the two interpretations of "significant"—a gap that seemed roughly the size of the crack my wife had fallen through.

Suddenly, I felt a little sick. But I wasn't sure if my nausea was caused by what I was learning about the drug or what I was learning about drug *approval.*

Until I started reading the application, I had actually always assumed that the FDA itself tested drugs before approving them. Or at the very least, I assumed that drug companies did preliminary testing and then the FDA came and redid the tests in its own state-of-the-art labs. Or at the very, *very* least, I assumed that the FDA vigorously reinvestigated every facet of the results presented by the drug companies.

Instead, I found myself reeling from the realization that all the agency did was read summaries of the results of drug company tests, offer a few comments and occasionally ask to see the raw data on which the summaries were based. Many of the medical officer's complaints involved clerical errors. The drug company seemed more likely to get in trouble for sloppy paperwork than for sloppy analysis of drug safety.

Whenever I found something interesting in the New Drug Application, I would run down the library's broad, worn-slippery marble stairs to the pay phone and call Diane to tell her about it. For example, there was a chart showing that females tended to have a higher incidence rate for some types of adverse effects, including CNS reactions, than males. Or an individual case would catch my eye, like the patient the medical officer singled out because he had been forced to discontinue the drug after severe hallucinations.

Further back in the application, the FDA medical officer was interested in ofloxacin patient 12311, who participated in a study of the drug's effects on uncomplicated, mixed sexually transmitted diseases. The report said that patient had a drug reaction requiring hospitalization for psychiatric treatment. The company had listed the reaction as severe on one summary chart but not in the results of the study itself.

I was interested in this case for another reason. It was the first reference I had seen to a hospitalization for a CNS reaction to the drug, and the study had taken place in Philadelphia, at Temple University. I thought the principal investigator in the study might know something useful for Diane's case. Even though the study was several years old, I assumed that a patient who ended up in a psychiatric hospital during a simple clinical trial for an antibiotic would be memorable. So I tracked the doctor down to his private practice in the Philadelphia suburbs. When I finally got him on the phone, he said it was a long time ago and he didn't recall any such patient in his trial.

But he inadvertently gave me a chilling insight into the drug development process. "I was principal investigator, but I was really just pushing papers," he said, sounding distracted. "We had a fleet of residents who were prescribing and signing patients up. I was just overseeing the collection of data. I had very little contact with the patients. The bureaucracy at the hospital was such a mess, and it was six or seven years ago. I couldn't really tell you any of the people who would have been handling the patient care. We were working with four or five chief residents, but I can't really remember anyone specifically.

"Doing that kind of research really isn't one of my passions, you know. That's why I don't do it anymore."

That's hardly the level of enthusiasm and intellectual engagement I'm looking for in the scientists who test the drugs I take.

What was interesting about the New Drug Application was that you could see which cases had led to which warnings on the label. A patient's experience would be mentioned, the medical officer would take note of it, and that's all it took: it was on the package insert. If only one patient in the trials reported a certain reaction, it was on the label in the singular: seizure, manic episode. If more than one, the event made the label in plural, and the drug caused seizures. Very literal, very legalistic.

At one level, I found this very encouraging: if a single patient's experience could change the label, then I felt better about my decision to make such a big deal about *my* one patient. At another level, however, this was scarier than not knowing how something got on the label. Because I was just beginning to realize how little is generally known about a drug before it comes on the market.

Exactly 3,296 patients took Floxin during the clinical trials leading to the drug's FDA approval. To me, that seemed like an absurdly, even shockingly low number. But then I paged through the *PDR,* where some companies (but not Ortho) list the number of patients who initially tested their drugs. It turned out that 3,296 wasn't unusual at all. In fact, when compared with other antibiotics, that 3,296 is actually a bit above average.

But a drug reaction that doesn't present itself in one of 3,296 patients could still be pretty devastating when the drug reaches the general population. Just do the math. What if the drug causes one in 3,297 people to just drop dead?

What if it causes one in 10,000 to just drop dead? And what if it is then taken by 10 million people? Well, a thousand people could drop dead. If a thousand people dropped dead from a drug, would it be yanked from the market? *Should* it be yanked from the market? That is assuming, of course, that doctors ever figured out that the drug was responsible for killing their patients, and then bothered to *report* the deaths as drug reactions.

Ever since I first read the *PDR,* I had wondered about this phrase that appears in the Adverse Reactions section of every drug label: "less than one percent." It seemed to be used rather dismissively, which I found strange considering what an arbitrary threshold it was. In all the Floxin trials, for example, if thirty-two people had a certain reaction, it was "less than one percent." But if thirty-*three* had it, it would be viewed differently.

I knew a little bit about how people misuse numbers because I had once done a story on John Allen Paulos, the Philadelphia mathematician who wrote the best-selling book *Innumeracy.* I called him to see if he could offer any insight into "less than one percent." He hadn't really thought about it before, but he pointed out that " 'less than one percent' isn't that small a number, even as a percentage. It's probably just a cover-all term that really means at *most* one percent, but probably one in thousands." The problem, which he tends to see everywhere, is putting the numbers in some context.

"Generally, the people who come up with these numbers are some obscure scientists in some back corner of the company," he said, "and the people who defend the numbers are lawyers who couldn't add two fractions if you paid them. The people who *know* aren't brought before the public, because the people in the company are afraid they might say something *true.* . . . You know, it's like 'our invisible people have told us . . .' " On the other hand, he said, a lot of psychological issues are involved in the reporting of medical complications—and whenever numbers rely on self-reporting, there are always confounding factors and the possibility of hysteria.

Paulos told me one of his favorite stories about math and medicine, involving his wife, Sheila, and a minor surgical procedure she was considering. "We went to the doctor, and he said the procedure had a one-in-a-million risk, it's nothing," he recalled. "The next time he said, 'It's ninety-nine percent safe.' And as we went out the door, he said, 'It usually goes quite well.' " The doctor seemed oblivious to the fact that he had just cited three vastly different risk/benefit ratios.

"Presumably doctors *know* the risks," Paulos said. "But I've found they bandy about numbers without any reference to their literal meaning. They say what sounds good."

What didn't sound good to me was that even though most of the patients in the clinical trials had taken Floxin without incident, the drug company seemed to be arguing that almost every adverse reaction was somehow "insignificant" or "not drug related." The medical officer seemed to be disagreeing in several instances, but it didn't appear to matter. The drug was approved, and nothing I could see on the label or in the promotional materials would lead a doctor or a patient to wonder if there was anything unique about the kinds of adverse reactions Floxin caused, or the kinds of patients who suffered them. Yet this was a class of drugs with unique CNS side effects: even the Japanese company that invented Floxin said so.

I finally decided to simply call the medical officer myself, to try to understand how the process works. Dave Flockhart helped me track down the doctor in what I was quickly realizing was the very small world of drug approval (and reproval) based in and around Washington.

Along the way, I spoke to several people at CDER, the FDA's Center for Drug Evaluation and Research. The agency has other divisions for food products, medical devices and vaccines (or "biologics"), but CDER regulates medicinal drugs and is the umbrella over government efforts to rule on drug applications and labeling materials, analyze drug advertisements, keep track of adverse drug reactions and investigate violations of drug laws. The medical divisions are divided by drug type. Floxin had been approved by Anti-Infectives. Many of the drugs Diane was now taking had been approved by Neuropharmacology.

I found myself pleasantly surprised at how nice everyone was whom I spoke with at CDER—secretaries, medical officers—and how curious they seemed about Diane's situation. I don't think they were just preening for the press, because I wasn't really calling them as a reporter; they knew I worked for magazines, but they also knew that I was inquiring about a personal matter. They seemed patient and encouraging but also eager to be understood, or aware that they were *mis*understood. They told me about drug reactions in their own families—"One of my kids took a drug," one explained, "and something I know can happen unfortunately *did* happen to her"—and tried to make me understand what they grappled with.

Finally, I hooked up with the medical officer who had overseen the Floxin application and whose commentary I had been psychoanalyzing at the library. Her name was Dr. Ana Szarfman, a reviewer in the anti-infectives division of CDER. She spoke hurriedly and in flurries, with a thick Eastern European accent. I had just started telling her a little bit about how I had become interested in Floxin when she asked if my wife had ever had a head trauma of any sort. I explained that Diane had been in two auto accidents when she was younger, one of which resulted in a concussion and a loss of consciousness. Stacy Phillips had told me something similar had once happened to her.

"Well, that's it, that's it," Szarfman said.

"What do you mean, that's it?" I replied. "Based on your understanding of Floxin, that could be enough to lead to this?"

"That's why, oh yes."

Well, hell, I thought to myself, shouldn't *that* be on the label? Don't more than one percent of the population ever hit their heads really hard? Shouldn't a doctor be told to ask about head trauma before giving the drug?

And what else do medical officers know about the drugs we take that never turns up on the label?

I inquired about some of her printed comments in the Floxin NDA. "In many of my comments," she said, "you must understand, I was a new reviewer. You need to realize, this was my first review."

Oh, great. She seemed almost apologetic about some of the comments she had made in the NDA, but in a very curious way. I couldn't tell if she felt she had been unnecessarily harsh about the inconsistencies in Floxin drug trials or whether she was just remembering how honest and bold she had been when she first came to the agency. Did she now feel her comments were rookie mistakes, or perhaps examples of the admirable youthful exuberance that bureaucracy eventually leaches out of you?

She said she had to run to a meeting. But before she hung up, she left me with a cryptic admonishment. "If you're thinking about this drug, if you're going to write about this drug, I am glad," she said. "Just be careful."

After surviving the six-hundred-page review of the Floxin application, I was ready to plunge into the second envelope the FDA had sent. It contained microfiches of what the FDA had compiled about the drug during its two years on the market in the United States—the pharmacovigilance on Floxin. The data came from the national Adverse Reactions Reporting System, which was CDER's early warning system for problems not detected during preapproval testing. When a patient experiences a suspected adverse reaction to a drug, the doctor is supposed to contact the drug company and the FDA with this information in what is called a "spontaneous report." This is to be filed even if there is no way to prove a causation. The reports then sit in the FDA's database until someone at the agency gets interested in a particular drug and decides to look for trends among the amassed data.

After I made fuzzy copies of all the microfiches, I had more than 150 pages of printouts, each with eight to ten cases and a warning emblazoned across the top: "Cause-effect relationship between each drug and reaction cannot be established with certainty in all cases." Each entry listed all the drugs the patient had been taking and the nature of the adverse reaction to Floxin. After that, there were spaces for the dose, route and duration of the Floxin therapy, as well as the patient's age and sex, and then the outcome of the case. There was also a space for whether the report was domestic or foreign.

What jumped out at me before I could even begin looking for cases like Diane's was how many of the spaces had been left blank. Most of the reports were ridiculously incomplete. Many didn't include the age or sex of the patient. On most, the "patient outcome" was "unknown" or "none." I had to wonder: How seriously were doctors taking the need to report adverse reactions? And how hard were the drug companies or the FDA trying to follow up on the reports, to make sure the database was as complete as possible?

I also noticed that while the domestic reports concerned reactions ranging from rashes and urine retention to sudden death, reactions in the smattering of foreign reports were, for the most part, nothing *but* deaths. Virtually no other reactions had been reported. This confirmed one of the things both Dave Flockhart and Ana Szarfman had told me: that while adverse reaction reporting was terrible in the United States, it was even worse in most of Europe, Asia and South America.

I was also interested in one reaction that showed up a number of times but hadn't really occurred to me as being an ADR. The problem: "no drug effect." Well, I thought, why not? Why shouldn't it be reported when a drug didn't work? We bother to maintain records of who writes prescriptions, who fills them and who takes them. We supposedly monitor when drugs harm patients. Doesn't it make sense to keep track of how well drugs do or don't perform?

The case reports on Floxin—or Tarivid, as it is called in Europe and Asia—were raw, but some trends did pop out. The adverse effects reported were overwhelmingly central nervous system reactions, the most common being insomnia. In each case report, the symptoms were listed alphabetically, and as I charted them, there were clear elevations at agitation, anxiety, confusion, convulsions, depression, dizziness, dream abnormality, hallucinations, headache . . . and on and on. A significant number of the CNS effects—significant to me, anyway—were reported in women, many of whom were in their thirties and taking Floxin in pill form, without other medications. This seemed to confirm what had been predicted in that chart from the clinical trials: women appeared to be having more CNS reactions.

I then separated out all the men, all the older women and anyone being treated with multiple medications, not because their reactions didn't matter but because their medical situations appeared dissimilar to Diane's. From the remaining cases, I counted sixteen reports of convulsions, twenty-five reports of hallucinations and twenty-six reports of other central nervous system effects: everything from depression and agitation to two cases of psychosis. Among this select group of younger women, there were three reports of deafness and six deaths, including one sudden death and one suicide the doctor associated with an "allergic" reaction to the drug. I even found Stacy Phillips's case. Her doctor reported she had had a convulsion after taking two 300-milligram Floxin tablets.

I called Diane from the library to let her know that now it wasn't just she and Stacy who had been Floxed.

The Floxin numbers were creepy but, of course, completely out of context—until I opened the third envelope the FDA had sent and looked at the reports on Omniflox, the quinolone that had been withdrawn. One chart, prepared by the FDA, compared adverse reaction reports for quinolones during their first 120 days on the market. Floxin accounted for almost as many reports as Cipro and Noroxin *combined.* But Omniflox generated nearly three times as many reports as Floxin— in fact, twice as many serious reports as all the other quinolones combined.

The chart convinced me that Omniflox had many more reported safety problems than Floxin. But it also reminded me that I had become interested in quinolones at what must be a very delicate time. Omniflox had been withdrawn only five months before Diane's drug reaction. Quinolone manufacturers must have been waiting for the other shoe to drop. The medical product liability lawyers were also closely monitoring the quinolone situation. In fact, they were about to descend on Acapulco to discuss strategies for a number of drugs and sharpen their teeth. A Philadelphia attorney who was planning to send associates to the meeting, Steve Sheller, promised to tell me all about it.

I had a long talk with Sheller, who had first introduced me to Stacy Phillips, after he got his report from Acapulco. He explained to me that the American Trial Lawyers Association (ATLA) sets up what are called litigation support groups so that lawyers around the country with individual product liability cases can share information and strategy. At the same time, he described the competition between the lawyers to become the "lead counsel" on a group of cases that might turn into something big, like a lucrative class action suit. Lead counsel directed the path of the lawsuits and usually got a bigger cut of the final payout.

The attorneys had a rapidly growing interest in medical product liability because they were right in the middle of the massive and controversial class action involving Dow-Corning silicone-gel breast implants, as well as a smaller group of suits concerning L-tryptophan, a natural sedative sold in health food stores. The breast implant suits were about the product itself; the L-tryptophan cases appeared to be focused on tainted batches from a single manufacturer. Sheller had a few clients in each suit.

The silicone-gel breast implant cases had been jump-started by the stunning decision of the FDA commissioner, Dr. David Kessler, to temporarily halt their use the previous winter, in January 1992. The size of the possible settlements in the cases had sent lawyers scrambling to make FOI requests from the FDA. Suddenly, the product liability bar was taking drug and medical device cases more seriously. At the same time, plaintiffs' lawyers were uncovering potentially damaging information during the "discovery" phase in these cases. During discovery in drug and device cases, lawyers make endless requests for company documents, some of which have never been seen by the FDA; they also often take depositions of key people the FDA has never directly questioned. The agency was taking the by-products of civil litigation very seriously as a major investigative windfall. Several major FDA investigations had been initiated, or broken wide open, by documents from civil cases. It was Dow-Corning internal memos, leaked to the press in 1991 after being sealed by the court during civil suits, that had led directly to Kessler's later ban on the implants. That same year, memos from a suit over the patent rights to the acne medicine Retin-A—which Johnson & Johnson was trying to have approved as the first prescription antiwrinkle cream—reinvigorated a stalled FDA/Justice Department probe of J&J's promotional practices.

At the same time, Sheller explained, trial lawyers were terrified by a new federal ruling by the First Circuit Court of Appeals in Boston. A woman who had allegedly developed autoimmune disease from collagen injections had sued the manufacturer. The court had held that since the collagen was an FDA-approved medical device, the case should be thrown out because FDA approval protected the product from being considered faulty.

The concept of FDA approval as a blanket shield against liability claims had been upheld at the state court level before. In fact, when Sheller had contacted ATLA colleagues before the meeting to see what anyone knew about quinolones, he heard about a couple of Floxin cases in the South which had been thrown out for that very reason. But there had never been such a ruling in a federal court, where it could become a national precedent.

The Boston ruling covered only medical *devices*. But drugs and devices are both regulated by the FDA, and a new legal interpretation of the scope of an FDA approval could eventually affect pharmaceuticals as well. Apparently, drug companies had been lobbying for years for just such a protection—which would put lawyers like Steve Sheller out of business. It would also stop the discovery process on many cases before it ever got started. "This decision," Sheller lamented, "says that if the FDA approved a product, even if the approval was based on false information, the consumer has no rights to do anything."

Sheller reported that there was little interest in Floxin cases at the meeting, because everyone was so absorbed by the Omniflox situation. Since Omniflox had been withdrawn from the market, it would be much easier to prove that it was a faulty product. And since it had been on the market for only four months, lawyers assumed they would be able to show there was a specific period when the drug company knew about the problems but continued to sell the product anyway. That would play well with a jury.

As far as the lawyers were concerned, Floxin was still FDA-approved, and only a handful of possible plaintiffs had been heard from. It was too early to know how actionable the seizures and neurotoxicities would be. The "discovery" process could easily run a law firm $50,000 to $100,000 in time, travel expenses and stenography fees. Unless a number of firms and clients wanted to share that cost, it meant that without a mid-six-figure settlement, the lawyers might not even break even.

In the meantime, however, Sheller wanted to know what *we* were doing about making sure Diane's case was brought to the attention of the FDA and the drug company. Regardless of whether we wanted to initiate legal proceedings—and we weren't sure that we wanted to—had we made a spontaneous report yet to the FDA? That's why the system doesn't work, he said. Nobody bothers to report adverse reactions.

So I called around to Diane's doctors to see if any of them had reported the reaction. None had. I spoke about this with Dr. Amy Finkelstein, the fine internist to whom Diane had been sent after the emergency room visit and who had since become our regular doctor. A towering, handsome pterodactyl of a woman with a raucous wit, Finkelstein volunteered to contact the drug company. I contacted them, too. She called the medical division, I called the public relations division. The responses couldn't have been more different.

Dr. Finkelstein called Ortho to report the incident and ask if the company had had any previous experience with such reactions to Floxin. She reported back that an Ortho physician had seemed genuinely concerned about Diane and had revealed that the company knew of three indexed cases of neurochemical changes in the same medical ballpark as Diane's reportedly brought on by Floxin. The doctor also said that the company was either contemplating, or was about to implement, wording changes in the Floxin label to reflect those reports.

Armed with this information, I called the company's publicist to see if she could help me find someone at Ortho who could discuss the adverse effects of Floxin and could address fears about quinolones in general in the aftermath of the Omniflox withdrawal. This seemed like a contentious but fair request: these fears weren't just *mine,* but were beginning to show up in the pharmacology literature Dr. Flockhart and I were swapping. And much of the Floxin press material describes the drug's side effects as "generally mild and comparable to other quinolones." I also wanted to speak to someone about how the drug was being marketed, and I wanted to verify the coming change in the labeling.

I received instead a carefully prepared statement from the company. It said: "It is important to note that while Floxin is from the same class of drugs, quinolones, it has a different chemical structure [from Omniflox] . . . a completely different safety profile and has been proven worldwide as a safe and effective drug. . . . In the United States alone, ofloxacin has been on the market for almost two years and millions of prescriptions have been written since that time.

"We're not aware of any labeling changes. Floxin continues to be a marketed product and the drug is doing very well."

It turned out that both the company doctor and the PR statement were wrong. The Floxin label had already been significantly altered. About a month after she told me there was no new label, the publicist sent me a copy of the new label—which had been approved by the FDA two months before I ever asked for it. The paragraph about central nervous system effects included new warnings about "agitation, nervousness/anxiety . . . paranoia and depression, nightmares, insomnia and rarely suicidal thoughts or acts. These reactions may occur following the first dose." The company also now warned that ofloxacin "should be used with caution in patients with a known or suspected CNS disorder that may predispose to seizures or lower the seizure threshold." There were also many additional adverse reactions, and seizures had been added to the list of hypersensitivity reactions. Of special interest to Stacy Phillips was a brand-new warning of an interaction with nonsteroidal anti-inflammatory drugs (NSAIDs), which "may increase the risk of CNS stimulation and convulsive seizures." That was certainly something Stacy's physician might have liked to know before prescribing her Floxin and the NSAID Motrin.

When I inquired what the company was doing to make sure prescribing doctors knew about all this new language, I was asked to submit my question in writing. Ortho's written response was, "We do not believe that the changes made to the package insert reflect any basic change in the well-established overall safety profile." In short, they hadn't done anything.

The company pointed out, once again, that Floxin "has been used by over 100 million people worldwide and has been shown to be safe and effective when used in accordance with product labeling recommendations. Like all prescription drugs it has a side effect profile which the doctor must weigh in treating the patient. As described in the labeling, serious side effects with ofloxacin are rare when used according to product labeling recommendations." The company said it had "evaluated in a number of volunteer studies the potential for CNS toxicity. In all of these trials, the results of which were submitted and reviewed by the FDA, *ofloxacin displayed no CNS toxicity* [my emphasis]."

By the time the new label showed up, I had decided to write a magazine article about Diane's situation and the adverse reaction we were having to her adverse drug reaction. As I was working on the story, I received word that Dr. Sidney Wolfe, the medical consumer advocate at Ralph Nader's watchdog group Public Citizen, was about to unleash an updated version of his controversial best-seller *Worst Pills, Best Pills: The Older Adult's Guide to Avoiding Drug-Induced Death or Illness.*

Even though it was quite impossible to get him on the phone, Wolfe did finally agree to fax me an advance galley of what his book would have to say about quinolones. He called them "one of the biggest selling and most overprescribed new classes of drugs in the United States." He noted that "no quinolone is the drug of choice for . . . bronchitis or . . . the commonest . . . community-acquired pneumonia. With rare exceptions, quinolones are not the drug of choice for other infections." The seven-day course of quinolone treatment, however, "can cost between seven and twenty-one times more than equally effective (for most infections) treatment with other drugs."

While writing my story, I became increasingly aware that *another* tall guy with salt-and-pepper hair was getting very interested in the whole legal drug business. Former Arkansas governor Bill Clinton had developed a passion for bashing drug companies during his campaign for president of the United States. While he probably knew that his hero, John F. Kennedy, had railed against high drug prices during his own presidential campaign, Clinton had inherited the issue more directly from one of his major political mentors, David Pryor, the Democratic U.S. senator from Arkansas. Pryor had become one of the most outspoken critics of the pharmaceutical industry after being given the platform of the chairmanship of the Senate Special Committee on Aging in 1989. He had breathed life into the issue of drug company practices by shifting the focus away from the scientific and regulatory questions I was pursuing, and going directly to dollars. Seen through the prism of price, pharmaceuticals were an industry almost anyone could hate. But it was especially loathsome to senior citizens with fixed incomes, bulging medicine containers and rising drug bills. These were the people who were truly being "pillaged."

Senator Edward Kennedy had long been holding hearings on a variety of pharmaceutical issues, and in the U.S. House of Representatives, Democratic congressmen Henry Waxman of California and John Dingell of Michigan had also been harsh critics of pharmaceutical pricing. The American Association of Retired Persons (AARP) had been strong supporters of the attack on the drug companies, along with a strident nonprofit group called Families USA, which sponsored studies of drug prices. They were often conducted by Steve Schondelmeyer, a crusading professor of pharmaceutical economics at the University of Minnesota. Along with Dr. Sidney Wolfe at Public Citizen, this group had, for some time, represented the front line in the small but tenacious consumerist assault on the omnipotence of drug companies. But it was Pryor's interest that had influenced Clinton most strongly, and a handful of Pryor's legal-drug point people were now working at the White House as advisers to the president.

Taking the drug companies to task appeared to be the centerpiece of Clinton's monumental health care reform strategy. To that end, Clinton was joining Pryor, Waxman and Dingell in turning up the rhetoric, providing the media with powerful "did you know" factoids that set the whole legal-drug culture in a new, darker light. Everywhere I looked, I began seeing stories about high drug prices and drug company profiteering. One of the best was a series in my hometown *Philadelphia Inquirer.*

The drug business was, and had been for some time, the single most profitable legal manufacturing industry in the world. Every year when *Fortune* magazine did its *Fortune* 500 issue, pharmaceuticals ranked at or near the top in return on revenues, return on assets, return on equity *and* total return to investors. In worldwide sales, legal drugs were a $250 billion business. But the $55 billion U.S. pharmaceutical market was the one where prices had most spiraled out of control. American drug prices outpaced not only the general inflation rate but even the inflation rate for soaring medical costs.

In the previous five years, the consumer price index had gone up 21 percent. But the price of the top twenty drugs bought by elderly Americans had risen almost 80 percent. Americans paid over 50 percent more than Europeans for identical drugs, and 32 percent more than Canadians. U.S. prescription drug prices seemed almost impervious to the market forces affecting most other products Americans bought; because doctors and patients were so clueless about what drugs cost, there had been little pressure on pharmaceutical companies to compete on price. It was not uncommon for a new me-too drug to enter the market at a price as high as, or even higher than, the drug it had been developed to compete against.

The companies blamed their high prices on unreasonable regulation by the FDA and, more important, on the massive research and development costs associated with bringing a new drug to market. The precise amount of the R&D costs was a source of debate. Individual compounds generally cost less than $50,000 to develop: some cost as little as $3,000. But when the costs of all the compounds that failed along the way to a marketed drug were added up, the average was $194 million per drug, according to the Office of Technology Assessment (OTA), a bipartisan congressional agency. Industry preferred the estimate of $231 million per drug arrived at by researchers at Tufts.

Whatever the figure, drug industry critics were quick to point out that the companies spent much less money creating new drugs than they spent creating new *demand* for drugs. As an industry, pharmaceutical manufacturers spent $10 billion a year on marketing, but only $9 billion a year on research and development. The $10 billion in marketing money was being spent largely to sway the opinions of America's 550,000 prescribing doctors. FDA chairman David Kessler joined the growing pharmaceutical feeding frenzy by suggesting that large promotion budgets were leading to inappropriate prescribing. "People will be hurt," he told the *Times,* because the "promotion is designed to create a market for a product . . . [but] not necessarily the market that will benefit from the drug."

Industry critics also pointed out that while the companies were spending $9 billion on R&D, more than half the medicines they were developing were me-too drugs. This assessment was based on the FDA's internal system for determining whether a new drug provided "significant improvement" over what was already available, "modest improvement" or "no improvement" at all; essentially, it was an official government "me-too rating." When the high percentage of me-too drugs became a public embarrassment and a potential liability on Wall Street, the companies took immediate action. They forced the FDA to abolish the me-too ratings.

The articles started hitting fast and furious in late February 1993, when eye-opening reports were released by Pryor's Senate subcommittee and then by Representatives Waxman and Dingell, who had commissioned a devastating study by the Office of Technology Assessment. The OTA report said, "The market for prescription drugs is broken" and went so far as to calculate how much "excess profit" the drug companies were making, even when compared with other high-tech, science-driven, risk-heavy businesses. OTA put the excess profit margin at a staggering $2 billion a year.

Clinton wanted companies to voluntarily lower their prices. He was threatening mandatory price controls—which most other countries had already enacted (chiefly because they had national health insurance, so their governments were actually *paying* for the drugs). He was also threatening to withdraw a massive tax loophole that was saving pharmaceutical companies over a billion dollars a year. The Section 936 tax credit was available to any U.S. company that brought jobs to Puerto Rico by manufacturing its products there. But it was the pharmaceutical companies that were benefiting most from the loophole. They had taken advantage of it more than all other industries *combined,* and they had the most to lose.

Clinton's threats were the same ones that Pryor had been making for years. But as the senator had made very clear in his committee's annual reports about pharmaceutical pricing, the drug companies seemed neither scared of nor particularly sympathetic toward those who couldn't afford the medications they needed.

Occasionally I would wonder if I was being too tough on Ortho, or its parent Johnson & Johnson. When that happened, I had only to listen to the president call the pharmaceutical industry "price-gougers" again. Then I knew my cause was just, or at least popular.

Diane was still not feeling much better, although she was beginning to, as doctors say, "climatize" to her symptoms. And as the holidays came, we got a chance to see if people were climatizing to her. I was curious to discover how our friends and relatives had processed the few tidbits of information we had let out about her condition. When you're cagey about someone's health problems, you never know how people are going to fill in the blanks.

We went to an annual holiday party that most of our friends in Philadelphia can be counted on to attend. This one offered a smorgasbord of reactions to Diane's drug reaction, most of them more reassuring than I had expected. I thought some people might find what had happened hard to believe. There were times when I still found it hard to believe. Diane looked fine, acted fine; in fact, since many of her symptoms were ones that only an attentive husband would notice, she would need to go out of her way to explain how she *wasn't* fine. But she wasn't about to do that at a party.

Actually, she didn't need to. Many of the guests had their own drug reaction tales to share. Diane was especially moved by a woman who told her a harrowing story about her preteen daughter and an antibiotic. After taking several pills, the young girl, who had never had any emotional problems, told her mother she was suddenly overwhelmed with the feeling that she wanted to kill herself. The frightened mother was even more shocked when her daughter stopped taking the drug, and the feeling simply vanished.

The onset and disappearance of that symptom, called suicidal ideation, was exactly the kind of neuropsychiatric drug effect we were learning about. Diane had experienced it acutely in the weeks right after the drug reaction—this unprecedented feeling that she could just jump out the window. She had quickly recognized it as a symptom and was relieved when medication alleviated it. But she wasn't sure how to explain this phenomenon to others. Hearing a suburban mom discuss her daughter's drug-induced suicidal ideation with such clear-eyed compassion—and not a hint of "it's in her head"—made Diane feel more reassured about how it would go when she explained it to her own mom.

Unfortunately, medications hadn't been quite so successful in addressing her other problems. The drugs, which the doctors had initially hoped would reverse all her symptoms in three weeks, had yet to do their jobs after three *months*. We were getting more worried.

Diane was primarily being treated by Dr. Michael Miller, a bright young biological psychiatrist and psychotherapist with an arch manner and impeccable taste in suits and office art. Initially, he had put her on the antianxiety agent Klonopin (clonazepam) to quash the insomnia and lithium to bring her mood down from the thought-racing highs of what he concurred with the internist and the neurologist was "acute hypomania." The Klonopin had made her *too* sleepy, zombie-sleepy, so she was quickly switched to a less powerful member of the same class of drugs, called benzodiazepines. The new drug was Ativan (lorazepam), which we called "lorz," and Diane was encouraged to regulate—or "titrate"—the dose herself. She jokingly referred to this prescription as "lorz, to taste." Since the normal dosage is between 2 and 6 milligrams a day, she was given 1-milligram pills. But sometimes even one of them was too strong. This is apparently a common problem for petite women, and Diane is tiny, just over five feet tall and just over a hundred pounds. Since the pills couldn't be cut in half, the doctor rewrote the prescription for the half-milligram tablet, which she called a "mezzo-lorz."

Lithium was the more disagreeable of her two drugs. Besides being used preventively—or "prophylactically"—as the standard treatment for manic-depressive illness (or what is now often called bipolar disorder), it is also used to counter temporary, severe mood symptoms brought on by drug reactions and other illnesses. I quickly came to understand that the medication carries a stigma: it's one of those drugs people don't want to take, simply because they hate the characterization of being "on lithium," and they don't appreciate their medication being the punch line of every mental health joke. All current Prozac jokes were originally lithium jokes.

Besides the stigma, lithium is also a very high-maintenance medicine. Diane was required to drink more water every day than she was accustomed to *showering* with, and she had to have regular blood tests to check her lithium levels. The reason was that lithium is a medication with a very fine line between an effective dose and a toxic one.

All drugs have what is called a therapeutic range—which is the amount you want to have in your bloodstream for maximum effectiveness. For all drugs, the dose itself is less important than how your body utilizes the dose. Doctors can roughly assess how a drug is working by asking how you feel, but it can be accurately determined only by measuring your blood levels. If the dose doesn't bring your blood level into the therapeutic range, the drug may not be doing anything. If it goes above the therapeutic range, you are technically overdosing and inviting some of the drug's worst side effects.

If it were practical, ideally doctors would test your blood levels for all the drugs you take; it's the only way to know whether you're getting the proper dose. But it is not practical, at least not at present, unless you're already in the hospital and having blood drawn every five minutes anyway. Outpatients are tested only for medications that, like lithium, have a very narrow therapeutic range and a high risk of toxicity. Even with those drugs, however, doctors aren't always religious about the testing. Why? Perhaps they assume that the patient can be relied upon to tell them if the drug is making them feel sick. Or perhaps they trust that, as healers, they will Hippocratically *sense* a brewing medication problem—especially in the case of psychiatrists, when they're seeing a patient weekly. They are probably also in a catch-22 situation with patients and insurers who could criticize them for ordering *too many* tests.

Why was I speculating about the reasons a doctor might not order yet another blood lithium–level test? Because the package insert said Diane was supposed to have two tests a week during the "acute phase" and at least one every two months after that. Regardless of my unfitness to determine when the "acute phase" ended, I knew she was getting fewer tests than recommended. Diane knew it, too, and had asked Dr. Miller about it. She was just more accepting than I was of his reassurance that he had treated many patients with lithium and had a more realistic idea than the *PDR* of how much testing was needed.

Diane and I almost never quarrel, but we did find ourselves arguing several times about her lithium-level testing. Dr. Miller is a fine psychiatrist whom I otherwise like very much and generally credit with saving Diane's life. But I thought he was being too cavalier about these tests. Diane felt I was being paranoid and trying to meddle in her care. It was hard for me to make her understand the way I felt. I continued to believe that if I had been more paranoid and meddlesome before she took the Floxin, this whole situation might have been avoided.

It was also obvious to me that Diane was having more problems with her current medications than she was letting on. The morning after my birthday—for which we have an annual pizza and bowling party in New Jersey—she admitted that she had had a terrifying experience while preparing for the festivities. After walking over to the bakery to pick up my cake, she got lost while carrying it home. She described standing at a corner a half-block away from our house and not being able to figure out where she was. It was heartbreaking.

We finally got our first relief in months by taking a long romantic weekend of tan lines and shellfish in St. Thomas. Diane started out the trip feeling as well as she had in months (and I have pictures of her in a bikini to prove it). But after five days in the tropical hot sun, she wasn't able to keep up with the amount of water she needed to drink with the lithium. By the end of the trip, she was dehydrated and a little neurotoxic.

Ultimately, the lithium levels became a moot point, because Diane and her doctor agreed that the drug hadn't done much to arrest her symptoms anyway. They decided to try another pharmacological approach, replacing lithium with Depakote (valproic acid), an antiseizure medication in a different family from the benzodiazepines. Depakote was being used experimentally as a mood stabilizer.

By this time, Diane's health problems had lasted too long to be viewed as an emergency by anyone but us. Unlike the first few weeks after she was Floxed, when we encouraged family and friends to believe it was a situation with a short-term "cure," we were now at a different place. When people asked, "How are you?" we were no longer sure they really wanted to know the answer—nor were we sure we wanted to give it to them. I found myself deflecting questions I had wanted to answer just weeks before, consciously rerouting conversations, especially health-related conversations.

And unfortunately, all of a sudden, there were a few other places for those conversations to be detoured.

In mid-January of 1993, my uncle Michael, my father's younger brother, died in Harrisburg. He was only forty-four years old, and left a teenage son and an ex-wife who didn't quite know what had hit them.

I was close to my uncle when I was a kid, and he still lived with my Nana and Pop-pop. I spent many Friday nights sitting in his bedroom being introduced to Bob Dylan and Stevie Wonder on his little record player. Later, when he went off to college, he inadvertently continued my education through the records he left behind. The one that made the greatest impact on me was called *Undercurrent,* by pianist Bill Evans and guitarist Jim Hall, which featured a mesmerizingly grim cover shot of a dead woman floating beneath the surface of a body of water. The music inside was similarly dark—complex, haunted versions of normally up-beat jazz standards—and I came to associate it with him. Michael was thin and handsome and always wore great clothes. But even though he had been a brilliant law student, he treaded water in the real world, always fighting against some kind of undercurrent. Eventually he was towed down.

As I carried Michael's casket to his grave, I couldn't pretend that I didn't lay some of the blame for his death on the dangers of legal drugs. He had migraines, for which he took too many painkillers. Several years before his death, Michael had had an operation on his stomach, and it was bleeding from his stomach that eventually killed him. I couldn't help but wonder if the damage hadn't been caused by some of his prescription drugs—the pain pills he took can gnaw away at the stomach lining.

Not long after Michael's death, my Pop-pop was admitted to the hospital for his emphysema and found out that he also had inoperable cancer. The diagnosis was irrelevant, because mostly what he had was a broken heart—after spending so long preparing for the death of his wife, he had instead lost his youngest son. Knowing Pop-pop would not last much longer, I came to visit him often. My first book was due to be published very soon, and I hounded my publishers to give me just one copy so he could see it before he died.

I hopped on the train to Harrisburg the day the book arrived so I could show it to him that very afternoon. I kissed him good-bye and felt the tickle of his mustache on my cheek for the last time. He died a few days later, and I was back home as a pallbearer for the second time in six weeks.

Then Diane's father was rushed to the hospital with a perilously high fever. Stoic that he is, Ed had ignored a bladder infection until it nearly developed into septicemia, a life-threatening condition. The doctor at the hospital wanted to put him on, of all things, Floxin. Ed refused it, so they gave him another strong antibiotic instead.

While his reaction was understandable, it did concern me. Certainly anyone with a daughter who had the kind of reaction to Floxin that Diane did might be at greater genetic risk for similar problems. But as I was beginning to understand more fully, it is not only risk that matters. All drugs have risks. It's a question of whether the potential benefit is *worth* the risk and whether the patient *understands* that risk—which depends on whether the doctor knows enough about the drug to really *explain* the risk.

From a risk/benefit perspective, Floxin was probably not the drug of choice for what had been wrong with Diane. Not only was it "too big a gun," but it was never clear that the specific bacteria she was infected with would have responded to Floxin. (Doctors are encouraged right on the Floxin label to administer the drug before results of lab tests are back.) But Floxin may very well have been the drug of choice for my father-in-law's potentially lethal infection, and he waved it off only because of what he knew had happened to Diane.

I felt much better, as did he, when the replacement drug killed the bacteria and brought his temperature down to double figures.

My article was about to come out in the April 1993 issue of *Philadelphia* magazine. The piece offered a fairly in-depth view of what had happened to Diane and what we had learned about the system that was supposed to have prevented it. I concluded with a discussion of "black boxes."

During my conversations with FDA doctors and Dave Flockhart, I would often hear about black boxes: big serious warnings placed at the very top of the package insert for certain drugs and then highlighted with, literally, a thick black box around them. A doctor in the FDA antibiotics division told me I could learn a lot from the story of the aminoglycosides—a class of injectable antibiotics, including gentamicin, that had come on the market in the late 1950s and were hailed as a new way of treating many of the same bacterial infections that quinolones combat. After the drugs had been on the market for some time, it was found that, in some patients, they caused both kidney damage and deafness.

They now carry a black box warning for both these adverse drug reactions. A black box doesn't mean the medication should be avoided: in fact, gentamicin is still commonly used in hospitals. It simply means that the drug can be dangerous and patients taking it should be closely monitored. Drug companies apparently hate black boxes, especially for products like broad-spectrum antibiotics, which they want physicians to feel comfortable throwing at anything. A black box calls attention to a drug's risk/benefit ratio. Doctors are always supposed to be taking that ratio into consideration, but too often they don't. Instead, they prescribe on automatic pilot.

A black box also alters the kind of print advertising a drug company can do. For most drugs, companies have a choice between regular ads—which, since they recommend a course of treatment, must be more than one page in order to include prescribing information from the package insert—and "reminder" ads or "promotional labelings," which simply call attention to a brand name and can be a page or less. A pen or a notepad that a drug company gives out is, basically, a reminder ad and is regulated as such by the FDA's Division of Drug Marketing, Advertising and Communications ("Dee Dee Mac"). Technically, the agency can act only if a false or misleading ad is published. While companies aren't required to submit their promotional materials ahead of time, DDMAC is usually asked to screen ads and press material before publication or distribution to see if it will consider them problematic.

Reminder ads can be cheaper (because they require less space) and can often be more "creative" because they provoke fewer arguments with the FDA about whether the scientific claims are accurate. But if a drug has a black box, its manufacturer cannot use reminder ads.

In my article, I called for a black box warning for CNS side effects to Floxin. I also urged the FDA to call a meeting of its Anti-Infectives Advisory Committee to put the drug's neurotoxicity on trial.

The piece included as much of Diane's story as she and I felt was appropriate. The debates we had over the inclusion of personal details were intense. Since we had both written about each other before, we had already navigated some of this territory, but the stakes seemed much higher this time. And it's always easier to tell a personal story when you know how it ends, which we didn't. Diane and her doctor were already talking about getting her off the Depakote, which she had been taking for only two months. The drug gave her terrible stomach pains and was making her already fine hair fall out in clumps.

Still, overall she was functioning better—no less symptomatic, but more accustomed to *being* symptomatic. Once Diane admits something is real or true—which can take a long time—she can adapt to almost anything. She was growing weary, however, of being sick and, worse to her, of being *perceived* as sick. She was still waiting for that combination of pills that would make her feel not just "better" but like someone she recognized as herself. So was I. Even after all the bitter pills we had swallowed, we were still awaiting the wonder drug.

I was proud that Diane had the courage to let me use her story to illustrate an important public health problem. But we both had serious doubts that anyone besides our family members would pay much attention to such an esoteric piece of pharmaconfessional journalism.

And then the phone started ringing.

CHAPTER 3

MedWatchers

The first call was from a Marlene Josephs, who said that her husband David had phoned the doctor to complain of severe flu and chest cold symptoms. Without an office visit, David was prescribed Floxin along with the antidiarrheal Imodium D and cough syrup. Less than an hour after taking the Floxin, he was having trouble breathing, and "by the time we called 911," she said, "he was the color of a fire engine." At the ER, David was rushed, gasping, into a treatment room. It was forty-five minutes before the doctor emerged and told Marlene that her husband was alive and starting to come out of shock.

She said the prescribing physician later told them he thought the reaction was to the cough syrup, which David had used before, and *not* the Floxin, which he had never taken. The couple had not known to ask if Floxin had any special neurotoxicity. But the doctor probably should have. David's vulnerability to central nervous system reactions could not have been a secret. He had undergone brain surgery five years earlier and was still taking preventive antiseizure medication.

The next call was from an elderly woman who had taken one sample pill of Floxin for a bladder infection. She became disoriented, her pupils dilated "like saucers," she couldn't sleep for days and she was having smell and taste hallucinations. "I took that wrapper and stomped on it and threw it in the trash can," she declared.

The next woman had taken Omniflox, not Floxin. She had been given the drug to bring down a fever just before her honeymoon— which, unfortunately, began only days before the drug was recalled. "I almost got divorced on my honeymoon, I got so sick," she said. It was six months before she was able to go back to work.

Then I got a call from a medical writer who lived several states away. She had been given Floxin for a urinary tract infection, and after the third pill, she had had two seizures. Her husband, a doctor, initially thought she was experiencing cardiac arrest. The seizures eventually subsided, but the neurologist she consulted said she shouldn't drive for several months. In fact, the driving was the reason she didn't want her drug reaction to be reported to the drug company, the FDA or anyone in authority.

"The motor vehicle code in most states is very restrictive," she said. "The physician is supposed to tell the state if you've had seizures, and then it's on your license. What most people do is lie: it's the only thing you *can* do."

The medical writer said that I had just scratched the surface of the entire problem of doctor-induced or iatrogenic disease. The problem went back to Hippocrates and was reinvented most recently in the mid-1970s by social critic Ivan Illich's provocative books *Tools for Conviviality* and *Medical Nemesis: The Expropriation of Health*. Since she maintained an elaborate system for devouring medical journals and filing the articles for her various projects, the writer offered to send me published reports she thought would or should interest me and Diane. Her faxes began arriving almost immediately.

The calls kept coming and only increased when, several days later, I discussed the article on the popular local morning television show *AM Philadelphia.* Its host, Wally Kennedy, was the one who had indirectly introduced me to the Floxed lawyer Stacy Phillips. Diane was invited to appear: in fact, they wanted her more than me. But she declined. She didn't feel up to it, and she knew that, since I had been a regular guest on the show, they could do it without her. In fact, Marlene and David Josephs, the first people who had called me about "Less Than One Percent," ended up appearing in her place.

Several viewers called in to report adverse reactions to Floxin. A woman who had previously taken Cipro without incident said she was now scared to death to take it again because of the article. I tried to explain that if she hadn't had a problem taking the drug before, it was unlikely she would have one now. And besides, Cipro was not exactly the same drug as Floxin. I also reminded her that I was not a doctor— although, suddenly, I was sort of playing one on TV.

After the show, the letters increased as well. I heard from a nurse in Massachusetts who had noticed that her elderly patients were complaining about insomnia, palpitation, restlessness and other abnormal CNS agitation when taking Floxin. And I was contacted by a pharmaceutical industry safety consultant, a physician who had worked for several major drug companies and had been involved in analyzing a quinolone antibiotic.

"I don't think the medical community realizes the potential danger of quinolones," he lamented. "They're promoted as high-tech, sure-fire *candy,* as drugs that are going to be effective for a wide variety of patients. But except for one drug interaction [with the asthma medication theophylline] and the need to adjust doses for people with renal failure, they only have a vague understanding that there may be other side effects. There is not yet an appreciation for the kind of CNS reactions your wife had, which are very serious because they can take ordinarily healthy people and ruin their lives."

He said that before he even read the article—his wife had mentioned its subject to him—he knew that my wife had private health insurance and that her reaction had been to *samples* of Floxin.

How had he guessed that? "If it was an HMO," he explained, "they wouldn't let the doctor use [Floxin] because it's overkill. For a basically healthy person, you don't want to go to drugs that are expensive or unnecessarily potent. I hate to say this, but your wife's doctor may have wanted to do her a *favor* by giving her free medicine.

"The doctor probably wouldn't have 'written for' [prescribed] ofloxacin. I'm willing to bet that. Heavy sampling contributes to its use."

One of our pharmacists agreed completely with this observation about samples, which are distributed to make it easier for physicians to get into the habit of using a new drug. The pharmacist recalled that her old boyfriend, a urology resident, had *piles* of Floxin samples in his apartment.

"He had, like, three hundred of those little boxes," she said. "He had to give them to *someone.*"

By the end of that first momentous week—which just happened to coincide with the publication of my first book, so we were pretty busy— Diane and I had been invited to appear on the national ABC morning show *Good Morning America.* Diane was torn. She had been as public as she ever wanted to be in the article, and she had been willing mostly because she was convinced nobody would ever read it. She had turned down Wally Kennedy, who was a friend of mine. And now she was being asked to make an appearance on national television, but instead of discussing her first novel—the way she might have dreamed it—she would be talking about her urinary tract infection.

She was ultimately swayed by the opportunity to use her situation to anchor a women's health segment on adverse drug reactions. Dr. Timothy Johnson hosted the two-part segment, which featured us and two doctors: a physician from the New York area, and Dr. Murray Lumpkin, the head of the anti-infectives division of the FDA, on whose watch Floxin had been approved. Diane and I agreed that the whole trip was worth it just to see Johnson turn to Lumpkin after the commercial break and ask, "Dr. Lumpkin, does the world *need* a drug like Floxin?"

Bald, with oversize glasses and a thin-lipped smile, Lumpkin looked a bit like Hunter Thompson turned pharmaceutical bureaucrat. He and Johnson went on to have a very lucid and informative discussion about the FDA and antibiotics. Johnson, who obviously knew the subject well, nudged Lumpkin into explaining matters that many consumers don't understand: like the fact that drugs don't have to be *better than* those in existence to get approved, just *as good as*. Lumpkin used the opportunity to chide doctors who don't report adverse drug reactions, carefully saying it was their "responsibility" (it's not a legal requirement) to let the FDA and the drug company know about ADRs, especially in the first few years after marketing.

After the show, Lumpkin approached us backstage. I was edgy because my article had questioned the FDA's ability to protect the public health and included quotes from several FDA doctors who had spoken to me without agency permission. And of course, I was the reason he had just been dragged up from Washington to be dressed down on national television. I figured I probably wasn't his favorite guy right then, and assumed he was about to tell me why.

Instead, he introduced himself by his nickname, which is Mac, and proceeded to ask us detailed questions about Diane's condition. Then he told us how much he and his colleagues had appreciated the article, and asked if his division could follow up on any other cases that came to my attention; I had about a dozen already, none of which had been reported to the FDA or the drug company. He even asked me what I thought should be on the drug's labeling.

Lumpkin also encouraged me to continue doing investigative journalism in this area. I was pleased but a little puzzled. Here was a former pediatrician who had worked at a drug company before coming to the federal government. This didn't sound like the résumé of someone who would deliberately invite media scrutiny. Yet here he was suggesting that I delve further into the whole process of drug regulation, which he knew that I believed to be deeply flawed.

Was he a glutton for punishment, I wondered, unaware that he was hanging a "kick me" sign on his own agency? Or did he know that the process was even more screwed up than I thought it was?

The TV appearance brought many more calls and letters. By the end of the week, I had been told of at least twenty cases of severe CNS reactions to quinolones—most of them to Floxin—that hadn't been reported to the FDA. Diane and I came to refer to this growing group as "the Floxies." Dozens of other people contacted me about other kinds of reactions to quinolones, or reactions to other medications. Some people wanted to bemoan the awful state of drug information for patients, or health care in general. Others just wanted to know how Diane was feeling.

One of the most interesting letters came from a licensed pharmacist and dentist in Indianapolis, Kent Smith. He and his wife Sue took an annual Christmas trip to Yellowstone National Park, where they stayed in the cabins maintained by the National Park Service and enjoyed sleigh rides around the snowbound geysers. During the past year's trip, Sue had taken Floxin for a mild pelvic infection and nearly died from the reaction.

Sue had been told nothing about Floxin. Almost immediately after taking the first pill, she felt headachy and disoriented: after six pills, she went into anaphylactic shock and stopped breathing four times. She had to be airlifted, unconscious, out of the park to a nearby hospital. But after she was fully revived, she continued to suffer from side effects. Four months later, she was still experiencing visual distortions, confusion and stabbing pains in her legs, which her doctors had diagnosed as toxic polyneuritis caused by the Floxin.

I called her husband, who, on the phone, sounded like a curious combination of mild mannered and completely pissed off. Kent Smith had been doing his own literature search and, since he was better at it than me, had found some articles I hadn't seen—including some in German, which he was trying to get translated.

One was a 1988 German study on quinolones that addressed the issue of head trauma and CNS reactions. While the study did not describe a large number of cases—nine reports of seizures out of some two million prescriptions for ofloxacin—it did point out that "in many cases these patients had a history of epilepsy or cerebral trauma." While the paper didn't specifically recommend that head trauma be listed among the contraindications for ofloxacin, it did say that "further information is needed on severe CNS reactions . . . unlike many antibacterial drugs, the quinolones can cause these severe CNS effects even after short-term use . . . in patients with no abnormal psychiatric history."

The study also raised the issue of the ophthalmic toxicity of quinolones, suggesting that some of the visual distortions brought on by Floxin reactions could be caused by changes in the eye as well as the brain. So we considered making an appointment with a neuro-ophthalmologist.

In the meantime, another doctor sent me an article on quinolones from the latest issue of *Infections in Medicine* (which had a very appealing cover shot of a "necrotizing streptococcal infection" on someone's leg). Adjoining the article was a commentary from journal editor-in-chief Dr. Thomas Beam, the Buffalo microbiologist who was America's Chief Justice of antibiotics: the chairman of the FDA Anti-Infective Drugs Advisory Committee, which I hoped would take a hard look at these drugs.

Beam announced in his written commentary that the bloom was off the quinolone rose. "For years, infectious disease specialists have discussed the characteristics of the ideal antimicrobial drug, such as infrequent dosing, low toxicity and high specificity," he wrote. "Unfortunately, this ideal can never be achieved, in part because the survival skills of bacteria are greater than the power of any antimicrobial. The fluoroquinolones as a group represent a significant advance . . . however, the advantages that patients have gained from their use have already diminished. . . . There are now chinks in the armor of these drugs . . . [and] the perception that [they] are uniformly safe has been altered."

In the middle of this journal article was a one-page "reminder" ad for Floxin. The doctor who sent it to me believed the ad violated FDA rules—although quite ingeniously. The main photos and text were, as required, nothing more than the brand name and the dosages. In the background, however, was a running list of the pathogens supposedly treated by the drug. But the names of the pathogens were cleverly positioned so that a few letters of each would be obscured by the photo, so the FDA couldn't say the company was overtly recommending Floxin to treat them.

While these journal articles were feeding my growing obsession with quinolone safety, I tried to take a step back and look at the big picture. Look how many months it had taken, I thought, for a reporter with pretty advanced investigative skills to dig up the information a doctor would need before even thinking *twice* about giving Floxin to my wife. What clinician has time for that? And if doctors get most of their information from pharmaceutical company "detail men," what drug salesperson would be stupid enough to volunteer all this bad news about the product he or she was selling on commission?

.   .   .

Later in April, I got an enraged phone call from a local hospital pharma-cist. He wanted to know if I was aware of what detail men from Miles Laboratories, the $7 billion Connecticut-based multinational company that makes Cipro (and whose German owner, the $28 billion Bayer AG, makes Bayer aspirin) had been doing with my article. Apparently they were clandestinely faxing it around, along with obviously desktop-published charts comparing CNS and gastrointestinal drug reactions of quinolones, to convince hospitals to drop Floxin and replace it with Cipro.

The faxes were completely misleading. The data weren't drawn from a head-to-head comparison in any recent study. They were just old num-bers copied from package inserts. And the faxes were probably against the law—not only did they violate my copyright, but they broke FDA rules about distributing unapproved promotional materials.

The pharmacist said it was exactly this kind of behavior that had led his hospital to ban the local Cipro rep from its grounds for six months. In recent years, the FDA had severely restricted what the detail men could do and say. But it was obvious that some detail men would still do almost anything to make a sale.

The pharmacist was calling the FDA to report Miles. And I called Miles to find someone who could officially put a stop to this. An execu-tive in the sales department called back very apologetically. "Our reps are trained not to use unapproved materials," he said sheepishly, "and hopefully this was just a misguided one or two. But we sent a message out to all our reps the day you called to let them know this should not be used."

He asked for the name of the hospital pharmacist who had alerted me. I told him I was certain that when the FDA complaint against Miles was processed, he would find out.

In the meantime, I continued to get phone calls and letters. Some were from obvious hypersensitivity junkies—people who said that because of a drug reaction, they were now allergic to everything. The term *allergic to* was being tossed around very casually. To some of these people, it had become a metaphor for any negative physical sensation following the ingesting of a food, drug or beverage. I tried to explain to them that, in fact, *allergic* means something much more specific and sometimes much more life-threatening. A drug that upsets your stomach is not the same as a drug that sends you into shock.

We also heard from a few crackpots. Our favorite was the doctor who called to inform us that Diane had been completely misdiagnosed. She hadn't had a drug reaction at all. She was, in fact, suffering from TMJ—temporomandibular joint disorder, the controversial dental condition of the lower jaw. He based his diagnosis on the fact that, during her appearance on *Good Morning America,* it appeared to him that her face was slightly asymmetrical, and that one of her eyes seemed slightly lower than the other. His office sent along his promotional videotape.

More than half the people who contacted me, however, seemed like ordinary folks who had become symptomatic while taking Floxin or just afterward. Some hadn't known there *were* such things as adverse drug reactions. Far too many of them reported being assured by their doctors that Floxin could not have caused such reactions. They were stunned when I told them that most of the reactions were listed on the package insert, which hardly proved causation but definitely suggested that their doctors hadn't known much about the drug. A significant percentage said that their physicians had told them to keep taking the medication, even while they were having reactions such as "restlessness, lightheadedness [or] confusion"—even though the package insert clearly states that quinolones should be discontinued immediately at the first sign of these reactions.

I spent hours on the phone with the people who seemed like true Floxies. While I didn't mind explaining what little I knew, one thought kept recurring. If these people were so desperate for help and information that they were calling *me,* how well could the FDA, the drug companies and prescribing physicians be informing the public about adverse drug reactions?

Late that spring, I got my answer when David Kessler announced in the *Journal of the American Medical Association* that he was scrapping the entire national Adverse Reactions Reporting System. His article was meant to create excitement for a new FDA program called MedWatch, which came complete with a new, simplified form, a PR campaign and toll-free numbers for reporting drug reactions. But to me, Kessler's announcement only confirmed my worst fears about how drugs were monitored for safety problems after being made available to the public.

Simply from focusing on the case of Floxin, I had come to the conclusion that pharmacovigilance—or "postmarketing surveillance," as it was called at the FDA—was pretty poor. According to Kessler, it was even worse than that.

You know that there's a big problem when the first word of a *JAMA* article on a subject is "Unfortunately."

How bad was the ADR problem? Kessler cited recently published figures showing that between 3 and 11 percent of all hospital admissions in the United States could be attributed to adverse drug reactions—which translated into as many as 3.7 million Americans a year who were hospitalized because of ADRs. He neglected to mention the people who suffered adverse drug reactions once *in* the hospital. Recent *JAMA* studies said that as many as 30 percent of hospitalized patients experienced ADRs from the medicines they received there. Complications from drug therapy were the leading cause of medical injuries in hospitals and were responsible for 0.31 percent of all hospital deaths. That was "less than one percent," but it still amounted to somewhere between 60,000 to 140,000 dead hospital patients a year in America alone. More than half of these deaths were considered preventable.

And how bad was the ADR *reporting* problem? Kessler said that 90 percent of all adverse events involving drugs and devices, and perhaps as high as 99 percent of the most serious adverse events, were never reported to the FDA. The reason, he speculated, was that when doctors were confronted with an unexpected outcome of treatment, they were more likely to blame the event on "the course of the disease" than on the drug they had prescribed. He blamed this on the "limited training" that medical students receive in clinical pharmacology and drug therapy, citing a study that found only 14 percent of American medical schools required courses in the core skills needed to understand how drugs functioned in the body and properly prescribe them. Most schools "taught only a few hours of clinical pharmacology," he said, and only in the early years of training. So it was hardly surprising that prescription errors are the second most common cause of malpractice claims.

British drug safety guru Dr. William Inman had once described the "seven deadly sins" of voluntary reporting as "complacency, fear of involvement in litigation, guilt, ambition to collect and publish a personal series of cases, ignorance of the requirements for reporting, diffidence about reporting mere suspicions, and lethargy."

"Physicians are caught in a double bind," one nationally known pharmacologist explained to me. "They swear to a Hippocratic oath, 'Do no harm.' And every time they write a prescription they're [taking a chance of] breaking that oath. It creates an environment in which it is better for the physician to become defensive and try to deny there was a drug reaction.

"It's hard for a doctor to say, 'I hurt you. I didn't mean to, but you were that one in fifty or whatever who developed a bad reaction to the drug. And I feel like shit.' So up come the defenses and the fear of litigation and it becomes better to stonewall."

Kessler said that reporting drug reactions just didn't seem to be part of the "culture" of medicine in America, the way it was in, say, the U.K.—where prescription drugs have been dispensed with "yellow cards" attached for patients to easily report drug reactions. But Kessler didn't mention that conditions in the U.K. still weren't that much better.

In one study, a hundred British doctors had their practices heavily scrutinized for a month—a total of 36,740 consultations and more than 20,500 prescriptions—to see how many adverse reactions they observed and how many they reported. Even though the doctors knew that they were being studied for their ADR reporting habits, they reported only 6 percent of the drug reactions they observed to the official government "monitoring scheme," as it is called. Of the two hundred reactions considered severe or moderately severe (which accounted for about a third of those observed, and one per every hundred prescriptions), only thirty were reported to the "scheme."

The Kessler article went on to promise how great an improvement there was going to be under MedWatch, the new reporting system the FDA was putting into place. But all I could think of was what Kessler was *really* saying.

He was admitting that the FDA didn't know nearly enough about the thousands of drugs the agency had already approved.

He was admitting that Phase IV did not work.

What is Phase IV? It is the most poorly controlled scientific experiment in the entire legal-drug world. And it is an experiment we unwittingly volunteer for every time we use a medication.

The process of clinical trials for drug approval is almost always referred to as having *three* phases, and those phases have been standardized in every country where medications are tested and monitored. Phase I is the "first time in humans" trials, in which a small number of healthy subjects take the drug to see if it is safe, and at what dose. Phase I trials are undertaken only after years of tests on individual cells, then on animals, and then on a handful of individual human subjects.

Phase II is the first test of the drug's efficacy in sick human subjects, also on a small scale.

Phase III is the large-scale testing, for efficacy and safety in sick human subjects, at the dose or doses that will actually be marketed.

Most consumers of medication are not even aware that there *is* a Phase IV. We either haven't been adequately informed, or just don't want to know, that the biggest test of a drug's safety and efficacy comes *when we take it.* Every time we are medicated—every pill, patch, shot and suppository—we are technically participating in an ongoing experiment, a Phase IV study of safety, efficacy, even the quality control for the specific "batch" of pills ours came from.

How is Phase IV meant to work? Basically, anything a drug does to a patient that is unusual, telling or simply interesting is supposed to be reported by doctors to the drug company and/or the appropriate government regulatory agency, such as the American FDA, the British Medicines Control Agency (MCA) and the Japanese Central Pharmaceutical Affairs Council. The moment a report comes in to a drug company, the clock starts ticking. Depending on the severity of the reaction and whether it is already mentioned on the label, the company has a specified period of days (for a serious reaction that isn't yet mentioned on the label), weeks or months to forward the information to the proper authorities in the various countries where the drug is sold. Once a drug is available in the United States, for example, a death possibly caused by the drug in the Netherlands is supposed to reach the FDA just as quickly as a death in Pennsylvania.

Drug companies and regulatory agencies have a separate staff for this postmarketing pharmacovigilance. The field is dominated by people trained in the emerging discipline of pharmacoepidemiology—which is referred to as "pharmaco-epi" or just plain "epi" (pronounced "eppy"). Epidemiology is a very inexact science that began as the branch of medicine that studied the cause and control of epidemics, and it grew into the statistical analysis of extremely raw medical data for early warnings—or omens—of unexpected problems.

The omens that pharmaco-epi people search for are called "signals," and in the postmarketing surveillance of medications, it doesn't take many serious adverse reaction reports before a signal is suspected. With a new drug, two or three unexpected and similar cases in the entire United States can be considered a signal—or can at least stimulate interest in turning up the volume to listen for one. There are some instances when *one* case becomes a signal, if it is particularly shocking, or the patient is being treated by a prominent, well-connected doctor who gets the case report published as a letter in a peer-reviewed journal or just talks about the case with people who matter.

Once a signal is identified by a regulatory agency, several things can happen. One of them is nothing, because the drug company's own epi-

demiologists will almost always argue—and sometimes convincingly—
that there is no signal at all, but only what epidemiologists refer to as
"noise."

But what often happens is that the drug company is forced to amend
its package inserts. If the labeling change is considered significant, the
company may be ordered to send a personal correspondence to all
the prescribing physicians in the country—that's 550,000 letters in the
United States alone—to let them know about the new information.
These are called "Dear Doctor" letters.

The drug company is sometimes urged to do additional epidemiological analysis, or even to enroll patients in a formal, controlled Phase IV
study in order to address a specific question. Or most severely, the regulatory agency can threaten to withdraw its approval. When this happens,
a drug company usually decides to "voluntarily" withdraw the drug from
the marketplace.

Some version of this process takes place in all of the industrialized
nations that regulate medications. But what happens in the United States
has more international resonance. America is the world's largest pharmaceutical market, and it has the largest concentration of prescribing physicians. Its Food and Drug Administration is the world's largest, richest
and most persevering regulatory agency.

So when the chairman of the FDA said that one of the cornerstones
of Phase IV needed to be replaced, because 99 percent of the data
required to keep drugs safe wasn't reaching the proper authorities, I
worried.

Stacy Phillips, our first fellow Floxie, called with bad news. She was
quitting her job because of the symptoms, which had never really
stopped since her drug reaction. She hoped that maybe staying home
with her kids would be a better, safer place for her to be. But there was
no question that she was crushed at having to make the decision.

She was also angry—angry enough to sue both Ortho and the physician who had prescribed the Floxin, even though she knew she might be
the first and perhaps the only plaintiff. She had chosen her old boss,
Steve Sheller, and his daughter Jamie, to represent her. In less than two
years, Stacy had gone from a very promising young attorney in the
firm—she had worked on a number of the L-tryptophan cases—to a
moderately promising client. She had obviously been severely damaged,
but her case wasn't going to be an easy one. In fact, if she couldn't get it
heard at the state court level, she might not have a case at all. Sheller told

me the discovery process for a case like this could easily cost $50,000 in document searches, interrogatories and depositions. I had no reason to doubt him. If I billed by the hour, like a lawyer, for the time I had spent investigating Diane's case, it would have added up to at least that. And I felt as though I had only scratched the surface.

Stacy was curious as to whether we were going to sue. It was an interesting idea, one we had swirled around in our mouths a number of times but always spit out. When Stacy decided she was going to file, we thought about it again and reluctantly decided to speak with a few lawyers. We met, in a very preliminary way, with Sheller and with lawyers at another Philadelphia law firm. But neither of us really wanted to go through with it. Diane was dead set against the whole idea and felt it was time to start putting the whole episode behind her. Indeed, she felt that people were pressuring her to sue. Some of those we talked to made her feel she would be a fool not to pursue legal action.

I felt strongly that once you enter a situation as a journalist, you can't rejoin it as a plaintiff. But I was curious about what a lawsuit might accomplish—certainly more curious than Diane. And I did wonder how we would react if Stacy went ahead alone and was given a big, easy settlement just to go away.

So we listened to the lawyers. And we decided to think about it some more. In the meantime, we tried to get back to our previously scheduled life, already in progress.

Diane's younger sister had a second baby, Anna. Her first child, Emma, was already a year and a half and starting to turn into a little person. In the meantime, my work was going well. My book got some publicity and was optioned for a feature film. I had to take a business trip to London and Munich for a *Vanity Fair* story, and Diane joined me. It was our first extended journey since the drug reaction, and Diane's first visit to England, and she held up pretty well. She had been concerned about going to museums and tourist sites by herself. After the birthday cake incident, she admitted to me that she had gotten lost walking around in our neighborhood one other time. But she paced herself, and judging from our end-of-the-day recaps over Indian food at Chutney Mary's, she had a better time than I did.

After we came back, we were treated to the only really good thing that had come out of Diane's drug reaction: she was given a New York reading of her unpublished first novel by the big Barnes & Noble store on the Upper East Side. The invitation had come the day we were in New York to appear on *Good Morning America*. After the show, we stopped in a few bookstores to see if they were carrying my book.

The manager had read my jacket-cover bio and knew we were both writers. While he was interested in having me come back for a signing, he seemed much more pleased by the notion of having a reading by an unpublished novelist—which B&N had never done before. So he put us on a double bill. Although Diane was still having trouble getting much new writing done, she was able to edit sections of her first novel into performable pieces. I was enormously moved to watch Diane, who had been through so much in the past months, get up and trust the muscle memory in her brain again.

While I was busy working on other stories, I continued to correspond with Floxies and talk on the phone with Dave Flockhart. The Georgetown clinical pharmacologist was amazed and appalled at the number of Floxin cases I'd heard about.

Among others, I had been contacted by Pennsylvania state representative Lita Cohen, whose district was just outside of Philadelphia. She had taken Floxin and Noroxin and had had "terrible" reactions to both drugs. She said she wasn't sure if the doctors who had prescribed them were even aware of their adverse effects. She was one of the many patients I heard from who, after having a bad reaction to one quinolone, were given another one—sometimes by the same doctor. This meant the doctors either didn't know that the first reaction was a good predictor of the second, or didn't understand that the drugs were in the same class. Representative Cohen said she was sending my article to her doctors and would now carry a card in her wallet stating her sensitivities to the drugs.

Flockhart was doing what he could to sow the seeds of interest in reactions like these at the FDA. There was a semipermeable membrane between the regulatory agency and the pharmacology department at Georgetown University Medical Center. By scientific osmosis, some of the concerns the FDA might not be ready to officially voice as a government agency would seep out through academics closely associated with the agency, either from Georgetown or nearby Johns Hopkins. Conversely, many of those academic pharmacologists knew shortcuts to getting the FDA's attention.

The FDA had a tiny annual budget to fund a handful of its own Phase IV studies; Georgetown was a primary recipient of those grants, along with Hopkins, Penn and the University of Maryland. The vast majority of Phase IV studies were done by the companies themselves. According to Flockhart, the FDA fund was for research that drug companies did not go out of their way to sponsor because it might limit, rather than expand, the use of their products.

The agency's budget for such outside research was about $12 million a year: a drop in the bucket compared with the $9 billion drug companies spend annually on R&D, but something nonetheless. The grants also served to formalize the intellectual underground railroad between Georgetown and the FDA. Georgetown graduate students could obtain fellowships at the agency. And the director of CDER, Dr. Carl Peck, was very friendly with the chairman of the Georgetown pharmacology department, Dr. Raymond Woosley.

I had, through pure dumb luck, fallen in with some of the right people. But besides his interest in Floxin, Flockhart also had a broader agenda. He explained that Woosley, his boss, was beginning to "get political" about the terrible shortage of unbiased information about medications. Woosley would soon be unveiling a radical proposal that could address some of the problems inherent in the FDA approval system.

Flockhart suggested that when I finished investigating what had happened to my wife, I should come down to Washington and talk to Woosley about the politics of pharmaceutical science.

What the hell had happened to my wife anyway? Nine months after I led her into the emergency room, we were still trying to authoritatively answer that question.

Well, maybe it's unfair to say "we." Diane's psychiatrist had already come to a diagnosis. Dr. Miller believed that Diane's drug reaction had set off a genetic predisposition to mood disorders, triggering full-blown manic-depressive illness. He believed that Diane had experienced some symptoms of mood problems before the drug reaction but had successfully incorporated them into her lifestyle as a writer; and they had never been extreme enough to derail her work or her life for any substantial period of time.

Now the symptoms were quite severe and quite debilitating. The "acute hypomania" he first diagnosed had lasted far too long to still be called "acute." It never shifted into the most extreme forms of full-blown mania—during which patients are known to stop sleeping altogether, spend all their money, become grandiose, hyperreligious or hypersexual. But it did downshift into stretches of severe depression and other periods of what is called "mixed state": a jumble of manic and depressive symptoms, the most dangerous combination being the agitation and impulsivity of mania along with the suicidal thoughts of depression. When I read descriptions of "mixed state" in textbooks, I had a hard time really conceptualizing what the feeling was like. Diane knew exactly what they were talking about.

Dr. Miller's diagnosis did not offer a complete explanation for all of Diane's symptoms—especially the visual distortions. People with manic-depressive illness do sometimes experience hallucinations, generally during the most extreme manic or depressed phases of the illness. They can see things, hear things, even smell things that aren't there. These symptoms are referred to as "psychotic" even though manic depression is primarily a disorder of mood and not of psychosis or disordered *thought,* such as schizophrenia. For either disease, these symptoms can often be successfully treated with various medications that were once referred to as "major tranquilizers" or "neuroleptics" and now fall under the umbrella class description of "antipsychotics."

But Diane's visual distortions were constant, regardless of her moods or her meds. She wasn't seeing things that weren't there; she seemed to be processing light and images that *were* there, but processing them differently from everyone else. The peculiar "melting" sensation she experienced when first being Floxed had largely abated. But the visuals were relentless. They were also the most profound symptom she had that was not easily attributable to a diagnosis of manic-depressive illness. I sometimes wished that they *were* hallucinations. Then medication might have given her some relief.

To me, the visuals were the clearest indication of what Floxin had done to my wife. And for that reason, I probably tended to focus on them more than the manic depression. Diane worried that this meant I was avoiding or resisting her manic-depression diagnosis. And maybe I was. In my defense, accepting such a diagnosis is nearly as difficult for the spouse as it is for the patient. The way Diane would sometimes recount the events of the past months and angrily say, "And now I'm a person with a *serious mental illness,*" suggested she wasn't having the easiest time with it either. We hadn't told anyone but close family about the diagnosis. And I was still very aggressively investigating her drug reaction, in the hope that I might discover some way to reverse its effects.

I did believe that Dr. Miller's diagnosis was probably accurate, and I had no doubt that he was keeping her alive by keeping her on the medication. And I had no other suggestion about her course of treatment. Yet I continued to be ambivalent about the exact nature of her medical problems. Nine months later, how much was the drug reaction still to blame: 100 percent, 90 percent, 60 percent?

And was psychiatry the best—or the only—answer to Diane's problems? It didn't take much research to figure out that her symptoms were among those that form a kind of rope footbridge over the chasm between neurology and psychiatry. She was, after all, now being treated with antiseizure medications, neurology drugs that were being tested for their ability to also stabilize moods in manic-depressive patients. She had recently been switched from Depakote to another such medication, Tegretol (carbamazepine). But if such a drug relieved symptoms, how could you prove that the problem was basically psychiatric or basically neurological?

I was further confused about this subject after reading the book *Seized,* which detailed the history of the controversial diagnosis of temporal lobe epilepsy (TLE), which is characterized by miniseizures, mood instability and hallucinations. According to the handful of experts on the illness, TLE is a neurological condition often misdiagnosed as a psychiatric condition, chiefly because the seizures are so small and so deep in the brain that TLE sufferers do not test abnormally on the standard electroencephalograph.

The EEG is a relatively crude device, yet in many cases it still determines if a patient will end up being viewed as neurologic or psychiatric. We had seen this firsthand. Even though many of their other symptoms were identical, Diane's EEG was normal, Stacy Phillips's was not. So from their respective doctors' points of view, Diane had a major mental illness with a side order of neurological symptoms, and Stacy had a seizure disorder with a side of psychiatric symptoms. But both would be prescribed the same course of medication. To me, the bigger difference between them seemed to be that Diane was getting regular medical care and seemed to be experiencing very slow but real improvement, while Stacy was avoiding treatment and getting worse.

Why did drawing lines in the gray matter *matter* so much to me? Because I was trying to protect my wife, and myself, from the stigma attached to mental illness. Even though neurology and psychiatry both deal with disorders of the brain, one field is considered physical in nature while the other is sometimes still dismissed as "merely" mental. Patients are never blamed for causing their own seizure disorder, any more than cancer sufferers would be blamed for their melanomas. Psychiatric patients are still more likely to be told by friends and family—overtly or subversively—that they should "snap out of it."

There is also financial prejudice. Medical insurers cover treatment for neurological conditions at their maximum reimbursement rate—usually 80 or 90 percent. Psychiatric care is usually covered at an arbitrarily lower rate—often 50 percent or less—and unlike neurological care, it often has an annual cap on reimbursement. Psychiatric drugs are sometimes covered at a lower rate as well. And if you get reimbursed for psychiatric care under a company plan, you always run the risk that your employer can find out and somehow use that fact against you.

So if you have a choice, you're rooting that your friends, family, physician and medical insurer will see your illness as neurological. It makes life less difficult. And I don't think it's just the patients who worry about this. I don't think it's any coincidence that some of the more pharmacologically oriented mental health practitioners have taken to referring to what they do as "neuropsychiatry."

It was easier to tell people that Diane had a neurological problem than to explain the different neurological and psychiatric subtleties of her condition. And I felt that, even if her main problem was manic-depressive illness, it seemed to matter that a serious mental illness had been ignited by a drug reaction instead of by a psychological stressor.

Some people might say that I was in denial about Diane's manic depression. But if I was, it was a very specific, very complicated form of denial. And it didn't mean I was wrong to think that her eyes were a window onto the soul of her illness. So I pushed her to get a second opinion about her visual distortions from a specialist.

The best neuro-ophthalmologist in town turned out to be Dr. Steven Galetta at the Hospital of the University of Pennsylvania. Galetta was thirty-six, which made him a year younger than Diane. We had already grown accustomed to the surprising lack of generation gaps between my wife and her doctors, because they were almost all in their thirties. But Galetta was different. Besides being our age, he had also been a classmate of mine when we were both undergraduates at Penn. We had been in the same freshman English class.

Back then, Galetta was on the lightweight football team. I was now going to trust the ex-Ivy-jock (which, luckily, is not exactly the same as a real jock) to treat my wife. It was an odd sensation. I got through it by reminding myself that I interviewed plenty of people who probably couldn't believe that they were trusting me with their professional reputations. I'm sure many of them would have preferred someone older, or at least someone with shorter hair, and I can't say that I blame them.

Before we came for Diane's first visit, Galetta had made a search of the neurology literature to see if any ocular toxicities—adverse drug reactions affecting vision—had been reported with fluorinated quinolones or any drugs even remotely similar to them. He found only a single mention, but even as a dry abstract in a medical text, it was a pretty startling one.

According to the passage Galetta copied for us, a class of drugs called halogenated hydroxyquinolines—especially clioquinol—had been responsible for an epidemic of subacute myelo-optic neuropathy, or SMON, which causes visual problems and permanent nerve damage sometimes leading to blindness or paralysis. (Despite the similar-sounding name, the hydroxyquinolines are structurally quite different from Floxin.) The majority of the SMON patients had been in Japan, and it had taken from 1956, when the syndrome was first reported, until 1970 for the medical establishment to figure out that the syndrome was being caused by products containing clioquinol, a popular treatment for diarrhea. This was discovered only after creative, multidisciplinary research was done, the same kind of intensive Phase IV research that was so difficult to get funded. The drug was eventually banned in Japan and many other countries.

Two things about the SMON epidemic immediately struck me as creepy. One was that the drugs in question were hardly being used to cure cancer: they were mostly over-the-counter treatments for gastrointestinal problems. The other was that Galetta, the neuro-ophthalmology expert at one of the country's top teaching hospitals, had never heard of SMON—even though there had been more than 10,000 cases, probably the drug-induced epidemic of the century in his field—before coming across it in a book. Was this because most of the cases had been in Japan, and American doctors didn't find the epidemic globally relevant? Or was it because physicians' training in drugs and therapeutics was so lame, as the FDA's David Kessler had suggested, that it had simply never come up?

Diane liked Galetta immediately. And I could see that even though she was firm in her acceptance of the manic-depression diagnosis—even when she really didn't *want* to believe it—she also took some comfort in the confirmation that her visual symptoms seemed to him neurological. Galetta was especially sensitive to the distinctions between brain diseases; he was married to a psychiatrist.

Since Galetta was our age, it was also easier to talk to him about whether recreational drug use could have had anything to do with Diane's continuing symptoms. One of the many things that had happened during our long night in the emergency room was that Diane had tested positive for marijuana—which the doctors knew early on but only told us about, rather sheepishly, as we were preparing to leave. The test results hadn't affected the ER doctors' diagnosis that Diane was having a CNS reaction to Floxin, as Poison Control had suggested. But we had pursued this subject with every doctor who saw her afterward, asking if residual marijuana could have caused or exacerbated the reaction that sent her to the ER. They all doubted it. Galetta did find one article in the *Journal of Clinical Neuro-ophthalmology* with case reports of visual illusions associated with previous recreational drug use, but those were cases in which all other possible causes had been ruled out.

Galetta examined her for any physical damage to her eyes: SMON had caused atrophy of the optic nerve, and I had also seen mentions in the literature of quinolones leaving deposits in the eye. Then he ordered a series of tests, first assessing the function of the eyes themselves, then doing more elaborate tests of brain function.

As we were learning about all the new brain research being done, Diane was curious what it would be like to have a positron-emission tomography, or PET, scan of her brain. These experimental scans were becoming the predominant visual aid in the effort to prove that serious mental illnesses were biological in nature, by showing pictures of the physical differences, in structure or in function, between a normal brain and a "broken brain." We had been frightened that something abnormal would show up on the CT and MRI scans that first night in the emergency room, but I was now almost hoping to see something on a brain scan that would help explain what being Floxed meant.

Instead of a PET scan, Diane was given something similar, called a SPECT scan, which also assesses inconsistencies in the flow of blood through the brain. Her SPECT scan did show a mild abnormality. Interpreting it was something else; brain scientists are still trying to figure out exactly what they are seeing in these scans. But Galetta brought in a cognitive neurologist, who he half-jokingly referred to as a "philosopher of the brain," to interpret the scans. This specialist agreed there was an abnormality in blood flow in the right occipital-temporal region that could be causing changes in visual processing.

The scan didn't explain what the presence of the abnormality signified. It could have been there before, and it might, in fact, have been the inconsistency that caused the drug to affect her central nervous system the way it did. It could have been congenital; it could have been caused by Diane's childhood concussion.

On the other hand, the abnormality could very well have been caused by the drug reaction. This could be a picture of what being Floxed looks like.

While Galetta found Diane's case intriguing, he continued to offer more questions than answers. He said he didn't think her visuals would get any worse, but he couldn't promise they would get much better. It was possible that taking a much larger dose of lorazepam might be helpful, but that would also mean Diane would feel even sleepier than she did already.

He wondered what would happen if she switched from Tegretol to one of the old-time drugs used expressly for seizures, like Dilantin (phenytoin) or phenobarbital. But that would mean changing our entire view of her "main problem" from a psychiatric to a neurological perspective.

This option was tempting to me, but neither Diane nor her psychiatrist saw any point to it. Diane wasn't feeling very well: she was experiencing "mixed state" depression, very agitated, or what I refer to as very "fighty." But she and her doctor both felt she had improved and that they were on the right course. Galetta was not insistent that they change direction.

Armed with Galetta's opinion that the visuals might be here to stay, Diane decided that her search for more answers about being Floxed was officially over. She wanted to get on with her life, treat the symptoms she could treat and "climatize" to those she could not. After a couple of meetings with lawyers, one firm very much wanted our case and another decided to pass. At that point, Diane reiterated that she wanted nothing to do with any of it, and we weren't going to revisit the subject. She was never going to pursue a legal action, no matter how convinced I was that the drug reaction had permanently damaged her, no matter how angry I felt toward the drug company. Lawsuits were for people with nothing left to lose. We still had *plenty* left.

Someone else would have to fight the fight. She had done her part. She had let me write about her. She had agreed to appear on *Good Morning America* to publicize my quest. She hadn't complained about the many hours I spent on the phone with other Floxies that I hadn't spent with her. But she wanted off at the next stop.

. . .

By now, the Clinton administration was mounting a full-on attack against the legal-drug business. The task force the president had assembled to map out his health care reform strategy—and create coalitions that might enable the reform to pass Congress—was making high drug prices its marquee issue. While pharmaceutical companies tried to calmly discuss voluntary price ceilings with the administration, task force members were not-so-subtly leaking their intention to call for a mandatory price freeze on all medications.

They even talked about setting up a government review board, like the ones in Canada, France and the U.K., that would monitor compliance with price restrictions. This review board might also have access to some of the proprietary drug company information that FDA medical officers are shown during the course of the regulatory process but aren't allowed to disclose publicly. The trade secret information provided to the FDA was deleted from application materials before they were made public. Some believed the drug companies were more afraid of their trade secrets being scrutinized than they were of price cuts.

The drug companies actually had quite a bit to *gain* from the Clinton health care plan: millions of Americans would get new insurance coverage for prescription drugs under the proposal. But to get access to that windfall, the companies had to agree to be pilloried. Both the pharmaceutical companies and their stockholders were in a panic: the *Los Angeles Times* was reporting that manufacturers were beginning to lay off workers, and industry stock prices had fallen 15 percent.

At the research level, two big scandals were hitting the newspapers—one finally drawing to an end, another just beginning. The one that was just beginning had been broken by *Washington Post* science writer John Schwartz in July; clinical trials of a new anti–hepatitis B drug being tested by the National Institutes of Health and Eli Lilly had been halted because test subjects suddenly started dropping dead.

The experimental drug was fialuridine, shorthanded as FIAU, and it had been tested once before in humans, but only on very sick patients, suffering from AIDS as well as hepatitis B, who were given the drug for just a few weeks. In what one NIH scientist called "a nightmare," the first time FIAU was given to less sick patients over longer periods of time, the test subjects became terribly ill: they were cleared of hepatitis B, but poisoned by the drug that cured them. When the story broke, two of the ten patients who had been given the longest course of the drug were already dead, after liver transplants failed to save them. Another patient was in critical condition awaiting a transplant, and eight others were in the hospital. The FDA, NIH and Congress all vowed to investigate.

Several weeks later, the long-awaited trial of nationally known child psychiatrist Dr. Barry Garfinkel got under way in Minneapolis. The forty-six-year-old teen suicide expert was accused of falsifying data in a $250,000 study of the antidepressant Anafranil (clomipramine), which he was testing for the Basel Pharmaceuticals subsidiary of the $1.25 billion Swiss drug giant Ciba-Geigy to assess its ability to control a different condition, obsessive-compulsive disorder (OCD).

Back in 1989 a study coordinator had reported to the University of Minnesota, where Garfinkel was an associate professor, that the prominent psychiatrist had told her to invent data on patient visits that had never taken place—eye examinations and physicals that were supposed to be done to make sure the drug wasn't harming the test subjects. But it had taken four years for the case to come to court, and after a two-week trial—in which he was accused of treating the study "like a joke"—Garfinkel was found guilty of two counts of mail fraud and three of filing false statements for which he would later serve six months in a halfway house and six months under house arrest, and pay $210,000 in fines and restitution. (Although the disputed study data were never used, the drug was later approved for treatment of OCD based on other, more reliable research.)

The comments of Garfinkel's lawyer to *The New York Times* were hardly a ringing endorsement of how drugs are tested. In discussing "protocols"—the predetermined, written rules of a clinical trial, in which the sponsor poses the question, defines its terms and decides what the participants will be asked about—the lawyer lamented that federal prosecutors "turned a breach of protocol into a crime. And scientists breach the protocol in many many studies all the time. If this case sets a precedent, there will be a lot of prosecutions."

Garfinkel's conviction couldn't have come at a more perfect time for Warner Bros. The next day, the studio released its big summer movie for 1993, a feature film version of the TV drama *The Fugitive,* with Harrison Ford starring as the falsely accused wife-murderer Dr. Richard Kimble. In the TV original, Kimble's enemy was his wife's real killer, the infamous "one-armed man." In the film, the enemy was the guy who *hired* the one-armed man, a fellow physician with whom Kimble had been involved in the clinical trials of a new drug. But the real enemy was the drug company sponsoring the research, which needed Kimble dead so he wouldn't blow the whistle on doctored trial data being used to gain FDA approval.

As we walked out of the theater after seeing *The Fugitive,* Diane said she was fascinated by how willingly the audience seemed to accept the drug company as corrupt, and how unapologetically the filmmakers had portrayed the industry that way.

Diane's theory was that, since the recent fall of the Soviet Union, writers of movies and books needed a new, generic "evil empire," something the public agreed to hate. The drug business fit the bill. Pharmaceutical executives had become Klingons in business suits. They were making nuclear power plant operators look like family farmers.

Crowds of people were waiting to get into the next show of *The Fugitive.* Nine months before, we had felt like a solitary couple questioning the pharmaceutical industry. Now, if you wanted to boo the drug companies, you actually had to wait in line.

CHAPTER 4

"Nobody Reads

the Label Anyway"

t was Mac Lumpkin from the FDA on the phone, and he wanted to know if I had heard the news. In the months since our meeting backstage at *Good Morning America,* I had worried that the agency had lost interest in Floxin. But now he was telling me that the Anti-Infective Drugs Advisory Committee was going to hear the case of quinolone safety. In fact, the committee was going to focus on the very issue I had discussed in my article: the neurotoxicity of this entire class of drugs. He wanted to know if Diane and I would come and testify.

I felt like a minor league baseball player being called up to "the show." In the world of drug regulation, that's exactly what an advisory committee meeting is: a public contest in which the world's most powerful regulatory agency takes its best shot, the world's most powerful drug companies take their best shot, and then a jury of doctors flown in from all over the country renders its influential verdict. Millions of dollars and millions of lives are at stake every time an advisory committee votes.

Much of the press coverage of the drug industry is generated by advisory committee meetings. (You can always identify these stories by the disclaimer near the end that "the decisions of the committee are not binding, but the FDA generally follows them.") The committees draw attention because they are used by the FDA to throw the more controversial issues open to public debate, instead of making its decisions about them internally. But the meetings also lend themselves to a kind of high drama that is hard to find in the day-to-day drug business. Data that are, in theory, available to the public in raw form are finally analyzed and synthesized into pointedly useful information. And drug companies will disclose private information about themselves, or their competitors, if they think it will help their cause.

Advisory committee meetings are carefully orchestrated events. Drug companies often run mock advisory meetings to prepare for them. And since the meetings are only a day or two long, with no postponements for last-minute witnesses, it is not unusual for a manufacturer to show up with dozens of company doctors and hired outside consultants—each with his or her own set of slides—ready to cover any contingency. Nothing is left to chance. So while I knew Lumpkin was trying to be a nice guy by calling me, I had no doubt that he felt there was some advantage for the agency in our being there.

Diane and I have home offices on the third floor of our house; only a door and a small step separate the work spaces. When I got off the phone with Lumpkin, I burst through the door and leaped in to tell her the great news. The system had worked. One very annoying man and one highly sympathetic woman had made a difference. We were going to get our day in FDA court.

Or actually, *I* was going to get my day in FDA court. Diane said she didn't feel up to testifying. I was welcome to speak for her and invoke her story, but she was feeling too anxious and depressed to speak before a large group. I was disappointed, as I know she was. But I was also a little confused. As her illness progressed, it was becoming harder for me to accept when Diane said she was *unable* to do something. I still wanted to interpret that as meaning that she just didn't want to. The old "you can't or you won't?" is an issue that all couples struggle with. Illness simply exacerbates the problem, because the sick person sometimes doesn't want to admit she is too ill to participate.

So while I was certain I would be making the trip to Washington alone, I wasn't sure why.

After Lumpkin's invitation, I immediately dropped everything to research my presentation and compile obscure papers I thought the advisory committee should see. I was extremely excited, convinced I could make a difference and determined to be an A-student in front of all those doctors. Kent Smith, the pharmacist whose wife had been Floxed in Yellowstone, redoubled his efforts to search for journal articles, as did Dave Flockhart at Georgetown.

In my presentation, I wanted to sound as reasonable as possible. For example, many people who called me wanted to know why Floxin shouldn't be banned. But I knew that calling for it to be taken off the market was not reasonable. Instead, I tried to focus on a handful of points I thought even Johnson & Johnson would have to admit were fair to raise.

As the committee discussed whether to change the neurotoxicity warnings, I wanted the members to keep in mind just how unaware doctors were about the differences in safety profiles between these drugs and the other classes of antibiotics they regularly used. I also wanted the committee to consider the fuzzy area between neurological and psychiatric side effects, and to make sure it paid equal attention to the patients in whom quinolones had ignited seizure disorders, and those who ended up with drug-induced manic depression, depression, psychosis or sleep disorders.

My suggestion was that the entire class of drugs carry a "black box" warning that they shouldn't be taken by people with seizure disorder, people with psychiatric conditions that are treated with antiseizure medications, or people predisposed to those conditions (because of, say, head trauma) unless it was an emergency, a last-ditch effort. I also planned to suggest the label include a newly recommended treatment plan for patients with CNS reactions to quinolones: an EEG, followed by Tegretol.*

I also wanted to suggest that if the FDA were *truly* concerned about medication neurotoxicities, it should reconsider one aspect of its new MedWatch reporting system for adverse drug reactions. In the old system, any drug reaction was supposed to be reported. Because the reporting was so pitiful, and many of the reports were of relatively minor events, the FDA had announced with MedWatch that it now wanted to hear only about "serious" events. But the checklist definition of "serious" was worrisome and exclusionary, full of the kinds of holes that some drug companies drive trucks through when justifying their ignorance of a safety problem.

What made a drug reaction "serious"? In the new rules, one criterion was that the event lead to or prolong hospitalization. But managed care companies were discouraging inpatient stays for a vast array of conditions. Another criterion was that the event cause permanent impairment or damage, or that it require medical intervention to prevent such dam-

---

* The journal *Neurology* had just published a case report from doctors at the Bronx VA Medical Center in which a sixty-year-old patient, with no previous history of neurological disease, had been given Cipro twice for ear infections. Each time, he became volatile and confused, experiencing visual and auditory hallucinations and paranoid delusions; his EEG was also abnormal. Dilantin was not helpful, but Tegretol did arrest the symptoms, which were diagnosed as "ciprofloxacin-induced complex partial status epilepticus manifesting as an acute confusional state." So Tegretol seemed as logical a place as any for a doctor to start with a Floxed patient.

age. But how many doctors were going to consider a problem like new and permanent *insomnia* to be serious? And how many of them could be counted on to follow up and see if troubling mental changes continued long enough to be considered permanent?

I was pretty sure that there were many central nervous system side effects that doctors would not consider serious. Their patients, however, might feel differently. They would consider any lasting change in sleep or mood or mental status that was directly attributable to a drug to be very serious indeed.

In fact, as I worked on my presentation, the legal-drug world was learning a painful lesson about discounting the complaints of people having drug reactions. In a stunning front page story titled "And Then the Patients Started Dying," *The Washington Post* detailed the cruelest irony of the unfolding FIAU scandal—which, by September 1993, had resulted in the deaths of *five* of the ten long-term test subjects and had left two others holding on for dear life after liver transplants. One of the dead was a former congressional aide who had become the liaison for the National Commission on AIDS.

It turned out that patients taking the experimental anti–hepatitis B drug had tried to warn their doctors that the medicine was harming them. But for months they had largely been ignored. Their complaints were doubted for the same reason that many patients are told that their symptoms are "probably not drug related." Some of the symptoms were blamed on the disease the drug was supposed to treat, not the drug itself. This was especially true of the symptoms that developed only after the patients had been taking FIAU for a while or, in some cases, had already stopped the drug. Other symptoms were viewed as temporary. Patients were told to keep taking the drug anyway; tough it out, and the pain would eventually go away.

The FDA scheduled its first hearing on the FIAU affair the same week as the quinolone advisory committee meeting, and other hearings would soon follow. The potential for scientific embarrassment was high, because the problem FIAU caused had been predicted in a journal article by a Yale researcher back in 1991. NIH researchers claimed the article had never come up in their literature searches, but the *Post* reporter said it took him less than two minutes to download it from MedLine using the most basic of keywords.

The Washington drug community was still trying to decide if the FIAU scandal had villains and, if so, how many. But a sort of patient-hero had already emerged. His name was Paul Melstrom, an outspoken fifty-three-year-old Phoenix man whom the *Post* had charitably described as "acerbic." He may have been acerbic when his ordeal began, but by the time I tracked him down and spoke to him, he was downright bitter.

Melstrom, whose other health problems had included a hip replacement and a recurring drinking problem, believed he had contracted hepatitis B at a Club Med in Mexico. He had been Patient 1A in the FIAU trial, and almost three months after he finished taking the drug, he developed a painful tingling in his feet. When his NIH doctors didn't take his complaints as seriously as he would have liked, Melstrom started educating himself via the Internet: although he did not have AIDS himself, he ran a computer online service for AIDS patients and had learned the intricacies of medical research on the World Wide Web. He also began to write cranky letters to the NIH, explaining that the pain was one thing but he was equally annoyed by "the insensitivity and denial from NIH . . . I came to feel like a number, a mere casualty to research objectives."

After many months, he finally got the letter from the NIH that he had been waiting for. "Dear Mr. Melstrom," it began. "Thank you for your letter. Recent events in our current study of FIAU have caused us a terrible shock and show us that you were indeed right about the toxicity of FIAU."

I wondered if Diane and I were ever going to get a letter like that.

Speech in hand, I strode purposefully into the meeting of the Anti-Infective Drugs Advisory Committee on September 23, at about eight in the morning. Much to my disappointment, the event wasn't being held at FDA headquarters. The location was the "Plaza Ballroom" at the Holiday Inn in Silver Springs, Maryland, a circular room with bird-patterned wallpaper and carpeting so boldly colored that it didn't even match itself.

The meeting was held in the round, with the eleven FDA advisers—nine physicians and two clinical pharmacologists, seven men and four women—seated around a table in the middle, and several hundred interested parties surrounding them. Each adviser, according to an offhand comment Mac Lumpkin made while introducing them, was being paid the princely sum of $150 a day to serve his or her country in this capacity. Before the meeting, each adviser also had to disclose in writing any potential conflict of interest—if, for example, he or she had been paid to research one of the drugs in question or worked for one of the companies affected—and then be declared eligible or ineligible to join the discussion or to vote.

The way the drug business works, it is nearly impossible for prominent researchers and clinicians like these *not* to be caught in a potential conflict of interest at some point. Medication experts shift easily between the government, academia and "industry." Because there are so many potential conflicts of interest, the FDA allows advisers to appeal their "conflicted" status after a number of years. For example, this advisory committee had met back in the fall of 1991 to discuss whether certain quinolones were as effective against streptococcal infections as their labels said they were. (It turned out that they *weren't,* and both Floxin and Cipro were forced to drop certain claims and relabel.) At that time, committee chairman Thomas Beam had disclosed a conflict because he had worked on a clinical trial for Cipro in the 1980s. Now, two years later, he no longer had to officially disclose this—even though the makers of Cipro, Miles Laboratories, had a considerable financial stake in the outcome of the day's meeting.

There had been two meetings of the Anti-Infective Drugs Advisory Committee concerning quinolones since 1991 (and only four others for all the other antibiotic drug classes combined). The committee had met after the Omniflox fiasco in the summer of 1992, and it had also met in the spring of 1993 to discuss Maxaquin, a new quinolone from Searle, the Illinois firm owned by the international Monsanto conglomerate. Maxaquin seemed to increase sensitivity to the sun in both the skin and the eyes, a side effect that had had to be added to the label.

This time the committee was meeting to address two very specific questions about the entire class of drugs. The first question was whether all quinolones should carry identical labeling information for CNS toxicities, so that doctors would basically view their safety profiles as identical. This was a loaded question. Before Omniflox was withdrawn, being seen as a me-too drug in this class was considered an advantage, and all the quinolones had been presented to the FDA as being interchangeably safe. After the debacle, me-too was not such an attractive position for a quinolone manufacturer. In fact, as the day went on, the theme of some company presentations was "not me."

The second question was whether the current warnings—identical or not—were adequate. Were the FDA and the manufacturers doing enough to "get the message out to physicians" about CNS toxicities?

After the questions were called, there was a brief presentation by a representative of MedWatch to explain the new program. Her talk included many amusing slides—the standard *New Yorker* and Gary Larson cartoons that doctors regularly insert between tables, graphs and pie charts to keep their audiences from dozing off. When she finished, the committee moved on to the first part of the meeting, which is open to anyone from the public who has requested time to speak. When patient groups and advocacy groups address the FDA, it is usually during this public section of an advisory committee meeting. Most of Dr. Sidney Wolfe's quotably impassioned pleas on behalf of Ralph Nader's Public Citizen Health Research Group are delivered during the open public hearing.

On this day, only one person had requested time to speak on behalf of the public. That would be me.

I had ten minutes to do my best *Mr. Fried Goes to Washington*. I opened by apologizing that I hadn't brought any slides. "You must not be a physician then," the chairman joked back. And then I gave my presentation, briefly recounting the story of Diane's drug reaction, the response to our media appearances, and my growing concerns about the drugs. I made my clarion call for a black box warning on the drugs, knowing I would probably have to settle for a "Contraindication"— which says the same thing, at the very top of the label, but not quite as loudly, and without the advertising restrictions—or perhaps a "Dear Doctor" letter, calling prescribers' attention to the neurotoxicities of the drugs.

During my speech, I felt really stupid only once. That was when I mentioned the articles I had Xeroxed in advance for the committee, and I realized that one of the articles had been written by one of the committee members.

I ended by playing the diarrhea card. Of all the absurd overuses I had heard for Floxin, the worst was a paper I had received recommending the drug for the *prevention*—not the treatment but the prevention—of traveler's diarrhea. When the committee considered how casually this class of drugs was really being used—"high tech, sure-fire *candy*," that safety consultant had said—I wanted them to wonder if it was worth the risk of being Floxed to try to prevent "the runs."

When I finished, nobody had any questions. But Dr. Beam, tall and stocky with glasses and thinning brown hair, was very cordial about encouraging me to remain for part of the discussion and raise questions if I had any.

Next up was an FDA medical officer, Dr. Michael Blum, who explained how the FDA had labeled different quinolone products for central nervous system side effects since the 1960s. Almost every class of drug has some regulatory history with the FDA, and the agency relies heavily on what it has already done, rarely starting from scratch even when a new question arises.

The first quinolone available in the United States, nalidixic acid, was approved in 1964 and, in fact, carried the very warning I wanted on the current quinolones: it had a Contraindication—the strongest official caution, appearing on the label above Warnings and Adverse Reactions—for patients with a history of convulsive disorders. The next two had the same Contraindications, but that changed when the first of the current fluorinated quinolones was approved by the FDA in 1986. That first fluoroquinolone, Noroxin, was marketed by Merck, the scientifically innovative New Jersey–based drug colossus. The Noroxin label did not have any kind of CNS contraindication.

However, it did carry a lesser CNS precaution, as well as another warning that was so unbelievably sensible that, as soon as I heard it, I couldn't believe it wasn't on *all* the quinolones. "Noroxin can cause dizziness and lightheadedness," the warning said. "Therefore patients should know how they react to [the drug] before they operate an automobile or machinery or engage in activities requiring mental alertness or coordination."

As soon as Noroxin came on the market, the FDA began getting reports of drug-induced seizures, and the label was updated. Its CNS warnings became the boilerplate for all the subsequent fluoroquinolone antibiotics when they were introduced in America: Cipro in 1987, Floxin and Penetrex in 1991 and then Omniflox and Maxaquin in 1992. But none of them were actually contraindicated for patients with known or suspected CNS disorders. You now had to wade deep into the fine print before discovering that the drugs should be "used with caution" in such patients.

In fact, the drugs were contraindicated only for patients who had shown hypersensitivity to other quinolones. They were labeled as having a potentially dangerous interaction with theophylline, but the asthma medication had troublesome interactions with many commonly used drugs, so this wouldn't strike anyone as a surprising safety issue. The quinolones carried a warning about immediate allergic or anaphylactic shock reactions, but all drugs can cause them, too. So basically, unless a doctor did a Talmudic dissection of the package insert, the CNS problems would not jump out.

After finishing, Blum took questions. One advisory committee member, Dr. Russell Steele, a pediatric infectious disease specialist from New Orleans, said all this information seemed out of context. He pointed out that during their lifetimes, about 3 percent of Americans will have seizures anyway, something worth keeping in mind when assessing the relative dangers of drug-induced seizures.

Steele also said he wanted to know how the neurotoxicity of quinolones compared with that of other kinds of antibiotics. Blum said he didn't have that data and asked if anyone else in the meeting did. Another committee member asked Blum why he hadn't just run the database for a couple of other antibiotics so they could compare the rates.

Just as it was beginning to get interesting, a gentleman from Johnson & Johnson asked to be recognized. He immediately changed the subject, addressing several points Blum had raised early in his talk—mostly having to do with why Floxin had more CNS adverse reaction reports than all the other quinolones. He referred to this increase in reports as "that little blip," then introduced a colleague from the company's Ortho-McNeil division, who was ready with slides that "may lend some insight into the blip."

When the J&J tag team, all of whom were sitting right behind me, finished up, I sheepishly raised my hand and asked to be recognized. I just wanted to go back to the point the committee had been asking about before all the blipsmanship began. The committee had asked if anyone knew how the quinolones compared in their CNS toxicity with other antibiotics. I knew full well that the Johnson & Johnson team had such information in its possession and simply wasn't sharing it. I remembered that paper Dave Flockhart had sent me: an Ortho-McNeil-sponsored study that compared the safety of Floxin and several older, better-established antibiotics. I also remembered that the drug had not compared favorably.

I wish I could say I was surprised that they hadn't volunteered the information, but I wasn't. This moment was such a microcosm of the legal-drug world, such a perfect example of what is so screwed up about it. These companies purport to be in the business of science, but it seemed clear to me that whenever science could hurt business, they quickly reverted to tactics from the courtroom rather than the laboratory. This wasn't even "Don't ask, don't tell," the Washington slogan of the moment. This was "Ask, and we *still* won't tell."

Or more succinctly, "Catch us if you can."

So I tried to catch them. I believe the people from Ortho-McNeil might be able to help, I explained, in my best "gotcha" tone. They have already done *just* the comparisons you are asking for, I continued. I think their results might be of interest. . . .

Without a beat, the woman with the blip-slides raised her hand and tersely admitted, "We *do* have some information relating to what Mr. Fried was addressing in terms of . . ." They probably already have the slides prepared, I thought. They offered to present the information right away, but the committee chairman asked them to hold it until the formal presentation the company had requested, which was scheduled for the afternoon.

I was going to have to wait until after lunch to hear them explain why, even though Floxin had, in some cases, 50 to 100 percent more reported adverse reactions than erythromycin or amoxicillin, it was equally safe.

Next up was Dr. David Graham, who had done the postmarketing analysis for the FDA's Department of Epidemiology and Surveillance. Bony, bookish and redheaded, Graham was trained as a neurologist, a clinical pharmacologist and an epidemiologist, so he knew well the differences between the disciplines and how they played out in the regulatory process.

Pharmacoepidemiology is a newer, "softer," more predictive, more *macro* science, which is threatening the traditional, harder, more micro, trial-based clinical pharmacology that has been the cornerstone of FDA medical reviewing. (Harvard, for example, no longer even has a clin-pharm department, but has a growing cadre of pharmacoepidemiologists.) Practicing physicians are sometimes suspicious of epidemiological safety analyses, since, of course, all the comparisons are of "soft" numbers. How many people have taken a drug? Well, you can get a good estimate of the number of "scripts" filled from the legal-drug world's version of television's Nielsen ratings: the National Prescription Audit (NPA), which is conducted by a company near Philadelphia called IMS America. Since drug companies do not easily release their own sales figures, IMS instead polls hundreds of doctors about their prescribing habits and makes estimates extrapolated from those polls. Another health care consulting firm in suburban Philadelphia, Scott-Levin, provides the number of drug samples given out in the same way. But even when combined, these pharmaco-Nielsens don't tell how many of the prescribed pills were actually *taken*.

And how many adverse reactions have there been? Well, you can find out how many are reported. But the percentage of reactions that *aren't* reported is open to broad interpretation. Kessler wrote in his *JAMA* paper that perhaps 1 percent of all serious drug reactions get reported; but is that figure firm enough to mean that every report should be multiplied by, say, 99 to get a reliable estimate? As is so often the case in the drug business, the "best available" information isn't very good.

Basically, an FDA epidemiologist is presented with a handful of drug reaction reports and asked, "What do these mean?" or in the language of epidemiology, "What *signals* do you get from this data?" If the FDA answer is "It's probably nothing," the drug company epidemiologist immediately agrees, and everybody goes home smiling. If the answer is "It's *something*," the drug company immediately digs bunkers, the FDA loads its weapons and Sidney Wolfe screams bloody murder to the press.

For that reason, a lot rides on the FDA epi-analysis. Every time the agency hears a "signal," it is likely to cost somebody a lot of money. So Graham took his time laying the groundwork. According to the IMS prescription audit data, the horse race in the quinolone market had begun when Noroxin debuted in 1986 with about 2 million scripts a year, but was quickly overtaken the next year by Cipro. By the time Floxin came on the market, Cipro had become one of the top-selling drugs in the world. Its sales growth was flattened briefly by the introduction of Floxin in 1991, and Maxaquin and Omniflox in 1992, but quickly picked up again and was headed toward 10 million scripts a year (about $394 million in sales), while Floxin hovered at about 2 million scripts ($104 million). Maxaquin was fourth but coming up fast to overtake Noroxin, which, even with eroding sales, was still bringing over $50 million a year in revenues to Merck.

Graham then talked about the Byzantine coding system the FDA uses to catalog adverse drug reactions. To give doctors the widest possible berth in describing their patients' problems, the FDA has a list of thousands of what are called "COSTART terms," which capture the subtle gradations in the color and texture of symptoms like a warehouse full of paint samples. There are 160 different COSTART terms just for different kinds of central nervous system reactions. The price the system pays for giving doctors so many options, however, is that it creates a lot of places for a troubling safety profile to hide. Many reactions very similar to each other can be spread out among different COSTART terms—as when, for instance, one doctor uses "restlessness" instead of "insomnia"—before any one of them approaches the "less than one percent" threshold.

Adverse reaction reporting had been very slowly improving since the first quinolones were introduced. In 1986 the FDA had received only

40,000 reports for all drugs sold in America; in 1992 it was closer to 100,000. But these improvements hadn't really changed the agency's view of the overall estimates of unreported drug reactions. Nonetheless, to be as fair as possible, Graham compared the first two years of reports for each drug and then adjusted for the reporting rise.

He found that, generally, the newer, stronger quinolones caused more seizures and more psychiatric problems than the older ones. In neurological events, Maxaquin led all the quinolones by a large margin. For psychiatric events, he saw a "potential signal" for both Maxaquin *and* Floxin.

And what were the actual signals? For Maxaquin, anxiety reactions, tremors, dizziness and seizures. The Maxaquin seizures were especially troubling to Graham because many had occurred in patients with no factors that might predispose them to seizures. The FDA has a history of being most concerned about serious side effects that come out of nowhere, with no apparent predictive factors.

For Floxin, he saw a signal for sleep disorders—although "the question is," he said, "what is the *nature* of the insomnia that this drug provokes?" That was exactly what I wanted to know because, as many people had told me, their insomnia seemed to have a peculiar quality.

Both Floxin and Maxaquin, he said, also had signals for major psychiatric episodes. Moreover, he said that not only did he believe that the Floxin psychiatric reactions "were *real* events . . . [that] *were* drug-related [my emphasis]" but they struck patients with "by and large a total absence of preexisting psychiatric disorder."

So these Floxin and Maxaquin psychiatric reactions were as unpredictable as the Maxaquin seizures. And the reporting rates for seizures were only slightly higher than those for major psychiatric events. Yet Graham recommended that greater attention be paid to the seizures. The only reason he gave was that psychiatric reactions are "very difficult to study . . . a decent study would . . . be very difficult to do."

The recommendation, of course, confirmed my worst fear about the differences between neurology and psychiatry. All serious side effects are not created equal.

The contingent from G.D. Searle & Company, the manufacturer of Maxaquin, was sitting directly across from me, on the other side of the circle. All through Graham's presentation, they coughed, fidgeted, rolled their eyes and yanked at their collars. It was going badly for them, and they knew it. They were next on the agenda, and their only shot was to do a really kick-ass presentation, one that made the committee rethink the agency's entire analysis. But from the start, they were talking defensively. The first sentence out of the mouth of Searle's lead doctor was that the company had had only a week to do its homework.

Searle had flown in outside experts from St. Louis and Philadelphia, as well as a battalion of employees from the company's home base in Skokie, Illinois. Their main theme was that the neurotoxicity signals for Maxaquin were noise; the drug's safety profile was actually no different from those of its competitors. Their message, in a nutshell, was "Hey, we're a me-too, too."

But their explanations for why the numbers *gave the appearance* of being signals did not seem to be impressing the committee. Their first explanation was that the extra reports were caused by the extra diligence of their detail people, who were out there making sure that the drug was supersafe.

Their second explanation was that the company had given away such an astonishing number of free samples of the drug that the statistics should all be cut in half. About 840,000 prescriptions had been written for the drug so far, and the epi-analysis had been done with that figure. But the company said its free samples had been given to at least as many patients as that; the FDA said that as many as 1.5 million people had received samples.

That would mean that every doctor in America had exposed an average of at least three patients to a brand-new drug, one that had nothing very special to recommend it except a strong sales staff.

In tag-team fashion, the outside doctors that Searle had brought along did their best to explain every seizure report, claiming to have "more information about individual cases" than the FDA. Searle then offered up Dr. Judith Jones, who had once been the head of postmarketing surveillance for the FDA and still had a lot of friends at the agency. She is now a consultant, largely to industry. Dr. Jones heads a company that studies drug safety and analyzes publicly available Freedom of Information data on postmarketing drug reaction reports.

Jones had been brought in, technically, to scrutinize the quinolone data for Searle. But her more important role seemed to be elucidating the problems of the postmarketing system she had once run herself. She was clearly there as an expert on the biases and failures of FDA pharmacovigilance. Until actual studies could be done to prove the incidence rates in volunteers, she insisted, the FDA shouldn't single out one of the quinolones just because of some . . . "signals."

This advice clearly irked committee chairman Beam, who quickly pointed out that Omniflox had been withdrawn from the market based on the same kind of "signal." Was Jones honestly telling the committee and the FDA that the response to the Omniflox deaths should have been "Go out and study the drug more because the *system is not good enough*"?

"Well," Jones said, "I think that's a very important question, and I think one has to put it in perspective."

At that point, the meeting seemed to lose all perspective and took a turn to the existential, as the participants began philosophically dissecting the very process of which the meeting was a crucial part. One committee member noted that all the quinolone labels said that the drugs should be used "with caution."

"I love that phrase," he chuckled, "because I haven't the foggiest idea what that means."

In response, the doctor leading the Searle delegation said something that almost caused *me* to have a seizure.

"As you know," he pointed out, "physicians will not even *look* at the package insert. If they do, it's for seconds."

When it was suggested that maybe the FDA just didn't have enough information to make a critical judgment on the quinolones, David Graham, the agency epidemiologist, became exasperated. "You have to make a decision *somewhere*," he insisted. "Otherwise, exercises like this are really futile and . . . reporting [adverse reactions] is generally futile."

If the FDA didn't have enough information about drug reactions, he went on to point out, maybe it was because the manufacturers were doing such a terrible job getting the information to the agency. He chose this moment to reveal that his department was studying how well the companies filled out the forms on which all postmarketing analysis was based. While the results weren't complete, Graham already knew the research would show that fewer than 50 percent of the reports coming from the major companies supplied even the *basic* information about the cases. The spaces on the forms were simply left empty.

And while he wasn't at liberty to name names, Graham was certain that when the companies were rated on the quality of their reporting, "none of the firms represented here today are number one or number two."

Five minutes later, the meeting broke for lunch. I called Diane on a pay phone in the hotel lobby to tell her what I had just seen and heard. She said it sounded like the Mad Hatter's tea party.

I now better understood why one member of an FDA advisory committee, clinical pharmacologist Dr. Marcus Reidenberg, had written an exasperated account of his experience advising the agency's over-the-counter drug division. The article was called "The Pinocchio Syndrome," and it appeared in the leading journal for clinical pharmacologists, of which Reidenberg is editor. In the piece, he excoriated colleagues who he said had come before the committee and lied outright on behalf of corporate sponsors. Accompanying the article was a cartoon that used Pinocchio's nose as the bottom axis of a graph about truthfulness.

After lunch, the next company up was Miles Laboratories, the very confident, almost arrogant manufacturer of top-selling Cipro—the quinolone all the others aspired to become. Dr. Roger Echols gave an extraordinarily polished presentation, in which he insisted that there was no need to relabel the quinolones. In fact, he wasn't even sure that Cipro deserved to have a warning as harsh as the other drugs in the class.

But he was sure what his main market competitor was: Floxin. Whenever there was an opportunity to make a point about Cipro by disparaging the Ortho-McNeil drug, he did so. Whenever Floxin and Maxaquin could be paired as the "new bad quinolones" and Cipro and Noroxin painted as the "old reliable quinolones," he found a way to do it. I found this amusing. After what Diane had been through, I must say I enjoyed watching multimillion-dollar companies throw one another under the bus. And all in the name of *science.*

After Echols's presentation, a member of the J&J team announced he had proof that, in fact, Cipro induced a higher rate of seizures than Floxin. I assumed this was a prelude to the company's presentation, and I sat back to enjoy the fireworks as the company finally got up to defend Floxin.

Instead, the committee chairman announced that Johnson & Johnson had decided not to give its presentation after all.

I felt as though I had been Floxed myself. That was *it?* Giving testimony during investigations of the safety of a drug taken by millions of people is, what, *voluntary?*

But, in fact, it is voluntary. And as outraged as I was, I completely understood J&J's strategy. Up until this point, the meeting had been focused primarily on Maxaquin—the newest and weakest-selling member of the class. The Cipro representative had even prefaced his comments by declaring that the entire meeting had been called only because of Maxaquin adverse reaction reports—a piece of deliberate misinformation that the committee chairman was later forced to correct for the record. With the manufacturers of Cipro trying to link Floxin to Maxaquin, and me sitting there on behalf of America's Floxed, any additional attention paid to Floxin could be dangerous to J&J.

A presentation could raise tough questions that would have to be answered. And since J&J was scheduled last, the possible problems with Floxin would then be freshest in the minds of the committee when they voted. Since the chairman had obviously forgotten about the research data he had requested after I mentioned it, J&J rolled the dice—and won. Their withdrawal passed almost unnoticed, and the committee adjourned to confer.

When they returned, a lively discussion broke out. One committee member asked why everyone was being so timid about putting something on the label that simply told doctors not to prescribe these drugs to certain patients unless the benefits clearly outweigh the risks. "If there's another good drug," he asked, "why take the risk?"

The answer from another member: "We've already agreed that the overwhelming majority of physicians aren't reading the labeling anyhow before they prescribe the drug."

It was exactly as the Searle doctor had said. Thanks, I thought, I'll make sure to let my wife know that this is your solution to the problem.

Only one committee member seemed upset that everyone else was ignoring the psychiatric side effects. She thought Floxin should be singled out for its sleep disturbances and the psychiatric episodes it had reportedly caused. "That's not an easy side effect, if you kick off a major psychosis in a patient," she said.

Another member agreed. The chairman asked for other comments. I leaned forward in my chair, wondering if it was appropriate to chime in during final arguments and hoping that another committee member would keep the tribunal focused on the issue long enough to actually *do* something.

But then one of the committee members made a joke. He wondered about how the sleeplessness could be "put to good use" for patients with "cerebral atrophy." The moment was lost, and the conversation returned to seizures.

·   ·   ·

Ultimately, the committee decided that the existing CNS caution should be moved up so that it would be the very first warning a doctor saw, and the language about seizures in the warning should be boldfaced. The line about being "used with caution" was to be changed so that doctors would "think twice . . . about the risk/benefit ratio" before casually prescribing quinolones. This new line was also to be boldfaced.

No black box, no "Dear Doctor" letter. No warnings on psychiatric side effects. No additional studies. Two lines in boldface. The net result of my year of haranguing the FDA and Johnson & Johnson about Floxin was two lines in boldface.

The consolation prize: one committee member came up to me afterward and said he liked my article very much.

Oh, and I did get to meet Dr. Ana Szarfman, the FDA medical officer who had approved Floxin in the first place and had spoken to me on the phone. She came up to me and introduced herself. The first thing she wanted to know was how Diane was doing. I told her the truth. When I said "not very well," Szarfman's face fell. She was shocked that, almost a year later, Diane was still having many of the same symptoms that had begun after taking one pill of Floxin.

"You must report to the FDA that she is still having symptoms," she said. "You must, you *must*."

At least somebody at the agency was still concerned.

CHAPTER 5

The Ray

and Dave Show

t was a good thing I had arranged to meet Dave Flockhart for beers after the meeting. I needed someone to tell me that the process of warning doctors and patients about reactions like Diane's wasn't as futile as this day in Silver Springs made it seem.

Flockhart, with whom I had maintained a year-long phone friendship but had never met, turned out to be an animated, almost cartoony character. Like Wallace Shawn with glasses and a bushy mustache, he is compact and balding with a mischievous grin. With him was his boss in the Georgetown clin-pharm department, Dr. Raymond Woosley, who wanted to talk to me about a drug safety bill he was trying to press through Congress. Woosley is also small but more southernly handsome, with chiseled features and a serious demeanor. The two finish each other's sentences like a clinical pharmacology comedy team: Flockhart excitedly chattering with his heavy Scottish accent, Woosley calmly explaining in his slight Kentucky drawl.

I told them how amazed I was at how much of the meeting seemed to have been about problems in the *system* rather than problems with the drugs. Their heads bobbed knowingly. This is what life in the legal-drug culture is like, they were saying, this is what is so maddening about it.

"We can tell you a story," Flockhart began, and they proceeded to recount their research into the antihistamine Seldane (terfenadine) and its ability to cause heart arrhythmias.

"Seldane was the tenth most prescribed drug in the country," Woosley cut in, "about $700 million in sales, and it was just about to go over-the-counter. Buried in the drug's experience were some arrhythmias, patients blacking out. . . . So there was a case at Bethesda Naval Hospital where a woman was on Seldane, and she had been given a prescription for ketoconazole [Nizoral] for a fungal infection. The next day she started blacking out."

The woman was admitted, and clinical pharmacology was called in to see if her problem was related to medication. The case ended up being presented to Dr. Carl Peck, who was the director of CDER. Besides his position as a pharmacrat, Peck was known as an astutely inquisitive clinical pharmacologist who, sometimes to the bewilderment of his more bureaucratized colleagues, still loved digging into an interesting case.

"Carl called me and said, 'You might want to come out and listen to this case,'" Woosley recalled. "'It's got an arrhythmia: I know that's what you like.'" Woosley did like arrhythmias and all sorts of drug-related cardiovascular problems. His father died of heart disease, and his department at Georgetown is known for its special interest in "heart stuff."

"It turns out the company had a bunch of these cases," Woosley said, "and they called them overdoses. They were sent to the company [by doctors] as drug reactions, or interactions, but they were sent to the FDA by the company as overdoses." The reason was that the drug's "parent compound" was found in high levels in the patients. When a drug is metabolized by the body, its parent compound is broken down into one or more metabolites, which are substances the body creates out of the drug. The company reasoned that if there was too much of the parent compound in the patient's blood, it was because the patient had taken too much medicine.

It is easier to blame one patient than a drug that brings in $700 million a year in revenues.

"The company stand is 'We didn't cheat, we thought it was an overdose. The parent compound was found in high levels,'" Woosley explained. "What happens, we now know, is when you take Seldane with this other drug, the parent compound builds up—and that's what causes the trouble. There were thirty to forty deaths in the database, clearly the same kind of arrhythmias, and the company was just going to overlook them completely. Carl Peck was telling me that the company wanted to come up and talk to him about going over-the-counter. Carl said, 'Why don't you come up, but the question is going to be if it stays on the market at all.'

"The president of Marion Merrell Dow, Fred Lyons, who was also a member of the Federal Reserve, flew to Washington that afternoon. It didn't go over-the-counter, and the drugs now carry this boxed warning."

The Seldane black box warned about that interaction with the antifungal, and a similarly dangerous one that was subsequently discovered with the common antibiotic erythromycin. I could tell that Woosley and Flockhart were very proud of this black box. They considered it their trophy. In hunting, there are stuffed lion heads. In clinical pharmacology, there are black boxes. It's a symbol of pharmacokinetic immortality, a sign that every once in a while, science can still box in commerce.

"This has affected the *whole* of pharmaceutical development," Flockhart chimed in. "This one story."

Actually, this was the *second* time Woosley had been involved in changing the history of pharmaceutical development. The first story hadn't ended quite so well for him—but it helped explain his zeal. Before coming to Georgetown in 1988, Woosley had made his name at Vanderbilt University, where he developed his reputation for incisive clin-pharm detective work. While there, he had tested an anti-arrhythmic—a drug for suppressing irregular heartbeats—called Tambocor (flecainide), for the pharmaceutical branch of the Minnesota-based multinational 3M, and had given the experimental medicine generally high marks. Woosley was also a member of the FDA Cardiovascular and Renal Drugs Advisory Committee, which, with some reservations, approved Tambocor in 1984, along with several other new anti-arrhythmics.

The FDA advisory committee's reservations about these new anti-arrhythmics, shared by the agency itself, had to do with the age-old problem of drugs approved for the very sick being prescribed for the *barely* sick. The FDA tends to prefer to approve drugs for precisely what they are good at. Drug companies prefer much broader approvals because they encourage physicians to use the drugs on a much wider variety of medical conditions—including prophylactic use to possibly prevent the conditions. When the FDA was considering a limited approval for Tambocor—allowing its use only in very sick patients—a 3M internal memo said that marketing the drug under such conditions had "little or no economic merit." The manufacturers eventually talked the FDA into the broader approval.

The debate over the breadth of the approval probably would have remained scuttlebutt for cocktail hours at cardiovascular conferences if it hadn't been for a monumental Phase IV trial commissioned by the National Heart, Lung and Blood Institute of the National Institutes of Health. The Cardiac Arrhythmia Suppression Trial (CAST)—a five-year, $40 million study begun in 1987—compared anti-arrhythmic drugs head to head in randomized, double-blind tests to see which ones saved more lives in mildly symptomatic patients.

Woosley was the vice-chairman of the CAST steering committee. So he was one of the first to find out, in the spring of 1989, that early CAST results showed a medical nightmare in the making. Patients being treated with anti-arrhythmics, especially Tambocor and Enkaid (encainide), were twice as likely to die from cardiac arrest—the very problem they were taking the drugs to *prevent*—as were patients taking placebos. And, in a stunning refutation of the "prevailing wisdom" that dangerous drug reactions usually arrive in the hours or days after a drug is first taken, the longer the anti-arrhythmics were taken, the more likely they were to kill. Estimates of the number of people who died from indiscriminate use of these drugs vary from several thousand to more than 50,000.

The CAST trials ended up setting off an FDA investigation, a congressional inquiry and many rounds of hand-wringing in the pharmacology community. Although many of the drugs involved are still on the market—relabeled to prevent use in less sick patients—the episode raised very troubling questions that are not only hard to answer but usually too expensive even to ask. These questions have haunted Ray Woosley ever since and have turned the churchgoing family man into a pharmaco-rebel.

"What is interesting about Seldane," Woosley continued, "is that there was a *disincentive* for the drug company to find out what was wrong with this drug. They couldn't *afford* to study it, because the reason for studying it would imply there's something *wrong* with it. So there's this whole disincentive to find out what's wrong with a medicine."

In fact, sometimes there's even a disincentive to finding out what's *right* with a medicine. Flockhart and Woosley regaled me with the tale of an older, less expensive but more sedating antihistamine compound, chlorpheniramine (now available over-the-counter as Chlor-Trimeton, Comtrex, Co-Tylenol and a slew of generics), which they had been given an FDA grant to study. "It's one of the best antihistamines in the world, and we've been misusing it for years," Woosley explained. "The reason Seldane was doing so great was because it was nonsedating. If you use Chlor-Trimeton right, it's nonsedating, too. If you get some at the drugstore, over the counter, the dose is four milligrams every four hours. Dave and a colleague have been working on it, and it turns out the dose probably ought to be two milligrams, twice a day. *Then* it's nonsedating. . . . But nobody would pay for this kind of research, because the drug is off-patent and available as a generic."

Flockhart jumped in: "Most research goes toward proving something is better than the competition. Very little is put into Phase IV kinds of questions—'What are the long-term side effects of drugs, how do they affect different genders, different races?' It's always how to find some better use for a patented drug."

Then Woosley: "In the last fifteen years, I have made the argument to drug companies over and over again that we can predict ahead of time, with lots of drugs, who will have those bad reactions like your wife did. But a company would never fund the research, because they are afraid it would limit the way doctors would have to use their drug. They want a *completely nonthinking doctor*. Sometimes research like this means that a doctor can't prescribe a drug until he checks a blood test. And they don't want a drug that has that problem.

"There is a drug that causes lung scarring. It kills one out of every hundred people who take it. Everybody knows that. Ten percent of the people who take it get lung scarring, and ten percent of those people die. So we went to the drug company and said, 'We think we can find a way to identify these people before they get the problem, before you give them the drug.' We came up with a test to prevent it, and they wouldn't fund the research. And I want to know, how can you *not* fund that kind of research?

"The company attitude was, 'We don't think it's such a big problem.' Deep down they think, 'If you study this side effect, it just magnifies it. We're going to go out and tell them it's *not* a problem. Hey, don't worry about this lung scarring bit!' And that's what their salesmen did."

"That's criminal behavior!" Flockhart said, slamming down his Killian's Red Ale.

After the day I'd just had, how could I *not* like these guys?

Woosley asked me how Diane was. I told him the truth. It's interesting, when you're ill or have an ill spouse, how you inhabit two separate worlds. There's one world in which you tell the truth, because the people in it already know or are capable of understanding, and another world in which you always just say "better," because it would take too much time—all of which is likely to be wasted—to explain how and why you're *not* better. Just because somebody is a doctor doesn't mean they're in the first world. But I sensed that Woosley understood Diane's situation.

"You know, now that you mention it," he said, "*my* wife is still having difficulty with her vision from a drug reaction eight years ago."

"You know, in the field we're in," Flockhart said, "it's hard to find a drug that *doesn't* have a problem—"

"And most doctors don't have a clue," Woosley shot in. "In clinical pharmacology, we have an attitude about drugs. We think drugs could be part of the problem. Doctors in practice just don't have that attitude. They *never* think about their drugs. They just think drugs are all wonder drugs, silver bullets—"

"Well, *that's* a disservice," Flockhart interrupted. "They're aware of the drugs you get blood levels on, and they know *why*. It's just that the information those doctors receive about drugs is heavily biased toward the pharmaceutical industry."

"No, it's all about how *great* this drug is, how *great* that drug is," Woosley insisted. "It's never 'Oh, don't forget to check the EKG, don't forget that this drug might cause your patients to act crazy!' You know, we have a lot of good doctors in this country, but they've sold out to the drug industry—"

"Well, it's not so much that they've sold out," Flockhart tried to break in. "It's just the information they get—"

"They're out on the circuit, giving talks about how great drugs are because *that's what the drug companies pay them to do!*" Woosley said. "We need docs whose livelihoods don't depend on the drug industry and who are willing to stand up and say there's something wrong with a drug!"

The point of the Ray and Dave show was not just to rile me up, but to sell me on Woosley's plan to save America from drug ignorance—and in the process, save clinical pharmacology from extinction. He called the plan CERT, and it had been quietly making the rounds in Washington for some time. CERT stands for Centers for Education and Research in Therapeutics, and it proposes a national chain of research centers, located in major universities with existing clinical pharmacology departments, that would be funded by the federal government and do ongoing research in consultation with the FDA and industry but wholly independent of drug company economics and regulatory politics. The CERTs would also serve as education and information centers so that physicians, pharmacists and patients could get economically unbiased facts about drugs—including fair comparisons of price, efficacy and safety.

This "less than one percent solution" is an updated version of a plan first suggested in the 1970s, and something like it was first proposed as an amendment to a bill by Senator Edward Kennedy in 1977. Woosley had received mixed reactions to his own plan. "I did a presentation to the Drug Forum at the National Academy of Sciences," he recalled. "The NIH said, 'Great idea, but we don't have money for that.' The FDA said, 'Great idea, but we don't have the money for that, you'll need legislation.' The drug industry said, 'That's the worst idea we ever heard.' One guy said, 'Ray, you and I used to be friends. That was offensive.'

"That's because the drug companies honestly don't think they're doing anything wrong—or that there's anything wrong with the system. There *is*. But it's going to take recognition that this country is spending billions on drugs—and if the only source of information about those drugs is the marketing that drug companies do, then drugs aren't going to be used in the most safe and cost-effective way. It's hard to even call this a *problem*. It's a built-in part of our economic system that *creates* a problem."

Woosley also thought the CERT plan might address what he perceived to be a malaise in the world of Washington drug doctors.

"Morale is low at the FDA," he said, "and I'll tell you why. There's a tremendous amount of expertise being crimped by being able to review only what drug companies give them. They have to take the labeling proposed by the company and work with that, and they can't dictate changes in therapy. They may *know*—'I reviewed three drugs, this one is better.' *But they can't tell doctors that.* They're restricted by law not to recommend treatments. Somebody besides drug reps should be recommending treatments!"

Woosley said he'd been lobbying for a bill that would improve the way the FDA worked, give it more power to do its job properly. But he believed that the FDA was afraid of encouraging any scrutiny of the laws on which its power was based, because too many powerful lobbies wanted to defang what little bite the agency already had. "This was told to me recently by a real old-timer at the FDA," he said. "The agency is afraid to let anybody interfere with their charge, because they're afraid of losing ground. They're afraid to lose funding, even afraid to lose the bill that gives them the power to say that drugs have to be judged 'safe' to be on the market."

Politically speaking, Woosley was crestfallen that his ideas about drug safety didn't appear to have found a place in the brand-new Clinton health care agenda, which had been announced the previous evening. Clinton had broadly outlined his plan during a long-awaited speech before a joint session of Congress. Copy shops inside the Beltway were reportedly doing a brisk business in bootleg reprints of the entire proposal, which had been sent only to members of Congress. A friend at the American Heart Association had slipped Woosley a copy. He already knew that all the proposed drug reforms were about price.

Why wasn't there a word about safety or efficacy in there? I wondered.

He shook his head. "That's just the political reality," he said.

We finished our beers, and I caught a late train back home to Philadelphia. It is a ride that goes through inner city and outer country, long expanses of urban blight and equally long expanses of the twinkling blue waters of Chesapeake Bay. I had just lived through one of the most provocative, infuriating, depressing, confusing, emotional days of my life. It was much more than one of those "everything you know is wrong" days; I had sped by that feeling sometime during the late morning, and by late afternoon, I realized I hadn't known that much to begin with. The legal-drug world is so much bigger and so much more troubling than I had ever guessed. I needed time to think and rethink.

Three days after the advisory committee meeting, Diane and I were flying to New Mexico, finally taking the trip we had canceled almost exactly a year earlier because of the drug reaction. We held hands at takeoff and landing—a superstitious habit to ward off crashes, but it hasn't failed us yet—and couldn't wait to get through the Albuquerque airport to our rental jeep and the big sky around Route 25.

It took almost an hour to make the flat drive to Pecos, a gas station of a town. There we stopped at Aiello's Town and Country store, where we got some groceries, a new fishing license and whichever spinning lures the bored guy behind the counter was recommending. Then it took another fifteen minutes to drive what seemed almost straight up the side of a seven-thousand-foot mountain to get to our friend's cabin, one of several in an old converted hunting lodge. Battling to keep the caretaker's stinky dog from following us inside, we unloaded the car, unpacked our stuff and started planning just how little we planned to do.

The next morning I woke up before the sun, when the three ponds near the cabin were still crusted with a layer of ice so thin that it disintegrated from the heat of my fingertips. After a quiet cup of coffee—I didn't want to wake Diane—I layered up just as the first hint of daylight began to melt holes in the ice. Then I went out and casted mindlessly, waiting for a rainbow trout to bite my lure. There was a lot of time in between for thoughts large and small.

Not surprisingly, I was thinking a lot about drugs and illness and couples and families. I was trying to make sense of what had happened over the past year, and trying to make some decisions, as a husband and as a journalist, about what would come next.

I was now married to a woman with, by my estimation, two chronic illnesses: manic depression, and a neuro-ophthalmologic problem. It was time to admit that however this had happened, whatever combination of drug reaction and genetic factors and plain old bad luck, it was not going to go away.

In my family, we are no strangers to chronic illness. When my father was twenty-nine years old and I was eight, he had a massive heart attack that ended with him crumpled on the floor of our den. Miraculously, he survived it—this was the mid-1960s, still the neolithic age for cardiac care—and he resumed his life with a low-cholesterol diet and a regimen of blood thinners. In fact, his drugs provided my first childhood lesson in the fine line between therapeutic and toxic doses of the same compound. During one family meal, a field mouse came slowly crawling across our breakfast room floor. Its steps were so labored that none of us bothered to scream, jump on a chair or even lift our feet. In a rodent's equivalent of one of those drawnout "you got me" scenes from a bad gangster movie, the mouse finally listed to one side, keeled over and died. At which point my parents explained to us that the mouse poison they had put out was warfarin. It was the same stuff that Dad's doctors used to thin his blood and prevent another heart attack.

I had recently started asking my parents what it was like to incorporate the fear of a second heart attack into an otherwise normal suburban life. They initially shrugged the questions off—"No big deal . . . we survived." But they eventually spoke a little bit about the aura of dread they had labored hard to hide from their children. I knew my father had changed careers after the heart attack, joining his own father in the family furniture business. But he was finally letting on just how much his health fears had formed him as a husband and a father.

My mother had endured her own medical crisis; two years before the heart attack, she had been badly burned at a family cookout when her own father was careless with some charcoal lighting fluid. But it was always my father's health on which she focused. And until Diane got sick, I had never really considered the depth of my mother's fear that my father could be taken from her at any moment, from any exertion.

These incidents had taught my family how to function during a medical emergency, and we had become fairly accomplished at it. Later, when my youngest brother, Dan, was diagnosed with juvenile diabetes at the age of nine, we became so proficient with the constant emergencies of the illness that the Juvenile Diabetes Foundation hotline was in our house. I sometimes wondered if we did better during emergencies than we did after they ended. We were great at banding together, but perhaps slightly less great at just *being* together.

I realized it was very easy for me to shift into "emergency mode," but terribly difficult to shift out. How did you treat a chronic illness if not by declaring a permanent emergency? I didn't know. In my family, we just left the siren running and adjusted to the noise. We're basically loud people: we never really liked the quiet much anyway.

But in the mountains of the Santa Fe Wilderness Area, with only the sound of the Pecos River bubbling nearby, there was a cacophony of quiet.

It seemed that Diane and I were experiencing what my friend Barry Jacobs—a clinical psychologist specializing in medical family therapy with people dealing with traumatic or chronic illnesses—has called the "locked embrace." He describes it as "a rigid pattern of interaction in which the patient is stuck in an underfunctioning role as other family members overfunction in an effort to protect [her]. It allows the family as a whole to avoid difficult feelings such as anger or overwhelming sadness, but can prevent the patient from recovering to the maximum extent possible." I understood that Barry was describing a sort of loving dysfunction, born more of fear than hope, that should be treated with psychotherapy. But what if certain people could thrive only while in the "locked embrace"? What if it was the most "normal" solution to a completely abnormal set of problems and relationships?

Locked or not, I often felt now that the embrace was our salvation. Mental contact was not quite as easy as it had been; we had always been such an intuitively together couple that it sometimes seemed we could mentally beam each other information. Now, when her symptoms were at their worst, she was far away—sitting right next to me, but lost in a world of melting brains, visual tricks and chaotic moods. So we became much more reliant on purely physical contact.

.   .   .

One thing about our emotional and intellectual relationship had not changed. When Diane and I first met, she immediately became my editor. Not someone who reads and pats you on the shoulder, "That's nice, dear," but a real, hands-on, fight-over-a-dash editor. We came to see this as her "real job," the payment for which was the freedom to work on her fiction. It was only because of her editing that I could churn out the volume of magazine work I did. Somehow she was able to remain rock-solid as an editor even now, her advice sound, her support unwavering. And when she couldn't help, she was self-aware enough to say so. She had what psychiatrists call "good insight" into her illness; she could usually recognize when she was symptomatic.

I assured Diane that I could handle the pressures of her illness. And even to my closest friends, I rarely admitted how difficult it was to see my wife sometimes battling her meds just to stay awake. This was a woman who, for years, had had to be literally dragged away from her desk, because she was so engaged in her fiction or poetry or drawing. While I was successful at keeping my psyche from bursting under the mounting pressure, some of what I was feeling seeped out in less conspicuous ways.

In the middle of the night I would sometimes blast awake from a strange dream. In one, my mind's eye did a tracking shot through a bustling pharmaceutical plant before finally stopping at a two-story-high vat and panning up over its lip to see thousands of brightly colored pills dropping in from a conveyor belt. Suddenly a hand, a woman's hand, burst through the surface of the pills, and then the other hand, and then a head, momentarily gasping for air before sinking forever—like the guy drowning in corn in the movie *Witness*. When I awoke from these dreams, I felt the need to make sure Diane was still alive, but without waking her up. If she was sleeping on her back, I'd put my hand under her nose to feel for breathing; if she was on her side facing away, I'd brush my lips across her neck and wait for the quick reflexive sigh I knew would come.

And I also noticed something that happened occasionally when I was at the gym. After doing a brisk hour on the recumbent bike, I would stumble, dripping with sweat, over to the thin blue-foam mats to do my stretches. Once on my back, the sweat would cascade off my face, arms and legs, puddling wherever it found an indentation.

As I groggily closed my eyes, too tired to even stretch yet, a feeling of sleepy sadness would come over me. I felt as if I were crying into my own sweat. But I was so wet already that nobody could be sure. Not even me.

What was wrong with me, experiencing my most private moment in a public place? Maybe nothing except logistics. When you can't bring yourself to cry at home and you shouldn't cry at work, doing it clandestinely—even while lying on the floor in the middle of a crowded, noisy gym—begins to make perfect sense.

CHAPTER 6

Pharm TV

While we were in Pecos, I decided I had had enough of writing about drugs. I would do one more short follow-up for *Philadelphia* magazine—to report on the results of the advisory committee—and I would keep my eye on Ray Woosley's CERT proposal and the Omniflox lawsuits. But it seemed like time to refocus on my other work.

I did, however, try to keep up with the drug industry in the newspaper, more as a hobby than as a beat. I was convinced it could be followed like any spectator sport.

The "sports pages" for this pastime in the United States are *The Wall Street Journal* and the business section of *The New York Times*. Neither pays a huge amount of attention to the legal-drug world but, in a businessy way, at least they let you keep up with the headlines. The stories are generally very bottom-line oriented, and it's always fascinating to see which subjects make the leap from the business sections to the medical or news sections. Most U.S. drug approvals weren't making the leap. Most advisory committees weren't making the leap.

The saga of Prozac had made the leap, but only years after its 1988 FDA approval. Prozac (fluoxetine) had outsold all other antidepressants combined in 1989 and rated a cover story in *Newsweek* the following year. But it wasn't until Peter Kramer's *Listening to Prozac* hit the bestseller lists in the summer of '93 that the mania for antidepression reached its peak. When I finally got a chance to read Kramer's book, I found it interesting, but for different reasons than everyone else. Certainly fluoxetine was a fascinating drug, and its enormous success for Eli Lilly was big news: the company was on its way to selling over $1 billion of the drug in 1993, and some 10 million people worldwide were reportedly taking it. But that only partially explained people's fascination with the book.

My theory, after reading it, was that most people were just bowled over because they had never before heard how these younger psychopharmacologists talk and think. The first generation of psychiatrists who don't use drugs grudgingly, they are generally very interested in what the action of medications can teach them about illnesses and about specific patients. Most of them know the boilerplate history of psychiatric drugs that Kramer wove through his patient anecdotes. And most of them—the good ones anyway—"listen" to all their drugs. All psychotherapists are in the business of "listening," just as astronomers call what they do "seeing." When you're being treated by them, you learn to "listen" yourself.

For example, Diane had recently added an antipsychotic drug, Trilafon (perphenazine), to see if it would make a dent in her "visuals." It didn't, but it did offer relief from some other jangly symptoms. They were, in fact, symptoms that she had never really identified as separate phenomena until they were diminished or gone. It was like a scene in a Tarzan movie, where nobody notices the sound of distant drums until they stop. But the drug also had another effect, which I've heard described as "taking steel wool to your brain." Just as when you Brillo a favorite cast-iron skillet, some accumulated flavors seem to get scraped off with the crud.

But while these younger psychopharmacologists represent a special, fascinating group within mental health care, I suspect Kramer's appeal goes beyond the subject of psychiatry. Deep inside, *all* patients want to know why *all* their doctors aren't as thoughtful about *all* the drugs they prescribe. What people responded to in Kramer was what I was responding to when I was around clinical pharmacologists: the gratifying feeling of being around clinicians who seemed to pay as much attention to drugs as the people who actually have to *take* them, clinicians who actually philosophize about drugs.

Actually Kramer wasn't all that thoughtful. In fact, he went out of his way not to "listen" very hard to certain aspects of his drug of choice. He admitted in his prologue that he "all but ignored certain issues," namely Prozac's side effects and its role in treating more serious depressions. In other words, he set out to hear mostly the good news about the least sick people. But even his selective view was well received, because patients were desperate for a doctor who thought about drugs before giving them.

· · ·

In the newspapers, the Prozac and Prozac-backlash stories were battling for space with the Clinton health care plan. As promised, the plan was going to include drugs in basic insurance benefits and cover 80 percent of drug costs for the elderly and disabled on Medicare—adding about 70 million people to the 174 million who already had coverage for medications. But Clinton's approach to price controls suggested that the administration had a provocative and radical notion of the direction the pharmaceutical industry should be pushed. According to *The New York Times,* the president believed drug companies needed to think of themselves more as "a crucial social service or public utility" than as "private profit-seeking businesses."

Until they agreed to do that, Clinton was going to portray pharmaceutical executives as the bogeymen of American medicine. A week after the health care proposal was released, the Justice Department blew away a plan that the Pharmaceutical Manufacturers Association (PMA) had proposed, to tie price increases to the Consumer Price Index. From the moment the drug companies had suggested it, the plan was dismissed as a "publicity stunt" and a "joke." But it could have been a crafty joke. The PMA argued that the only way these voluntary price ceilings could be put into place was if the drug business were exempted from antitrust laws.

You had to admire their pluck.

What would the legal-drug world look like without government regulation and antitrust laws? The answer may have come in the bribery scandal unfolding in Italy, where the $10.6 billion-a-year drug industry was the world's fifth largest pharmaceutical market and perhaps its most corrupt.

The scandal centered on Duilio Poggiolini, a sixty-two-year-old academic pharmacologist who was the Italian government's top health minister involved with pharmaceuticals. But Poggiolini's power extended beyond Italy; he was also the closest thing Europe had to a "legal-drug czar." He headed the committee that was charged with creating a European Medicines Evaluation Agency, which would harmonize drug regulation for the European Community (EC) countries and allow manufacturers to apply for "multistate" approvals. And he was a leading figure in the World Health Organization (WHO), the division of the United Nations that, among its other activities, sets international standards for medication use.

So when Poggiolini was accused of accepting more than $100 million in bribes from drug companies, there was no question what the firms had been trying to buy.

For more than a year before Poggiolini's name came up, the Italian government was being rocked by a white-collar crime scandal referred to by some as the "Bribesville" affair. By the summer of 1993, the members of the health ministry's pharmaceutical pricing advisory committee—which was responsible for keeping Italian prices unnaturally high—came under tremendous scrutiny. One member, the chairman of the pharmacy department at Naples University, committed suicide. Several others were arrested or put under cautionary warrants, and several pharmaceutical company executives—including the head of a SmithKline Beecham subsidiary in Italy—were charged with making illegal campaign contributions that were really bribes to speed up approval and keep prices elevated.

Then Poggiolini disappeared suddenly. When he failed to show up at several meetings of his EC Committee for Proprietary Medicinal Products, he was publicly replaced. Several months after vanishing, he was discovered at a private health clinic in Lausanne, checked in under a phony name. After he and his wife were arrested, their amazing wealth was revealed. About $70 million was discovered hidden in Swiss and Italian bank accounts. Then police raided their home close to Rome and found a safe filled with, according to published reports, "over 100 bars of gold bullion, as well as sterling gold coins, hundreds of South African Krugerrands, Swiss francs, U.S. dollars, Dutch florins, gold ecu coins, twenty uncut diamonds, rubles from the Czar Nicholas era and gold watches."

Poggiolini told police the haul had been "a present from my wife."

A week later investigators returned and, on a tip from an arrested former colleague, ripped open the sofa in Poggiolini's drawing room, where they found $6 million in government bonds. The total value of the bribes, said to come from fourteen major pharmaceutical companies, including SmithKline Beecham and Glaxo, was estimated at $120 million. Many of the payments were alleged to have been funneled through Farmindustria, the drug industry trade association.

Not long after Poggiolini's arrest, Italian newspapers were reporting that he had told police the corruption scandal even involved the Vatican. He reportedly implicated Cardinal Fiorenzo Angelini, Pope John Paul's top health authority, who oversaw the church's 40,000 medical institutions worldwide. Angelini denied any wrongdoing.

Soon Poggiolini's entire twenty-year tenure was being reconsidered. Consumer advocates claimed that his industry-friendly pricing policies had created "unjustifiable profits," the Italian version of Clinton's "excess profits," of more than $1 billion a year. They also claimed that Poggiolini (who is still awaiting trial) had allowed potentially dangerous products to be sold in Italy and had allowed companies to disregard drug safety warnings.

This was especially troubling to those American academic pharmacologists who had been wondering for years about the flight of clinical drug trials from the United States to Europe. For much of this century, drugs could be approved by the FDA based only on trials performed in the United States. In 1985, the FDA announced it would begin to consider trials conducted in other countries as part of a New Drug Application. The change was made primarily so that drugs already in common use in Europe or Japan might be more quickly approved in the United States. It had the unfortunate side effect of allowing American drug companies to move trials overseas that normally would have been done in U.S. academic medical centers. Drug companies claim that the trials—often the "first time in human" Phase I trials, which usually determine both dosage and the general safety profile—are being moved to Europe because it is cheaper and the regulatory environment is more reasonable than what the FDA has created in the United States. (The FDA sends inspectors to foreign labs, but it has a far smaller presence overseas than it does domestically.) The companies neglect to mention that adverse reaction rates in European trials tend to be uniformly lower than in the same trials performed in America.

Italy has always been considered to be pretty lax even by European standards: at the FDA, an Italian trial submitted with an application was considered something of a red flag. But they were sometimes submitted. And it was perfectly legal. And more and more, U.S. medication approvals were built on the sometimes shaky foundation of what a prominent American researcher once described to me as "offshore drug development."

This researcher—a man who invented one of the world's top-selling drugs and has worked with many of the major pharmaceutical firms—told me a story about the emerging attitude among the drug companies. "People come to me and say they have this new compound, and they want me to have a look at it," he said. "I tell them I don't think it's active. But that's not what they want to hear. So I say, 'Look, I'll tell you who to go to in France or Italy. Give them twenty thousand bucks, and they'll get whatever results you want.' That's absolutely true. They *get* you good results. . . . The Italians are very cordial people: Give them money, and *they'll* study your drug."

．　　　．　　　．

Through that fall of '93, I really was trying to stay away from the drug business and concentrate on my other work. And then Oprah called. After that, nothing was quite the same.

Actually Alice McGee called. Alice is one of Oprah's longtime producers. She worked her way up from an intern to become a veteran of the Oprah studio in Chicago. One afternoon early in November, she called Diane to ask if she and I would appear on a show about adverse drug reactions. In the small world of daytime TV, Alice had heard about us from a producer who had just moved to *Oprah* from *Good Morning America.*

More amazing than her finding Diane was the reason she was interested in the subject in the first place.

Alice McGee had been Floxed, too.

She had been given Floxin by her gynecologist for a fairly serious urinary tract infection. Not long after she started taking it, her brain began, in her words, to "hiccup." She was dizzy and disoriented. She began hallucinating and having vivid nightmares. Her vision became so impaired that she was repeatedly bumping into other cars when she parked, and she found herself avoiding the long marble staircase in the *Oprah* studios. The surface of the steps appeared completely flat to her, like a long slide, and she was afraid of slipping down. Her fellow producers, and finally Oprah herself, started whispering, "Is Alice on *drugs* or something?"

Yeah, girl.

Unfortunately, McGee didn't realize she was having a drug reaction. She thought it was job-related stress. When Alice went to get her Floxin prescription refilled, she looked at the package insert and saw most of the side effects she was having listed there. But she *still* continued to believe that she was just under too much stress at work, and kept taking the drug.

Finally, the executive producer at *Oprah* told Alice to take a day off—she was just acting too strangely, and people were concerned. She had mistakenly left her Floxin in her office, so she wasn't able to take it the next morning. And by midafternoon, some of her worst symptoms were starting to clear. It was only then that she realized what their source was.

Diane was extremely reluctant to do the show, afraid she might appear to be some kind of freak. She became a little more interested when she learned that Alice McGee had also been Floxed, but she began considering the offer seriously only when she heard that Alice was talking to some of the other women we knew who were still suffering from Floxin reactions. Stacy Phillips, who had appeared in my original article, was thinking about going public, and Sue Smith, who had gone into shock in Yellowstone, was considering it as well. But both said they didn't want to come on unless Diane did. Together they would make an interesting cross-section of American women affected by Floxin: Stacy, a hard-nosed East Coast litigator and working mom; Sue, a good-natured midwestern real estate sales rep, married without kids; and Diane, a fiction writer and artist, all blown out of their lives by a drug reaction. In that context, Diane agreed to do the show.

During that fascinating twenty-four hours in Chicago at Grand Old Oprahland, I found myself constantly comparing the experience with the day I had recently spent at the advisory committee meeting in Silver Springs. The topics were almost exactly the same, as was the level of orchestrated button-pushing. But in what turned out to be a one-hour *people's* advisory committee meeting on Floxin, and on adverse drug reactions in general, the final vote was, of course, quite different.

In the backstage green rooms at Oprah's studio, I watched with great interest as Diane, Alice, Sue and Stacy met fellow Floxies for the first time. I listened to how each responded to the simple but in this case terribly loaded question, "How are you?"

Alice said she was much better and thought the worst of it was behind her. Everybody said, "Oh, good, good," but I could see a glint of "Yeah, right," in their eyes: how many times had they tried to convince themselves that the episode was truly over, that they were no longer feeling Floxed? Alice had been trying to recover for only several weeks. Stacy was going on two years.

Of the three women, Stacy seemed to me in the worst shape. Everyone was a little nervous about appearing on national television, but Stacy had the fear of something much bigger in her eyes. She wasn't shaking so much as vibrating. Her husband pulled me aside to ask if I had learned anything new about ways to treat the Floxin reactions. But mostly he seemed to want to connect with someone who had shared this weird nightmare. The difference was, he and Stacy had kids, and Stacy was still resistant to taking any medication at all. Diane had been slowly coming out of a deep depression and wasn't feeling all that great herself, but she had, over the year, been able to put her symptoms into some kind of medical context. Stacy was still in some strange form of denial: she knew she was sick, but she denied that she needed to take medication to get better, even though giving up her law practice had not helped as much as she had hoped.

My heart went out to the Phillipses. I knew how hard this was to deal with even if you trusted your doctors and participated in treatment. I could only imagine how Stacy and her husband had coped on their own. He seemed to be subtly trying to enlist the support of Diane and Sue to lean on Stacy to get treatment. At the same time, the three women were all attempting, as nicely as possible, to tell Alice to be careful and give herself some more time.

The taping opened with Oprah introducing Alice—who apparently didn't know until the last minute that she was going to appear on camera—and the two of them discussing how Alice's drug reaction had spawned the show. Featuring someone whose job it is to find "real people" for a talk show as the "real person" was remarkably effective; it took what I had done with Diane's story one better.

From Alice, they quickly cut to shots of Sue and then Stacy, with the words "suffered devastating drug effects" superimposed under them, and then to Diane, who was the first one Oprah actually interviewed. To me, Diane looked poised and pretty, but in her own estimation, she appeared terribly depressed. Either way, her blue-on-blue outfit suited the moment.

Diane did really well. Unlike her thirty-second spot on *Good Morning America,* this time she had the opportunity to set the whole chilling scene. Then Stacy and Sue told their stories. Stacy was very lawyerly and controlled. Sue was, frankly, scared to death. She actually forgot to mention the most horrific part of her story—about going into shock in the national park and having to be airlifted out—although she did have one of the best lines. When Oprah asked what special, detailed instructions her doctor had given her when prescribing Floxin, she said he told her, "Good drug, take it with water."

I came on and talked about my work. After a break, they brought on Joe Graedon, the advocacy-oriented pharmacist who, with his wife Teresa, a Ph.D. medical anthropologist, writes the best-selling *People's Pharmacy* books, does a radio show about prescription drugs and has a nationally syndicated column that is often the only place in the lay press where newly emerging drug safety issues are even mentioned. With his salt-and-pepper beard and broad glasses, Graedon is a rapid-fire huckster for drug safety, a model of a type I had come to think of as the "adverse drug reaction buff"—experts who don't do drug research themselves but serve as clearinghouses for safety concerns. And as ADR buffs go, he's one of the most effective. His every example is audience-tested for maximum impact.

Graedon hit the ground running with his pronouncement that more people died every year from adverse reactions to arthritis medicine than died from all illegal drug use (based on figures from the FDA and a leading rheumatologist). He talked about the dangers of food interactions with drugs, noting that the heart medication Lanoxin (digoxin) can be deactivated if taken with oatmeal or bran. He also ran through some of the appalling research about taking medications with grapefruit juice. I had heard about some of this before from Dave Flockhart, who had done some of the research. While exploring the toxicity of Seldane, Flockhart had discovered that taking it with grapefruit juice dramatically increased blood levels of the antihistamine; so high, Graedon said, "that it could cause death."

Flockhart had told me that after doing that work, he believed that doctors should always warn their patients never to take any drugs with grapefruit juice, because it was too easy to accidentally overdose yourself even with standard doses. (Something in the juice inhibited the Cytochrome P450 system in the liver, Flockhart's research passion, so drugs stayed in the body much longer than normal.) At the same time, he and others at Georgetown were quietly experimenting with using the grapefruit juice effect to lower the required dose of extremely expensive drugs. The brother of one of the department's pharmacologists was taking the very pricey antirejection drug Sandimmune (cyclosporine), and they were wondering if he could halve the dose with the right amount of Tropicana.

Graedon then moved on to the problems caused by drugs interacting with other drugs. His concern was not only adverse reactions but unpleasantly surprising drug *inactions.* He ticked off several different kinds of drugs that could alter the absorption of birth control pills, including some common antibiotics. Ironically, he said, the Pill was more easily affected by other drugs now than it was ten years ago because the hormone dosages had been lowered to reduce some of the troubling side effects. He also explained how the antibiotic tetracycline could be inactivated not only by milk—as patients are often warned—but also by vitamin and mineral supplements, and even antacids.

Oprah looked dead into the camera and said, "This is *shocking!*" And during the break, we found out why.

She said that a doctor had prescribed her a medication that she had never thought to mention to her other physicians. Apparently she never realized until that minute that there could be an interaction risk. I looked over to Diane and realized that she had heard something shocking, too. I had neglected to mention anything to her about what Dave Flockhart had told me about grapefruit juice. So when discussing the variables that influenced her drug reaction, we had never seriously confronted what she had had for breakfast the morning she got Floxed. It was the same thing she had every morning. Cheerios and a glass of grapefruit juice.

After the next break, Oprah spoke with a woman who had suffered a stroke while taking birth control pills. The woman described waking up one morning and feeling an arm on her chest: she assumed it was her husband's draped over her, but when she lifted it, she realized it was *her own.* The entire left side of her body had been paralyzed, and several years later she was still walking with a cane. She and her husband had sued the drug company, but she had been found partially responsible for her fate. She had been smoking cigarettes while on the Pill—which is strongly contraindicated, and her doctor had specifically cautioned her not to do it.

Oprah cut to an audience member, who just wanted to show how many pills she took each day. She had a little blue plastic pill case, compartmentalized for the days of the week, and for each day she had three blood pressure pills, one pill for allergies and a birth control pill (which she was taking for endometriosis). She had a nasal inhaler, and because her blood pressure medication gave her headaches, she carried a bottle of aspirin. In the aspirin bottle, she also carried Maalox tablets, because she often got an upset stomach. Oprah found this volume of pill-taking "unbelievable."

The show finished with a discussion of "addiction" to over-the-counter drugs. Graedon had brought along a woman from St. Louis who had so abused her OTC nasal spray that she had actually blown a hole in her nose. Other audience members testified to their overdependence on such inhalers.

All in all, it was a pretty scary hour of television: if the theme of the advisory committee meeting had been "don't worry," the theme of the *Oprah* show was "panic." The program ran several weeks after we taped it, and my office voice mail started filling up with messages before it was even half over. Producer Alice McGee (who was by then feeling back to normal) said it was one of the highest-rated programs they had ever done that didn't include a celebrity. The mail began to arrive a day or two later. It was the same mix of people—half bona fide Floxies, half people who had had reactions to other drugs or just wanted to talk about the subject. There were so many that I gave up trying to physically pass the cases on to the FDA myself. Instead, we gave people the new MedWatch numbers and suggested they call the agency personally.

Because of the *Oprah* show, various drug-related groups I had never heard of tracked me down. There was an organization of mothers whose children had been among the small percentage who are irreparably harmed by reactions to routine vaccinations. There were organizations that represented people with low-incidence illnesses that could be treated only by so-called "orphan drugs," which the pharmaceutical companies said they couldn't produce profitably and so were reluctant to manufacture. There were organizations of senior citizens who were angry about high drug costs and low safety standards. There were countless individuals who had begun letter-writing campaigns, via their U.S. senators and representatives, about specific drugs they had taken or their general frustration with the world of legal drugs. Because *Oprah* is shown in England, too, there were outraged British patients who sent copies of the letters they had been writing to their own government and regulatory officials.

And I was still hearing from that doctor who diagnosed Diane with TMJ based on her eye position during her earlier TV appearance. He wanted to know when we would be returning his promotional videotape.

I wasn't looking for any of this to suck me back into writing about the drug industry again. Unlike beat reporters at newspapers and magazines, I have always tried to spend as long as it takes to do one great big story on a subject and then move on to something new. But I just couldn't get off the drugs. I found myself asking my editors at *The Washington Post Magazine* if they'd be interested in the political efforts to get Woosley's proposal for centers for independent drug research and information services into the health care plan. They said I could write about it, but only if I reprised some of the material about our own personal story.

At the same time, my growing interest in drugs came up in other situations—like a medication information swap with best-selling cookbook author Sheila Lukins, whom I was profiling for *Vanity Fair*. Lukins was slowly recovering from a sudden, massive cerebral hemorrhage and several brain surgeries that had left her permanently combatting seizures, for which she had been prescribed a barrage of anticonvulsants. In between our interviews (during which she prepared a lobster and mango salad I can still taste), we got to talking about Diane. Sheila asked if we knew about an experimental anti-seizure med she was trying. I asked if anyone had warned her about avoiding quinolones while trying so valiantly to control her seizures. She knew nothing about quinolones, and asked me to write down the names of the drugs on the back of my business card, which she stuck in her wallet. Several weeks later, she called to report that she had been in Oaxaca, Mexico, came down with something, and a doctor there tried to give her a quinolone antibiotic—which she refused after consulting the back of my card.

While I was finishing those pieces, my drug articles for *Philadelphia* were chosen as a finalist for a National Magazine Award, the magazine equivalent of the Pulitzer Prize. I had been part of a group from *Philadelphia* that had won an award the previous year. But this was my first time as an individual finalist.

The *Post* piece came out the first week in April 1994, and the phones were ringing off the hook. Luckily, this time, it wasn't just my phone but Dave Flockhart's. Dozens of new Floxies tracked him down because he was the guy pictured in a white doctor's coat in the article looking as though he could help. Dave got all kinds of interesting calls, including one from an aide to Hillary Rodham Clinton who wanted to discuss the first lady's interest in adverse drug reactions.

The magazine received quite a few letters itself, some pro, some con. The one I was particularly interested in came from Dr. Eugene Sanders of Creighton University's School of Medicine. He called my article "understandably emotional but regrettably scientifically unbalanced." He correctly noted that "all drugs are potentially hazardous. Aspirin may cause serious bleeding. Penicillin continues to elicit severe and occasional lethal allergic reactions; in fact, were it discovered today, it could not receive FDA approval for human use because it uniformly kills guinea pigs." He suggested that "it would have been prudent for Mr. Fried to indicate that 'new' and 'potent' do not necessarily equate to 'toxic,' and that older and less expensive is not always as effective nor [is it always] safer."

In general, Dr. Sanders, whose papers on quinolones I had read, was "deeply concerned that as a result [of the article] many in the readership may avoid necessary or even lifesaving treatment with the quinolones or other potent new therapeutic agents." He neglected to mention that at least part of his concern may have grown out of the fact that he was a member of Ortho-McNeil's outside advisory board on anti-infectives. His bio was included with the Floxin press kit I received.

But the highlight of the *Post Magazine* experience came when Ray

Woosley called from Georgetown one afternoon. "Well, you finally got your 'Dear Doctor' letter," he said.

He had a copy of a letter that had been sent to all Washington-area doctors by Ortho a week after my article appeared. But instead of warning these doctors about the newly documented risk of CNS side effects from Floxin, the company was writing to warn doctors about *me*.

Woosley read me the letter. It said only that in the magazine "a journalist describes his wife's unfortunate 1992 experience and attributes it to our quinolone product. . . . We bring this to your attention recognizing the story might stimulate some questions from your patients." It went on to point out that "Floxin has been used by over 100 million people worldwide and we at Ortho-McNeil stand behind its well established safety profile." The company enclosed a package insert for reference, but since they were still wrangling with the FDA about the new language for CNS toxicity, the warnings were those the advisory committee had already deemed inadequate.

"These guys really are unbelievable," Woosley said.

A week later, I was sitting in the balcony in the Waldorf-Astoria ballroom with Diane and my colleagues from *Philadelphia* magazine when my name was announced, among the other nominees, from *The New Yorker, Atlantic Monthly* and *Common Cause,* for the National Magazine Award for public interest journalism. After only a brief pause—no envelopes for this award ceremony—our magazine's cover appeared on the twenty-foot-high screen, the spotlight shot our way and Diane gave me a buzzy victory kiss.

When I returned to the real world the next morning, I couldn't help thinking how complex and weird the whole experience had been. The highlight of my professional career had been spawned by the lowlight of my wife's life. It's not uncommon for writers to mine their own lives and the lives of others around them for their work. But I wondered how much you can dig up and drag to the surface before the mineshaft itself collapses around you.

Still, the award and the reaction to the *Post* piece seemed like clear signals that I wasn't really finished writing about the pharmaceutical industry. Diane, however, was adamant that whatever I did next shouldn't include her, except as an editor. A year and a half after being Floxed, she was finally trying to get back to her own writing again. She insisted that I find a bigger story than hers, or perhaps the bigger story that hers would allow me to tell.

I thought about what would drive me to find that bigger story, if not her. It had to be something more specific than the omnipresence of legal drugs in our society, and the amorphously huge dangers of their power not being taken seriously enough. A former high-ranking FDA official had recently looked me straight in the eye and insisted that "the amount of preventable harm done by the misuse of drugs and the lack of properly identifying drug side effects exceeds the sum total of all occupational and environmental hazards in the United States." It was quite a call to arms, but it still wasn't enough reason to keep taking the subject so personally.

Then the pictures came back from the awards luncheon. Looking through the shots, I noticed that I was grinning tight-lipped in most of them, never once showing a broad, toothy smile. And I remembered for the first time in years that *I* had once been the victim of a permanently disfiguring adverse drug reaction. As a child, I had very high fevers. My pediatrician gave me tetracycline, not knowing at the time that the drug could cause problems with the development of tooth enamel. When news of the side effect began reaching embarrassed doctors in the mid-1960s, it was too late for kids like me. When my permanent front teeth came in, the top ones, the most visible ones, were permanently mottled brown and pockmarked.

In my early teens, I had the worst of them covered with an elementary enamel-bonding procedure. But by then, I had already learned how not to smile—or at least how not to smile fully.

I looked at my face in the bathroom mirror. For the first time in years, I deliberately unpursed my lips, so I could stare hard at those teeth. The bonding material had lasted years longer than the orthodontist had promised. It was only now beginning to chip off, exposing the discolored, pitted mess beneath.

In the shadow of my smile, I found what I needed to push on. For better or for worse, I was going back to the drugs again. But this time I was going to start fresh. I was going to stop seeing the pharmaceutical world through the prism of Floxin. Instead, I was going to try seeing Floxin through the prism of the whole pharmaceutical-industrial complex.

So it was time to start checking obscure books out of the library; luckily, there's rarely a long waiting list for *Responsibility for Drug-Induced Injury* by Dukes et al. It was time to interview the people I saw referred to passingly in trade journal stories. It was time to find out, once and for all, how the world of legal drugs got so messed up in the first place.

PART II

CHAPTER 7

Nit-picking

I n the summer of 1962, Dr. Frances Kelsey became the Eliot Ness of the FDA. That's when her role in preventing the sedative thalidomide from being sold in America—sparing the United States the epidemic of birth defects it caused in other countries—suddenly hit the front page of *The Washington Post.* John F. Kennedy was so eager to give her a medal that her name and citation were added to the program of the annual President's Award ceremony only four days before it took place. And she became the first public face of modern drug regulation, along with the so-called "Kelsey's Cops" from her fledgling Division of Scientific Investigation. True to their image, they did much to clean up the drug business and set many international standards for cracking down on pharmaceutical manufacturers.

These days, Frances Kelsey is the ghost of FDA past. Many in the legal-drug world are surprised to hear that, in her mid-eighties, she is not only still alive but still working at the FDA.

I went to visit Kelsey at her office, which is in one of the squat, anonymous red-brick buildings that the agency leases in Rockville, Maryland. The FDA long ago outgrew its nearby suburban headquarters, where it had moved from downtown Washington in 1969. Funds to put the entire agency under one roof—which might help fill in the large cracks that drug problems can fall into between geographically distant departments full of overworked, underpaid people—are perennially voted down by Congress.

I came because I assumed Frances Kelsey would be a treasure trove of memories and insights about the 1960s and 1970s, when most of the world's drug regulatory systems—some complex and exacting, some frighteningly cursory—were established. Instead, I found that she could provide institutional memory all the way back to the 1930s and a personally guided tour through some sixty-odd years of the legal-drug culture. She could put a human face on the dozens of books and hundreds of articles I was poring through.

Kelsey sat behind a large wooden desk, piled high with new computer equipment and old papers, some of which were scrunched under a large black cast-iron bug. It was a "nit," she explained, given to her by a colleague because of her reputation as a nit-picker. When it comes from someone in industry, "nit-picker" is meant as the ultimate trivializing insult. But inside the agency, it is a compliment, paid most highly to Kelsey because she is the queen mum of nit-picking.

In her top desk drawer was the bag lunch she brings every day. She said she brown-bags it because she no longer drives and there is no place nearby to walk for lunch, but I wondered if it wasn't just agency-ingrained frugality. People at the FDA have historically made far less money than their counterparts in industry, and when they sit across the table from each other, there can be a noticeable socioeconomic difference. I once took a shuttle bus to an airport with three adverse reaction specialists who, like me, had been attending an annual clinical pharmacology convention. The three had clearly been peers at one time in academia: now one ran the safety department of a major pharmaceutical firm, and the other two worked for the FDA. While the industry guy listened, with some disbelief, his friends told him they had been forced to pay many of the convention costs—including part of their hotel room charges—out of their own pockets because the FDA couldn't afford to reimburse them beyond some absurdly low amount.

Frances Kelsey has the kind, fine-lined, genderless face of an elderly doctor. Her hair is thin and gray—she wears it short and unadorned, as she always has—and her voice is gravelly. Like many people I've met at the FDA, she can be almost inhumanly exacting and scientific when discussing technical matters. But her whole demeanor changes when a personal question gets past her radar: then she has an explosive laugh, and her face looks like someone startled out of a happy dream. She wore a paisley dress and bifocals, and on a chain around her neck was her plastic agency ID tag, prominently stamped with an expiration date in the year 2001. She was amused at the ID tag's optimism that she might "see the century out after all." She had seen a great deal already.

．　　　．　　　．

While Kelsey is an old-timer, there is, of course, some history that predates even her. The basic friction between the people who make drugs and the people who take them—refereed by some third party that draws the lines between medicine and snake oil, chemotherapy and poison, consumer protection and hysteria—has been documented since biblical times. In Muslim nations during the fourteenth century, a health inspector called a *muhtasib* was supposed to keep apothecaries honest. He was cautioned that it was necessary to make drug sellers "fearful, try them and warn them against imprisonment."

Until the 1600s, drug regulation focused on the apothecary, the retail pharmacist of the time, because medicines were primarily sold by the people who prepared them. The response to the Great Plague of London in 1665 made the first commercial production of medicines—or what passed for medicines—possible. The rise of the newspaper in Britain at about the same time created a medium for the first mass advertising of these medicines. Eventually, British doctors began calling for "examination, analyzation and approbation of every medicine before . . . it should be vended in any manner whatsoever."

By the 1800s, some of that responsibility was shouldered by the "pharmacopoeias." These were independent national boards in various countries, including the United States, that began by simply publishing official lists of available drugs, then branched out into creating standards of formulation and quality. The pharmacopoeias did not concern themselves with such esoteric issues as efficacy or safety. They were worried about purity of ingredients and false advertising, making sure that if a medicine was supposed to contain 10 percent of a substance we might today consider a poison, the customer was not cheated. Since many drugs and raw chemicals were imported, often from large companies in Germany, pharmacopoeial standards were important for screening out substandard ingredients at ports of entry.

The first calls for more medical regulation came in response to the rise of "patent medicines" during the Industrial Revolution. Although many of these medicines were the mild laxatives, sedatives and cough remedies similar to those still sold over the counter in pharmacies today, there was also heavy advertising for patent medicines that claimed to cure cancer, syphilis or tuberculosis, such as Warner's Safe Cure for Diabetes and Kick-a-poo Indian Sagwa. Several countries would later pass laws outlawing the advertising of cures for such diseases.

To differentiate itself from the patent medicine business, the chemical/pharmaceutical industry came to refer to its products as "ethical drugs." And by the late nineteenth century, the ethical drug business was changing. Fewer medicines were being made from scratch by apothecaries; the "retail chemist" was becoming the "dispensing pharmacist." (Patients who didn't use physicians often had their treatment dispensed directly by pharmacists, leading to a smoldering relationship between the two professions.) Chemical companies were growing more sophisticated at both synthesizing new compounds and manufacturing on a larger scale. And a number of family pharmacy businesses grew into large wholesale and retail operations to take advantage of the changing U.S. and European medicine markets. These large "ethical drug houses" were multinational decades before the countries they sold to could coordinate any serious regulation of the safety and efficacy of medications.

Much of this mass production was made possible by the pharmaceutical equivalent of the cotton gin: the "tableting machine" that made the first compressed pills. First done in England in the 1840s, tableting was perfected in the United States in the 1870s, and some major companies were built solely on their pill-making ability. One of the better known was Burroughs Wellcome, which was started in London in 1880 by two young Americans trained at the Philadelphia College of Pharmacy. The company became known for offering many popular medicines in compressed pill versions it called "tabloids." (Its promotional device was a "kit" of compressed drugs and foods, which was used by prominent adventurers like the first team to scale Mount Everest.) In 1894, Burroughs Wellcome also became one of the first pharmaceutical companies to set up in-house research facilities and actually try to discover its own new drugs. Until then, the major drug houses were primarily involved in international manufacturing, distribution and marketing. The few actual treatment innovations, such as diphtheria antitoxin, came from individuals: academic researchers, treating physicians and inventive pharmacists.

The first serious U.S. laws concerning medications were passed in 1902 and 1906, in a series of events that would keep replaying themselves throughout the twentieth century. What happens is that a critical mass of physicians, pharmacists, legislators and executives at the more high-minded drug houses begins a call for new regulations. Other politicians and big-businessmen block the path of reform. Then a highly publicized medical disaster kept the legislation from dying on the vine.

The initial patient disaster was in 1902, when twelve children died in St. Louis from diphtheria vaccine that had been contaminated with tetanus. The vaccine had been formulated by the city's own health department. Unfortunately, this wasn't the first occurrence of urban biological contamination: something similar had happened in Camden, New Jersey, the previous year, when eighty patients got tetanus from a commercially produced smallpox vaccine. The outcry over the St. Louis incident led to the passage of several laws to prevent adulterated drugs from being sold in the United States, which, for decades, had been considered the world's dumping ground for contaminated medicines. For vaccines, there was a specific Biologics Control Act in 1902. The same year, Congress passed a more sweeping bill, supported by the pharmacy trade association and the major American drug houses, that required the secretary of agriculture to investigate adulterated drugs. A drug laboratory was established at the department's Bureau of Chemistry in Washington. That lab would grow into the Food and Drug Administration.

Dr. Harvey Wiley, who directed the lab, was already known in the Bureau of Chemistry as the country's first drug safety crusader. But he used his new platform and mandate to drum up even more public attention. He set up a volunteer "poison squad" to test foods treated with chemical preservatives, and he lectured widely about his work. It wasn't until the February 1906 publication of Upton Sinclair's novel *The Jungle,* however, that he could amass enough political support to ensure the passage of broader legislation. *The Jungle* was a gritty drama set in the Chicago meat-packing yards, and it was meant to highlight the terrible labor conditions for immigrant workers. Instead, as the twenty-seven-year-old Sinclair noted with some dismay, the public was more horrified by the graphic descriptions of unsanitary conditions and tainted meat. "I aimed at the public's heart," Sinclair wrote, "and by accident I hit it in the stomach."

The public outcry over the book brought together the so-called "pure food movement"—a grassroots group that had sprung up after the Civil War—and Wiley's drug safety crusade and led to the passage of the Pure Food and Drug Act in June 1906. This was the first law that allowed the government to remove a food or drug product from the market if it was proven to be unsafe. It was also supposed to protect the public from drugs that didn't work.

This episode forever associated Chicago with the safety of medicines and consumer protection in general. The city had also recently become the national headquarters of the growing physicians' organization, the American Medical Association, which responded to the new law by setting up its own Chicago laboratory to test new drugs before they were written about in *JAMA*. So when Frances Kelsey retold the story of American drug regulation, as she was often called upon to do, she usually began with Chicago and the 1906 law.

She then would explain how the Pure Food and Drug Act failed. The statute didn't require the manufacturer to prove a product was safe before marketing it; instead, it required the government to prove the product *unsafe* before removing it from the market. Patent medicine manufacturers also mounted a legal challenge to the statute's efficacy provisions. And in 1911 the Supreme Court ruled that the Pure Food and Drug Act didn't prohibit even provably phony health claims—specifically those on Dr. Johnson's Mild Combination Treatment for Cancer—but only covered false statements about the *ingredients* of the medicines. An amendment was passed in 1912 to close the loophole, but it still forced the government to prove that the drug manufacturer had not only lied but lied deliberately. Prosecutors referred to this as the "fraud joker" that stacked the deck against them in most legal actions.

The problems with U.S. drug regulation statutes became increasingly important during World War I, when hostilities against Germany—still the most powerful nation in the drug world—deprived German firms of their markets and, more important, their U.S. patent protections. This allowed the American pharmaceutical industry to finally come into its own, leading to the first of two postwar booms in U.S. drug innovation. Recognizing that the safety net wasn't growing with the industry, the U.S. government made the Food and Drug Administration a separate unit of the Agriculture Department in 1927, but the limitations of the existing laws didn't allow the FDA to do much to protect consumers from questionable remedies. The public didn't become sensitized to the true toothlessness of the FDA's legal mandate until 1933, when another muckraking book, *100,000,000 Guinea Pigs: Dangers in Everyday Foods, Drugs and Cosmetics,* was published by the noted public advocacy group, Consumers' Research, and became an enormous best-seller. The book detailed people getting cataracts from an untested weight-loss drug, women being blinded by eyelash paint and a number of patients whose illnesses defied diagnosis until it became clear that what they all had in common was their hair-removing cream—which turned out to contain thallium, a deadly rat poison.

The book's charges presaged the elixir of sulfanilamide disaster, which revolutionized drug safety standards. In the fall of 1937, the S. E. Massengill Company of Bristol, Tennessee, put out a drinkable version of sulfanilamide, the new antibacterial wonder drug. The drug had been introduced the previous April with great fanfare; by summer, Squibb,

Merck, Eli Lilly and Parke-Davis all had pill or powder versions on the market. By early October, sulfanilamide drugs were so popular that *JAMA* was already warning doctors against their indiscriminate use.

Then suddenly, small children in the South who had taken the elixir version started dropping dead, most from anuria—an inability to pass urine—leading to severe kidney and liver damage. On October 20 the American Medical Association received an urgent telegram from Massengill about elixir of sulfanilamide.

"Please wire collect by Western Union suggestion for antidote," it said.

The rising death toll and the quest for an antidote was front-page news across the nation. The FDA and the AMA ordered immediate testing of the elixir. Most of the work was done in Chicago by the AMA's drug laboratory and by clinical researchers at the University of Chicago, which had one of the world's finest pharmacology programs. Dr. E. M. Geiling, the university's renowned research pharmacologist, was enlisted to do the emergency animal toxicology tests on the elixir and all its individual components.

Among his eager graduate students was twenty-three-year-old Frances Kelsey—then Frances Oldham, a Canadian who had come from McGill University for the opportunity to study with Geiling. Like the entire nation, she was waiting for the results of his pharmacological detective work. The suspect ingredient in the elixir was the liquid into which the sulfanilamide had been dissolved. Because sulfanilamide is difficult to dissolve in water or alcohol, a Massengill chemist had used diethylene glycol, an industrial solvent in the same chemical family as antifreeze. It had never been tested for safety in humans—and it was not even mentioned on the elixir's label.

"I was watching the tests with the rats, the dogs and the monkeys," Kelsey told me. "In next to no time, you could tell it was the diethylene glycol. The rats that took it got sick and shriveled and the urine got red and they would shortly after die. I was mostly just observing the experiments because the students had to do a through-the-night vigil, and it was considered rather dangerous for women to be out at night."

The elixir of sulfanilamide fiasco eventually took more than one hundred lives—including that of the Massengill chemist responsible for choosing the diethylene glycol, who later killed himself. But its aftermath was what galvanized Kelsey's interest in drug regulation. "The only thing that the company was in trouble for was that the elixir was misbranded," she recalled, still incredulous after all these years. "It wasn't illegal for a drug to be *unsafe*. The onus would fall on the FDA to show it was dangerous, and that's not always easy: people will give testimonials for virtually *anything*!"

In fact, one of the doctors who lost a patient to the elixir received this letter, signed by S. E. Massengill himself: "We . . . regret very deeply the fatal result that you had when administering [our] product . . . but as we violated no law and made no error in our manufacture, I do not think that we should be blamed by the unlooked for action of this product."

It was an interesting choice of words, because there is a difference between a truly "unexpected" drug action and one that is merely "unlooked for." The difference is one of the essential, built-in quandaries of drug safety—the danger of the unpicked nit. But the existing laws didn't recognize such subtleties. "The technicality on which the company was fined," Kelsey recalled, "was that to be called an 'elixir,' a product could only be mixed with alcohol. That's how they got the drug off the market."

Her mentor, Dr. Geiling, believed that the sulfanilamide situation was an opportunity to "really bring home to people that the nation's drugs had to be more carefully examined and reviewed," she recalled. Congress had been periodically debating a new drug bill for years, and after the highly publicized deaths, the debate began anew. A new federal Food, Drug and Cosmetics Act was finally passed by Congress in June 1938. For the first time, drug manufacturers were going to have to prove that their new products were safe before putting them on the market. "Proof of fraud" would no longer be required for the government to stop a firm from making false therapeutic claims, and the FDA was given authority to inspect factories.

The new law didn't really establish a viable system for drug regulation and labeling. But it was such an improvement over existing laws that it took years before its shortcomings became obvious. Over the next decade the FDA would try procedurally to close the loopholes in the statute without actually getting involved in the politics of drafting a whole new one. That process, which is still used today, involves writing new "regulations" or "guidelines" for how existing laws will be enforced and publishing them in the Federal Register, the government's daily proclamation of rule changes. But even with all these changes, the FDA's primary method of enforcement still centered on charges of "misbranding." Rather than being able to focus on whether a drug actually worked, everything came down to the accuracy of its label.

Yet at the time, the United States had some of the world's most advanced, aggressive laws for regulating drugs. Only Norway and Sweden had statutes on the books that allowed their tiny regulatory bodies to ask whether new drugs brought onto the market did what they were supposed to do. There had been an efficacy requirement in a U.S. bill originally proposed in 1933, but it had been killed by lobbyists along the way. Most Western governments would not develop the courage to actually legislate efficacy for decades to come. In fact, drug regulation in most countries amounted to little more than drug registration, an administrative formality.

Frances Kelsey got her Ph.D. in pharmacology in 1938, in the same month the Food, Drug and Cosmetics Act was passed. Her specialty was animal testing on the pituitary glands of mammals, especially armadillos and whales, and she began teaching at the University of Chicago the next fall. It was the beginning of a heady time in the drug world. The coming World War II era was to be a period many in pharmacology would consider more important than any other before or since.

It was the start of the pharmaceutical wonder years known as the Age of Antibiotics, when new medicines and vaccines were wiping out major diseases like tuberculosis. The breakthrough drug was penicillin, which had been discovered by Sir Alexander Fleming in 1929 and was known to have strong antibacterial action without being toxic to human cells—a much "cleaner" anti-infective than the available sulfa drugs. But it wasn't until 1939 that a team at Oxford began figuring out how penicillin could be used therapeutically and how it might be manufactured on a large scale. Not long after entering the war in 1941, the United States brought over two of those British researchers to try to speed up the process of mass-producing the drug. Because it was wartime, the government was eventually able to twist the arms of drug manufacturers—who could not patent the naturally occurring penicillin, which derived from a mold, but were busy trying to patent the various processes involved in making it—and force them to collaborate. Eventually the Department of Agriculture patented a process that was made available without charge, and by 1945, when the war ended, the drug became available for civilian use at a low price. It is easy to understand why people in the legal-drug world continue to romanticize penicillin. Not only was it arguably the biggest single leap forward in the modern history of therapeutics, but it was accomplished with minimal markups.

Although Kelsey was not involved with the antibiotic research, she did participate in the other large drug-related effort during the war: the search for new antimalarial medications.

"The United States realized," she explained to me, "that if it entered the war, it would have to improve its way of supplying antimalarial drugs—particularly after the Japanese became involved, which wiped out our quinine supply by putting it in the hands of the enemy. So the government started this big project, directed from Washington, and a number of research centers were involved. They went and *grabbed* chemicals off the shelf, and everyone tossed in many thousands of preparations to see what would work. Our group was largely involved in testing the new compounds in animals. The university also ran a Phase I study facility at the Statesville Prison: it was manned by army doctors, and the promising compounds that made it through our animal trials were tested there on human subjects."

Many pharmaceutical manufacturers and university pharmacology departments were involved in the effort, which Kelsey believes laid the groundwork for modern drug development. Unlike penicillin—which was already known to work and was difficult only to refine and mass-produce—the search for a new antimalarial involved systematic testing of natural compounds and attempts at synthesizing new ones. "The project introduced many people to the orderly development of drugs," she said. "After the war, these people went out to drug firms or universities, they set up testing companies."

In their rush to develop new products, pharmaceutical manufacturers began wide-scale testing of any substance, natural or synthetic, that might have a marketable drug action. In 1950, for example, Eli Lilly sent a directive to all its personnel, worldwide, to collect soil samples wherever they went, to be tested for antibiotic activity. One of these samples, found in a field near the Philippine town of Ilo-Ilo, led to the discovery of erythromycin.

This post–World War II period was also the beginning of wide-scale patenting of individual drugs by large American pharmaceutical companies. Previously, only German firms had patented the chemical entities themselves; part of the way American firms defined themselves as "ethical" was by avoiding patented medicines. But drug patents were becoming more important in the United States because the new "wonder drugs" were a wonder for more than just their effectiveness. The first big, broad-spectrum antibiotics after penicillin and streptomycin were also the first important drugs manufactured and sold *only* by the companies that had patented them. The patents meant that the companies could control the prices of the drugs and keep them high.

In a tradition that still continues today, a new drug would be marketed at a certain price point, and when a competing drug was developed, it would be sold at the identical price or an even higher one than the original. When confronted with the peculiar economic rules of their market, drug companies were fond of saying that medicine was too important to be sold as a price-sensitive commodity: ethical drug houses competed not on price but on "quality."

More and more, the firms also competed on salesmanship. And the postwar era saw an increased reliance on battalions of pharmaceutical sales representatives, the "detail men," who went door-to-door to doctors' offices. It was a very American way of doing business, and it was one of many examples of the Americanization of the world's pharmaceutical industry in the late 1940s and early 1950s. The industry power shift from Germany to the United States was so clear that Schering—the Berlin-based producer of laxatives and hormones, which also had large facilities in New Jersey—decided, after being nationalized by the U.S. government during two world wars, that it might as well stay put. By the time Schering began marketing its phenomenally successful antihistamine Chlor-Trimeton in 1948, it was an American firm (which later merged with the U.S. firms Plough Inc. and White Laboratories).

After the war, Frances Kelsey was forced to make a career change. She had married Ellis Kelsey, a biochemist in the same department at the university, and the antinepotism rule that had been waived during the war came back in effect. They decided that one of them should go to medical school, and she volunteered. During that time, she and her husband, together with Dr. Geiling, wrote a well-received pharmacology textbook.

They also had two daughters, Susan and Christine. I asked Kelsey if she had taken any medicines during her pregnancy. "When I was pregnant? You better *believe* I didn't," she exclaimed. "I wouldn't even take an aspirin. Late in one of the pregnancies, I did get a flu vaccine—which seemed like the lesser of two evils. But I still remember worrying about that. Hey, I even gave up drinking! I *never* believed the myth that the placental barrier protects a developing infant from the indiscretions of the mother."

In 1950 Kelsey received her M.D. and soon after went to work at the American Medical Association as an editor at the *JAMA*. She was there during some of the last days of the "old AMA." At the time, the AMA still maintained its own drug-testing laboratory and issued a seal of approval to worthy medications. The AMA seal was not only respected by doctors but, since the 1920s, it had been required before a company could advertise a drug in *JAMA*.

The relationship between physicians and drug companies had never been more important. Through World War II, the power of the prescription had been ill defined. Only a handful of drugs required a doctor's prescription, and drug regulation was viewed as a means of saving the public from the quackery of patent medicines and the dangers of living in a largely self-medicating society. But in 1951 the prescription-writing power of American doctors was etched in stone by a law cosponsored by Minnesota senator Hubert Humphrey, himself a former pharmacist. The law finally defined which drugs should be available only by prescription—which turned out to be most of them—and prohibited refills without authorization from the prescriber. It made doctor-to-pharmacist-to-patient the path of most major medicines and ushered in the golden age of drug promotion.

In 1953 Frances Kelsey and her husband relocated to Vermillion, South Dakota, where she did her internship, taught and saw private patients while he focused on research. She also did some research on radioisotope drugs for thyroid disorders. "I was the first one in South Dakota with an AEC [Atomic Energy Commission] license," she recalled.

Kelsey couldn't have picked a better time to be a general practitioner. Physicians had always been respected, but now they could be infallible, all-knowing and all-prescribing. The American physician was lavished with the love, respect and docility of patients, and luxurious tokens of gratitude from the drug companies. For decades, newly minted doctors received their first black leather bags as gifts from drug firms, and the complimentary *Merck Manual* was the standard desktop reference of illnesses. No one even thought to question the ethics of this largesse. Nonetheless, now that ethical drugs could actually cure major illnesses, they had become big business—and as in any big business, if sales and marketing practices went unscrutinized, there were likely to be abuses.

While the drug industry had more marketing successes than true therapeutic breakthroughs in the 1950s, some important new products were developed. The anti-inflammatory corticosteroids revolutionized the treatment of arthritis, allergies and many other disorders, and Darvon (propoxyphene) was part of a new generation of painkilling narcotics. Several new mood-altering drugs and tranquilizers—among them Thorazine (chlorpromazine) and Tofranil (imipramine)—brought the first effective treatments for serious mental illnesses. But with each new heavily promoted wonder drug came the possibility of overuse, and

many of the new medicines of the decade would later become synonymous with overmedication and pill-popping.

Only a handful of people were paying attention to the side effects of all
these new drugs. Dr. Leopold Meyler, a fiery, brilliant Dutch pharmacologist, had become interested in the problem of drug reactions the hard
way: at a young age, he had had a severe reaction to a medication called
para-amino-salicylic acid, which he had been given while in a sanitarium
being treated for pulmonary tuberculosis. In 1952 Meyler published a
surprisingly readable 128-page book called *Side Effects of Drugs* to help
doctors learn about the small but growing literature on adverse reactions—information that was not high on the priority lists of drug company detail men. The book would grow into a quirky annual review of
the less-than-wonderful news about the new wonder drugs. And Meyler,
who also produced a series of books on drug-induced diseases, developed an undeserved yet unshakable reputation in the industry as an
"antidrug man."

The same year that *Side Effects of Drugs* was first published, Albe
Watkins, a country doctor in a small town near Pasadena, California,
watched his ten-year-old son James die slowly and painfully from the
blood disorder aplastic anemia. The death was all the more horrifying
because Watkins believed he had inadvertently caused it by treating his
son repeatedly with a new, popular, therapeutically important antibiotic
being marketed exclusively by one of the world's largest and most repu-
table drug houses, Michigan-based Parke-Davis. The drug was Chloromycetin (chloramphenicol). Watkins's regular Parke-Davis detail man
told him that the drug had been used safely by millions of people during
its two years on the market, and that it had clear advantages over the
sulfa drugs, penicillin and even the new tetracyclines. It didn't have any
of the side effects those drugs had, the detail man said, and infectious
organisms didn't seem to have developed any "resistance" to it. So Watkins hadn't worried about using it on his son three times in two years to
treat a recurring postoperative infection.

It was only when his son was nearing death that Watkins began to
hear about other cases of aplastic anemia associated with Chloromycetin.
He convinced one of his patients, an aviation writer for the *Los Angeles
Times,* to do a story about this. Watkins and two other bereaved families
he met through the article sued the drug company, which quickly settled.
The Watkins family got $15,000, an enormous amount of money for a
settlement at that time; they gave the money to their church. But the

settlement did not quiet Watkins. In the summer of 1952 he closed his medical practice, packed his family into the car and drove cross-country to hook up with other afflicted families and present his findings to the AMA in Chicago, then to the FDA in Washington.

Albe Watkins's efforts set off an investigation by the FDA that in some ways has never really ended. Yes, the label was changed, and yes, Parke-Davis was unable to really overcome the negative publicity caused by its unflinching support of a drug that still causes many doctors to flinch. But Chloromycetin remains available for sale today. Although it has been eclipsed by other antibiotics in industrialized nations, it is still widely used in less-developed countries and remains one of the most effective treatments for typhus.

Its powerful legacy, however, makes it a poster pill for the consequences of promiscuous overpromotion and overprescription. Chloromycetin was the first, and may still be the best, example of a drug with unique therapeutic qualities and unique toxicities that was done in by its wonder drug status—and by the arrogance of drug company executives and prescribing doctors who didn't want to be told what to do. It was destroyed by its risk/benefit ratio.

Experts would later estimate that, in the United States, Chloromycetin would have been appropriately prescribed for about 200,000 patients a year, whose serious infections would warrant its increased risk of serious adverse reactions. But Parke-Davis continued to push its use for even the mildest of infections, and prescribing physicians followed the company's advice. So, during its peak of popularity in the 1950s and early 1960s, it was actually taken by closer to 3.5 million American patients a year, many of whom were put at risk for its deadly side effects for no compelling medical reason.

A truly important drug with a truly scary side-effect profile, Chloromycetin might have taught the legal-drug world much about how to intelligently approach adverse reactions like the one my wife had to Floxin. The drug did, in fact, inspire the world's first formal postmarketing surveillance system, set up in 1954 by the American Medical Association and later subsumed into the FDA. But instead of helping solve the adverse reaction dilemma, the Chloromycetin experience became a cautionary tale about its unsolvability, and about the international battle between drug companies, government regulators, physicians, politicians and consumer advocates that breaks out whenever a popular medication develops a drug problem. The company continued all-or-nothing marketing with full deniability, physicians refused to be more selective about their prescribing, patients didn't know any better and the political fallout created an atmosphere of mutual distrust that continues to this day. Chloromycetin was the first time the international pharmaceutical community saw the modern version of what I have heard pharmacologists call "The Cycle."

"All drugs go through The Cycle," one noted drug researcher told me. "First they're the silver bullet. Then they go into the trash. And then we come up with some mature reading of the thing. There's usually a category of patients for whom they are valuable. Unfortunately, we are very bad at deciding who is in that category."

CHAPTER 8

The Summer

of Drugs

Frances Kelsey came to Washington in the summer of 1960 to work for the federal government. She was hired as one of only seven full-time FDA medical officers who screened all of the nation's human drug applications, about three hundred a year. Her husband took a job as a biochemist at the National Institutes of Health.

When they arrived, the pharmaceutical industry was in the hot seat. Tennessee senator Estes Kefauver, who had been making life miserable for a series of industries by grilling top brass at public hearings of his Antitrust and Monopoly Subcommittee, had recently focused his attention on medicines. The dramatic hearings were a source of constant entertainment and revelation. When the Kelseys were on their lunch hour, they often would go with their new colleagues to watch the Kefauver hearings.

"It was such a hornet's nest," she told me. "Oh, my God, the fighting back and forth."

Kefauver was mostly interested in drug prices and drug company marketing practices. The economics of the antibiotics market was of particular interest—especially the chloramphenicol situation—and the hearings became the American public's first opportunity to understand the ethics of the "ethical" drug business. It wasn't just the drug companies themselves that were being implicated, but the whole system, including private physicians and the FDA itself. Dr. Henry Welch, the director of the agency's Division of Antibiotics, resigned after being accused of improperly accepting $287,142 in honoraria from two medical journals supported primarily by antibiotics manufacturers and, in at least one case, letting a drug company rewrite part of a speech so it better jibed with the language of its current advertising campaign.

The U.S. government wasn't the first to wrestle with high drug prices—politicians in Canada and Great Britain were also called to action. But the Kefauver hearings had the loudest international reverberations, and they created a virtual encyclopedia of ways to criticize the drug world. Look up "pharmaceutical research" in any of the library of provocative books the hearings spawned, and you'll come to the still-resonant comment of former Squibb medical director Dr. Dale Console, who agreed that drug research was expensive and that there were many failures for every success.

"The problem," he said, "arises out of the fact that they market so many of their failures."

Look up the troubling issue of "creating need" for drugs by promoting them directly to potential patients, and you'll come to the timeless comments of former Pfizer clinical researcher Dr. Haskell Weinstein. He warned the Kefauver committee of "a rather intense effort to reach [doctors] through the patient. . . . It is an unfunny joke in the medical profession that the very latest information on new advances in medicine most often appears in the eminent medical journals such as *Reader's Digest, Time* and *The Wall Street Journal* . . . [often] placed by the public-relations staff of the pharmaceutical firms."

And look up how patients and physicians cause their own drug problems, and you'll find the chilling story about the misuse of antibiotics that one prominent physician related to the committee. He told of a woman with asthma who came to the doctor with a common cold and demanded penicillin. The doctor refused because "it is not a good idea to give asthmatics penicillin." She stormed out of the office, saying she would find a doctor who would give her what she wanted. She did, and five minutes after the new doctor had given her the injection, she was dead from an anaphylactic reaction to the medicine.

Before coming to Washington, Frances Kelsey had wondered if she really wanted to be in the middle of this kind of political crossfire. When she arrived, she was relieved to spend her first month in orientation. Then, for her first drug application, she was handed something "simple and straightforward," she recalled, a sedative and sleeping pill that its German manufacturer, Chemie-Grunenthal, had already gotten approved in several European countries. It was being marketed under the brand name Kevadon, but as is true of all preapproval compounds, at the FDA, the drug was known by its generic name: thalidomide.

The sponsoring firm was the William S. Merrell Company of Cincinnati, which had licensed the drug for sale in the United States (and would later become part of Marion Merrell Dow). Merrell's new drug application arrived on September 12, 1960, in four bound volumes, each the size of a metropolitan telephone book. Despite the huge submission, Kelsey was taken aback by the shoddiness of the work, although, looking back years later, she agreed that she might have been shocked by the quality of whichever application she saw first and conceded that it wasn't "uniquely bad . . . particularly for a drug that wasn't exactly pushing any frontiers of science." (Her husband, who did the chemistry analysis of the thalidomide application for the FDA, was more critical, declaring that the company's absorption studies were "completely meaningless.")

Under FDA regulations, Kelsey had sixty days to notify the company of any deficiencies in its application. If she didn't, the law said the drug was automatically approved. She quickly let the company know there were paperwork problems and missing studies, but it wasn't until two sixty-day periods had already elapsed, with procedural problems still unsolved, that she found out about any real medical concerns. In February 1961 she discovered a letter about cases of thalidomide-induced peripheral neuritis—"tingling of the nerves"—in a December issue of a British medical journal that had just made it stateside after a shipping strike. When she inquired further about the cases, she found out that the British and German drug labels had been carrying a warning about this side effect for several months—which meant the company had known about it even before then. Yet the Merrell company had neglected to mention this side effect to the FDA.

Kelsey thought the delinquency in safety reporting was probably an oversight. "I couldn't believe that anyone would purposely hide it, I must confess," she said. "Perhaps if I had been at the FDA for a few years, I might have been less trusting. But at that point, it was just interesting." When inquiring about it, she also asked for additional information about using the drug during pregnancy—not because she suspected anything but because the company had provided so little information. The application had reported only on its use for insomnia, and the data was only from the third trimester. Kelsey wanted to pay careful attention to the drug's pregnancy warning. During the antimalarial project, she and her husband had studied how quinine could affect enzymes in the liver differently in the mother and the fetus. She wanted to make sure Merrell looked into the possibility of fetal abnormalities.

·   ·   ·

While she waited for more thalidomide data, the drug industry was on the defensive in Washington. In April 1961 Kefauver proposed a bill that would overhaul the 1938 Food, Drug and Cosmetics Act. Among its more revolutionary proposals, the new bill would have cut exclusive patent protection down from seventeen years to only three years—after which the patent-holder would be forced to license the drug to any qualified *competing* manufacturer at a royalty that could not exceed 8 percent. Kefauver was going after the pharmaceutical manufacturers' profit margins, the enormity of which had been one of the key factors in convincing him to investigate drugs in the first place. Two of his key staffers had come from the Federal Trade Commission, which in 1958 had decided to stop including drug companies in the chemical manufacturing sector and gave pharmaceuticals their own listing in the FTC annual estimate of corporate profits. The staffers had been stunned by how much more profitable drug companies were than any other American manufacturing business, and they shared their astonishment with their new boss. (One of the staffers also knew something about adverse drug reactions: his wife and brother-in-law had taken cortisone shots for their rheumatoid arthritis, and both got, as he recalled to *New Yorker* writer Richard Harris, "peptic ulcers and moonface, where your head swells up like a basketball.")

To battle the me-too drug problem, Kefauver wanted to deny patent protection for slight variations on existing drugs unless the new compounds proved therapeutically *better*—not just more of the same. The me-too problem was even more complex then than it is today because of the plethora of what were called "combination drugs." Most popular prescription drugs were marketed not only as single entities but in several different combination preparations, many of dubious value and questionable safety, regardless of the efficacy of the core medicine or medicines. (Today's multisymptom, multi-ingredient, nonprescription cold remedies are among the last vestiges of the kind of broad combination-drug marketing that then dominated the entire prescription drug business. Although the practice is still common in less-developed countries and remains especially popular in Germany, most remaining prescription combination drugs in the United States are older painkillers mixed with aspirin or codeine.)

Kefauver also held another revolutionary belief: that drug manufacturers should have to prove that their products actually *worked* before they could be approved by the FDA. This idea of requiring proof of efficacy was opposed by the powerful Pharmaceutical Manufacturers Association, which generally believed (and still seems to believe) that the drug industry is entirely capable of regulating itself. At the time, the efficacy legislation was also opposed by the American Medical Association, which had jettisoned its drug seal of approval and other oversight activities; Kefauver accused the AMA of getting out of drug analysis because *JAMA* had grown reliant on drug company advertising. (Political concerns also played a part in the AMA's stance. At that time, Congress had the new Medicare bill on its agenda, and the AMA, which strongly opposed it as "socialized medicine," needed the pharmaceutical manufacturers' support to defeat the bill.)

In fact, everything about the Kefauver bill was being lobbied against heavily. It was not considered very likely ever to become a law.

While Kefauver was pressing on, the Merrell company had been hounding Frances Kelsey about approving thalidomide. "We had been dickering away with it," she recalled, "and we were sort of chicken. They said, 'We must have it released before flu season.'"

Then, in mid-November, a German pediatrician named Widikund Lenz told a group of doctors meeting in Düsseldorf that he believed he could explain the epidemic of hundreds of gross birth deformities, including seal-like flippers instead of arms and legs, that his country was experiencing. He said at least 50 percent of the mothers had taken a certain medicine, later revealed to be thalidomide, during pregnancy. (The percentage was probably higher, but since thalidomide was also commonly sold as a combination drug with, among other things, cough syrup and aspirin, it was nearly impossible to know this with certainty.) Several weeks after Lenz's presentation, Merrell informed Kelsey that the German manufacturer was removing the drug from the market in Germany and notifying its licensees in twenty other countries, including England, Japan and Australia. Merrell said it was stopping all its U.S. studies of the drug. The company didn't immediately withdraw its application, however, because it felt there might still be a place for the drug in cancer treatment, provided it wasn't used by pregnant mothers.

None of these actions precipitated anything resembling the international scandal they would cause today. In fact, at the time, the Merrell company was taking far more heat at the FDA for its recently approved cholesterol-lowering drug MER/29—the company's best-selling prescription product. Doctors had been alerted to reports that MER/29 caused baldness, skin damage and serious eye problems, including cataracts, although the drug was still being marketed as safe. Then in February 1962 an FDA supervisor in Cincinnati was told by a carpool-mate about the reason his wife had quit her job as a Merrell lab technician: she had observed company doctors falsifying animal trial results on MER/29, specifically covering up serious changes in the vision of test monkeys.

It wasn't until early April 1962, several months after thalidomide had been taken off the market worldwide, that Dr. Helen Taussig—a renowned Johns Hopkins pediatric cardiologist who had codeveloped the heart surgery technique used to save "blue babies"—returned from a trip to West Germany and briefed Kelsey about the appalling birth defects, which she had finally seen with her own eyes. Also at the briefing was Dr. John Nestor, a former medical resident of Taussig's who had also just become a medical officer at the FDA. From then on the thalidomide situation began to cause reverberations at the highest levels of policy-making. In the weeks to come, Taussig addressed the annual meeting of the American College of Physicians in Philadelphia, and then a House committee, successfully linking the thalidomide disaster in Europe with the need for stricter regulations on new drugs in the United States. It was perfect timing, because Kefauver had just submitted a new version of his drug bill.

In another piece of perfect timing, several days after meeting with Taussig, Nestor flew to Cincinnati and was able to prove that Merrell had indeed falsified some of the monkey data on MER/29. The drug was withdrawn from the market two days after his visit. (The company and several of its scientists were later indicted by a federal grand jury, pleading no contest to most of the charges and paying large fines. MER/29 also attracted what became the first of the modern class action lawsuits against an American drug manufacturer, coordinated by Ralph Nader's law school classmate Paul Rheingold. It has been estimated that Merrell paid out over $45 million in judgments and out-of-court settlements of some fifteen hundred suits on MER/29.)

Then the agency got into a fight with Congress over releasing confidential FDA files on MER/29 to an oversight committee. The committee also wanted files on another drug that had also recently been withdrawn after scandalous accusations that a manufacturer had withheld dozens of reports of liver damage from the FDA. The company was Johnson & Johnson's newly acquired McNeil Laboratories subsidiary. The drug was a popular muscle-spasm reliever called Flexin.

With all these new controversies, Kelsey was no longer thinking much about thalidomide. Merrell had ultimately withdrawn its application on March 8, "and life," she recalled, "went on."

The thalidomide situation didn't explode into the American public consciousness until Sunday, July 15, 1962, when *The Washington Post*

ran a front-page story with the headline " 'Heroine' of FDA Keeps Bad
Drug off Market." The article finally brought appropriately high drama
to the ongoing birth defect problem and linked it inextricably to the
waning drug bill—which was exactly what Kefauver staffers had hoped
would happen when they urged the *Post* to do a story. In fact, it is
believed they pushed the story when the *Post*'s regular medical writer,
who had already overlooked it, was on vacation. The assignment went
instead to a *Post* city desk reporter named Morton Mintz, who had been
busy covering a savings and loan scandal. Mintz filed the one-shot article, went on vacation and returned to find himself lead reporter on the
country's biggest story and his life forever changed. (He went on to write
several groundbreaking books, becoming a Jessica Mitford of drug
safety.)

Three days after Mintz's story, Kefauver proclaimed from the Senate
floor that President Kennedy should give the heroic FDA medical officer
a gold medal for Distinguished Federal Civilian Service. He followed up
with a publicly released letter to the White House. By the end of the
week, Frances Kelsey had become an international icon.

Morton Mintz's story, quickly embraced by the entire Washington
press corps, became even more interesting when it was discovered that
the United States hadn't dodged the thalidomide bullet after all. When it
stopped all its thalidomide studies, Merrell had told the FDA that approximately sixty American doctors had used the drug experimentally—
and it assured the agency that they had all been warned promptly about
the birth defects. In late July it became clear that more than twelve
hundred physicians had been rather indiscriminately handing out the
drug Merrell had provided to them for what are called seeding studies.
These are "studies" in which physicians are recruited by company sales
reps and paid for each patient they can "enroll" in a broadly vague
"survey" of users. (Seeding studies are still done today and often get
funded instead of truly rigorous postmarketing research projects, because they deliver mostly good news.) A Merrell internal memo conceded that thalidomide was not being given out for true clinical research
but "to gain widespread confirmation of its usefulness." The memo went
on to suggest that sales reps "appeal to the doctor's ego—we think he is
important enough to be selected as one of the first to use [thalidomide]
in that section of the country."

Some of the doctors who had given out thalidomide weren't even
aware that the drug was experimental—no law specifically said they had
to be informed of this—so they had neither mentioned that fact to their
patients nor kept any records about the drug's effects. Also, it turned out

that some of the physicians had not been told about the birth defect risks until five months after the drug had been recalled in Germany at the end of 1961. On July 25 the problem acquired a human face. A Phoenix television personality, who had taken thalidomide brought from England by her husband, announced she would seek a legal abortion of the fetus she assumed (correctly, as it turned out) had been deformed by the drug.

The inability to quickly round up all the thalidomide that had been dispersed around the country and dispose of it became a cause célèbre. In fact, because the drug had been sold internationally under so many different names in so many different places, it would be years before all thalidomide use could be halted worldwide. Eventually, seventeen cases of U.S. birth defects were identified: ten from American seeding studies, and seven others in which the drug had been obtained abroad. But those numbers would pale in comparison to the final tally of nearly 10,000 babies affected in twenty different countries.

On August 1 Frances Kelsey made her first public appearance since the *Post* story, as a witness at a Senate hearing that wasn't supposed to be about thalidomide but quickly shifted to it. That afternoon, President Kennedy announced that the Senate drug bill—which his staff had quietly helped undermine only weeks before the headlines—was now too weak. Two days later, Kennedy approved a last-minute President's Award for Frances Kelsey, to be given at the ceremony that had long ago been scheduled for August 7. On August 10 the FDA published new guidelines that placed clinical trials under stricter supervision by the agency. Two weeks after that, the Kefauver bill was amended to include new protections for human drug test subjects (including, for example, *consent*) and a requirement that drugs be tested first on animals.

The bill came to a vote in the Senate on August 23. At the last minute Kefauver tried to rekindle interest in lowering "immoral" drug prices—his original obsession, long since swept aside by thalidomide safety issues—by an amendment limiting patent protections on drugs sold with a markup of over 500 percent. His amendment was tabled, and the bill was passed 78–0. It was headed for approval by the House—where a second sponsor's name would be attached for political posterity, making these officially the Kefauver-Harris amendments—and certain signature by the president.

And as the summer ended, word was slowly beginning to spread about reports of a new drug safety problem with the first generation of birth control pills. Each era has its emblematic drugs and drug problems. A sedative for ladies that causes birth defects was an ironic commentary on the late 1950s and early 1960s. Dangerous blood clots from the Pill would be medicine's cruel joke on the sexual revolution to come.

By the end of that Summer of Drugs, the world of medicines had been changed forever. A new design for the entire structure of the legal-drug world had been sketched out, and most major nations would eventually use this design concept in drawing up blueprints for their own modernized drug regulatory systems. But it would take years—or in some cases, even *decades*—to do what many people agreed in the summer of 1962 needed to be done. In many ways, we are still trying to figure out how to implement some of these changes today.

The Kefauver-Harris amendments had some built-in problems. Like so many laws, they were too focused on preventing the identical disaster from happening again. They failed to systematically address some of the larger problems that had *caused* the disaster. If thalidomide had actually been approved in the United States before the epidemic of birth defects was discovered, it might have been seen as an indictment of both premarketing and postmarketing regulation, and the new law might have placed greater emphasis on maximizing drug safety for the entire length of what European regulators refer to as a drug's "career." Instead, the major thrust of the new drug laws was to stop drugs with dangerous side effects from ever being approved in the first place. The thinking was that if drug approval was turned into the most rigorous obstacle course possible, everything else would take care of itself. After thalidomide, the FDA did take over responsibility for postmarketing surveillance from the AMA. But it did not make it a priority. Its real efforts were focused on creating a monumental barrier to approval. Scaling that wall was costly and time-consuming, and since that time was subtracted from the life of a drug's patent, companies were understandably eager to market their drugs quickly and aggressively the moment they were approved. Companies quickly realized that the FDA had been given far less statutory muscle to flex in the postmarketing period. After approval, it was an unimpeded sprint.

In retrospect, the U.S. regulatory process probably should have been reinvented as a long flat course with periodic hurdles to leap—before and after approval—to encourage a slow roll-out of new drugs and regular reassessment of their safety profiles. Other countries set up systems somewhat more attuned to postmarketing concerns, but America was the biggest drug market and the FDA was the dominant regulatory proving ground. The United States threw the most time and money at solving the problems of drug regulation. The deficiencies of its solutions became the world's.

Frances Kelsey took one of the most impressive victory laps in federal bureaucratic history. After the medal ceremony—which she recalled mostly because "some of the astronauts were there, they got an award, too, and I can still see them *bounding* across the grass"—she spent "about six months pretty busy with answering letters and writing." She had originally expected to spend about three years with the FDA and perhaps return to journal editing. But the next summer, on her third anniversary, she was named chief of the new Investigational Drug Branch of the FDA and set about revolutionizing the way new drugs were tested.

"When I joined the agency," she recalled, "a number of us were getting intrigued by these clinical investigators who would investigate *any* drug. No matter what it was, they'd do some studies on it. You've got to wonder how they could handle all that. We found some real problems there. And that's when people started talking about 'Kelsey's Cops.' At first, we'd just concentrate on individual 'bad actors' and later on vulnerable situations like prisons or mental hospitals—where there would be abuse of test subjects."

Kelsey's husband, Ellis, had taken a job as a special assistant to the surgeon general. He had grown interested in the flow of medical information, especially about drugs, between doctors as well as between the medical communities of different nations. Thalidomide had demonstrated just how bad communications were, and the U.S. surgeon general, along with officials in many other countries and the World Health Organization, became heavily involved in creating better lines of medical communication. Ellis Kelsey was also interested in computers and how they could speed up the practice of pharmacology. But he was not to see the future of the CANDA—the computer-assisted New Drug Application—or many of the other innovations that grew out of that pharmacologically fertile period in the early 1960s. He died of a heart attack in 1966.

Widowed at fifty-two, with her two daughters already in college, Frances Kelsey made the FDA her life. She never again did anything that drew as much media attention as thalidomide. To this day, she has many detractors in the drug industry who recall her role as nothing but a lucky hit after eight and two-thirds innings of typical bureaucratic sloth—the right result for all the wrong reasons.

But within the agency, she is revered not only for picking the nit heard 'round the world, but for her far less glamorous efforts to, for example, help create local institutional review boards (IRBs) to approve and administer protocols of clinical drug trials, and build a division of "compliance" to make sure companies keep to the protocols. The idea of forcing the creation of a local IRB anywhere a study was being conducted—a system already in use at the NIH—grew out of a series of high-profile cases in which Kelsey's Cops found widespread abuses in studies conducted at prisons, hospitals and nursing homes. But like many aspects of drug regulation, the problems are fascinating, the solutions dull. Setting up a system for inspecting foreign labs, as Kelsey did after the FDA decided in 1985 to accept studies done outside the United States, is grueling, tedious work. It only gets interesting if a field inspector picks some really amazing nit.

Kelsey took her lunch out of the desk drawer and carefully spread out two paper towels on her desk to avoid making a mess. I had brought mine, and as we ate, she seemed especially interested in making sure I understood how much progress had been made since the early 1960s. So much of the rhetoric is still the same, and so many of the problems seem encoded into the DNA of the agency and the drug companies, that it is easy to forget how much has changed.

"We've certainly gotten rid of some of the horrors of the old days," she said. "But things change and new problems pop up. There is a desire, obviously, to get new products on the market and a *pressure* to get them out there. And you still have to make that same judgment: How safe does something have to be? When can you afford to release it? And no matter what, you can't know everything about a compound. There is no absolutely fail-safe method to know. . . . And you can err on the other side of condemning a drug for something that turns out later not to be so.

"Look, there's a natural feeling on the part of the drug company that 'We have a good drug here, we'll help people, save some lives, make some money.' And it's natural that we would have a different feeling in a regulatory agency that says, 'Look, we have to see that the public is protected.' "

Kelsey paused and took a bite of her lunch.

"But ultimately more people can be educated about the good sides and the bad sides of drugs," she said. "And maybe they can learn not to press so hard for miracles."

CHAPTER 9

Psychopharm

Diane had been wise to insist that my work and her life should part ways. It was all getting a little too close for comfort, but more important, it diverted attention from the problems at hand. The drug reaction had taken place over eighteen months before. Grappling with manic-depressive illness was Diane's current reality. The way the symptoms may or may not have been triggered were simply part of her clinical history. How she felt today, and what she was supposed to do about it, were her issues of the moment.

But, of course, whenever you have an illness that's treated with medications, the medications themselves invariably become the issue, too. That is especially true for people with manic-depressive illness who also happen to be artists, because the drugs they are given to rein in their moods have a tendency to dampen their creative impulses as well. There are hundreds of examples of drugs that exact high prices for their curative powers. But the dilemma of the artist who needs mood stabilizers is one of the more dramatic. If you don't take your drugs, there's a good chance you'll kill yourself; the suicide rate for people with untreated manic depression is believed to be around 20 percent, and two-thirds of all suicides can be linked to mood disorders. But if you do take your drugs, there's a chance you'll kill, or at least wound, what often feels like the most vital part of yourself. It is a bitterly perplexing decision.

Diane had made the medically correct decision: she was aggressively treating her symptoms with medications and supportive psychotherapy. But this didn't keep her from sometimes having what are called "breakthrough symptoms," when the depression or mania breaks through the medicinal barrier and leaves you swamped in minutes, or even hours, of unprompted, uncontrollable sobbing.

Some days, when I called home just to say hello, I could tell that Diane had been crying. I was never sure how to react. Ignore it, I thought, and she might feel I was ignoring her pain. Acknowledge it, and she might feel embarrassed or even more depressed. Because I have no talent for keeping a safe distance, I always asked. For the most part, it turned out to be the right thing to do.

To treat the depression, Diane's doctor had recently added the antidepressant Wellbutrin (bupropion) to her mood stabilizer Tegretol. Wellbutrin is less well known than the selective serotonin reuptake inhibitors (SSRIs) such as Prozac, Paxil (paroxetine) and Zoloft (sertraline) and was slow to catch on because of some early concern about its causing seizures. But this side effect is rare, and psychiatrists were starting to pay more attention to this unique antidepressant.

This drug combination worked better for her than anything else she had taken so far. And only as the blue fog of depression lifted somewhat could we see how seriously it had been affecting her. You really don't know how bad you were until you're better.

Although Diane was making progress, we were constantly amazed at how much harder psychopharmacology is than it is sometimes advertised to be. Increasing numbers of print ads and public service announcements were trying to convince people to get medicinal help for mental health problems. The message they delivered was that once you agreed you needed, say, antidepressants, your problems were basically solved.

It goes without saying that the ads didn't prominently mention side effects. But what they also didn't convey was the frustration of waiting for a medication to work—for weeks, sometimes months. Nor did they point out the very real possibility that the first drug you took wouldn't be the right one for you, and you'd have to start all over again with a second, or a third. While everyone talked about the agony of untreated illness, hardly anyone mentioned the agonies of treated illness.

That's probably why one of Diane's greatest sources of solace and information about her illness was the work of Dr. Kay Redfield Jamison, a psychologist at Johns Hopkins who had cowritten the thick standard text on manic-depressive illness (with Dr. Fredrick Goodwin, the former director of the National Institute of Mental Health). Diane referred to the book as "the Bible," and when her symptoms were particularly bad, she read passages in it over and over to remind herself that what she felt was at least normally abnormal. She focused particularly on the sections Jamison had written, which did a remarkable job of capturing the patient experience, especially the difficulty of staying on psychiatric drugs once you've started them.

Jamison had also written a provocative book about mood disorders and the artistic temperament that discussed some of the issues Diane faced—like the possible trade-offs between creativity and mood stability. Jamison believed, ultimately, that it is always better for people with mood disorders to treat them with medications and psychotherapy. She felt this was especially true for creative people. Her studies of the great writers, musicians and visual artists she had posthumously diagnosed with mood disorders showed that most of them lost so much working time to depression—and then, in many cases, committed suicide—that the risks of nontreatment simply could not justify any possible rewards. Still, she knew her position had not prevented some of her patients, among whom were well-known writers and artists, from occasionally going off their medications in order to work at a manic pace.

After watching Diane pore over Jamison's work, I got interested in it myself. I convinced *The Washington Post Magazine* to let me do a profile of Jamison. We met at the Four Seasons Hotel in Philadelphia—she was in town to give a talk at a professional seminar on manic-depression treatment that Diane and I were attending as "press"—and I arrived with the breaking news of Kurt Cobain's death. Jamison didn't know much about Cobain; she's not really the Nirvana type. But she said she wouldn't be surprised if he had manic-depressive illness. (It later turned out he *had* been diagnosed with manic depression but couldn't stay on his medication—lithium, about which he had once written a song.) We spoke for about an hour, and while the conversation was intriguing, it was a little more uncomfortable than most first interviews. That's probably because we were both hiding something. Jamison hadn't asked, but I was deliberately withholding the real reason I had become interested in her work. I *did* ask, and I wondered if she was deliberately withholding the real reason she had become interested in doing that work.

Days later, she called to say she wanted to have an off-the-record conversation about something she might eventually share on the record. She thought I should know that she suffered from manic-depressive illness herself. She had been working on a memoir of her illness, but she decided she would first "come out" in my article. I then admitted to her why I knew so much about the illness. She asked a lot of questions about Diane's situation, and suddenly we were speaking on a much more comfortable, personal level that continued throughout our many interviews.

She sent me a copy of a partial draft of her book, and when it arrived, Diane snatched it up and read it in one sitting. It inspired her to be more open about her own illness.

Much of my time interviewing Jamison was spent talking about medications. One of the subjects she had written about quite extensively was why people stop taking their medicine, especially lithium. Jamison had a fascinating love-hate relationship with lithium, going back over twenty years. Given her literary tastes, I could picture her considering a Lithotab like Hamlet contemplating Yorick's skull. While studying the drug, she had even become friendly with Dr. Mogens Schou, the Danish researcher whose work had established lithium as a treatment for manic-depressive illness. She believed Schou, among others, had saved her life. But she had also once tried to *take* her life with lithium, by swallowing an overdose and chasing it with a medication to keep her from throwing it up. Fortunately, she survived, but only because her brother called when she was semicomatose, and she forgot that she wasn't going to answer the phone. In the years after the attempt, Jamison struggled to stay on the medication she sometimes hated for making her well, because she missed the hypomania that lithium dampened, and like everyone else, she hated the routine of taking pills. On several occasions she stopped taking her lithium altogether, always with disastrous consequences.

When she finally surrendered to her need for the drug, life wasn't that much easier. She was a "good lithium responder," and back then, there were few options if you didn't respond to the drug. But her prescribed dose, the standard at the time, was too high, so she suffered through years of unpleasant side effects, including a period of many years when she was essentially unable to read. "It's a rare side effect," she explained, "a form of neurotoxicity that causes blurred vision mixed with some inability to concentrate. I had to work very slowly, rereading over and over again. It was a period of enormous frustration and throwing books against the wall."

For years, Jamison hid her personal feelings about medication issues in her professional work; some of the "patient quotations" she used in her textbook and lectures were really excerpts from her own journals. Now that she felt freer to be more open about her own experiences, it was interesting to see her insights recombine. When you got her going, she dropped her academic formality and became like a stand-up comic with a very obscure brand of observational humor about taking meds. She could be the Jerry Seinfeld of compliance. And compliance certainly needed a Jerry Seinfeld.

.   .   .

The word *compliance* may be the single most telling term in the legal-drug world. Taken in all its various meanings, compliance describes, in one word, the tense relationship between every constituency in the pharmaceutical food chain.

In regulatory and industry circles, compliance generally refers to a manufacturer complying with a nation's laws governing the testing and sale of medications. To physicians (and savvy patients who like to use the jargon), compliance refers to whether you're actually *taking* the medicine you've been prescribed, and whether you're taking it correctly. In either case, it's a loaded word that can hold up to Talmudic-style interpretation and commentary. It begs a never-ending analysis of whether the rules to be complied with are proper, rational and scientifically defensible. It also speaks volumes about who is to wield power over whom.

The power issue inherent in compliance has become so troubling to some that I have heard people call for the word to be banned as politically incorrect. "We're trying to use the word *adherence* instead," one prominent clinical researcher told me. "Adherence is less of a loaded term. It sounds more like *doctor-recommended.*"

Patient compliance is an area with little hard data but lots of room for psychological interpretation. Kay Jamison is fond of noting that the classic literature on compliance includes studies of how well physicians themselves complied when prescribed antibiotics for respiratory tract infections. Even though the doctors knew better than anyone that if they didn't finish the full course, the pills wouldn't work, about 50 percent of them were still noncompliant.

"You hear doctors complain, 'I just don't understand why this guy stopped taking his medications,'" Jamison griped, "yet the same doctor can't stay on antibiotics for ten days when his infection will come back. And this is a medication that has nothing to do with the mind or free will. There's no stigma attached, no side effects. Unlike lithium, you don't have to take the antibiotic until you die. And this doctor can't understand why psychiatric patients who suddenly feel normal stop taking their medications?"

Another person with interesting ideas about compliance is Dr. John Urquhart, a Hemingway-esque clinical pharmacologist who has become a growly voiced guru of the human aspects of taking medication. Shuttling between his home in California and the Netherlands, where he helped found the crusading pharmaco-epi program at Maastricht University, Urquhart is an expert on many drug issues, but he is especially thoughtful on the subject of why people don't take their pills. He's good at coining terms like *white-coat compliance,* which means taking your pills only when you know you're about to go see the doctor who prescribed them. He is interested in the phenomenon of "drug holidays," which is when you give yourself a little "vacation" from your pills, regardless of how dangerous this medicinal siesta might be. While physicians will occasionally put patients on such a holiday, with careful monitoring, Urquhart is talking about patients who take it upon themselves to stop their medication for more than three consecutive days. In one study he analyzed, of ninety-one patients who were monitored for four weeks, fourteen of them gave themselves at least one "holiday" and several took two or more.

"These are all well-educated, mostly university-educated patients who were being treated for partial vision loss," he said incredulously. "And even *that* didn't concentrate their minds on taking medicine."

He refers to the money spent treating the medical problems caused by these drug holidays as "the noncompliance tax . . . like the $9,800 Medicare bill for the little old lady in San Diego who skipped her heart drug regimen for three days." He also talks about how the holidays contribute to the underappreciated "toxicity from underdosing. We all know about the toxicity of *overdosing,* but this is different. And with certain diseases, we are creating a Darwinian incubator for drug-resistant organisms." To Urquhart, the luckiest thing for patients is that many drugs are, in his words, "forgiving" of our mistakes. "Sixty percent of patients make errors too small to catch the attention of more forgiving drugs," he said. "A third make errors large enough to matter, with fifteen to twenty percent having recurrent relapses because of dosing."

Urquhart believes there has been "a systematic ignorance of drug misuse. The industry has turned its back on patient compliance," he told me. "Periodic lip service is given to it, but until somebody figures out how to make money on compliance, it won't be a big thing." He even feels that some steps taken to increase compliance have backfired. "The industry has gone to great lengths to make dosing convenient," he said. "In making it convenient, they've *trivialized* it. Suddenly it's 'Hey, just pop this pill.' We're moving toward daily [once-a-day] medicines, which is an absolute technological marvel. But it also makes it easy to brush it off.

"And if you have a chronic-use medicine, well, take Zocor [simvastatin, a cholesterol-lowering drug]. If you look at the curves of 'survivorship of use,' you see a huge drop-off. They're not dropping off because of side effects. They just figure nobody really cares. Or they hear something on television about how there's too many chemicals in our lives."

Patients can play strange psychological games with their physicians when it comes to medicines. Anything the doctor doesn't refer to specifically during an office appointment can be considered open for patient interpretation. "It may take a doctor a *year* before he figures out that they quit taking their medicine," Urquhart said. "In an eight-minute visit, it may not come back up on the radar screen."

I was becoming immersed in both psychopharmacology and the psychology of drugs. Besides my need to get whatever information I could for Diane and the research I was doing on the Kay Jamison profile, I had begun work on a massive project to capture in words the life of one of America's oldest, grandest and most endangered psychiatric facilities, the Institute of Pennsylvania Hospital in West Philadelphia. Diane's psychiatrist had his office there, as did 120 others—more psychiatrists under one roof than anywhere else in the country. But it also had a large inpatient facility with a heritage dating back to the first progressive psychiatric care done in America, by Dr. Benjamin Rush in the 1750s. The Institute's long corridors of closed white doors—many of the old patient rooms had been converted into doctors' offices—had borne witness to the entire history of mental health care, from bloodletting and leg irons to Prozac and interpersonal therapy.

Many of the interviews I did there were about how drugs are changing psychiatry—for better or worse. The Institute had been a mecca for psychoanalytic training, and its heyday had been in the 1940s and 1950s, when psychoanalysis was the predominant method of treatment for all mental illness. When psychiatric medications became available, many psychiatrists at the Institute, like their classically trained colleagues around the world, resisted using them; drugs were believed to "cover up" or "mask" symptoms, unlike psychoanalysis, which supposedly had the power to cure the "underlying disease."

This resistance helped set up a conflict between talk therapy and drug therapy, even as both treatments evolved and grew. This conflict exists in all aspects of medicine, the so-called "holistic" or "humanistic" approach versus a "medicalized" approach more driven by treatments or procedures (that is, drugs and surgery). The conflict raises interesting, often unanswerable questions about how drugs work. How, for example, do you prove that symptom relief is curative, especially with illnesses for which the mechanisms are not well understood? (If damming up the neurotransmitter serotonin in the brain reduces symptoms of depression, does that mean low levels of serotonin *cause* depression—or are they a by-product of depression?) The conflict raises other, also unanswerable questions about what actually heals, the therapeutic intervention itself or the entire human process of intervening?

But the conflict has been particularly divisive in mental health care, because brain diseases are so divisive to begin with. And it made life increasingly difficult for psychiatrists and their patients as it became clear that the future of mental health care was a combination of medication and psychotherapy. In many ways, the new drugs were helping to create breakthrough ideas in understanding the brain. Some of the old-timers were appalled that this was the case. But the younger doctors at the Institute were struggling to balance the old and new approaches: they had more training in psychotherapeutic techniques than most modern shrinks, but they were equally fascinated by the role medications played in defining diagnoses.

Illnesses, especially brain-related illnesses, have a history of being seen as clinical syndromes, constellations of vague problems experienced or imagined, until a medical treatment comes along that works. At that point, the syndromes become "real" illnesses—as if legitimized only by the pill that treats them. Early anticonvulsant medications (phenobarbital in 1912 and Dilantin in the late 1930s) helped to finally separate epilepsy from the psychiatric illnesses, most of which then fell under the umbrella diagnosis of "schizophrenia." In the 1950s the first useful antidepressant, Tofranil, helped separate out those patients suffering primarily from unipolar depression. In the 1960s manic-depressive illness, which had been described in the literature for decades, was finally teased out of the jumble of psychiatric symptoms because some patients with such symptoms responded to lithium. In fact, lithium response became a major way to diagnose manic depression and separate it from schizophrenia. The medicine became widely viewed as the "insulin" of this particular chronic mental illness, making sick people "well" if they "stayed on their lithium." Each new drug that worked was a huge step in the "medicalization" of serious mental illness, thereby making a set of symptoms more societally acceptable to treat. ("Psychotic" symptoms, unfortunately, have yet to reach that point; the word itself is still stigmatizing because of its derogatory use to describe any aberrant behavior.)

In the 1960s and early 1970s Tegretol, the anticonvulsant drug Diane was now taking, became the major new drug in the treatment of epilepsy. It was tested as a substitute for lithium in manic-depressive patients as early as 1973 but wasn't the subject of wide experimentation as a mood stabilizer until the mid-1980s. By then researchers were beginning to experiment with several different anticonvulsants, to see if they had value as mood stabilizers. They did, and experts in the field began to speak more openly about the substantial percentage of patients who clearly had manic-depressive illness but did not respond to lithium. In a way, the basic concept of the illness had to be broadened to encompass this new category of patients who responded only to anticonvulsants, or to lithium and anticonvulsants together.

At some larger psychiatric facilities, these changes had been more ideologically welcome than at the Institute. Kay Jamison had been trained at UCLA before coming to Hopkins, two academic centers that had championed a more biological approach to the treatment of mental illness. In the biological psychiatry utopia, drugs would help strip away the symptoms, and regular psychotherapy would help repair the psychological damage of living with the illness—and reinforce the need to stay on the drugs. And in this utopia drugs wouldn't be seen as medical commodities, like hair dye that should be counted on to make your hair darker or lighter. They would become some combination of diagnostic tool and treatment, with the patient, physician and drug constantly interacting, not unlike the diabetic's intense day-to-day relationship with insulin.

But utopia is expensive, and both the Institute and Johns Hopkins were facing terrible economic pressures. In the United States public and private health insurance reimbursements were shrinking. (Even outside the United States, where most countries had national health insurance and costs were traditionally lower, the reimbursements were shrinking.) "Medicalization" had originally been criticized for depersonalizing health care by "treating diseases rather than patients." Since the rise in the early 1980s of the Diagnosis Related Group (or DRG) system for insurance reimbursements (beginning with state-funded programs and later crossing over into private health insurers), doctors had complained about having to pair every patient with a formal diagnosis or "disease" and every symptom with a formal "disease state." But for a while at least, treatments and hospital stays were ultimately paid for. Then, instead of merely systematizing reimbursements, the DRG infrastructure began to be used for cost containment, too.

The age-old debates in psychiatry—talk therapy versus drug therapy, as well as long-term hospitalization versus outpatient care—were being decided not so much by science as by commerce. Managed care firms were now casting the tiebreaking vote themselves or hiring others to do it. While insurers handle most areas of health care in-house, they often subcontract to companies that manage benefits requiring specialized expertise. Mental health care and pharmaceutical use were two such benefit areas, and psychiatrists found themselves at odds first with behavioral health management firms and later with pharmaceutical benefits managers.

Together, these two groups of cost containers convinced each other of the pharmaceutical company party line that, yes, drugs could cure virtually all problems and eliminate most if not all hospital stays. More effective drug treatments were no longer seen as an adjunct to hospitalization or outpatient psychotherapy; they were viewed as a cheaper substitute. This trend was ravaging all of health care, and many hospitals were in economic trouble because these drugs were being used as an excuse to shorten inpatient stays. But the problem in psychiatry was more extreme. The medical reimbursement system was losing its ability to distinguish between a broken leg and a slashed wrist.

The Institute, long a dinosaur, was facing extinction. The timing was especially ironic because the Institute had been the birthplace of the American Psychiatric Association, and to commemorate that, the organization had chosen Philadelphia as the site of its big one hundred fiftieth anniversary annual meeting in late May 1994. I got press credentials for myself and Diane. While she was interested in a handful of seminars, I wanted to observe the commercial courtship rituals of physicians and pharmaceutical manufacturers in their element.

The meeting was held in the city's sprawling new convention center. Clutching the snazzy green tote bag everyone received at registration to lug all manner of handouts, I wandered into the main exhibition hall the opening day of the conference. It was like a Disneyland of drugs, with large colorful Prozac pagodas and elaborate Paxil education centers featuring interactive videodisk displays with names such as "Depression: The 3D Challenge." The only things missing were a Wellbutrin brew pub and a Zoloft petting zoo, but all of the major drugs and drug companies were there in full force, their grand display areas dwarfing those of every care facility, scientific publisher and patient advocacy group. The two exhibits hawking the older antipsychotic Haldol were almost as big as the combined spaces of thirty-four of the top psychiatric care facilities in America. It was a perfect visual metaphor for how drugs fit into the treatment of mental illness, or any other illness.

Walking down the aisles, I saw the major competitors in the market for trendy antidepressants: Eli Lilly was there with Prozac, Burroughs Wellcome with Wellbutrin, SmithKline with Paxil and Pfizer with Zoloft. The major competitors on the neuroleptic front were also making their presence known. There were the two Haldol booths, one from manufacturer McNeil, the other from Scios-NOVA, which was comarketing Haldol as well as a handful of other old-faithful psychiatric drugs whose manufacturers no longer paid much attention to them, including SmithKline's Stelazine (trifluoperazine), Thorazine (chlorpromazine) and Parnate (tranylcypromine). There were also large displays for the exciting newer antipsychotics, Sandoz's Clozaril (clozapine) and Risperdal (risperidone), which the J&J subsidiary Janssen was trying to position as a safer me-too of Clozaril. Upjohn was there with its aging anti-anxiety pill Xanax (alprazolam), Wyeth-Ayerst was there with its new one, Effexor (venlafaxine), and Searle was pushing its new sleeping pill Ambien (zolpidem).

Each exhibit was a cornucopia of promotional *stuff*—more pads, cassettes, videotapes and flyers than you could fit into your APA tote bag unless you tossed out the two-pound schedule of the scientific programs. It brought to mind the disparaging remarks I'd heard doctors make about colleagues willing to "sell themselves out for the price of a pen."

These were the pens.

I knew I should scorn these implements. They were part of the problem, overpromotion incarnate. On the other hand, they were pretty great pens. Solid without being too heavy. Well balanced. Smooth gliding. A pleasure to write a prescription with.

And above all else, they were free. I took several.

A few days after my visit to the Prozac Pagoda, Diane and I attended one of the APA convention's "industry-supported symposia." As is true at most medical meetings, these symposia are held before and after the regular, unsponsored daytime sessions. It is curious that the organizations bother to separate the sessions anymore. Much of the research presented during the day is also sponsored by the drug companies, and most of the better speakers lecture at both types of events. I recently heard a prominent AIDS doctor complain about one marquee researcher, whom he referred to as the "Michael Jordan of HIV," not because of his talents but because of his drug company *endorsements.* "He was the featured doctor at the seven-thirty A.M. sponsored symposium," he recalled, "then the eight-thirty A.M. sponsored symposium for another company, then the early evening symposium for a third company. It's ridiculous!"

The biggest difference between the sponsored and unsponsored sessions is usually the food. At the daytime sessions you get water, coffee, tea. The food at the industry-sponsored symposia, however, is breathtaking: shrimp as big as boomerangs, balletic desserts of puff pastry, cream and spun-sugar plums.

The symposium we attended was about optimizing treatment of manic-depressive illness. We had seen a couple of the experts on the panel at seminars on mood disorders, and since there are always more talks to give than new research findings to present, we weren't expecting to hear anything earth-shattering. This is one of the rude awakenings of being an "informed" patient, reading as many studies as possible and attending professional seminars. You think you're going to hear exciting stuff before your doctor does and save yourself months or years of needless suffering. Once in a while that actually happens. But for the most part, you just hear the same "new" research over and over. It's natural to start reading between the lines, because you've heard the lines themselves so often.

I had been wondering why there was such a variation in the amount of useful *new* information available for the different drugs Diane had been given. It made sense that there would be mounds of lithium literature. Lithium is what doctors refer to as the "gold standard" treatment for the illness, meaning it is the treatment 'against which all others are measured, either because it was the first, or the best, or both. The gold standard is the drug most doctors would be expected to try first after a diagnosis. Lithium had been the gold standard for over twenty years, as the only drug approved by the FDA for treating manic-depressive illness.

As we already knew, below the gold standard were the two anticonvulsants, Depakote, which Diane had tried without success, and Tegretol, her current mood stabilizer. The two drugs appeared equally promising for manic depression. Yet much of new research and all of the buzz was about Depakote. It wasn't until this symposium that I realized why.

Once a drug is approved by the FDA, your doctor can prescribe it to you for absolutely any condition, regardless of whether this condition is officially "indicated" on the label. These so-called "off-label" uses are not only perfectly legal but critically important to medical care. It is not uncommon for drugs to end up being most popular and useful for something other than their original label indication. And many drugs end up being used at a different dose than originally indicated, because of off-label exploration. On a level playing field, off-label uses would get explored because of their medicinal promise. In the real world, they get explored because of patent protection.

Lithium and the two anticonvulsants all had been around for decades and were off patent in their original forms, with inexpensive generic versions available. But Abbott Laboratories had been able to get a new patent on a buffered version of valproic acid, which it was selling in regular and time-release pills under its brand name Depakote. The company was actively funding research aimed at getting Depakote officially approved by the FDA for treating manic-depressive illness. The company that owned the spent patent on Tegretol, Ciba-Geigy, which also made one of several brands of lithium tablets, hadn't bothered.

So seminars on the care of manic depression were beginning to feel like Depakote pep rallies. People in the field were pleased to see how Abbott's promotional expenditures were helping to raise the profile of manic-depressive illness and its treatment. But I knew Kay Jamison was not alone in her concern that the successful campaign for Depakote—which she thought was a good drug—tended to "minimize" the value of lithium, which had a much more established record of efficacy and safety. And I worried that if Tegretol ended up being Diane's permanent mood stabilizer, she would always be at the wrong end of the anticonvulsant research budget.

One of the highlights of the APA convention was a star-studded symposium about the stigma of mental illness. The panel included actor Rod Steiger, author and columnist Art Buchwald, actress Suzanne Somers and writer Kathy Cronkite, daughter of the CBS anchorman, who had compiled a book of celebrities' reflections on their problems with depression. Interspersed between the celebrities on the stage were the leaders of the three major advocacy groups in mental health, the National Mental Health Association (NMHA), the National Depressive and Manic-Depressive Association (DMDA) and the National Alliance for the Mentally Ill (NAMI).

Only Laurie Flynn from NAMI had enough star power to hold her own with the celebrities, making Steiger and Buchwald appear shy. She seemed like someone I should meet, so I got an assignment to write about her for *The New Yorker*. And not long after the APA convention, I found myself in a Tex-Mex seafood restaurant in San Antonio with her discussing the politics of pills and mental health. We were talking over beers and enormous servings of fish, including a stuffed flounder the size of a manhole cover.

Short and moon-faced with darting blue eyes, Flynn is one of the great political animals of medical-consumer activism. She is executive director of NAMI, the most powerful lobbying group in mental health, but she is also a constituent. Several months after she took the job in 1984, she became a "NAMI-mommy" when her teenage daughter Shannon was diagnosed with schizoaffective disorder. At that time, NAMI was a loose confederation of local self-help groups for parents of schizophrenics. Its main goal, besides providing shoulders for each other to cry on, was to convince psychiatrists that bad parenting did not cause schizophrenia, and good parenting alone couldn't cure it. At the time, this was an open debate.

So the NAMI-mommies were much more pissed off than the usual disease-charity group. They were still being blamed for *causing* their children's disease. Until the AIDS advocacy group ACT UP came together in the late 1980s, NAMI was known as *the* most in-your-face medical lobbying organization. And the most successful: it got a stranglehold on the government research budget for mental health, in large part because the daughter of Senate budget committee chairman Pete Domenici has a serious mental illness, and Domenici's wife is an active NAMI-mommy. But the NAMI ethos is not without its own political victims. In an effort to separate from the broader mental health community, the group can be undiplomatic. They dismissively refer to neuroses and personality disorders—as well as any other afflictions considered to be psychological rather than biological—as "problems of living." It's a shrill echo of an earlier day in psychiatry when treatment of such problems was referred to as "mental hygiene." This strident position separates NAMI politically from the larger NMHA, which advocates on behalf of all mental illnesses, including "problems of living." NAMI has even been accused of favoritism among the serious mental illnesses, allegedly pushing harder for psychotic-disorder research than mood-disorder research because even though the group now includes depression, manic depression, OCD and panic disorders under its advocacy umbrella, the core NAMI-mommies have children with schizophrenia.

One of NAMI's biggest political weapons has always been pills, which it jams down people's throats, figuratively and, in the view of some, literally. If symptoms can be checked by medication, the group argues, very loudly, then serious mental illnesses are biological, not psychological: *not our fault.* This admittedly reductionist position is meant to help destigmatize serious mental illnesses for people who have them, treat them and study them. It has also been a perfect way to get the right people on NAMI's side.

For many years, there was little downside to NAMI and the drug companies being on the same side because they were both selling the same product: biological psychiatry. Flynn refused to take any drug company money, in part because she was urged not to by the group's medical advocate and patron saint, radical Washington psychiatrist E. Fuller Torrey, a close associate of Public Citizen's Dr. Sidney Wolfe. In 1989 NAMI began taking some drug company contributions, but only for events that the group could *claim* it completely controlled. Such claims are often only half-truths, because every charitable organization and academic conference knows what it has to do—or *not* do—to keep a large corporate sponsor happy, even in a "hands off" situation. But initially there were no major problems. And then came the great Clozaril crisis of 1990.

Clozaril is a drug that in every way lives up to its class description as an "atypical antipsychotic." Developed by a subsidiary of Swiss-based Sandoz Ltd. in the late 1960s, it was quickly seen as having some unique antipsychotic properties, but some equally unique toxicities. It caused agranulocytosis, a potentially fatal suppression of white blood cells, in 1 or 2 percent of patients. Because of the extreme sensitivity of the FDA to such side effects, Sandoz withdrew its application to have the drug approved in the United States. It was approved in Europe, however, and has been used there, cautiously, for decades.

Without Clozaril, Americans with schizophrenia had few cutting-edge treatment options. They were basically stuck with the older neuroleptics such as Haldol and Thorazine. These drugs are often more sedating than symptom-reducing, and they can cause tardive dyskinesia, involuntary movements of the mouth and tongue that are often irreversible.

In 1988 the first major U.S. study was done comparing Clozaril with Haldol, the gold-standard antipsychotic. Suddenly this twenty-year-old drug was seen as having a stunning, almost curative effect on many "untreatable" schizophrenic patients. Its power was being compared to the effect of L-Dopa on the patients in the Oliver Sacks book *Awakenings*. And it didn't cause tardive dyskinesia.

NAMI, the APA, and Sandoz's own in-house researchers urged the company to try and get Clozaril approved in the United States. The company was somewhat reluctant to spend the money on a drug that had only a few years left on its patent and was certain not only to carry a black box warning but also to require regular blood monitoring. Several European countries were requiring patients on the drug to have blood tests weekly. In the United States there were many drugs that were labeled with *suggestions* that doctors do regular blood testing. But there had never been a successful drug, used outside of the hospital, that required patients to get their blood tested every week before receiving their next dose. Most companies would simply assume that any drug so inconvenient to take would never make it, especially for people with schizophrenia, who have trouble staying on their medications as it is. The company would also be reluctant to put such a drug on the market in the United States because of the possible legal risks.

Just below the surface of the Clozaril dilemma was, to me, a problem basic to all drug-taking. The company was probably assuming, and probably correctly, that both doctors and patients would be unable to properly assess the risks and benefits of Clozaril and would opt to avoid it because the specter of blood tests made it seem too dangerous. So here was a drug that many believed was the most significant therapeutic breakthrough for psychotic disorders in decades—perhaps the last best hope for one of the truly doomed populations in all of medicine. And it was unmarketable because *too much was known about its safety profile.*

For treatment-resistant schizophrenics and their families, it was like not being able to buy a car because seat belts and air bags made the risk of collision too palpable. Here a system of blood tests had been created that would catch the small but significant percentage of patients at risk—a system that, as patients, we should probably want for *any* drug we take, to avoid getting, say, Floxed. Yet this system was what made the drug appear unattractive commercially.

It was up to groups like NAMI to convince Sandoz and the FDA that patients were ready and willing to take on the risks associated with Clozaril. The company finally agreed, many NAMI family members ended up being test subjects in clinical trials and the drug was approved in 1990, the first new antipsychotic on the U.S. market since 1975. It was greeted with great enthusiasm until people got a look at the price tag. It was initially priced at $9,000 a year, making it one of the most expensive drugs in history. The price was so high because it included the weekly blood testing, which Sandoz insisted on controlling itself, through its affiliate Caremark.

And NAMI, which had developed a reputation for screaming bloody murder about even the smallest injustice against its constituency, said absolutely nothing about Clozaril pricing. "I was naive and overly enthused," Flynn admitted to me. "We didn't know whether or not this price was appropriate, and it *is* expensive to develop drugs. But I was slow to understand what was really going on. I learned a great deal the hard way with Clozaril."

.   .   .

Part of what she learned was that when you accept money from pharmaceutical companies—and at that point, NAMI had received only a small amount from Upjohn to subsidize the printing of some brochures—you are easily accused of selling out to them. That's what Flynn was hearing from some NAMI members, as well as Sidney Wolfe, who was normally a NAMI supporter. Eventually Flynn realized that the interests of NAMI and Sandoz were no longer so mutual.

"The pricing came to us packaged as 'the fruits of our research,' " she recalled. "It came to us packaged by scientists we respect. I thought, 'Why should these people be selling snake oil?' Well, you know, I guess I just wasn't cynical and mistrustful enough. I was not wise enough. I was getting called daily by families with great recovery stories, and it was an emotionally charged environment." Flynn finally turned on Sandoz. "We tried to work with the company to help people who couldn't afford the drug," she recalled, "and it was clear they were unresponsive. We were slow to figure it out, but we did figure it out and issued increasingly strong denunciations of their policy. I went up twice and met with the president of Sandoz. I said, 'Not only is this a higher price than you should be ethically charging, but you won't get the market.' "

By that time, Sandoz faced a more formidable adversary: thirty-eight of America's state attorneys general, who filed an antitrust lawsuit against the company. They were led by the crusading attorney general's office in Minnesota, which was on its way to becoming an alternative FDA by using state antitrust and consumer protection laws to stop drug companies from practices not covered by the Food and Drug Act—anything from unfair pricing to failure to warn about adverse reactions. The effort was spearheaded by attorney general Hubert Humphrey III, the son of the late U.S. senator. To settle the suit, Sandoz and Caremark had to agree to rebate $10 million to Clozaril users, donate $7 million to the states, the Veterans Administration and the National Organization for Rare Disorders for "scholarships" for needy patients, and pay $4 million in legal fees.

The company also lowered the price of Clozaril and allowed the blood tests to be done by others. The cost for the drug and the testing quickly fell. But Clozaril remains too expensive for many of the patients who need it most. And because of the blood testing, the drug itself will forever carry a stigma. Its success spawned research on a whole new generation of antipsychotics, each one of which is promoted as "just like Clozaril, without the blood tests." So far, however, none has surpassed the abilities of this nearly thirty-year-old "new" wonder drug.

And no patient advocacy group or medical charity has entirely solved the problems underlying NAMI's experience with Clozaril. Drug companies and patient groups have so many common goals—and they are often so intertwined by the relationships between the groups' favorite researchers and their corporate funders—that everyone is shocked when a controversy arises. The leaders of the advocacy group are then left to choose between the members who drive the organization, and the companies that sponsor the major events that help define the organization.

The Arthritis Foundation, for example, had just accepted a million-dollar donation from McNeil in exchange for the opportunity to use the foundation's logo on a line of pain relievers. Several other major medical charities depended on pharmaceutical company donations for substantial portions of their annual budgets. But even in situations where there weren't such formal links, medical charity groups often counted on drug company promotional campaigns for "disease states"—which sold the *idea* of treating heart disease or mental illness as a backhanded way to bolster drug sales—to spread the word. And there were many situations when their commonality of interests played out in medical politics.

In the spring of 1993 a furor erupted over a $4 million print and broadcast advertising campaign about depression. The campaign was put on by the National Mental Health Association, but it was paid for by Prozac manufacturer Eli Lilly. The company also gave the NMHA another half-million dollars to run a public education program through local mental health associations. The campaign was controversial because it was one of the largest of its kind, and because psychologists—whose treatments come under the umbrella of the NMHA even though they can't write prescriptions—felt it was propaganda for biological psychiatry and drug therapy. In many ways, the campaign benefited the causes of NAMI and the DMDA as much as or more than the National Mental Health Association.

Interestingly, some of the ties between Prozac and the mental health lobby had developed during the political struggle over the psychiatric side effects of Prozac—specifically reports of suicides that may have been caused, rather than prevented, by the antidepressant. Back in 1991 the FDA's psychopharmacology division had an advisory committee meeting on the subject that quickly turned ugly. On one side was the Church of Scientology, which, through its Citizens Commission on Human Rights, opposes all psychiatric medication. It wanted the drug banned, as did Dr. Peter Breggin, the antibiological psychiatry activist whose Luddite book *Talking Back to Prozac* includes a torturous analysis of the FDA approval of the drug.

On the other side was the mental health consumer lobby—including NAMI, the DMDA, the NMHA and the American Psychiatric Association—all of whom believed that even the addition of new label warnings would further "stigmatize" patients treating depression. They supported a position that the alleged psychiatric side effects were, in fact, preexisting symptoms that the Prozac had failed to treat.

Since suicide is all too often the outcome of depression, this complicated issue deserved a cool-headed discussion. Yet even though more than five hundred suicide attempts had been reported to the FDA as possible drug reactions, and the chairman of the advisory committee believed there should be a label change to at least *mention* the possibility of a suicide risk, the panel chose to take no action whatsoever. It's not easy to sanely debate drug science amid the crazy politics of mental health.

CHAPTER 10

The Temafloxacin

Syndrome

While I was purposely trying to keep my interest in quinolones on the back burner, in the summer of 1994 I found myself haunted by a handwritten letter I had received a year earlier. It was from a woman in South Jersey named Joan Hiddemen who said her husband had been given samples of Omniflox.

"He took two pills a day for six days," she wrote. "On the seventh day, he died."

The woman had asked me for information about legal actions against the drug's manufacturer. In June 1992 Chicago-based Abbott Laboratories had withdrawn Omniflox worldwide after only sixteen weeks on the market because of unexpected severe adverse reactions, including hemolytic anemia (a widespread destruction of red blood cells), renal failure, anaphylactic shock, severe hypoglycemia and, in some instances, multiple organ failure leading to death.

At the time, I had given Hiddemen the name of an attorney from New Mexico who had called me trolling for Omniflox patients, and I put her letter in a file with all the others. But I kept thinking about her and about Omniflox. Her husband had died on April 12, 1992, only six weeks before the drug was withdrawn. And he had been given the drug, according to her letter, for bronchitis, an ailment for which it was not even approved. It seemed like such a stupid way to die.

Every once in a while, I would reread Joan Hiddemen's letter. And I tried to make it jibe with what my pharmacology friends at Georgetown and the FDA had told me about the drug. They claimed that Omniflox was one of those rare situations that proves the system *works*. That was also their explanation for why the me-too antibiotic, only the ninth drug in modern FDA history to be withdrawn, had received almost no media attention. Even though Abbott was facing several hundred product liability lawsuits from people who had taken Omniflox in America—as well as a class action by its stockholders—the situation was so low-profile that even Sid Wolfe had never bothered to be outraged by it. In the U.K., too, where temafloxacin had been marketed under its European brand name Teflox, little attention had been paid to the withdrawal, other than a comment in the *Drug and Therapeutics Bulletin* that the drug had been the subject of "explosive" marketing techniques.

I was intrigued that nobody else seemed intrigued by Omniflox. At the very least, I wanted to know how well the system could possibly work if a drug that dangerous had gotten approved in the first place. And with all those lawsuits, I guessed there were probably many fascinating internal Abbott documents sitting in boxes in some lawyer's office, just waiting for a journalist to ask to see them. Since lawsuits against drug companies are invariably settled out of court, such sensitive documents do not stay available forever. They appear, like Brigadoon, for a brief time during the pretrial "discovery" process of a legal action, and disappear as soon as a deal is cut.

After I finally called Joan Hiddemen up and asked her to send me more material about her husband's death, I was intrigued by Omniflox for another reason as well: it would be a chance to watch the dance of litigation, how a drug reaction becomes a lawsuit.

In the packet she sent were three letters from lawyers. One was from the best product liability firm in Philadelphia, which had turned down her case in 1992 because there hadn't been an autopsy, so there were no postmortem tests to prove Omniflox had killed her husband. The second was from the lawyer in New Mexico who had contacted me. In 1993 he had also turned down her case for basically the same reason. The third letter was from the same firm in New Mexico, written nine months later. Much to my astonishment, they were now representing Hiddemen and updating her on the status of her case.

The letter said that, as part of that discovery, Abbott had produced more than thirteen hundred boxes of documents relating to Omniflox. I couldn't stand the idea of all those documents going back without anyone but a bunch of settlement-happy plaintiffs' attorneys ever looking at them. My editor at *Vanity Fair* encouraged me to look into it.

When the lawyers from New Mexico were, surprisingly, reluctant to cooperate after repeated phone calls, I decided to fly to Chicago and just show up at the courthouse on the day I knew they were scheduled to appear before the federal judge overseeing the Omniflox cases. After the hearing, I cornered the father-son team who were lead attorneys: Turner Branch, a compact, tough-talking Texan known for his courtroom dramatics, and his ex-jock son Brian, who was as sun-baked and laid-back as the New Mexico capital where their nationally known firm was based. They still said they had no time for me, but with annoying persistence I finally convinced them to at least let me ride with them in their limo to the airport.

Once I got him going, Branch the elder pulled no punches. He said that after looking at confidential documents, he believed that Abbott "either knew or should have known" that Omniflox would cause hemolytic anemia and organ failure before the drug was put on the market. "They did more thorough testing on *thalidomide* than on Omniflox," he insisted. "We're finding too much data that's inconsistent."

After pumping the Branches for information during the traffic-snarled trip to O'Hare, I was finally able to wangle an invitation to come to Albuquerque and go through their Omniflox documents. They would also take me to meet their very first Omni-Floxie: Velva Conrad, the seventy-year-old woman who had filed the first suit in their class action.

Barbie Conrad pushed her stringy, sunburned hair behind her ear as she retold the story, her Early American rocker burrowing a groove in the green shag carpet of her home in the sandy garden suburb of Corrales, New Mexico. Her mother, Velva, wiry and fine-featured, sat quietly on a nearby couch, straining to summon what was left of her fabled feistiness. Mostly, she nodded at the parts of the story she recalled strongly.

In April 1992 Velva Conrad had gone to the doctor with a simple urinary tract infection. Ten days after the visit, she was comatose and dying in an Albuquerque hospital with multiple organ failure, the decision to pull the plug on her life support already made. The cause of the catastrophe—she had only felt a little flu-ish, until her urine turned the color of coffee and her kidneys began to fail—was unknown. She had either been infected by some unidentifiable "pathogen from hell," or she had ingested something unbelievably toxic.

Was it possible, the doctors asked, that Velva could have accidentally swallowed something like, maybe, *carburetor cleaning fluid*?

Then Velva's sister, who had been summoned from Seattle to the deathbed, called home with the grim update. She was told that the situation sounded very similar to that of a woman the family knew in Seattle who had also experienced a sudden, unexplainable kidney failure. The woman was forty years younger than Velva, and in comparing their stories, the two had nothing else in common except that they both had recently gone to the doctor with minor problems. The other woman had had an ear infection, and her kidney failure was being blamed on the free samples of a brand-new, heavily promoted antibiotic her doctor had given her to treat it. Had Velva been given a drug called Omniflox for that urinary tract infection?

"We rushed to the doctors and said, 'We finally figured it out, it's the drug, it's the Omniflox,' " Barbie told me. "And they immediately became very angry. One demanded to know where we got our medical license. . . . I think doctors are so scared of being sued that they immediately try to shut the door." Eventually they tracked down a kidney specialist who thought their theory had some merit. So did the doctor who gave Velva the drug in the first place. Among the suggestions on his handwritten note attached to her hospital chart was "rule out reaction to quinolone."

But it appeared to be too late to do anything with this information, so the family agreed to pull the plug on Velva Conrad. Much to her doctor's surprise, she kept breathing faintly. The family decided to at least restart her dialysis—mostly because they heard that the woman in Seattle had eventually recovered through dialysis. After five days she regained consciousness. About a month after all the trouble started, she was strong enough to consider leaving the hospital, although she was never going to be the same, and she and her husband were going to have to sell their house and move in with Barbie's family.

"This was like the biggest betrayal you could imagine," Barbie told me. "I mean, you trust that when you go to the doctor, he's going to give you medicine that will make you better! And you assume that by the time it reaches the level of public usage, it has been tested, it has been tried, it has been proved that you don't need to worry about taking it."

Still, the Conrads originally had no intention of suing Abbott. They contacted the company, which they say told them it planned to take care of all Velva's hospital bills. When the family mailed in the first of what would be many sets of receipts, they got a check from Abbott for $860.14. But it was stamped "final Omniflox settlement."

That's when they hired an attorney. According to that attorney, if the Conrads had cashed that check, Abbott would have been absolved of all further claims against it in her case.

"You know what the best part was about my contact with Abbott before we sued them?" Barbie asked. "It was the name of the department the person worked in. It was called 'risk management.' I was thinking, isn't that nice of them? They have a whole department that worried about the risks of the people taking their drugs. That's so nice.

"It wasn't until I saw the fine print on that check that it dawned on me, you know, that it wasn't *our* risk they were managing."

The Conrads contacted the Branch law firm, which is well known in Albuquerque for big verdicts and huge annual Christmas parties at its plush adobe compound on Rio Grande Boulevard. Velva became the Branch firm's first Omniflox client, but many others soon followed. The day after I met the Conrads, I showed up at the law firm's document annex, just down the road from the main office courtyard, and was led into the Omniflox war room. There a paralegal named Shariesse McCannon sat at a desk wedged between an overstuffed horizontal file cabinet and a U.S. map, with red pushpins and little typed-out names at the location of each Omniflox client.

Next to the map was a handwritten chart on a big piece of posterboard. It listed the status of each Omniflox case and how the fees were going to be split between the originating firm and the Branch firm. The chart was the final score sheet of two years of legal wrangling by liability lawyers from all over the country, each trying to corral the Omniflox suits for themselves. During much of the jockeying, the lawyers believed that Omniflox might be the next monster class action suit with sky's-the-limit settlements and fees: the next silicone breast implant, the next L-tryptophan, two products the Branch firm was already deeply involved with. Omniflox seemed like a slam-dunk case, because the company had already withdrawn the drug under FDA pressure.

But the liability lawyers were disappointed when no court would certify a "class" of injured patients. Even though a class action had been allowed for Abbott shareholders whose stock value might have fallen because of Omniflox, the patients who had actually taken the drug—many of whom were found through ads in *USA Today*—had to settle for the next best thing: a "multidistrict litigation" (MDL), in which only the pretrial motions and discovery are consolidated under one judge, and then the cases go back to their original jurisdictions for trial or settlement. Each state has its own laws concerning liability in drug cases. Some put more emphasis on the physician's responsibility as a "learned intermediary" than on the drug company, while others view the situation more as a strict product liability issue for the manufacturer. States also have differing ideas about the responsibility of the patient and the legal ramifications of a drug's warning label. Evidence that almost assures a win in New Jersey is a sure loser in, say, California.

While MDLs can be lucrative for the lawyers who tie up the most cases and get to run the steering committee, they still aren't as highly coveted as class actions because the pie gets cut up into many more pieces. The Branch firm had beaten out law firms from Chicago, Seattle and South Carolina for control of the Omniflox cases. (The South Carolina lawyers had finally taken the case of Joan Hiddemen, which is how she ended up being represented by a firm that a few months before had told her she had no case.) But the individual settlements weren't turning out to be as huge as they had hoped. And there had been little media attention to the drug—the best TV magazine show they could get was Connie Chung's ill-fated *Eye to Eye*—and no big congressional follow-up investigation of Omniflox that might pump up the volume. The whole legal effort was already beginning to feel like a situation where losses were being cut.

Shariesse loaded depositions into boxes for me to take down to the conference room to read. As she did, she told me about her own visit to the Abbott document depository in Chicago, where much of this material came from. She described it as a huge decrepit building, with holes in the wall and no air conditioning. While they were searching through files, she recalled, "a weird guy at the copy machine bounced a soccer ball off the wall with his feet and head."

Even in the more hospitable confines of the Branch firm's air-conditioned annex conference room, going through the documents and depositions was arduous. This material had already been culled through several times to highlight only the best potential needles in the haystack. Nonetheless, there were three huge binders of documents, some of which had been removed by the firm because Abbott had marked them confidential so they couldn't be shared with a journalist. There were also thousands of pages of transcribed depositions with Abbott employees. Each document had been stamped with an ID number for the purposes of the case, and the numbers reached well over 2 million. The story of one of the worst drug disasters in modern history was somewhere in this mountain of information. But it was nearly impossible to find. I felt as if I had just been handed the footnotes for a book but the book itself was missing, and it was up to me to figure out what it had said.

Certainly, Abbott was not going to help tell the story. I had called them for comment when I did my story for *The Washington Post Magazine*—which mentioned the Omniflox situation in passing—and they had declined to comment because of the ongoing litigation. When I called again and said I was now writing specifically about Omniflox, they still didn't want to cooperate in any way. But the truth is, Abbott has a reputation for rarely cooperating with anyone—not even other drug companies. The only major research-oriented pharmaceutical manufacturer in America that refuses to join the main industry trade group, Abbott is a drug company with an attitude. Arrogant and pugnacious even by industry standards, the company is also known for being aggressively entrepreneurial and is admired on Wall Street for the very reasons it is sometimes derided in regulatory and scientific circles.

Abbott's research efforts are organized into semiautonomous cells called "ventures." As the story unfolded in the depositions and memos, the "quinolone venture" had begun in 1979, when Abbott decided to create a me-too drug to compete with Noroxin and Cipro. After going through a thousand different compounds, researchers invented the temafloxacin compound, along with four other quinolones the company hoped to develop into drugs. One Abbott internal memo I read inadvertently provided a good picture of the demand for excellence in the quinolone venture.

"Differences among the competitors will likely be minimal . . ." it said; "being early even if not the best will improve the chances of success."

Concerns were also voiced early on that the quinolone venture might be a little *too* entrepreneurial. In one internal memo, the company's director of regulatory affairs, Roland Catherall, the point person in all dealings with the FDA, worried that Abbott's "desire for a product-line extension appear[s] . . . to have an overriding influence on the concept of the development plan being based on good science."

In 1988 Abbott applied to the FDA for Investigational New Drug status for temafloxacin, and a year later, it began applying for approval in the United States, Europe, Asia and South America. By 1991 Omniflox had been approved in nine countries, had approvals pending in twenty-two others and was speeding its way toward the most important milestone: FDA approval. Several thousand patients had been studied, and no major trends of unexpected, troubling adverse reactions had been reported. Omniflox's safety profile appeared similar to that of other drugs in its class.

Abbott was gearing up for the biggest drug launch in its seventy-five-year history. The company was so convinced of Omniflox's medicinal value—or at least its extreme marketability—that it decided its normal sales force just wouldn't be strong enough. Instead, Abbott entered into a marketing agreement with a British drug company, Imperial Chemical Industries, which was looking for a new drug because its hypertensive medication, Tenormin (atenolol), was about to go off-patent and its salespeople would need another product to maintain their commissions. Under the comarketing agreement, many doctors would have two different sales reps visiting them to pitch Omniflox.

Abbott's sales force was excited, and a large advertising budget was in place. A rush of articles about Omniflox were set to appear in major journals. The company apparently hadn't taken any chances that the articles wouldn't toe the party line. One revealing internal memo about some of those articles described an industry practice I had heard about but never seen so clearly documented: scientific papers being written by the marketing department instead of by the scientists. Dr. Reid Patterson, Abbott's director of drug safety evaluation, was complaining in the memo about publications on Omniflox in an upcoming supplement of the *American Journal of Medicine.* "[C]ertain manuscripts," he wrote, ". . . were being labeled as being authored by more impressive, outside, expert consultants, who had nothing to do with the design or generation of the data." In the memo Patterson, a company drug safety expert, seemed less concerned about the academic fraud than with the "loss of recognition" for the people who had actually done the work, as well as the possible "impact on their advancement within Abbott." But he was also concerned that "marketing has decided that our data will be assembled by ghostwriters . . . reviewed by us, then published as though they were authored by us or by some better known consultant."

In fact, many of the preapproval internal memos had similarly embarrassing passages. One noted in amazement that an Italian researcher had done four large studies, all of which had been completed by every single one of the patients who had entered them—a nearly impossible feat—and also pointed out that the paperwork for all the patients had been mysteriously misplaced. "I don't quite see how 800 patients on our drug could just 'disappear,' " the memo said, "[and] I'm not sure the FDA would accept this."

But it was hard to know if the Omniflox documents represented anything other than standard operating procedure for the drug industry. They had been assembled mostly to make Abbott appear generally suspicious to a jury. It was difficult to make sense of what I was seeing. So after a solid week of reading and taking notes, I had everything Xeroxed and shipped back to Philadelphia and came home to figure out what I had.

.   .   .

Since I was now treading into what I regarded as Sidney Wolfe territory, I thought it was time I finally met the man whose name had become so synonymous with pharmaceutical muckraking. I arranged to see him at his office in Washington's Dupont Circle area, in the building where Ralph Nader's other organizations were also housed. I waited for Wolfe in a small, jammed law library with a conference table.

For the past twenty-five years, Dr. Sidney Wolfe has been the most consistently controversial man in medicine. Calling him a medical Ralph Nader is almost too easy, because he is much more of a fixture in health care than Nader is in the various worlds he has invaded. More accurate, perhaps, is the description I once heard from one of the world's most respected drug researchers. He called Wolfe "the Malcolm X of medication," and he meant it in the best and worst possible senses.

Sidney Wolfe continues to have many fans in medicine, and among the millions of readers of his *Worst Pills, Best Pills* books and newsletters. "Sid is, on one hand, a loose cannon, but on the other hand an enormous resource," one prominent drug researcher told me. "He shoots from the hip, usually too early, but usually correctly. He serves an enormously important public role, although sometimes he goes beyond what the science will support." Some former supporters, however, think he has gone over the edge. "I think he has become hysterical and flaming enough that he undercuts the cause," said another drug researcher.

"Sid Wolfe is not a positive force, because he sees drug companies as evil," one drug safety analyst told me, "and without for-profit drug companies, we'd still be treating headaches by sucking on tree bark."

Love him or hate him, Wolfe is still the most cunning and fearless free safety in the drug game, often the last guy a pharmaceutical company has to get by before scoring a commercial touchdown. He has made more than his share of game-ending open-field tackles.

Wolfe credits three events in his young adulthood for his medical activism. As an undergraduate in chemical engineering, the Ohio native worked one summer at a chemical plant on the Cuyahoga River (which itself became famous for catching fire) and regularly came home with first-degree burns on his hands and face from the acid they were manufacturing. After college he took a year off and worked in the local coroner's office, where he became acutely aware of how often prescription drugs caused death—and not just in suicides. Then, during medical school, he worked in a hematology lab where they were studying bone marrow suppression caused by the antibiotic chloramphenicol.

By the mid-1960s, Wolfe was a researcher at the NIH, studying alcohol withdrawal and the effects of drugs on blood clotting, while following a fairly traditional academic medicine track until he met Ralph Nader, who was just becoming known for consumer activism. Wolfe's first major consumer action, in early 1971, was against Abbott Laboratories, which controlled much of the U.S. market for intravenous fluids. Some of the fluids had become contaminated with bacteria, but the company was reluctant to take them off the market, and the FDA hadn't forced the issue; it had simply warned doctors that any patient who got the infection should be taken off the Abbott IV fluid. Wolfe and Nader hand-delivered a letter demanding a recall to the commissioner of the FDA and released it to the news media. Abbott announced a recall the next day, and Sid Wolfe, although he didn't know it at the time, had launched a new career.

Nader's umbrella organization, Public Citizen, was founded that year, and its health activism began on the fall day that Wolfe and Nader demanded the recall of Red Dye number 2. By the beginning of 1972, Wolfe had left the NIH to run Public Citizen's Health Research Group full time, raising as much medical hell as possible. He developed a true gift for repackaging large, shapeless public health concerns into media-friendly and sometimes even commercially marketable form. Who else but Sid Wolfe would have thought to take the government's own list of older medications that, years after efficacy testing was mandated by the 1962 Kefauver-Harris bill, still hadn't been officially proven effective and publish it as a book (in 1980) under the catchy title *Pills That Don't Work*? The book is a perfect example of what Wolfe does best: take already published material from the most credible sources and use it against drug companies, the FDA or prescribing doctors.

Wolfe burst into the small conference room and greeted me by saying, "You have fifteen minutes." Tall and ruggedly handsome, with wavy dark brown hair, horn-rimmed glasses and a seriously cleft chin, he has an air of intense impatience about him, and his know-it-all edginess can be contagious, making a visitor feel the need to verbally joust. I told him I had been looking into Omniflox and asked him why he had never pursued the drug. He launched into a rapid-fire description of all the drugs he had moved on over the years.

"There are a number of drugs on the market for less than a year that wind up being taken off the market after dozens of deaths and hundreds of injuries," he said. "There are some we sued the FDA to get off the market, like Suprol [suprofen], an anti-inflammatory drug used for pain from athletic injuries that caused several hundred cases of acute renal failure. And in each of these instances there was enough information, or should have been, prior to approval to stop the approval. In an increasing number of cases it turns out that information was criminally withheld from FDA . . . a pattern of withholding data. There is no evidence right now that Abbott withheld data. We got the adverse reaction reports and none of them seemed to have illegally long intervals between the reactions and the reports. . . .

"We are besieged with things to work on . . . and when we looked at the Omniflox documents, nothing screamed out. Usually, on the things we pursue, the documents scream . . . but, I must underscore, I haven't looked extensively at the drug."

He did, however, have a general rule of thumb on these types of cases. "The sage position I choose to take," he said, "is when something like this happens, I believe that until evidence to the contrary arises, there's a strong suspicion that a company has withheld information from FDA or misinterpreted data—or something else in the process has gone wrong. There are these instances where one in a million people gets a rare reaction that nobody could have anticipated, and lo and behold, when it gets into wide use, three or four people get killed. I acknowledge there might be circumstances like that. But most of these events are hardly rare."

Then he looked at his watch. "I can give you five more minutes," he said.

Like any good politician, Wolfe was able, even during the course of our brief conversation, to tick off all the major cases Public Citizen had been involved with where such pharmaceutical fraud had been proven. The big three were when Eli Lilly pleaded guilty in 1982 to criminally withholding adverse reaction data on Oraflex (benoxaprofen), including a number of deaths in the U.K.; when Hoechst executives admitted to withholding data on Merital (nomifensine) in 1986; and when Johnson & Johnson yanked Suprol in 1987 after it was banned in Europe. But there had been several others. Somebody at the FDA had once faxed me the short list of drugs that had been officially withdrawn over the past twenty years. I had it hanging on the bulletin board over my desk.

What most of those drugs had in common was that their withdrawals had led to intensive investigations, first by the FDA and later by the legislative committees that do oversight on the FDA's parent department, Health and Human Services. Ted Kennedy's Senate subcommittee had done painstaking investigations regarding drugs since the 1970s, with which Wolfe and Nader were often associated. In the 1980s the focus shifted to, among others, the Human Resources and Intergovern-

mental Relations subcommittee headed by Democratic New York representative Ted Weiss, who died in 1992.

The lead counsel for Weiss's subcommittee had been a lawyer named
Dan Sigelman, who had worked briefly for Public Citizen before going
to the Hill. Sigelman had a gift for poring over documents like the ones I
had obtained and quickly separating the sloppy from the criminal. It had
been his job to tell Weiss what to scream about. Sigelman had since left
Washington and gone into private practice. I tracked him down at a
litigation firm in Atlanta and told him a little bit about my interest in
Omniflox. Unlike Wolfe, Sigelman was *very* intrigued.

I had asked the FDA if I could interview the medical officer who
approved Omniflox and had recently been informed that my request had
been granted. When I told Sigelman about the upcoming appointment
at the FDA, he urged me to come to see him first, promising to make it
worth my while. So I booked a triangle flight from Philadelphia to Atlanta to Washington and went to my local travel store to buy a lightweight rolling handcart. I was going to be lugging a box of more than
fifty pounds of bound documents through three major airports and into
the FDA's main building. I thought a cart would make me look less
suspicious—and perhaps prevent my back from going out.

I showed up at Sigelman's Atlanta office early in the morning, and we
started paging through the documents. He is a slight man with thinning
gray hair, a mustache and the nasal, insistent voice of a New York prosecutor. While we read, he offered a running commentary on the glory
days of government oversight of the FDA and the drug industry. He
clearly missed working for the government and was frustrated by his
position in the adverse drug reaction diaspora.

"I have a philosophy," he said. "The way agencies like FDA let down
the public is in the mundane, the day-to-day. Some decision that wasn't
very sexy or an omission that wasn't very sexy. You have to get down to a
detail level. But we're reaching a point where people have to sell things
quickly in media. Congressmen don't want to have multiday hearings: it
has to be a quick story, the press wants a quick one-line lead. And
there's a symbiotic relationship between Congress and the press. The
result is less oversight.

"In the oversight we do have, the emphasis has always been on pricing policies of drug companies—which are also very questionable. But
we're not seeing the detailed investigations into whether these giants are
adequately complying with federal regulations and carrying out functions that are protective of public health. You don't see much of *that*
anymore."

Sigelman believed that the entire approval process was stacked against the FDA. He felt the medical officers didn't have nearly enough time or access to raw, unspun data to take a truly independent look at a drug before it got onto the market. "Something can be seriously missed," he said, "because no one really has the time or inclination to look at the massive submission to see if summaries [on which almost all approvals are based] accurately reflect the more broad data. The people who write those summary reports are making certain choices that can create obvious omissions . . . nobody has the time to look at all the data and see what else might be going on." He thought this was particularly true of data from the increasing number of clinical trials done outside the United States. He had recently written a piece for the *American Trial Lawyers* magazine about the problem of foreign drug reporting.

Between diatribes, he made passing comments on the Omniflox documents. "Oh, this *stinks*," he said. "This is dirty, this stinks. God, I wish I had one of these cases. I *love* to get into this shit." Besides the actions of the FDA and the drug company, he had some advice for the lawyers. "This is not *digging*," he said. "Digging would be going through the documents and finding discrepancies. . . . They're probably sitting back waiting for a settlement, and they don't want to spend the extra money."

There were a handful of documents I had guessed might be important when I first saw them in New Mexico. Sigelman zeroed in on many of the same ones and offered a more expert interpretation of what they might mean.

He identified two basic issues with Omniflox, issues that went to the very heart of how our drugs are kept safe. Had Abbott had any inkling that Omniflox could cause a deadly syndrome of hemolytic anemia and organ failure before the drug was put on the market? And if not, how soon after the drug hit the market did the company realize there was a problem, and did it act responsibly in protecting the public?

Several particularly interesting documents seemed to speak to these issues. In the spring of 1990, for example, the medical director of Abbott U.K., Dr. Christine Carnegie, had asked the U.S. office for further information about cases of certain types of reported adverse reactions to Omniflox in test patients. Many of the reactions were the very ones that later caused the FDA to force the withdrawal of the drug. In the course of a week, Dr. Carnegie received three memos from the U.S. office. The first one detailed nine patients who had developed various blood disorders. The second one detailed twenty-seven patients who had abnormalities in laboratory blood levels measuring kidney and liver function. The third discussed three Omniflox patients with blood coagulation abnormalities.

It was unclear if Abbott U.K. needed this information to respond to questions from drug regulators at the British Medicines Control Agency (MCA)—which, because the British regulatory system has no Freedom of Information Act, we'll never know—or if it had an inkling of a problem with Omniflox and wanted to satisfy its own internal curiosity. Certainly, this document was evidence that someone at Abbott had been asked to compile information about such cases.

But much more troubling was a document marked with ID numbers 2858791 through 2858794. It was called Table 7 and was innocuously titled "List of Temafloxacin Patients with Certain Adverse Events for Phase II and III Oral Studies." The "certain adverse events" were nearly the exact same ones for which the drug would be withdrawn: blood disorders and organ failures. According to the cover page, the list had been generated so the company could start retrieving medical records of patients and analyzing their cases.

More stunning than what was on the list, however, was *when* it had been created at Abbott. It was dated March 31, 1992, more than a month before the company had ever even hinted to the FDA that it knew about any such problems. Many if not most of the approximately 500,000 people who had taken Omniflox—including Velva Conrad and the late husband of Joan Hiddemen—had done so after that date.

I wasn't sure if Table 7 was a smoking gun. But Sigelman agreed it was quite a piece of ammunition for me to be packing on my visit to the FDA.

CHAPTER 11

Table 7

Two days later, a cab dropped me off in front of the Parklawn Building, the once-modern concrete, stone and stainless-steel structure in Rockville, Maryland, that serves as the FDA's headquarters. It had been almost two years since I began my quest to investigate drugs and drug approval, and while I probably had made several thousand calls to offices inside the building, I had never actually been there.

The Parklawn Building is almost devoid of personality and uniqueness, like so many buildings associated with the government. It is as if the more powerful the federal government becomes, the less it wants to call attention to itself. Parklawn is the center of one of the most powerful bureaucracies on the planet. A full 25 percent of America's gross national product is regulated by the inhabitants of the building: almost anything eaten or drunk by humans or animals (until recently, the agency had an office in New York specifically for testing tea), anything taken as a medicine or vaccine by humans or animals (even vitamins and herbal remedies are regulated, but as foods or food supplements instead of as rigorously approved drugs), anything used as a medical device, anything used as a cosmetic (except soap), and of course, all the labels, advertisements and marketing materials associated with these products. Because of the agency's impact on imported and exported goods, the FDA ends up regulating a substantial portion of the rest of the world's economic output as well. While many of the people who work here may deserve their reputation for grayness, their mission is anything but boring.

One hand gripping my suitcase, the other dragging my metal luggage-cart, which was now listing to one side under the weight of the boxed documents and transcripts, I began roaming and rolling through the long, wide, interchangeable hallways. Eventually I found myself seated in a small conference room, preparing to interview Dr. Michael Blum, the FDA medical officer who had approved Omniflox. Sweaty from lugging the cart, I appeared more nervous than I really was—the recognition of which then made me nervous.

Blum sat across the table. Like many people on the medical side of the drug business, he reminded me of the oceanographer character Richard Dreyfuss played in *Jaws*; he was a slim, thirty-seven-year-old physician with thinning red-brown hair, a trim beard and wide fascinated eyes behind his horn-rimmed glasses. I recognized him from the quinolone advisory committee meeting where I had spoken; he had given the history presentation and had impressed me by actually having a sense of humor, referring to one factoid as "another interesting piece of quinolone trivia." Also in the room with us were Blum's boss—Dr. James Bilstad, the lanky director of the Office of Drug Evaluation II at CDER, who asked to sit in—along with an FDA press officer.

Four months after he had approved Omniflox, Blum had been a driving force in making sure the drug was forcibly removed from the market. More recently, he had published a provocative postmortem on the most severe reactions to Omniflox. He gave the paper a title that sounded more like a Michael Crichton medical thriller than a study in an obscure infectious disease journal. Using the drug's generic name, he called it the "Temafloxacin Syndrome."

Blum knew he was about to be subpoenaed in the shareholders' suit to testify about his work on the drug. I had come to interview him, but I knew he had his own questions for me. He wanted to know what was in the box I was wheeling around. He wanted to know if what was in there made him a hero or a fool.

Frankly, I wasn't sure yet myself. There were things I needed to know from him first. I usually do my interviews as slowly and chronologically as possible. That way, I can lay each person's time line side by side and try to understand who knew what, when—or more important, who *didn't* know what, when.

But this was also my first real opportunity to find out in great detail what it was like to be a medical officer in today's FDA. I was going to ask every question I had ever had before reaching into that box.

Blum explained that he worked four and a half days a week for the FDA, one of them from his home, and spent a half day treating patients in a hospital. At any given time, he would be overseeing fifteen to twenty drug applications simultaneously for the anti-infectives division, where he had been assigned during his fellowships at the agency in pediatric infectious diseases. Omniflox was a drug he had inherited just before it was about to be approved, in late 1991, because the original medical officer, Dr. Theresa Reed, was retiring. Reed was a lifetime FDA doctor who had been the principal reviewer of quinolones for more than twenty years: Omniflox was her last assignment. Blum initially felt positive about the drug. He didn't see it as just another me-too quinolone but as a medication with some significant advantages over the ones that were available.

While discussing antibiotic use, Blum said something that stopped me in my tracks. He said authoritatively that he didn't "perceive quinolones as first-line therapy"—that is, the first drug a doctor should try—for *anything*. That would include the infection Diane had had.

"There are definite niches where quinolones are important to have, like limiting hospitalizations of patients," he said, but for anything else, they are "second- or third-line therapy." I asked if he was aware that many doctors were using quinolones first. He said he was. I asked what he and other medical officers had done to let prescribing doctors know that this could be a problem. He conceded that the FDA "had not really tried to get out" the word on this issue.

This is the kind of information that all medical officers know, but aren't supposed to share with the public—because, technically, they aren't allowed to recommend therapies. This is one of the cruelest scientific ironies of drug regulation: the only people in the world who are in a position to actually see and compare all the proprietary information on competing drugs are not permitted to tell doctors and patients what they have learned. But "first-line" or "second-line" recommendations are a subject medical officers discuss privately, because they know that in most situations the drug companies will fight to the death to keep these recommendations off their labels. No company is eager to mass-market a new drug that is specifically labeled "second-line," and industry has a history of going to great pains to lobby the FDA against second-line status. Blum implied that such a lobbying effort was going on regarding quinolones even as we spoke. "But I'm not at liberty to say what the negotiations are with the companies," he said.

As I asked questions about how an FDA medical officer pursues information, I became increasingly distressed. Even after all I had learned, I *still* had imagined the process to be much more rigorous, much more scientifically aggressive than it really is. The course of FDA approval can seem interminably long to drug companies that have millions of dollars on the line, and the dropout rate is very high. But the final exam is, essentially, a pass-fail essay test, and a drug can retake the course and the final as many times as its sponsor can afford. And while there is always the possibility of cheating, the overworked FDA runs largely on the honor code. I was astounded by how many of my questions were being answered with "they never told us otherwise" or "we requested that information from the company and assumed what they gave us was accurate."

The first clue Blum had that he should pay closer attention to Omniflox came in the form of a hypoglycemia case that was called into Abbott by an osteopath in Michigan on February 27, 1992—three days after the first prescription for the drug was written. The osteopath had an eighty-two-year-old patient to whom she gave Omniflox for chronic bronchitis and walking pneumonia, as her sales rep had suggested. Soon the patient was in the emergency room with dangerously low blood sugar. He was an adult diabetic, so blood sugar problems weren't a complete surprise. But what was unusual was that they hadn't been able to get his blood sugar back up to normal.

Blum didn't know why this particular case—and two others just like it—caught his eye. The company had mailed the FDA the 1639s, the standard forms for reporting such events, with no particular fanfare. And even though this adverse reaction wasn't yet on the label, the hypoglycemias had not been "flagged" by FDA epidemiology as a possible "signal." It was just something that would eventually end up in the numbing litany of "events" listed on the amended label. But for some reason, the reactions bugged Blum, and he soon found Omniflox getting a little bit more of his divided attention.

Until those first hypoglycemia cases came in, Abbott's only trouble with the FDA had been over its slogan for the massive Omniflox launch campaign: "designed to exceed the reach of other quinolones." The agency's Division of Drug Marketing, Advertising and Communications felt this was a claim of "total superiority" over its competitors, but there was insufficient clinical proof the claim was true. The division warned the company not to use the slogan because it violated the law, but Abbott used it anyway in a journal ad. Abbott officials were then called to Washington for a two-hour meeting on March 16, during which, according to an internal company memo, "FDA vented a lot of hostility toward us" and threatened "corrective action" if the unsupported slogan ran again.

This threat of a slap on the wrist is apparently how the majority of violations of drug advertising laws are handled. It is an example of the give and take between the agency and industry, in which each side believes it is giving more than it is taking. And of course, the honor code is in effect.

"If the company has additional data on adverse reactions," Blum explained to me matter-of-factly, "we would expect that information to be submitted without having to *ask* for it."

On cue, I reached down into the box, pulled out a black binder of documents and opened it to Table 7. As Blum scanned the document, his face fell.

"They did *not* bring this to our attention," he sputtered incredulously, as he calibrated its significance. "I have *never* seen this." The memo suggested that he was more of a hero than he ever realized—and perhaps more of a fool as well.

He pointed to the date at the top of the page, March 31. "Why, that was at a time when the hypoglycemia had just been ID'd, but the anemia hadn't come into play *at all.* And here they've searched through for the whole spectrum of events that, um, unless . . ." He started to sound frustrated. "They searched through for coagulation, renal disorder, blood dyscrasias, thrombocytopenia, they looked at *all the elements we put together months later.*" He sighed in confusion, caught himself before saying what he was thinking, and then sat back down to restart the interview.

After seeing Table 7, Blum was suddenly less guarded in discussing the Omniflox experience, more open to wondering if Abbott had deserved the benefit of his doubt. He retold a story he had mentioned only in passing earlier, highlighting the details that Table 7 made seem even more troubling. It was about the first face-to-face discussion he had had with Abbott about Omniflox side effects: "the May seventh meeting," as he referred to it with typical FDA exactitude.

At that point he knew nothing about any hemolytic anemia reactions. He had called Abbott in only because he knew there were a bunch of hypoglycemias—more had been reported since those first three caught his attention—and he wanted to talk to the company about adding them to the label. He also wanted to make sure that Abbott continued sending him any new cases immediately, by fax. If a serious side effect isn't yet on a drug's label, the FDA must be informed in writing of any additional cases reported to the company within fifteen days of receipt. Blum had already asked Abbott to start faxing them as well. But once the side effect is on the label and the public has, ostensibly, been warned, the company only has to report quarterly. Blum, wary, wasn't satisfied with that, and insisted that Abbott continue faxing new cases.

Then, when the "May seventh meeting" was ending, in what seemed to Blum to be almost an afterthought, an Abbott official said that since the label was already being changed, the company would also like to add hemolytic anemia. Abbott had, at that moment, reported only three cases of this serious side effect, and the FDA wasn't requiring the label change, but Blum agreed to it. He also said, however, that any new hemolytic anemia reports should also be faxed in immediately.

This offhand request, he believed, had serendipitously uncovered a looming public health crisis.

Six days later, Abbott was suddenly reporting that in fact it had twenty cases of hemolytic anemia and was hiring hematology consultants. Blum recalled being suspicious and checking to make sure that the company had reported every one of those seventeen new cases within fifteen days of receipt. But everything checked out.

"From our standpoint, it looked like they were being up front about it," he said, somewhat wistfully. "I *felt* they were up front."

Blum must have been less convinced after speaking with me, because when I got back to my office in Philadelphia the next day, there was a phone message from his boss, Dr. Bilstad. He wanted to know if I would be willing to share a copy of "that Table 7" with the agency. Specifically, Bilstad wanted to know if I'd share it with the FDA's Division of Compliance—still Frances Kelsey's Cops, although the new head of scientific investigations was a woman named Mary Richardson. I said I would think about it, but only if I could share the information in the form of an interview with Richardson and her staff. I wanted to know what kind of investigation they had done when Omniflox was withdrawn, and what, if anything, they would do with Table 7.

Three weeks later, I was sitting across from a tribunal of FDA Compliance officers including Richardson, a strong-jawed, middle-aged woman, and George Praeger, an affably overburdened, heavyset investigator with tinted glasses and a beard who had done some of the original legwork on Omniflox. At the far end of the table was Dr. Alan Lisook, the longtime head of the clinical investigations branch, whose gaunt, kindly visage brought to mind a time-lapsed version of children's TV personality Mr. Rogers. Lisook had seniority by decades—he had worked under Kelsey in the 1960s—and he was the sole M.D. in the group, so it made sense for him to be the one to explain what part Compliance played in the FDA approval process.

As the FDA grew in the 1970s and 1980s, each division got bigger, and the role of Kelsey's "scientific investigators" changed. Once an integral part of the medical evaluation of drugs, the Compliance police are now a wholly separate division to which cases and suspicions get reported only if the medical officer on the beat can't handle them. It is a much bigger effort, but more separated from the day-to-day work of the Center for Drug Evaluation and Research.

Compliance officers don't feel much like sheriffs anymore. And they still don't walk a beat. They don't regularly stop by drug company labs unannounced to see if a patient is having an adverse reaction or if a lab assistant is writing down the correct blood cell count. Basically, until a screamingly obvious problem presents itself for investigation, Compliance has only one main responsibility. Before a drug is approved, the division's Office of Drug Evaluation is supposed to double-check the handful of studies that the manufacturer and the FDA agree are the most pivotal in proving that the drug is safe and effective. For each malady a drug is approved to treat—each "indication" on the label—the company has to have two of what are called "adequate and well-controlled studies." Compliance officers are supposed to reassure the agency that the studies were in fact controlled *well,* by traveling to the sites of the clinical research—where the subjects were actually seen and tested—and then comparing the raw data in the file cabinets to the summaries submitted to the agency. The FDA maintains field offices in many major U.S. cities, from which Compliance officers are dispatched to do domestic inspections. If the studies have been done in Europe or in the Far East, a Compliance officer is supposed to hop on a plane from Washington and fly to the remote location to do an inspection.

Dr. Lisook took great pains to explain that the FDA has an actual checklist of things that must be done before a drug can be approved, and inspection reports of the sites for the "adequate, well-controlled trials" was on the list. The checklist isn't in the regulations, he said, it's just a practice that developed over the years. I told him that, of course, I'd like to see the Omniflox site reports, as well as its actual checklist. He assured me there would be no problem.

Our conversation moved on to how Compliance had responded to the Omniflox withdrawal. What had they done to satisfy themselves that

Abbott had always been up front with the FDA about any problems or potential problems with the drug? The truth was, they had done very little. Mostly, they had rechecked the notes of a minor investigation the agency had done in 1989 of one research facility in Fort Myers, Florida. It was a small, for-profit lab, exactly the kind of place that pharmacologists at major universities feel is undermining the credibility of industry drug research. Large drug studies were once done in a few big nonprofit institutions with hundreds of volunteers, among whose experiences trends might emerge. Now the same studies are more likely to be subcontracted to a for-profit firm—a contract research organization (CRO)—which will further subcontract to smaller, for-profit labs in the United States or Europe that might study fewer than a dozen patients each. Some pharmacologists believe that the reason Omniflox's severe toxicities weren't picked up in preapproval testing is because contract research firms had studied too few people at each site.

The problems at the lab in Fort Myers grew out of a dispute over the number of adverse reactions to Omniflox that the researchers were reporting. In 1988 Abbott had become generally worried about high rates of reported adverse reactions to Omniflox in several trials comparing the drug with another company's quinolone. The company decided that the reason for these reports was not that the drug was causing more adverse reactions, but that something was wrong with the forms that the clinical investigators were using to *report* the reactions. The forms didn't have a space to allow the investigator to blame "concurrent conditions"—whatever was wrong with the patient in the first place—for a new symptom rather than an adverse reaction to the drug.

To address this problem, the company had to bend a principal canon of science and change the protocols—its written code of rules and definitions under which any scientific study is conducted—for all eight of its ongoing experiments. It created a protocol amendment, which appeared to be minor to the FDA and was routinely approved.

But down in the clinical trenches, the amendment was a paperwork nightmare. The researchers in Fort Myers fought with Abbott over what information should be transferred from the old forms to the new ones. The researchers claimed that Abbott was leaning on them for overreporting "minor reactions that other clinical investigation sites were ignoring." Abbott framed the dispute as an argument over redoing paperwork—which it may very well have been, because a lot of the lab's paperwork turned up missing.

The FDA had looked into this matter in 1989, and again after the drug was withdrawn, deciding both times it was a red herring. The only other issue Compliance had noted was that several months after Omniflox was withdrawn, Abbott reported two international cases of deaths associated with the drug. This was well after the deadline for such reports, but since the FDA did not have any evidence that this slowness was deliberate or part of a pattern, it didn't pursue Abbott for this technical violation of the law. The company hadn't even received a warning letter.

It sounded as though the Omniflox investigation had been dead until Dr. Bilstad called Compliance and suggested they talk to me. Now, they were "very interested" in the documents I had. "I would like to get my hands on them," said George Praeger, who would actually be looking into the paperwork I would be handing over.

I asked if they could share anything about the investigation with me. "I can tell you it's still active," he said.

CHAPTER 12

"What If Things

Go South?"

Back at home, I finally had a chance to compare all the different chronologies of what had happened with Omniflox. From the FDA, I had Dr. Blum's personal version, Compliance's version, and the version that was presented by various FDA people at a postmortem advisory committee meeting several months after the drug's withdrawal.

While I had no official chronology from Abbott, I had copies of lengthy depositions that the Branch law firm had taken from more than fifteen of the top people involved with the drug. In Chicago, I had also gone through the public documents available from the shareholders' class action suit against Abbott. I was certainly less sympathetic to the stockholders' cause. After meeting Velva Conrad, it was a little hard for me to feel weepy for investors who felt betrayed when Abbott's stock price temporarily dropped and the company took a $215 million write-off for lost development, marketing and legal costs associated with Omniflox. But I was impressed with the stockholders' legal team, which was headed in Chicago by a very bright, careful lawyer named Ron Futterman. Judging from their interrogatories and their questions during deposition, the lawyers in the shareholder suit seemed to have a much more specific understanding of the Omniflox situation than the patients' lawyers did.

Sitting at my computer surrounded by piles of documents and binders, like a rock musician encircled by more keyboards than he could possibly play, I tried to piece together the last days of Omniflox. Down the hall, Diane was at her computer working away as well. For the first time since she had been Floxed, she appeared to be engaged in a new writing project. She wouldn't tell me what it was, but the fact that she felt inspired again both heartened me and freed me to concentrate on a drug other than the one she had taken. Whenever I made a really essential connection between two seemingly disparate documents, I would call her in to try and explain why I was so excited.

"Good, good," she would say, "but can't I just read it when you're *done*? I'm trying to *work* here."

Who knew what, when? The trail began in the early winter of 1991, just before Omniflox's January 1992 approval. In the weeks after the drug was handed off to him, Blum had been working on getting the final labeling prepared and doing the final review of safety information. Of the 4,261 test patients whose experiences would form the basis of the Omniflox approval, nearly a third of them were added only weeks before that approval to justify a new indication for lower respiratory tract infections. Abbott pushed hard for that indication at the last minute because the FDA had just taken it away from its main competitors. On November 1, 1991, Floxin and Cipro had been stripped of their lower respiratory tract indications by the Anti-Infective Drugs Advisory Committee, because they appeared to have lost their ability to kill strep pneumonia. A pharmaceutical stock analyst predicted that these two relabelings could be worth an additional $200 million a year in Omniflox sales to Abbott, which submitted the safety data on 1,314 new patients to Blum on December 14, 1991.

Blum spent as much time as he could with the new information, considering that he had a dozen other drugs to worry about and the holidays were approaching. His final safety update, submitted only a week before the drug was approved, didn't focus on any of the new cases, but he did single out a case that had been reported to Dr. Reed, his retired colleague, the previous fall. A fifty-seven-year-old woman had enrolled in an Omniflox trial in October 1990 after being diagnosed with a bacterial infection on top of her chronic bronchitis. It was a double-blind trial, two unmarked drugs, and the patient initially got better. But after ten days on her study drug, she was hospitalized with kidney failure and disseminated intravascular coagulation (DIC), a life-threatening blood coagulation disorder. This was serious dysfunction in two separate body systems. Four days later, the study "blind" was broken to reveal that she was taking Omniflox.

The patient's physician believed that the antibiotic had caused both of her conditions, and indeed, she recovered from both ailments after she stopped taking the drug. However, when, as is customary, Abbott sent a letter about her case to all the other Omniflox clinical investigators who were testing the drug, the company reported her doctor's findings in a more equivocating manner, saying that the "precise relationship of the study drug . . . is difficult to ascertain" because the patient had not been "rechallenged." To be rechallenged is to agree to take a drug that made you sick to see if it makes you sick again. It rarely happens— who in their right mind would do it, except by accident?—but drug companies invariably note that it wasn't done.

The case went down in the books as a drug-related renal failure and DIC, a very rare, very serious adverse event. Blum noted the incident in his medical review, which Dr. Reed had not, and suggested the incident be mentioned in the labeling. But after further internal discussion, Blum's superiors decided not to force Abbott to add it.

On January 30, 1992, Omniflox was officially approved by the FDA. From what the people in Compliance had told me, the drug should not have been approved unless a field inspection had been done of the labs that had conducted the key studies leading to approval, including the studies for the last-minute lower respiratory indication. Dr. Lisook's office had been slow in getting me copies of those inspection reports, so I called him up looking for them.

He said he had just discovered that the inspections were never done.

"I couldn't find that we had done any assignments for validating any studies for the drug approval," he said sheepishly, although not quite as sheepishly as I would have expected. "It appears this must have fallen through the cracks." More amazing than his words was his ability to say them without betraying any feeling that this was a really crucial problem.

"I don't think this is of any practical concern," he explained, "because *if we can ignore the documents you have seen and provided* [my emphasis] and make the assumption that the major problem . . . was something of a low incidence and only occurred when the drug was marketed, it's not what we look for in our inspection anyway."

"*Shouldn't* you be looking for that in your inspection?" I wondered aloud.

"Well, only in the past year have we developed an activity that is aimed at the nonreporting by the sponsor [the drug company] of important data," he said. "We have been checking what the [clinical] investigator has done, but had not checked on what the sponsor had been submitting to us."

As he double-spoke, I began to realize that everything I had been told about Omniflox was true. It *was* a perfect example of how the system works. And a perfectly frightening example at that.

.   .   .

Regardless of whether the site inspections were done, or even ordered, the first prescription for Omniflox was written on February 24, 1992. It wasn't until April 22 that Blum first contacted Abbott to inquire further about the hypoglycemia reactions. He called Jeanne Fox, Abbott's assistant director of regulatory affairs, to talk about the three reports of Omniflox-related low blood sugar that had made their way to his desk.

By that time, however, the company's medical affairs division had received at least eight more reports of serious low blood sugar, including one patient who eventually died from it and another who had hypoglycemia *and* kidney failure. But according to Fox's own memo, she didn't mention any of these other cases to Blum on the phone, even though she had signed one of the hypoglycemia reports that very morning.

She also didn't mention that the company had received at least twenty-seven other reports of serious adverse reactions that were even more ominous. There were seven cases of kidney failure, five cases of hemolytic anemia, four cases in which patients experienced kidney failure *and* hemolytic anemia, six cases of lesser hemolytic, kidney or liver problems, and one death from anaphylactic shock.

Jeanne Fox particularly neglected to mention to Blum the flurry of activity within the company concerning these reactions, even though the 1639 reports were all being sent to the FDA by regular mail, as if they were nothing much out of the ordinary. Meetings were being held, numbers were being crunched and databases were being searched. Table 7, the list of drug reactions reported *pre*approval that were similar to the ones Abbott was surprised to be seeing *post*approval, was just one of the many documents produced for internal use during that frantic period inside the "quinolone venture."

Nobody at the FDA—and apparently nobody within the massive sales force out promoting Omniflox—was clued in.

Blum called Jeanne Fox at Abbott again five days later, after receiving two more hypoglycemia reports. This time she mentioned that five or six more of them were on their way and Blum requested she start faxing him the hypoglycemia reports in addition to putting them in the mail.

"He seems to be getting quite concerned," she wrote in the memo she always sent around to the top regulatory and medical personnel after a contact with the FDA.

But Fox still didn't say anything to Blum about the company's mounting concern about the hemolytic anemia and kidney failure reports, even after the FDA told Abbott it wanted to have a meeting in Washington to discuss the hypoglycemia cases. As Blum had told me, Abbott agreed during "the May seventh meeting" to add a hypoglycemia warning to the Omniflox label and disseminate information to physicians via its sales force. They also agreed that if the reports didn't subside after a month or so, Abbott would send a "Dear Doctor" letter to all prescribing physicians about the problem. The tail end of the meeting was when Abbott brought up hemolytic anemia reactions to Omniflox.

At that moment, the FDA had received three reports of hemolytic anemia, and Abbott neglected to mention that any more were on the way.

In fact, seventeen more cases were already on the way or, at the very least, had already been reported to Abbott—according to a handwritten chart discovered by plaintiffs' lawyers. When Blum agreed to add hemolytic anemia, he told the company to fax him any new reports *immediately*. But it wasn't until six days after the meeting that Blum got that call from Jeanne Fox that the company suddenly had reports of twenty cases of hemolytic anemia. When he received the actual 1639s on the cases, he checked to see if the company was technically "in compliance"—that the forms had been mailed within fifteen days of the date each had been received. Apparently they were. But clearly Abbott had not done what Blum had asked. And clearly its corporate posture was that this was probably not any big deal. In fact, the company had hired two hematology consultants to verify that it wasn't any big deal.

To the physicians reporting the reactions, however, it was a *very* big deal. I was able to track down the upstate New York internist who reported the first hemolytic anemia case. "The most severe drug reaction I've seen in my forty years of practice," he told me. "I usually don't use drugs until they've been out for a while, but . . . I think probably the advertising was so good, it swayed me."

In the meantime, the Abbott sales force pounded away at doctors, trying to get them to write more prescriptions for Omniflox or try their patients on samples. On May 8, after visits from two different drug reps extolling the virtues of the drug, Dr. Thomas Hayes, a family practitioner in Albuquerque, New Mexico, decided to give his patient Velva Conrad samples of Omniflox for her urinary tract infection instead of the Floxin she had used the last time. All over the world, doctors were doing the same thing. In less than four months, U.S. physicians alone would write approximately 250,000 scripts for Omniflox and distribute untold thousands of free samples. The salespeople would be the last to know about the reports of problems with the drug, because most of what they were hearing back from their customers, the doctors, was pretty positive.

While the sales reps were kept in the dark, Abbott was frank when addressing its corporate executives. In a May 18 memo to all the international offices—marked "Urgent!"—Dr. Romeo Bachand, vice president of scientific affairs and quality assurance, explained that there had been twenty-four instances of hemolytic anemia coincident with the use of Omniflox. He described what Dr. Blum would later call the Temafloxacin Syndrome: "the syndrome is characterized by abdominal pain, fever and chills and jaundice, dark urine and hemoglobinuria," he wrote. ". . . A direct cause-and-effect relationship has not been established, but is suspected for at least some of the cases."

After detailing other severe reactions, Bachand went on to tell his international affiliates they should be on the lookout for hemolytic anemia and hypoglycemia cases. But they were not to mention any of this to their local regulatory authorities until the company had developed "a global regulatory strategy." He promised a package for submission by the end of the week.

At the same time, the company was drafting a "Dear Doctor" letter that seemed far more protective of its product than the public's health. "Dear Doctor," it read, "During routine postmarketing monitoring, Abbott Laboratories has received a low incidence (in the range of one in 10,000) of reports of serious adverse events in patients who were taking Omniflox. A number of these [adverse drug reactions] have been reported under the putative diagnosis of hemolytic anemia, but many may have been misclassified. The pathogenesis of these disorders is unknown."

Meanwhile, Mike Blum sat in his cramped office in the Parklawn Building trying to figure out what could be causing these Omniflox reactions. For the moment, all his other drugs would have to wait. He began flooding Abbott with questions. He wondered if it could be a problem with the dosage of the drug, or perhaps a flaw in the manufacturing process. He wondered if it was a problem with its basic chemical structure, which led him to ask the company about another quinolone it had invented at the same time, tosufloxacin. That drug, which for years had been considered more promising than the compound that became Omniflox, made it all the way to Phase III before the company found that it caused crystals in the urine, which was often predictive of drug-related kidney damage. Tosufloxacin was abandoned for possible U.S. approval but was approved with no problem in Japan, where it was being successfully marketed. As chemical compounds, tosufloxacin and Omniflox had something in common structurally that was different from all other quinolones. Blum hoped the Japanese experience with the drug might shed some light on the situation. But it didn't.

Blum also started asking more questions about that one case of kidney failure and DIC he had flagged just before the drug was approved. He felt that case was very similar to the ones he was starting to see.

Abbott management either failed to grasp just how precarious the situation was or simply believed they could market their way around any safety problem. The company proceeded as if the worst that could happen was that Omniflox would get a harsher label warning. As Blum's concern mounted, he learned on May 28 that Abbott actually planned to go ahead with its delayed "launch campaign" anyway. The FDA's division of drug advertising and labeling had just approved the revised slogan, and everything was immediately sent to the printer. Blum was concerned that a dramatic boost in advertising would cause even more patients to take the drug, and later the same day, Abbott regulatory affairs got a call from Dr. Bruce Burlington, then the deputy director of the Office of Drug Evaluation II at CDER. Burlington suggested they hold off on the launch, which they did, and consider halting all further promotion of Omniflox.

Four days later, Abbott executives were summoned back to Rockville. The two sides couldn't have been further apart. The FDA was there to convince Abbott to stop promoting Omniflox altogether or perhaps even to withdraw it. Abbott, however, showed up armed with reports from its hired hematology consultants that many of the cases had either been incorrectly blamed on Omniflox or misdiagnosed as a serious blood disorder.

While hemolytic anemia is sometimes a judgment-call diagnosis, Abbott pushed its luck when it then tried to convince the FDA that the reported adverse reactions to Omniflox were no different from reports for other quinolones. The way that Abbott epidemiologists appeared to jerry-rig their analysis only raised even more suspicion. The company had prepared a table comparing the first three and a half months of Omniflox reports with the first twelve to fourteen months of Cipro. They justified the disparate time frames, which just happened to make the total number of reports nearly equal, by claiming that Abbott had so many more sales reps working on Omniflox than Miles had in the first year of Cipro that this was the only fair comparison.

The FDA didn't buy it, but agency epidemiologists were intrigued by the idea of comparing Omniflox with its competitors. They set out to make a chart of their own. On June 4 Abbott received a fax of the FDA's version of the quinolone challenge. The numbers were horrifying. When adjusted for the number of prescriptions written and the differences in marketing budgets, the other quinolones had between thirteen and twenty-five reported adverse reactions per 100,000 prescriptions in the first 120 days on the market. Omniflox had 108. For serious adverse reactions, the others had between three and six reports per 100,000 prescriptions. Omniflox had twenty-eight.

These data had just been presented at the FDA to all the various regulatory officials who had been involved with Omniflox, including Burlington and his boss, Dr. Carl Peck, the top man at CDER. In case anyone there had any doubts, three reports of Omniflox-related deaths had just come in that week. After the meeting Burlington told Abbott's representatives he wanted to see them *the next day* to discuss the very dim future of Omniflox.

If the handwritten notes taken by Abbott's Dr. Romeo Bachand are any indication, the June 5, 1992, meeting at the FDA was a bloodbath for Abbott. The company apparently still believed it could convince the agency that all these adverse effects could be handled through labeling. The best deal the FDA offered was that, instead of withdrawal, the company could suspend its sales of the drug, do more research and resubmit the drug for a less broad spectrum of indications. Abbott's counteroffer was a "Dear Doctor" letter, hand-delivered by sales reps, and an agreement to stop promotion and let the reps use only minimal printed material in their sales pitches. Anything more, Abbott said, and the product "will be dead . . . and it's too early to take that step."

Burlington was finished playing around. "We must halt patient exposure," he said. The agency had already prepared a press release about Omniflox safety. If Abbott wouldn't voluntarily withdraw the drug, the FDA planned to send out the release without the company's imprimatur.

The agency was even willing to go a step further. Burlington threatened a criminal prosecution. "He invoked Justice," Abbott's Roland Catherall recalled in a deposition. "Which meant . . . if we weren't ready to do something . . . they were ready to go to the Department of Justice."

Omniflox was dead. The leaders of the Abbott contingent trudged off to call their president and COO, Thomas Hodgson. The leaders of the FDA contingent trudged off to call their chairman, Dr. David Kessler. The final press release was prepared, and frantic phone messages started going out to all the Abbott sales reps. It was a Friday, and the story of the emergency worldwide withdrawal was going to be in the papers Monday. The company wanted to make sure its salesmen heard it from them rather than reading it in *The Wall Street Journal*—which is where most doctors got the news.

The next day, a letter went out to all the sales and marketing reps telling them to stop the promotion of Omniflox and destroy all promotional materials, including pens, magnets and mugs. According to the reps' "Discussion Guide," they were to hand the prescribing physicians they worked with a letter about the recall, and while they could respond to doctors' questions, "conversation on this matter should *not* be initiated." The letter went on to say "it is unfortunate this has occurred" but there were "enormous opportunities" available with the company's other drugs. In fact, they would immediately begin selling Biaxin (clarithromycin), Abbott's other new antibiotic. "You will be receiving training and other information on Biaxin," the letter said, "to prepare you to promote this exciting new product."

It was only after the fact that regulatory officials in some of the other countries where Omniflox was being sold found out about the problems with the drug. Because most of them do not make their correspondences public like the FDA, it is hard to know exactly how they reacted to the news. But a letter from the British Department of Health, discovered in Abbott's files by plaintiffs' lawyers, gives a good indication of the outrage.

Three days after Abbott was forced to withdraw Omniflox in the United States and then decided to withdraw it worldwide as well, Abbott U.K. sent a letter about the withdrawal to the Medicines Control Agency (MCA) office on Nine Elms Lane in Southwest London. With the letter were a number of new adverse reaction reports about Teflox, as the drug was known in the U.K., some dating back five months. Apparently this was the first time that anyone at the MCA had been informed of any serious adverse reactions to a drug that had been on the market there for eight months. According to the letter from Dr. Susan Wood, the head of pharmacovigilance, the MCA was "extremely concerned" that the reactions hadn't been reported previously, and she suggested that Abbott had failed to comply with its statutory obligations. The tone of the letter suggested that if the drug *hadn't* been withdrawn, the MCA might have revoked Abbott's license to sell it anyway because the company hadn't reported the serious reactions.

Dr. Wood expressed her additional concern that Abbott might not have fulfilled its ADR reporting requirements for its other drugs licensed by the MCA. While it remains unclear what actions the MCA took against the company, internal documents show that Abbott began taking steps to reorganize its international system for reporting adverse reactions.

.   .   .

As I sat in my office piecing together the last days of the drug "designed to exceed the reach of other quinolones," I continued to wonder what lessons the drug development process should have learned from Omniflox. What I saw was that once the drug was off the market, nobody was very interested in learning anything from it at all—except for Mike Blum, who had nervously made what he considered "the ultimate judgment call" against Omniflox and kept wondering if he had guessed correctly. A month after the drug was withdrawn, the Omniflox situation was presented by the FDA at an Anti-Infective Drugs Advisory Committee meeting. After all, there were still four other quinolones on the market, with many others in development, and anything new that could be learned about their toxicities would be important to public health.

Abbott was urged to send scientists and executives to Rockville to be part of the meeting. But the company flatly refused. According to Blum, he also urged the company to do some postwithdrawal studies to help figure out why the drug caused these side effects and why they hadn't been picked up during development. If the company ever did those studies, they were never shared with the FDA or the public. Several months after the withdrawal, Blum was encouraged when the manufacturers of some of Omniflox's competitors expressed interest in further research on such reactions during the big annual international quinolone meeting. But it never happened.

With little new information available except what Abbott legally had to continue to report to the FDA—just the adverse reaction forms—Blum and his colleagues could satisfy their curiosity only by doing a statistical analysis of the very raw data and publish that. They focused in on the ninety-five clearest cases and made the bold pronouncement that Omniflox "causes immune hemolytic anemia . . . [or] what we have chosen to call the temafloxacin syndrome." Their conclusion of an immune response to Omniflox—basically that, in some people, the drug caused the body's immune system to create antibodies against the drug and attack its own red blood cells—is a controversial one. The FDA does not regularly force antibiotic manufacturers to test for antibodies against their compounds. Blum also found that those patients who developed the syndrome after taking just one pill of Omniflox were more likely to have used another quinolone previously.

Another very interesting side finding of Blum's analysis was how doctors had prescribed Omniflox during its brief time on the market. Half the patients he and his colleagues studied had been given Omniflox for illnesses that the drug was not even approved to treat. Off-label use itself is no surprise. But so large a percentage of off-label prescriptions with a new, unproven drug does raise some troubling questions about prescribing practices.

This is especially true because patients don't always have the same rights to legal redress if a drug is given for an off-label use. At least one Omniflox case, in which a doctor who gave the drug to *himself* later died from multiple organ failure, was thrown out of a federal court in Delaware simply because it was an off-label use. After that decision, several other cases were quickly settled when plaintiffs' attorneys feared the same thing could happen to their clients.

While I thought the paper Blum and his colleagues prepared raised some very provocative questions that should interest any physician who prescribes antibiotics, the major journals did not agree. "We tried to get it into *JAMA*," he told me, "but they had trouble with it and felt it was for a more narrow audience. We were hoping for a broader primary-care audience. We wanted to get the idea out in the community that this can happen with a drug. So they should be especially cautious about off-label use just after a drug is approved." After *JAMA* rejected the article, it appeared in the smaller journal *Clinical Infectious Diseases.*

Other small journals weighed in on how these severe adverse reactions had avoided the radar of the FDA approval process. One theory was that Abbott had done no wrong, and the adverse reactions were simply the unavoidable result of testing the drug on only 4,500 patients before approval; statistically, some serious reactions will happen less frequently than that and show themselves only when the drug reaches the general population.

What was creepy about that assessment was that a version of this syndrome *did* show up, full-blown, at least once during the clinical trials. It was the case of that fifty-seven-year-old woman with renal failure and DIC. The company had disagreed with the prescribing doctor over whether the drug was definitely the culprit, but the case was clearly known to the FDA in 1990, more than a year before approval.

To satisfy my curiosity, I then compared the number of serious hemolytic incidents reported postmarketing with the number of patients who had taken the drug during its four months on the market. Ironically, the ratio was almost exactly the same: about one in five thousand.

So in essence, Omniflox was withdrawn from the market for having *the identical safety profile it displayed in clinical trials.* In a way, it all had been predicted by that one case—a case that, by itself, probably wouldn't have kept the drug from being approved even if Sid Wolfe had been the FDA medical officer.

As I pondered this, I found myself wondering if the Omniflox story might actually reflect more poorly on the regulatory process than on Abbott. Maybe the FDA approval process was every bit as onerous and stupid as its harshest critics said it was. Maybe Abbott's behavior with the FDA was nothing more than a cynical response to a dysfunctional system. Maybe I should have a little more sympathy for a company that had wasted hundreds of millions of dollars on a drug that passed all the government tests, but still failed.

Then I got hold of the Weisberg deposition. After that, my sympathies returned to their rightful owner.

Dr. Gerald Weisberg had spent ten years in private practice in Chicago as an endocrinologist before coming to Abbott in late 1991. His new job, as associate medical director of medical services, put him on the front line of all adverse drug reaction reports, as well as inquiries about Abbott products. If a practicing physician called with a question or complaint about an Abbott drug, that doctor would speak with Weisberg, or one of his staff.

Weisberg had been deposed not by the Branch firm for the patients' suits but by the lawyers for the shareholders. I previously had read through dozens of depositions with Abbott executives. All of them had been well prepared to dodge provocative questions with "I don't remember." Many even claimed that they really didn't understand why Omniflox had been taken off the market.

Either Dr. Weisberg hadn't been prepped, or he just refused to toe the company party line. His deposition began at 9:15 A.M. on October 28, 1994, and well before the lunch break he had already made it clear that from very early on he disagreed with his superiors about the way they were interpreting the adverse reactions to Omniflox. Weisberg said he recalled that when the first hypoglycemia cases came in, he met with his bosses to discuss how they were being *framed,* what *context* they were being put in, for the FDA. He was told that the company believed that all the hypoglycemia cases were patients who were elderly or had preexisting impaired renal function.

It was his medical opinion that some of these cases could *not* be so easily explained away. But Weisberg recalled that Abbott regulatory affairs chief Roland Catherall, who was not a medical doctor, dismissively told him "that's the way it was discussed and agreed upon with the FDA." When Weisberg tried to pursue the point, he recalled being told, "Let's move on."

Weisberg also said that he had begun to notice the frequency of hemolytic anemia and renal failure reports in the latter part of March, almost six weeks before anyone bothered to mention them to the FDA. After noticing the disturbing reports, he created special data sheets so that additional information about hemolytic and renal failure adverse reactions could be collected when phone calls came in. This was also done in March. Then in early April, he called a hematology expert and asked "whether in his opinion a quinolone could cause hemolytic anemia."

Later in April there was another meeting where the six new cases of hypoglycemia were discussed. Weisberg remembered being told by a nonphysician member of the quinolone venture that the reactions were to be blamed on drugs other than Omniflox—one on a beta-blocker the patient was taking, another on aspirin. Weisberg found these explanations "unlikely, based on the real world clinical experience."

During his second day of depositions Weisberg made an oblique reference to a conversation he had in mid-April with his boss, Dr. Ralph Stoll, the director of Abbott's medical drug risk assessment and communications department. He recalled that Stoll "offered information relative to the frequency of adverse events seen or allegedly seen with Omniflox." It wasn't immediately clear why this interchange was important, but the shareholders' attorney, Ron Futterman, pursued it doggedly. After a hundred more questions, each only minutely different from the one before, and several vigorous objections by defense counsel, Futterman was finally able to get Weisberg to come out and say what he seemed so torn about saying.

During this conversation in April, Dr. Stoll apparently had discussed drugs that had been withdrawn from the market for serious adverse reactions. According to Weisberg, Stoll said that Omniflox was already exhibiting "the frequency of adverse events and the particular adverse events that historically had led to compounds which had been on the market no longer being on the market." Stoll had actually prepared a typewritten list of six or seven drugs that had been withdrawn, along with the incidence figures for the adverse reaction that got each in trouble. He gave Weisberg a copy of the list and made it clear that Omniflox could soon be on it.

Weisberg also recalled that after his conversation with Stoll, and a subsequent conversation with his immediate superior, he and various members of the quinolone venture and the Abbott marketing department began running numbers to produce "incidence estimates" that might predict how many more patients could be expected to experience such serious adverse events. Weisberg wasn't exact with his dates, but he made it clear that some of the estimates had been done before "the May seventh meeting" with the FDA at which hemolytic anemia was brought up as a seeming afterthought.

After several more hours of questions, Weisberg was asked if he had ever discussed the Omniflox situation with Abbott's president and COO, Thomas Hodgson. He said he had been summoned to be part of a Sunday Omniflox briefing for Hodgson. Abbott officials were to meet with the FDA the next day and pitch their chart showing that Omniflox was no more toxic than any other quinolone. Weisberg, who was the person who had actually spoken to the doctors reporting the cases, clearly did not share his company's opinion.

Weisberg described his recollections of the meeting. He said he felt that he and his department were being made scapegoats in front of the company's president for all of Omniflox's problems because they had somehow "overreported" the serious adverse reactions. He recalled Paul Clark, the nonphysician who headed Abbott's entire pharmaceutical products division, suggesting that some changes needed to be made in the way adverse reactions were being reported to the government. Weisberg had responded that he "followed the regulations set forth by the FDA."

The discussion turned to what was going to happen at the FDA the next day. Weisberg remembered President Hodgson asking two or three different times, "What if things go south?" Each time he asked, someone in the group gave him an answer.

At the very end of the meeting, Weisberg recalled, Hodgson had only one more question. He asked "if anybody in the group thought that Abbott had done anything unprofessional or unethical."

The room fell dead silent and stayed that way.

Three weeks after Weisberg finished his second deposition, Abbott settled the shareholders' case for $32 million. Most of the personal injury cases, including Velva Conrad's, were eventually settled for under $500,000—many *well* under. Joan Hiddemen, the widow who first got me interested in Omniflox, settled for $35,000. After legal fees, she was left with $16,000.

In the end she was told that she should have had an autopsy done. And she couldn't stop replaying the conversation she had had with a hospital doctor just after her husband died. She had worked in that hospital, so when the doctor told her an autopsy was unnecessary— because her husband had recently been to his own physician—she said fine. "I have regretted that ever since," she said.

CHAPTER 13

Generation Rx

While I was deep into the Temafloxacin Syndrome, the Clinton health care plan, ill for many months, finally died. Its official time of death was late in the afternoon on September 26, 1994, when it was clear that the 103rd Congress would not act on the measure.

The pundits had been busy speculating on what the defeat meant for Clinton's political future, and for health care as a whole. I was more interested in how it affected the legal-drug business. When I came up for air after doing all I could with Omniflox—the FDA had officially reopened its investigation, and it was up to them to decide whether laws had been broken or just bent into very peculiar shapes—I started calling around another part of Washington. I wanted to hear how Clinton's health care debacle had played in the world of bitter pills.

One high-ranking White House aide was still defending the wisdom of using the drug companies as scapegoats for the high medical costs and selling the health care plan as an antidote to industry's high prices. "When you're launching a campaign like the effort to expand health care coverage, there have got to be enemies," the aide explained to me. "And the drug companies were not only a good enemy in terms of consumers, but they were also a good enemy in terms of policy. If our policies would have been adopted, it would have been fine. If they had thought it through, they would have recognized they were being singled out—they were a bogeyman of sorts—but the ultimate financial impact might have been helpful to them. If we had expanded the Medicare drug benefit [as the plan proposed], there would have been a lot more drugs being sold. They should have understood they were going to be a target, take it in stride and look to the long run."

To put the administration's decisions into perspective, this aide explained a little bit about how Clinton viewed the political clout of the drug companies. "There were not huge drug company contributions to the Democratic Party," he said. "I don't think there were any at all. But when you're attacking pharmaceuticals, you're attacking major employers in important states. In New Jersey, for example, or Ohio, there are major companies out there."

He noted, however, that while drug company power was concentrated in certain states, the pharmaceutical industry had always been divided as a national political force. The drug companies were so competitive that they rarely agreed on anything. Clinton hadn't counted on their finding a common enemy—in *him*. But the president's incessant attacks on industry, and his administration's refusal to let the companies save *any* face, allowed them to accomplish something they probably never would have otherwise: he taught them how to circle their wagons.

"We created a momentary truce among the pharmaceutical companies," the aide said, not very proudly. "The companies had never been well organized as a force on the Hill. They *became* well organized, thanks to what we did."

Another well-placed White House aide was more openly critical of the administration's tactics with drug companies. "It's all about the 'inside' strategy versus 'outside' strategy, and we tried to play it both ways," he said with a sigh, sitting in a restaurant near the Old Executive Office Building. "On the inside, we were working on members of Congress without being too negative against the drug companies. But on the outside, it felt like we were demonizing them. So with the outside strategy, we gave the industry incentives to spend all kinds of money against us. But if we were going to use that outside strategy, we should have gone all out. If you don't take them *out*, you can't keep up that level of debate. If you go after them, it can't be halfhearted. You either *do it* or you *don't*."

The aide took a long draw on his drink. "Personally I don't care," he said. "*They* make the political decisions. But this inside/outside strategy didn't seem to score many points. The Hill was pissed off. They would call up and say, 'Don't be mean to my drug industries.' But if you asked most of the public, it didn't seem like it was a strongly repeated message."

The aide saw this inside/outside strategy as emblematic of Clinton's inability to understand Washington during his first two years in office. But he felt that using the tactic against drug manufacturers was particularly ill advised. The aide had a lot of experience working on pharmaceutical issues, and he had come to believe that drug manufacturers were the last people on earth you should attack subtly.

"These are CEOs who, if someone says their hair is parted wrong, they call up their PR person," he said with a chuckle. "Anything that in the least bit sheds negative public *whatever* on them, they go crazy. . . . Few people have the expertise to take them on. And there are so many reasons why *not* to take them on. For most politicians, it usually becomes 'Oh shit, let's not do it.'

"They are very influential in key states: Connecticut, New Jersey, Pennsylvania. But the bigger problem is that it's so easy to be overwhelmed with their information. They just *bore you to death.* Senator David Pryor used to say that going after the drug industry was like following someone into a forest, but the forest grows up right behind them. They leave no tracks, and they have all these lawyers who make sure they find no documentation."

Six weeks after the health care bill breathed its last, Clinton and the Democratic Party were stunned by a massive Republican victory in the midterm elections and the seemingly overnight rise to power of conservative House Speaker Newt Gingrich. Only a pharmaceutical conspiracy theorist would believe that the drug companies were the main driving force behind this Republican revolution. But it did seem more than just coincidence that Gingrich's broad antiregulation message was being sold politically through attacks on only one regulatory body: the Food and Drug Administration.

Gingrich had taken to describing the FDA as "the leading job-killer in America." He was spouting the anti-FDA rhetoric of the conservative think tanks to which the pharmaceutical industry had turned in its hour of need. Both the anti-FDA rhetoric and Gingrich's deregulatory stance had been well known before the election, but the Speaker's newfound political power suddenly brought the issues to the national agenda. Full-page ads were beginning to appear in national newspapers with the slogan, "If a murderer kills you, it's homicide. If a drunk driver kills you, it's manslaughter. If the FDA kills you, it's just being cautious."

The rhetoric was so heavy-handed, it could only be seen as a payback for the lashing the industry had absorbed, like a recent pronouncement from Democratic representative Pete Stark during a hearing about a doomed proposal to force doctors to report fatal adverse drug reactions. "These crumbs at the Pharmaceutical Manufacturers Association [are] the worst people in this country," he railed. "They do not want the FDA to do anything. They would kill everybody for a nickel if they had their way."

While Gingrich was leading the charge, the anti-FDA campaign was being funded and orchestrated by the Washington Legal Foundation (WLF), a conservative public interest law firm that views itself as a sort of ACLU for business. The WLF had been founded in 1976 by a former U.S. Interior Department lawyer, Dan Popeo, who opened a one-room office with a small bank loan and had his wife typing at night. By the mid-1980s *The Washington Post* was reporting that the WLF had a $2 million budget and nearly 200,000 dues-paying members, although nearly half of its money came from conservative foundations and large corporations.

The WLF had gotten interested in FDA issues, not coincidentally, within a year of Clinton's election. The group had filed a petition in 1993 to stop a proposed rule change about how the FDA regulated the way information about off-label uses of prescription drugs was given to doctors. It is an extremely delicate issue that goes to the very heart of the FDA's precarious mission, and the WLF was attacking it with a sledgehammer.

There is, clearly, a free speech dilemma at the heart of the FDA's off-label drug policy. Companies want doctors to "learn" about off-label uses, but they are prohibited from actually "promoting" these new uses until they have done the testing required to get the drug formally approved for a new indication. Since almost all continuing medical education on drugs is funded, directly or indirectly, by pharmaceutical companies, it would take an electron microscope to see the line between education and promotion. Consequently, many judgment calls are made concerning the boundaries of propriety.

The FDA wanted new, crystal-clear rules on this issue. The WLF saw any rules as "censorship" and "suppression" of medical information; their ads noted that in the name of "protecting" the public, the outdated FDA rules had prevented aspirin makers from publicizing the off-label use of the drug to prevent heart attacks and slowed the flow of information about new cancer treatments. Its 1993 petition turned into a June 1994 lawsuit, in which the WLF was joined by an unlikely coalition of conservative groups and often liberal journalistic organizations, who were in it for the free speech. By early 1995 the lawsuit had become merely a springboard for an all-out attack on the FDA and everything it stood for. One full-page WLF ad in *The New York Times* would carry the slogan, "The problem with health care in America is the FDA."

But unlike the past twenty years, when the faceless bureaucracy of the drug industry had attacked the equally faceless bureaucracy of the FDA, the war now had very public, recognizable gladiators. It was Newt Gingrich against the man he had recently called "a thug and a bully": Dr. David Kessler, the most ambitious, high-profile, politically adept chairman the FDA ever had.

David Kessler had confounded and amazed both his critics and his sycophants. The youngest FDA commissioner ever—five years into his reign, he still hadn't hit forty-five—he was also the first to take the power of the office seriously enough to wield it himself.

Unlike regulators from the Frances Kelsey era, Kessler didn't wait for somebody in Congress to hear about a new drug problem and run with it. He played his own politics. And for a man who was as nervous in public as he was bold—his words came out in clumps, even when his pronouncements were pre-scripted—he didn't frighten easily. He had a pediatrician's heart and a prosecutor's brain, with training in medicine and law from Harvard, Hopkins and Chicago, and he was the first to publicly acknowledge what everyone in the legal-drug world had known for decades: the FDA was never going to have the manpower, the money or the mandate necessary to do what the public *assumed* it was doing. The agency's budget was no larger than that of the New York hospital where he had served as medical director at the age of thirty-three. The FDA's only option was to regulate entire industries through fear and intimidation, publicly hanging those firms stupid or arrogant enough to get caught red-handed as a deterrent to everybody else.

To do that, Kessler first had to clean up the FDA itself.

For decades, Americans had been bemoaning the unfulfilled promises of the 1960s. But nowhere was the failure of that decade's idealism more chronic than at the FDA, which was once going to save the world but by the late 1980s could barely save itself. The post-thalidomide era had started with regulators, legislators and consumer activists marching arm in arm against the drug companies. But by 1973, when Long Island–born David Kessler graduated from Amherst and headed to Harvard, the situation had grown more complex.

The undermanned agency was still digesting the problems it had bitten off in the early 1960s. It took ten years after thalidomide for the United States and the other major industrial powers to get their new drug regulatory statutes in place and even vaguely operational. Not only did the testing of new drugs have to be revolutionized to meet new standards of safety and efficacy, but manufacturers were also required to prove to the FDA that all four thousand of the drugs approved since 1938 actually worked. It was years before all those older drugs were either proven effective or withdrawn from the U.S. market, and much of that time was spent in court. The drug companies challenged the government's right to demand efficacy—instead of the "testimonials" and "clinical impressions" of physicians that had previously been enough to get drugs approved—while the consumer advocates decried how slowly the drugs proven "ineffective" were being forced off the market. The Supreme Court eventually had to step in, ruling in favor of the FDA's mandate in June 1973. But it wasn't until the mid-1970s that randomized, double-blind clinical trials were regularly used to prove drugs worked.

In addition to the mounting difficulties of regulating medications, Congress decreed in 1976 that the FDA had to begin regulating medical devices as well. But it was what is known as an "unfunded mandate"— when the agency asked Congress to pay for the twelve hundred new employees needed to handle its new responsibilities, the request was turned down. The difficulties of this period were searingly explored in the groundbreaking book *Pills, Profits and Politics* by San Francisco physician-turned-medical-journalist Milton Silverman and UCSF pharmacologist Dr. Philip Lee (who would later become a high-ranking official at the FDA).

By the early 1980s the legal-drug world was changing, growing more aggressive and promotion-oriented as the companies fearlessly raised both their prices and their financial expectations. David Kessler brought his dual degrees to the Washington area in 1981, taking a day job as a health consultant to conservative Republican senator Orrin Hatch—after the more ideologically compatible Kennedy staff couldn't find room for him—while doing a pediatrics residency at Johns Hopkins at night. Soon after, drug scandals began erupting that reflected as badly on the agency as they did on industry. The 1982 congressional investigation of Oraflex, for example, showed that manufacturer Eli Lilly had criminally failed to report adverse reactions to its new, highly hyped arthritis drug—which ended up being yanked off the market in three months. But the Oraflex investigation also showed that the FDA's system for gathering those ADR reports was a disaster. The system was massively overhauled in 1983 by an outside epidemiologist, Jerry Faich, who is said to have been greeted by "rooms full of crates of unread reports . . . the stories you hear are hair-raising."

As the decade continued, the antiregulatory zeal of the Reagan administration punched the teeth out of the Federal Communications Commission, the Federal Aviation Administration and the Environmental Protection Agency. The FDA had had only baby teeth to begin with, so it didn't take much to dull its bite and render the agency nearly helpless. Not only did regulation come to a near standstill; so did approval of New Drug Applications. The major, research-oriented pharmaceutical companies had always dreamed of getting the FDA off their backs, but they hadn't counted on its slowing down drug approval even more.

And the slowdown came at the worst possible moment, because in 1984 Congress passed the Hatch-Waxman Drug Price Competition and Patent Term Restoration Act, a bill Hatch's staff had worked on while Kessler concentrated on food laws. The first major revision of the FDA law in two decades, Hatch-Waxman offered huge incentives for companies to make lower-priced generic versions of drugs. It included an exemption to the traditional FDA process that allowed generics to be preapproved, so manufacturers could make their investments, build their plants and be ready with cheaper generics the moment the patent expired. As a payback to the brand-name manufacturers, the bill also allowed those companies to apply for a patent extension of up to five years.

The law was not an immediate success. Doctors didn't switch patients to generics nearly as quickly as Hatch and Waxman had hoped. Old prescribing habits die hard, and study after study proved that doctors didn't know enough about drug prices to focus on changing prescriptions. For that reason, much of the time cheaper generic drugs didn't cause the name-brand products to come down in price—they just created two separate markets. The brand-name manufacturers that also owned generic manufacturing concerns simply learned how to compete more profitably against themselves.

But the bill did have one immediate impact. By making it ridiculously easy to get FDA approval for a generic, it brought many untested firms into the business. Some were less than scrupulous; others simply didn't know what they were doing. The FDA's naive honor code was quickly violated.

By the late 1980s the FDA was embroiled in a generic drug scandal, much of which was played out in the House Subcommittee on Oversight and Investigations of the Committee on Energy and Commerce, chaired by Michigan Democrat John Dingell. FDA employees were accused (and were later convicted) of taking bribes to push through the applications of certain generic firms faster than others; the generic business is based on speed, and whichever firm gets the first low-priced generic out there has a big advantage. At the same time, several firms were found to be making substandard generic medicines. Some pills were adulterated because of unsafe manufacturing processes. But others simply were not formulated correctly, so they weren't "bioequivalent" to the name-brand or "pioneer" drugs for which they were supposed to be substitutes. ("Bioequivalent" medications can have some differences in formulation and appearance, but they must deliver equal amounts of the same active ingredient.) The public grew fearful that generic drugs weren't such a medicinal bargain after all, and it blamed the FDA for approving them.

The agency was also under attack for being even slower than before in approving new drugs and medical devices. After the embattled commissioner of the FDA resigned in the fall of 1989, David Kessler, who had left Washington and spent the next six years as medical director of Albert Einstein Hospital in New York, was an obvious candidate to lobby for the job. More important, his influential former boss, Hatch, lobbied, too. Kessler's adversaries would later argue that the Bush administration botched its investigation into his background, never understanding that the heavyset, bearded and bespectacled New York doctor was a liberal Democrat in conservative Republican clothing. As soon as he got the job at the FDA, Kessler quickly shed that clothing—literally, because he proceeded to lose over fifty pounds—and metamorphosed into a much larger-than-life character than anyone in either party had ever expected.

Four months after taking over at the FDA in December 1990, Kessler stunned Washington and all the industries he would regulate by flexing muscles nobody remembered the agency having, and setting off the first in a series of corporate panic attacks. When the all-too-typical ten months of fruitless talks broke down with Procter & Gamble over taking the word "fresh" off the label on its Citrus Hill "Fresh Choice" orange juice (which was made from concentrate), Kessler exercised the only real statutory power the FDA had. He declared the juice "misbranded," and he had 15,000 gallons of it seized in a warehouse in Minnesota.

"In that instant," he recalled, "I believe that people began to understand what I meant by providing adequate incentive not to cross the line."

From Citrus Hill on, Kessler did everything loudly and boldly. His enemies interpreted this as grandstanding and egomania. His fans saw it as

Kessler being an aggressive doctor for America, a country whose food and drug industries didn't want to take their medicine. Either way, nobody could doubt that Kessler had ushered in a new era at the FDA: Generation Rx.

Because Kessler's actions were often popular with the public, and he shared at least one key belief with the Republican administration—that drug approval needed to be faster—the Bush regime was unable to dump him when he started stepping on too many toes. In his first year, Kessler forced "fat free" and "no cholesterol" claims off many foods. He also went after Bristol-Myers Squibb for illegally promoting off-label uses of a cancer drug, and Syntex for making misleading claims about a popular anti-arthritis drug. And then he banned silicone-gel breast implants.

To increase funding without getting much more money from Congress, Kessler pushed for an experimental system of "user fees" in which companies would pay $100,000 per New Drug Application, allowing the agency to hire more staff. The enabling legislation was called the Prescription Drug User Fee Act (PDUFA), referred to in FDA circles as "pedoofa." The drug companies agreed to the user fees on one condition: PDUFA money could be used *only* to speed up drug approval and not for postmarketing surveillance or compliance investigations.

While all approval times were supposed to be speeded up by PDUFA—in an attempt to rectify what had been dubbed the "drug lag" between approvals in other countries and the United States—Kessler responded to the cries of AIDS activists by creating a separate "accelerated approval" process for drugs that fought HIV. This new "fast track" for AIDS drugs would allow them to be sold on a conditional approval based solely on improvements in what was called "surrogate end point" data—laboratory tests that might be indicative of medicinal progress—instead of waiting to see if the test patients' health actually improved. Accelerated approval was risky, but it was a risk that AIDS patients demanded that they be allowed to take.

When Clinton beat Bush, he kept the FDA commissioner, who had earned the nickname "Eliot Nessler," and the agency continued to get headlines. Kessler made so many major pronouncements that on any given day he could be branded anti-industry, anticonsumer, antidoctor, even anti-FDA.

As a medical consumer, I had to admit there was something rather heroic about Kessler. When he entered a room, he brought with him a sense of urgency that made the entire tedious enterprise of regulating drugs seem as important as it actually is. He stood out in most crowds with his red-blond hair and beard and his wide-open blue eyes behind thick glasses, but he did not pretend to be smooth. When I finally was able to interview him, I was surprised by how scattered he could be, even when discussing something about which he had strong, well-considered opinions. For a man so well known for manipulating the media, he was somewhat klutzy about it, repeatedly announcing he was going off the record even when there was no reason to do so. But I was interested by his tenacity, even in the way he pursued our dialogue. He would be called away to put out some fire, and then have his assistant ring me back repeatedly until she got past my voice mail—once he even dialed me himself—and our conversation picked up right where it left off.

Kessler didn't act like a typical Washington bureaucrat. He acted more like what he was: a hotshot doctor with a law degree. One of the highest compliments he could pay to a colleague (in this case David Feigel, head of the AIDS drug division) was, "I can just be another doc around him." And like any hotshot doctor or lawyer, he liked to zealously jump on any exciting new case, leaving the tedious day-to-day stuff to someone else—or sometimes to nobody at all. Kessler stayed with his special cases as long as they were exciting, and he was willing to overreact to new health concerns because so many of his predecessors had underreacted to almost everything.

Many people in the legal-drug world had waited their whole careers to have someone as strong and politically adept and *medical* as David Kessler at the FDA. That's why some were surprised when Kessler announced that one of his major initiatives would be taking on a problem that wasn't yet his: cigarette smoking, particularly among the young. While the FDA did regulate nicotine gum and patches to help stop smoking, the marketing of cigarettes themselves had always been regulated by the Federal Trade Commission, and health concerns about them were voiced by the U.S. surgeon general. But the Clinton administration had political problems in the surgeon general department, so Kessler took the ball and ran with it. He announced in 1994 that the FDA would fight vigorously for the right to regulate cigarettes as a drug-delivery system for nicotine. His justification was that smoking-related illness killed more Americans than many of the diseases for which the FDA approved drugs, and that with tighter controls, teen smoking might be lessened.

Many applauded Kessler's efforts to take the cigarette problem so seriously. He was, in many ways, the right person for the job. But some in the legal-drug world wondered if he was in the right position to *do* the job and were concerned about the cost of focusing Kessler's powerful attentions and the FDA's limited resources on something other than medications. It was bad enough that, as commissioner, his time was already split between drugs, devices and food products. Why then add smoking, which everyone already knew was dangerous, when so few patients and doctors seemed aware of the dangers of "the other drug problem"? Why expend so much energy grilling tobacco company executives about a risk that all smokers take voluntarily, when patients were still unwittingly taking so many medication risks?

I began hearing complaints that Kessler didn't prioritize basic problems crucial to drug safety, or that he would call attention to issues without really addressing them internally. For example, he had made a big announcement about replacing the adverse reaction reporting system with MedWatch. But he then did little to make sure that the FDA's embattled epidemiology department, which had been cut out of the PDUFA pot, had the resources to actually analyze all the new reports.

"I'm delighted he's gone after tobacco," one top drug researcher told me. "But he's acting as if he has an entity in the FDA that actually knows what to do with all these new reports. . . . The agency has a trivially small program in postmarketing surveillance, which has been level-funded for years. . . . When you talk to people at the FDA, you get the sense they are the same sort of bland bureaucrats who staff agencies. The best way is for the FDA to find vigorous investigators, not federal hacks who are there waiting for their pensions to kick in. Even under Kessler, the FDA hasn't done this."

I discussed this situation with Dr. Brian Strom, one of the few pharmaceutical researchers who successfully shuttles between the FDA and industry, and between academia and the real world of patient care, while maintaining both his independence and his funding base. An affable, elfin physician and teacher with one of those pens that writes in four different colors peeking out of his breast pocket, Strom had so many people waiting to see him at his University of Pennsylvania office the first day I visited that he got right to the point.

"The epidemiology program at the FDA has been stripped to nothing," he said. "It was allowed to really die. Adverse reactions that occur less commonly? We don't know about them. In special populations? We don't know about them either. All sorts of problems are found, yet they are left in the hands of the companies who spent $250 million to develop the drugs. I've had companies say to me, 'What we don't know won't hurt us.' . . . I've also been told, 'Why should we do that study? It can't help us.' You need a government agency that will study it instead. How do you get docs to use fewer or cheaper drugs? That has to come from the government.''

Strom was especially concerned that the FDA was devaluing pharmacovigilance at the same time that drug companies, facing bottom-line pressures, were laying off their postmarketing surveillance specialists and hiring outside private firms. "There will be another crisis or two before they realize [what they've done]," he said. "The companies see the issue as strictly financial, part of company belt-tightening. But the outside researchers know they don't want to hear bad news. Some of these outsiders are known as 'results for sale' places. . . . A company was recently talking to us about a study, and they were shocked that we wouldn't guarantee certain results. There was another group I know that would, and I told them to take the study there.

"These are very sophisticated people. They know it's easy enough to guarantee a negative result by getting a study that's too small to pick up an effect."

While the drug safety community wondered how Kessler's actions would affect pharmacovigilance, no one had any doubt that the commissioner had been remarkably effective in one area: he had managed to create a powerful coalition against himself and, by default, against the FDA. Food producers and medical device manufacturers rarely had much in common before Kessler went after orange juice, then spawned hundreds of lawsuits by banning breast implants. Even though drug and device companies had also been in different worlds, the pharmaceutical indus-try was able to appropriate some of the outrage over the implant suits. To these newly unified food, drug and device lobbies, Kessler added the tobacco lobby as well as the antiregulatory conservatives and all their lobbies. There were also quite a few disgruntled former FDA employees who had been pushed out as deadwood in an attempt to streamline the agency. Together, they attacked Kessler relentlessly, demanding a priva-tized, defanged regulatory apparatus that would basically trust industry to police itself and allow market forces to root out substandard prod-ucts. They were calling for a moratorium on any new government regula-tions, no matter how necessary they might be.

The whole situation was painful to watch. The FDA didn't have the free time or resources to waste defending itself against Newt Gingrich, who wasn't actually interested in solving the FDA's problems—just exploiting them. It was all politics, pills as metaphor rather than medicine. Within the Clinton White House, I was told, the discussion had turned to how to "inoculate" Kessler and the FDA against this epidemic of deregulation fever.

PART III

CHAPTER 14

Detail Men

During that fall of 1994 and early winter of 1995, Diane had been percolating away on a project in her office. It was a thrill to see her so engaged again, and even a thrill to have her be so secretive about what she was doing.

For many years I had found it irksome that Diane was so protective of her work until it was finished—more than irksome, actually; I found it a little threatening. I often complained that she never gave me anything to read. Then she got Floxed, and one aspect of her illness was that her privacy had to be regularly invaded. When I worried she was hiding symptoms from me, I couldn't take "Don't ask" for an answer anymore. This had created a newly heightened sense of intimacy between us, and Diane realized that some of the things she had been reluctant to share with me were not such big scary secrets after all. But over the course of the illness, she had been forced to relinquish a little too much of her privacy. And I had probably helped to compromise her ability to write freely. While I had been enjoying the opportunity to have more of my curiosities about her satisfied, it felt healthy for her to be cagey again about her writing.

In mid-January 1995 I was presented with the fruits of her labor as a thirty-seventh birthday present: a collection of forty-five poems and sonnets, many of which, I was elated to see, had been written *since* her drug reaction. She had printed out a special copy of the manuscript for me on lovely marbled paper and put it in a portfolio bound with a blue silk ribbon.

· · ·

The one thing I had appreciated about my many months spent piecing together the Omniflox saga and following David Kessler's exploits was that none of it directly involved Floxin or Ortho. I felt that after two and a half years, Diane and I finally had been able to put Floxin's impact on her health problems into some healthy perspective. The previous fall, the two-year statute of limitations on any possible lawsuit we might have brought against Ortho had finally run out. We knew that Stacy Phillips and her husband had filed suit because they had asked if we wanted to join them in litigation. But we had allowed the deadline to pass almost effortlessly, and it felt good to finally let it go.

While I was still planning to do more investigative work on drugs, it had been a long time since I saw the whole project as being about Floxin. I was glad I had resisted the temptation to turn my quest into a moral crusade against Ortho and its parent, Johnson & Johnson.

But then I discovered that my wife was being counterdetailed. Ortho sales reps were disparaging her and flat-out lying about the reaction she had had, in order to sell Floxin. Suddenly, I wondered if I had let them off too easy.

I found out about it at a dinner party. A young writer on the staff at *Philadelphia* magazine, who had done some medical stories and was himself recovering from a medical emergency that turned some of his sources into his caregivers, came up to me to say he had heard something really disturbing from one of his doctors at the Hospital of the University of Pennsylvania. He had mentioned my Floxin article in casual conversation, and his doctor said she had recently asked her Ortho sales rep about the piece and Diane's drug reaction.

According to this writer's account, the doctor was appalled that the rep was completely dismissive of Diane's case. It was nothing, the rep said, and besides, did the doctor know that Diane had tested positive for marijuana in the ER? The doctor said no, she hadn't heard that. But, she asked, even if that were true, what *possible* difference could it have made to whether or not she had a reaction to Floxin?

The rep, apparently not expecting that response, conceded that it wouldn't have made any difference at all and promptly changed selling tactics.

When I heard the story, I became blisteringly angry. We hadn't thought about that toxicology screen in ages. When Diane's case was finally entered into the FDA's database of spontaneous reports of adverse drug reactions, I assumed that the positive test would make the list of what was found in her blood. I also assumed that if the FDA or the drug company wanted to follow up on her case, they would call the doctor who reported the reaction and get her opinion, which we already knew.

Neither the FDA nor Ortho ever called the reporting doctor to follow up, which was fine. But apparently someone had given the information to this sales rep. And in the privacy of a doctor's office visit, reps can't be prevented from saying whatever they want—even though legally they are allowed to disseminate only medical information that meets FDA standards.

I was livid because Diane's confidential medical records had been violated. The ADR reports were supposed to be anonymous. Still, while I was curious who exactly had violated her doctor/client privilege— probably one of the ER physicians—I figured this was the price she paid for my writing about her in a small town. The same Ortho rep could conceivably have been servicing the hospital where Diane was treated as well as the hospital where my writer friend heard the story. Maybe it was just an isolated case of malicious gossip.

Weeks later, however, I got a letter from a concerned physician in Washington, someone with whom I had no personal connection at all. She was very disturbed about a conversation that had taken place when an Ortho sales rep was in to make a breakfast presentation to her clinic staff about a new line of oral contraceptives. She wanted me to know what the Ortho sales rep had said when one of the nurses asked about Diane's case, which she had read about in *The Washington Post Magazine*.

The sales rep was dismissive, saying, "That was the only case," and "she was on drugs."

The physician, startled, asked, "She was on drugs? Which ones?"

"Cocaine and antidepressants," the sales rep said. The physician had no idea whether this was the "company's line" or the rep's own opinion, but she found the interchange "shocking."

So did I, since everything the rep had told the clinic staff was provably false. Diane was neither taking nor had she screened positive for cocaine or antidepressants in the emergency room that night. But more appalling was the notion that a sales rep would tell doctors and nurses that Diane's was "the only case." By that point, the company had reports of many such cases, and the FDA advisory committee had already recommended label changes because of them. In fact, this doctor was writing to me from Georgetown Hospital, where she worked in the Student Health Service. Several buildings away, Dr. Flockhart was currently treating at least half a dozen patients for similar CNS reactions to Floxin. But to a detail person trying to sell a drug, these were just—well, details.

.   .   .

From the very beginning, being counterdetailed had been one of my worst fears about making Diane's situation public. I had always doubted that the drug companies would ever come after us publicly, because I knew they didn't have to. They have thousands of sales reps, making private, unmonitored visits to physicians. In an era of increased centralized buying, pharmaceuticals is one of those remaining industries that still relies primarily on traveling sales reps making house calls.

I knew all about sales reps. I grew up in the middle of the family furniture business, and some of my father's best friends were sales reps. They could become extremely involved in your life; we often went fishing with the Willy Loman of bedroom sets. And on any given day, a good rep could sell you anything. In the give-and-take of sales, if a rep convinced you to buy the wrong thing, somebody had to, in my father's words, "eat it." A good rep "ate it" himself, or offered markdown money to help you digest. A bad one made you eat it yourself.

Unfortunately, when the product being sold is medicine, the mistakes are generally "eaten" by the unwitting patient.

I also knew quite a few pharmaceutical sales reps. Philadelphia, with all its drug companies and medical schools, is crawling with them. My youngest brother, who is single, would sometimes date them: if you talk to women in bars in the Delaware Valley, the law of averages says you're going to make out with at least a few drug reps. Since my brother is diabetic, he was particularly delighted when he once found himself dating a rep from a company that sold insulin.

In just the past year or so, several people I knew had given up careers in, for example, construction and banking to join training programs and become pharmaceutical sales reps. These people represented what I assumed was the broad range of people in the job. On the one end was a guy my brother had gone to college with, who was one of the most honest and forthright people I knew. At the time, he was working for Burroughs Wellcome, which had a reputation as a high-end company with particularly scrupulous reps. On the other end was a guy I didn't think much of at all, who probably couldn't be trusted to tell you the time of day. Yet he was now part of the army of people "educating" doctors on the proper use of today's most sophisticated pharmaceuticals.

Those sales reps were under more pressure than ever. Their numbers were dwindling—in the previous two years, 1993–95, the total U.S. detail force had fallen from 41,000 to 36,000, mostly because of corporate belt-tightening set off by fear of Clinton price reforms that never came. Managed care was changing the playing field, so that prescribing choices once driven by a persuadable individual physician were now second-guessed by some corporate "suit" more interested in volume discounts than salesmanship.

So the reps—or the "knock squad," as some called them—had to cover more territory, more aggressively than ever before. The Student Health doctor from Georgetown told me a hilarious story about how competitive it was getting.

"Two reps who had arrived simultaneously at our office got into a fistfight in our parking lot," she recalled. "It was the battle of the non-sedating antihistamines. While our entire office staff gaped at them through the windows, these two suits duked it out, till they both left in a huff, shouting epithets. Later, one of the reps had a catered lunch delivered to our office, hoping, I guess, that we'd forget the spectacle."

But physicians were not above reproach either. A drug company executive told me that her firm knew which doctors were "high writers" and which were "low writers," and, she said flatly, "we don't detail people who are low writers." I've heard Dr. John Urquhart lecture about how sales reps "find the docs with that special light in their eyes," the ones who would give a brand-new drug "to everyone who came in the door." He feels the early clinical profile of a drug is unfairly dominated by a small number of doctors with that "special light."

In a study of Dutch doctors he did with his Dutch protégé Dr. Herbert Leufkens, Urquhart found that 4 to 6 percent of doctors accounted for 50 percent of the prescriptions written for nine brand-new drugs. Urquhart believes drug companies don't really understand how this practice of shotgun prescribing could hurt their new drugs, by exposing them early to a disproportionate number of patients who might not need them but who might get drug reactions that would damage the drug's safety profile. He discussed how a "defrocked rep" had owned up to the fact that there were doctors who "get a blank check from the company . . . if they prescribe for their whole practice. Companies *always* deny they do this sort of thing, but they don't deny that they put high targets on sales levels."

One sales rep lamented to me the difference between what he told doctors and what doctors told patients—in this case, his own aging parents. "I talk to my parents, who are in their sixties," he said. "I *know* that what the physician is telling them is wrong. I question my physicians based on the minimal knowledge I have as a drug rep and—well, it's not that the physicians are *stupid*. It's the amount of information they have to know. It's just phenomenal."

My former intern, Sabrina Rubin, who had done much of the research for my first drug articles and was now a full-time writer, had gotten interested in drug reps and did a piece about them. One of the characters in it who was a local rep for a top company had been arrogant enough to talk to her frankly and even pose for pictures without getting permission from his employers. Don, as I'll call him (to be more protective than he was of himself), had sold mailing and shipping equipment before changing industries because, he said, "Nobody's gonna stop getting sick." He was trained for a month, and then sent out on the road.

Don discussed cruising hospital elevators at lunchtime to "bump into" doctors, holding pizza parties for hospital staffs and showing up at the ER every morning with donuts—all pretty standard fare. When asked if he ever broke FDA rules, he said, "Oh, sure, yeah," especially when selling antibiotics because that market "is extremely competitive, and people start lying. . . . With antihypertensives, you're taking them for the rest of your life, a pill a day . . . [with antibiotics] the doctor's only gonna write you something for ten days. Then you get better. So the market is ruthless."

Apparently in drugs, like everywhere else, sex sells. "Women do real well," he explained, "because most doctors are guys. I make it past the receptionist real easy, easier than those ladies do, but once I get to the doctor, they'd much rather see a tight skirt than a suit . . . there are a *lot* of tight skirts on the street pushing drugs, I'll tell you."

Don thought little of the ethics of some of his doctors, who he referred to as "money-grubbing . . . bastards. . . . They schedule two patients every ten minutes. They say, "What's wrong with you, what do you want? You got a cough, here's an antibiotic." I hate to say it, but 90 percent of my doctors I would *never* go to for medical attention."

Doctors often wanted to be taken only to the best and most expensive restaurant in town, Le Bec-Fin. He was at a disadvantage because other companies allowed their reps to take doctors to the restaurant, but his did not. "If he's a big enough doctor," he said, "I'll find a way to take him to Le Bec-Fin."

Other doctors wanted to be taken to lunch at strip clubs where they "have blank receipts . . . I have this one [doctor], and all he wants is Phillies tickets. I say, 'You know, that's really illegal.' And he says, 'Okay, forget it, I'll just wait for the rep who comes in and gets them for me.' Sometimes I'll be sitting there in the office waiting for the doctor and I'll see this other rep walk in with samples . . . with tickets sticking out of his pocket. How am I going to get this doctor, walking in there going, 'My product's better because it's dosed once a day as opposed to twice a day?' . . . [He's] dropping off tickets in the fourth row because his manager is burying the receipt."

Don went on to reveal some of the other ways that reps get around FDA rules about sales materials. He mentioned the homemade charts, like the one I had seen after my Floxin article came out, and even the creative use of baked goods. "A lot of people use cakes shaped in the form of their products because people eat the evidence," he told Sabrina with a smirk.

When the article came out, Don, naturally, was fired.

In the legal-drug world, there is never a shortage of hard-sell horror stories. Sales reps are the most visible symbol of the most commercial aspect of the drug business, and doctors will often wear their stated "position" on them as a badge of incorruptibility, especially the growing number of physicians who ban them from their offices altogether. In Scandinavia, some doctors avoid one-to-one contact but periodically gather to let reps "inform" a group of them.

There is, however, very little empirical evidence about how sales reps actually influence which drugs we take. Much of the hard data has been provided by Jerry Avorn, a Harvard physician who is legendary as the father of the ultimate counterattack against pharmaceutical marketing campaigns.

Avorn and his colleagues did a lot of the pioneering work on drug marketing and prescribing practices. He was one of the first to prove, for example, that much of what doctors know about medicines comes verbatim from pharmaceutical industry advertisements and not from journal articles, as the doctors themselves believe. But he is best known for inventing the very elegant idea of "academic counterdetailing." To study how physicians might unlearn the commercially driven science they were being taught by drug reps, Avorn had the brainstorm of sending in independent do-gooder "reps" to hawk economically and scientifically unbiased prescribing, information such as alternative studies that gave a more balanced view of a drug or drug class. His "counterdetail men" even considered giving out product-free pens (which a program inspired by his later did).

The study, first done in 1983, showed that so-called "rational drug prescribing" could be taught if it was sold hard enough. Avorn's research, done with his colleague Dr. Steven Soumerai, has since been invoked in almost every critique of drug marketing. While few places have the money to fund large academic counterdetailing programs—for obvious reasons, drug companies don't readily finance them—variations on his model are used in many hospitals around the world. (One of the more successful programs is the Drug and Therapeutics Information Service in Adelaide, South Australia, which provides bound books of international reprints that give "medicos," as physicians are referred to there, a quickly digested, unbiased syllabus on a particular prescribing topic.)

I went to Boston to see Avorn at his office in Cambridge, where he is an associate professor at Harvard and runs an active clinical research program at Brigham and Women's Hospital. I found an infectiously exuberant man in his late forties, somewhat turtlelike in stature, with fuzzy chin whiskers, longish hair and the air of someone who was on the conservative side of "hippie" in the 1960s, so he didn't have to change as much as others to still be employed in academia in the 1990s. Even as a radical med student at Harvard, he wanted his revolutionary ideas to be presented in establishment forums. The reason his work on drug detailing made such a big impact is that it was published first in *JAMA* and *The New England Journal of Medicine*. Avorn is among a core of younger clinical researchers who do much of the more credible contrarian work on drug issues, a small group whose studies are often the most provocative at any pharmacological gathering and whose journal contributions provide a running reality check to the cheery news about new drug treatments.

Avorn and his colleagues represent the second generation of the group I was coming to see collectively as the Bad News Bearers, experts from all different walks of life and academic disciplines who have in common the feeling of being hated by the commercially driven drug establishment. I have heard them refer to themselves as "skunks at an otherwise lovely garden party." One of the world's top Bad News Bearers once told me, "We are regarded by the medical community at large as sort of doom and gloom merchants." Then he sighed: "It's rather an unattractive occupation." Some second-generation Bad News Bearers are primarily clinical pharmacologists who teach, treat patients and do clinical research, like Ray Woosley and his colleagues at Georgetown. Others, like Avorn and his group at Harvard, see themselves primarily as clinical pharmacoepidemiologists who treat patients but primarily do more statistical, macro research. Only a few show up at both the clin-pharm and pharmaco-epi conventions.

What the second generation has in common is age and a postmodern approach to drug problems; they were all in school in the 1960s and

1970s, long after their mentors and heroes had been mythologized by thalidomide and the consumer movement. They remind me of post-Watergate journalists, born too late to be afforded the luxury of seeing the world in black and white, and wanting to feel like informed insiders with real jobs rather than complete outsiders.

"Coming out of the sixties and the student movement, you sort of knew to ask, 'Who are the corporate bad guys I can be against?' " Avorn told me. "But as I became a physician and realized there has never been a reported case of a company putting a gun to a doctor's head and making him prescribe, we can't blame everyone else for what we prescribe. It's not 'the devil made me do it.' We're all grown-ups, all responsible for our actions. I was drawn to these issues. And I had, perhaps, the naive view, with my postsixties hangover, that these studies might help."

Avorn started his first controversial study on how drug company advertising seeps into doctors' consciousness as a medical student at Harvard. He called up a sample of primary care doctors and asked questions designed to help him figure out where they got their information. "What they believed about Darvon matched perfectly with what they read in the ads and not what was in the studies," he recalled. "I concluded that what doctors may believe they are learning from journals is actually coming from commercial channels. From day one of medical school, people thought I was wasting my time on this garbage. In the beginning, I think I was demonized. In the climate of the early eighties, the industry had the sense that everything would be fine if we didn't have these rabble-rousers spoiling it for us."

After his first studies on detailing, Avorn was tempted to make a career out of his observations. "Yes, we could have had Avorn's Counterdetail Men," he chuckled, "but it became a personal choice not to go into business like this. I wanted to be in research rather than have an information product to sell around the country."

Instead of counterdetailing, Avorn shifted his focus to geriatric drug issues. "The elderly consume the most drugs," he explained. "They get into the most trouble with drugs. When people ask me why study drugs in old people, my reaction is, 'Why doesn't everyone do it?' " Avorn and his colleagues have done a lot of the work that others use to call attention to medication problems with the elderly. Some of the more jarring statistics are: one in four prescriptions given to the elderly are unnecessary or dangerous, 40 percent of nursing home residents receive inappropriate medication orders, and more than half of ADR-related deaths are in people sixty or over.

"In caring for the elderly, there is often a limited number of things we can do for them," he said. "So when you identify a drug problem, you can often do a risk-free intervention and the patient can get better in a day or two. You take somebody who's cruising toward a nursing home, and you stop their sleeping pill, and suddenly they're Grandma again. Until we're able to fix Alzheimer's, this is where we can help the most."

A big part of the problem in geriatric pharmacology is that drug companies are usually reluctant to test drugs on the elderly, even if they will be used primarily by the elderly. Avorn understands why. "The elderly are messier to do clinical studies on," he said. "They tend to be taking other drugs, and they have a distressing predisposition to dropping dead. If you want to get data out there, the last thing you want is to enroll a bunch of complicated old people who get side effects, because what you're more likely to learn in a study of the elderly is the side effects.

"If the FDA doesn't make you do that study, you don't do it. It's not the drug company's fault that nobody makes them do it better. I've come to peace with that."

While Avorn had put certain of the old fights behind him, he was still excitable about the future of pharmacoepidemiology, which he believed could save the drug world. And he was extremely encouraging about the research I was doing, offering to help in any way he could. He insisted that I come to the annual international pharmacoepidemiology convention, where he thought I would learn a lot about the legal-drug culture. And he offered to make introductions to a much wider world of Bad News Bearers than I had met before. I typed out their names phonetically on my laptop, and when I returned home from Boston, there was a fax from Avorn's office with the names spelled properly.

At the same time, I got some help widening my search from a protégé of Dave Flockhart's, a very ambitious, advocacy-oriented doctoral candidate from Pakistan, Syed Rizwanuddin Ahmad. Rizwan, as he was known to colleagues, was about to return to Pakistan for several months to see his family, but he offered to post a letter about what I was doing on a computer service called E-Drug—short for Essential Drug, a reference to the World Health Organization's restrictive list of drugs that are essential for the health care systems of less-developed countries. Many top drug safety experts around the world subscribe to E-Drug. While I had been using computers for years, I was still unaccustomed to working with the World Wide Web. So Rizwan said that when he returned, he would let me know if anyone had responded.

·   ·   ·

With the mounting political pressure on drug regulators and economic pressure on drug companies, I had to wonder whether more matters than usual were falling through the cracks at the FDA. The media was beginning to raise the issue of whether fear of political reprisals would stunt regulatory action.

For example, whatever happened to those new warnings on quinolones that the FDA's anti-infectives advisory committee had ordered nearly two years before? "Well, that's a very good question," Mike Blum said, somewhat embarrassed, when I asked him about it. "I'm not at liberty to say." The FDA was still "in negotiations" with the companies. A year hadn't been enough time to agree on two sentences. "I can't give you any details," he shrugged. "It takes a lot of to and fro to arrive at labeling that's acceptable."

While the FDA dawdled, a brand-new adverse reaction was being reported for Floxin and the other quinolones, one that would be even more surprising than seizures and psychiatric disorders to a physician who might casually prescribe the drugs for a minor infection. Quinolones now appeared to cause spontaneous tendon ruptures, especially in the Achilles tendon. A letter in *JAMA* about one such case had alerted American doctors to the problem, and follow-up letters from the FDA confirmed several dozen cases in the United States, including one of a physician who found his tendons repeatedly rupturing when playing football.

While this was news in America—where women's magazines were soon running warnings about quinolones and aerobics—I discovered that it had been well known in France for some time, having been first reported in a rheumatology journal in 1992. The French had reports of one hundred patients with tendon disorders, including thirty-one ruptures; all the quinolones were implicated, including one not available in the United States, pefloxacin. Some of the cases were downright bizarre.

"A French elderly gentleman is sitting holding his coffee cup," Bernard Begaud, the head of pharmacovigilance in Bordeaux, reported at a conference, "and all of a sudden, his Achilles tendon goes pop. Very strange story." In another French case, a patient had ruptures in both legs at once.

One French pharmacovigilance center was even using the new quinolone reactions to test a theory about drug reaction reporting in general, comparing hands-off "spontaneous" reporting to more aggressive ways of securing reports. In the study, only one report came in spontaneously, but when all doctors were asked if they had seen such reactions, suddenly there were eighteen reports. And when the center tracked down doctors known to have prescribed quinolones and asked if they had seen such reactions, suddenly it had 342 reports. French pharmacovigilance officers were also tracking neuropsychiatric reactions to quinolones, collecting more than 450 cases in just two regional centers.

Unfortunately, French "signals" on adverse drug reactions are sometimes disregarded, one FDA epidemiologist told me, because the surveillance system in France is considered unusual. It is regional instead of national, and it pays more attention to exploring individual cases for causality than simply compiling raw numbers. While patients might appreciate the French attention to human detail, epidemiologists prefer to stick to the countries with similar systems so they can be assured of comparing similarly acquired raw data.

It is too bad that French pharmacovigilance has second-class status and that the French market isn't always in sync with that of other nations, because the country has what many top pharmacologists consider the world's best publication on drugs. *Le Revue Prescrire* is a *Consumer Reports* of medication that rates new drugs on a six-point scale, with little cartoon drawings ranging from "not acceptable" (the little guy in the hat drop-kicks the pill) to "nothing new," "possibly helpful," "offers an advantage," "a real advance" and simply "bravo." Editor Gilles Bardelay's monthly publication even gives out annual "golden pill" and "bitter pill" awards. (It's in French, but there is a quarterly English-language digest, *Prescrire International.*)

The fact that a drug "signal" from France could take two years to make it to America is appalling. The drug industry is entirely international, and it can largely ignore the national boundaries that separate the drug regulatory systems. If they were truly in the business of science, drug companies would make sure that *all* new insights about their products—not just the "good" news—were freely circulated to doctors around the world. Instead, the opposite appears to be true. Apparently, the companies often do their best to play down as idiosyncratic "signals" from smaller countries in which regulators are in closer contact with the patient population.

One country with a long reputation for picking up signals early is the Netherlands, a place where all drugs—legal or not—seem to be taken very seriously. The country has several excellent university programs with strong government support and an active adverse reaction monitoring system. Moreover, its signals tend to be amplified because some

Dutch regulators have been actively involved with the World Health Organization, which is based in Geneva. And Dutch concerns are often picked up by the very loud consumer group Health Action International (HAI)—a network of about a hundred groups involved with health and drug issues in sixty countries. HAI is based in the Netherlands and has coordinating offices in Malaysia and Peru, so it can spread the word quickly.

One day I was paging through a book Brian Strom had given me that compared postmarketing surveillance programs in different countries, when I came to an article on drug monitoring in the Netherlands. It included a table of the most "serious drug-induced diseases in the past 100 years." I started reading down the list of all the great drug tragedies of the twentieth century: 1938, elixir sulfanilamide; 1952, chloramphenicol; 1961, thalidomide.

And there on the list was ofloxacin—*Floxin.*

Back in 1987 the antibiotic had made the Dutch drug reaction hall of fame for causing psychosis. I stared at the page in disbelief. After many phone calls and faxes, I tracked down the Dutch doctor and drug regulator who had written the article, Ronald Meyboom, and we later met at a conference. He said the CNS problems with Floxin were very well known in the Netherlands, but he thought the original signal had come from Germany.

"Oh, yes," he said. "I understand that in Germany they call it the, how do you say, the 'flashing blue light' drug. This refers to the blue lights on the German ambulances."

I told Meyboom a bit about my personal interest in the drug, and about my quest for information that might help Diane. A quirky and confrontational man who vaguely resembled TV anchor Ted Koppel, he paused and then asked philosophically, "Are you willing to accept the possibility that there is no answer? Or that her illness would have manifested itself anyway?"

I pondered for a moment. Yes, I was willing to accept the possibility that there was no answer. And yes, I guess it was *possible* her illness would have manifested itself anyway—although I didn't believe it would have reached this level of severity without the drug reaction.

It was an interesting question for Meyboom to be asking, because he had played a key role in the almost-twenty-year multinational battle over the psychiatric side effects of the popular benzodiazepine sleeping pill Halcion (triazolam). He had been one of the Dutch regulators who first noticed a signal on psychiatric reactions back in the late 1970s, nearly a decade before the drug caught the attention of the British and American press. Meyboom had been permanently embittered by the Halcion experience, as had almost everyone else associated with the saga of the best-selling medication. The roll call of Halcion victims included officials at its manufacturer, Kalamazoo, Michigan-based Upjohn, countless experts brought in to testify in lawsuits in the U.K. and America, regulatory officials in many countries, and even President George Bush, who reportedly had one of the world's more famous drug reactions to Halcion in 1992, when he threw up and collapsed at an official dinner in Japan.

The debate over Halcion had turned into much more than an argument about drug reactions. Social policy analysts considered the controversy a symbol of a "general crisis of legitimacy in the efficacy of medical treatments" and a "fracturing" of the very concept of expert authority. Meyboom tended to compare it to the *Challenger* disaster. The difference was that the *Challenger* spacecraft had blown up only once, while Halcion exploded again and again.

At the center of the initial controversy were Meyboom and his former boss in the Dutch regulatory authority, Dr. Graham Dukes, a quintessential first-generation Bad News Bearer whose name I knew from several of his books and articles that I had read. Dukes had taken over editing the internationally known annual volume *Side Effects of Drugs*—which always opens with a provocative essay from some other prominent Bad News Bearer—and he has played a major role in the World Health Organization's drug efforts. He and Meyboom became the first of many internationally known drug safety experts and consumer advocates to be kept up nights by the little blue sleeping pill.

Halcion is an enigmatic drug, born to be argued about—not exactly the qualities one looks for in a casually popped sleeping pill. As far back as 1976, when an FDA medical officer first assessed the medication and recommended against its approval, it was clear that it worked well for certain patients, but in a very narrow therapeutic range. There were originally three dosages—a quarter-milligram, a half-milligram and a full milligram—and for many people, each size was going to be too much or too little: it could cause memory impairment and other CNS side effects in some people at a dose that wasn't high enough for others. In 1977 the FDA Psychopharmacology Advisory Committee overrode the medical officer's opinion and declared the drug approvable. But it wasn't actually approved until five years later. There were the usual paperwork mix-ups, as well as a less-than-usual disqualification of the clinical investigator who did one of the three pivotal studies. But the bigger problem was what happened in the Netherlands. About a year after the 1978 Dutch approval of the drug, the Netherlands Centre for Monitoring of Adverse Reactions to Drugs began receiving spontaneous reports that Halcion had caused psychosis, paranoia, amnesia, depersonalization, nightmares and a withdrawal syndrome. A Dutch physician named van der Kroef wrote a highly publicized article about such cases in *The Lancet,* which set off a firestorm in the pharmaceutical world.

The Netherlands then yanked Halcion off the market—and was quickly accused of condemning the drug in a "trial by media," by American experts who were brought together in Boston by Upjohn and allowed to review confidential company data on the drug. Most prominent among these American critics was Dr. Louis Lasagna, who has been a major presence in clinical pharmacology since the late 1950s, first at Hopkins and later at the University of Rochester. (He now runs the Tufts Center for the Study of Drug Development, which does a broad range of research, sometimes with confidential information and/or financial support from drug companies; some Tufts studies played prominent roles in the recent deregulatory attacks on the FDA.) Upjohn pulled out all the stops because it assumed, correctly, that the Dutch situation was holding up its more important U.S. and U.K. approvals.

After six months of investigation, Dutch regulators, believing that many of the effects were probably dose related, offered to reapprove only the lowest-dose Halcion pill in the Netherlands with new labeling. Upjohn took an "all or nothing" approach and chose not to market in that country; the Dutch signal was portrayed by the company as either idiosyncratic—something peculiar about Netherlanders—or illusory. Upjohn argued that spontaneous reports were unreliable, especially those of psychiatric side effects to a psychiatric drug, because drug reactions are so hard to separate from the underlying disease.

While this was going on, the U.K. approved Halcion, but only at lower doses: the one-quarter milligram and a one-eighth milligram. The drug was approved in the United States in 1982 at doses up to a half-milligram, over the objections of the FDA medical officer (who preferred only the lower doses approved, and also wanted patients to stop taking Halcion after two weeks). But while it was wildly successful in the marketplace, the drug never completely shook free of the early controversies. Some of the controversy belonged to Halcion itself, because the drug did make some people psychotic. But Halcion also carried the baggage of some of the other medicines in its class: the benzodiazepine tranquilizers like Miltown (meprobamate), Librium (chlordiazepoxide), Valium (diazepam), and later Xanax (alprazolam). These very successful drugs were originally marketed as nonaddictive alternatives to barbiturates but later turned out to be addictive as well, and they had a nasty withdrawal syndrome that their manufacturers were conspicuously slow to appreciate or even admit. When Valium became the biggest-selling drug in America in the 1970s, it spawned an overdose of media hand-wringing about the "Dr. Feelgood" society we had become. (This happened again when Prozac began topping the charts and we became a "Dr. Feelbad" society.) Xanax, used largely to treat panic, became the Valium of the 1980s. Like Halcion, it was manufactured by Upjohn.

So even though Halcion was more a sleeping pill than a tranquilizer, it was ripe for being viewed metaphorically as well as medically—by consumers, by industry and by the lawyers who filed all the thousands of benzodiazepine-related lawsuits in the United States and the U.K. In regulatory circles, Halcion also became something of a referendum on which country's safety experts were most qualified to properly assess the risk/benefit ratio. The Dutch, especially, were growing incredulous about the way their findings had been disregarded. Top international drug people were taking Halcion very personally.

In 1988 the sleeping pill was back on the front page. Ilo Grundberg, a fifty-seven-year-old Utah woman who had killed her mother with eight bullets to the head and body, was judged by court-appointed psychiatrists to have been "involuntarily intoxicated" by Halcion (and other drugs she had taken) during the shooting. Then San Francisco writer Cindy Ehrlich, a veteran of the early days of *Rolling Stone* magazine, did an award-winning two-part article in highly regarded *California* magazine called "Halcion Nightmare: The Frightening Truth about America's Favorite Sleeping Pill," which detailed her own horrific CNS adverse reaction to the drug, reprised the European controversy and demanded FDA action. Press attention to the Grundberg case and Ehrlich's articles led to an agency investigation and raised British regulatory concern. The FDA combed its database of spontaneous reports, and Public Citizen called for the drug to be withdrawn. Upjohn again argued that spontaneous reports, especially for psychiatric drugs, are unreliable.

The debate within the FDA about Halcion grew bitterly personal. "It's the one drug I feel really badly about," Carl Peck, the former director of CDER at the FDA, told me, "because it was terribly poorly worked up, and once it was marketed, the agency basically turned its head on the safety problems. Behind closed doors, there was a *lot* of fur flying between Leber and Temple." Leber is Dr. Paul Leber, the head of the agency's psychopharmacological drug division; Temple is his superior, Dr. Robert Temple, the director of the Office of Drug Development I at CDER and arguably the agency's most powerful and hands-on pharmacrat. The battles between them—over everything from drug safety "signals" to whether the FDA should talk to *Time* magazine—became so intense that someone illegally broke into Leber's private computer diary and printed out excerpts of his accounts of Halcion-related discussions. These were then circulated with a glossary attached. According to a copy of the purloined diary excerpts I was slipped, Leber wrote that his longtime colleague Temple is "to manipulation what Sinatra is to song," criticizing what he saw as Temple's "lack of judgment" and "grandiosity." He went on to describe Temple as "oozing slime" and "a shit." (Ehrlich's drug reaction was described as "possibly due to Halcion—also possible, however, is that she's a bit loosely wired and her crusade against Halcion is all part of a grand denial of her weakness.")

In the diary, Leber also called the FDA's department of epidemiology "obnoxious" and said it had "a total lack of comprehension about the agency's mission." While much of this is the loose personal name-calling that might be found in anyone's diary (and Leber and Temple are still working together ten years later), it does very colorfully sketch the basic schism in the FDA—and medicine at large—between hard-number clinical pharmacology and more interpretive epidemiology. It also shows how angry Halcion can make drug safety experts.

The FDA's Psychopharmacology Advisory Committee ultimately decided not to take any major new action on the drug, but the lawsuits piled up—including one from Ilo Grundberg, who successfully avoided a murder conviction with her Halcion intoxication defense. Upjohn would settle with Grundberg out of court in the summer of 1991, but documents and experts' depositions from her case—including the strong opinions of retired Scottish psychiatric researcher Dr. Ian Oswald—made their way to regulatory authorities. Then the company informed the FDA that during a review of files for the suit, it had discovered errors in a clinical study submitted to approve Halcion. The study had underreported the number of patients who had paranoid reactions to the drug and overstated the number who had similar reactions to a placebo, confirming some people's long-held fears. This information, and mounting adverse reaction reports, caused the British MCA to suspend the license for Halcion in the fall of 1991.

The move came as a shock to Upjohn, especially because the MCA apparently has a reputation for being among the *last* regulatory authorities to take serious action against a drug. "The U.S. system started as adversarial, and in the U.K. it never was," one leading British drug safety expert told me. "In the U.K. there has been a basic attitude that regulators would trust industry to do the right thing. The danger in the U.S. is that everything has to be documented and proved, and it's much more labor intensive and unpleasant. The U.K. system has the danger that regulators get too close to industry people and there's a sort of friendliness that becomes too great. . . . So it's only when the MCA knows it has been misled that it gets tough."

The FDA did not follow the lead of the MCA—although the two agencies were in close contact and American officials actually took a field trip to London to discuss the British regulatory actions—but it did instigate its own investigation, and according to one agency spokesman, "We basically did a whole new NDA for the drug, overseen by scientists other than those who originally worked on it." The new FDA inquiry came at a crucial time for Upjohn; it had only a year left on its valuable patent for the world's best-selling sleeping pill, and its sales were already being affected by the bad publicity. In early 1992 *The New York Times* did a front-page story on Halcion that was fairly critical of Upjohn and included accusatory quotes from Grundberg's expert witness Ian Oswald. Upjohn went on to sue Oswald, the BBC news program *Panorama* (which did an explosive show on Halcion) and the newspaper *Sunday Express* in the U.K., where libel laws are somewhat less protective of journalistic freedoms than in the United States. (The *Express* suit was settled in Upjohn's favor, and the pharmaceutical firm won large judgments in the other two cases—including the largest judgment ever against the BBC—although Oswald did win a small judgment in a countersuit.)

At the end of 1992 the FDA decided that none of the paperwork inconsistencies it had found while investigating Upjohn changed its opinion that the drug could be safe and effective with proper labeling. But in June 1993, the British regulatory authority permanently revoked the company's license to sell Halcion in the U.K., followed by thirteen other countries.

"Where Upjohn slipped," one expert witness associated with the case told me, "is, they felt that in a competitive situation you can't afford to admit to any weakness of your drug. Society as a whole would have been better off if they had just admitted it, and the drug would still be benefiting many people. It's a pity it was thrown off the market." He felt, as many had throughout the years, that the Halcion affair wasn't really about drug reactions. The company denied for so long that its drug could be causing *any* of these severe psychiatric side effects that the denial became the issue, and disproving it a cause unto itself.

For a while Halcion quieted down. Then in April 1994 an investigator in the FDA's Kalamazoo office completed a report on an inspection that he had done at Upjohn two years earlier. The report contained allegations of significant wrongdoing, and the investigator explained its extreme tardiness by stating that he had been "directed to discontinue the investigation . . . before its conclusion." A task force was impaneled by David Kessler to investigate the FDA's investigations. Two years later, it would release a report critical of several FDA procedures and actions but still supportive of the safety and efficacy of the drug as labeled— even while noting that doctors were still prescribing Halcion for longer periods and at higher doses than the label recommended.

Needless to say, Americans and Europeans who actually had to decide whether to take the sleeping pill were very confused.

CHAPTER 15

Countries unto

Themselves

While I shared the confusion over Halcion, I was also intrigued by the more broadly international character of the drug's saga. By following Halcion back and forth across the Atlantic, I was finally getting a better view of the big picture of the pharmaceutical world. It made me want to step back and try to make some global sense of it. I had decided long ago to follow the industry as if it were a spectator sport, but it had been difficult to move beyond the handful of big-name drugs and high-profile scandals that reached the front page. I needed to develop more of a scout's perspective on the drug game.

I began with the companies themselves, which are sort of like baseball teams. Each team has a couple of rising or fading drug stars, some dependable role players to fill out the roster and a farm system. And as in baseball, there were a *lot* of teams. Fifteen major international drug companies controlled over 60 percent of the world's drug revenues, but unlike more consolidated industries, no single company controlled more than 5 percent. Some companies did only brand-name drugs, others only generics or over-the-counter drugs and some did all three (along with medical testing devices). But much of the industry trickled down from the big research-oriented brand-name firms. There was an American League of multinational companies that were based in the United States. And there was a European League of similar companies based in Europe, mostly the U.K., Switzerland and Germany. The American League was historically led by Merck. The European League, more in flux with recent consolidation, was, at the moment, led by British-based Glaxo.

All the major companies had headquarters, research facilities and sales offices scattered around the world. But they also had hometowns, and the fertile crescent of the pharmaceutical industry turned out to be right around where I live. This area was referred to in the industry as the Pharm Belt, because the majority of the world's major drug companies were headquartered in and around Philadelphia, in and around New York, or close to an exit on the turnpikes that connect the two cities. Dozens of smaller drug firms, and thousands of ancillary businesses that service the majors or have spun off from them, were also located in this relatively compact space. If I had nothing better to do on a Saturday, I could probably do a driving tour of the entire Pharm Belt and still make it home for supper.

From my house, I would head south on 95 to Wilmington, Delaware, and see Du Pont. Then I would come back up through the Philadelphia area to see SmithKline, which was just a few blocks from my office in town, but had several big facilities in the suburbs, and then Wyeth-Ayerst, which had a big complex on the Main Line. Both firms were now owned by other companies—SmithKline by the British Beecham, Wyeth by New Jersey–based American Home Products—but they still felt like local concerns, and their main operations were still here. Just outside of Philadelphia was the U.S. base of Rhône-Poulenc Rorer, the drug company owned by the French chemical firm Rhône-Poulenc, which was only a short drive from one of the two major campuses of Merck. If I took the scenic route from Rhône-Poulenc to Merck, I could pass by McNeil Laboratories, the Fort Washington division of Johnson & Johnson, as well as the Ambler offices of IMS, the company that does the National Prescription Audit and provides the "Nielsen Ratings" of drugs, as well as other pharmaceutical information services for companies (and journalists).

From Merck, I could go east to begin my sweep through New Jersey, the druggiest state in the union, where 25 percent of all American-made drugs were produced. I'd begin in Titusville at Janssen Pharmaceutica, the U.S. site of the Belgian firm owned by Johnson & Johnson. Then on through Princeton, where the main research facilities for Bristol-Myers Squibb were located, until I reached the heart of J&J country, with its main campus in New Brunswick, and both Ortho-McNeil and the R. W. Johnson Pharmaceutical Research Institute in nearby Raritan.

The international headquarters of Merck was just up the way in Whitehouse, and north of it was a ten-mile stretch crammed with five huge conglomerates. The world headquarters of both American Home Products (which owns, besides Wyeth-Ayerst, generic powerhouse Lederle and the merged over-the-counter giants Whitehall and Robins) and Schering-Plough were in Madison; followed by the American offices of two major Swiss-owned companies, Sandoz in East Hanover and Ciba in Summit; and then both Warner-Lambert and its subsidiary Parke-Davis in Morris Plains. In neighboring Nutley was the home of Hoffmann-LaRoche and its research branch Roche Laboratories, all part of the Swiss pharmaceutical giant Roche Holdings Ltd. Then on to Manhattan, where I'd breeze by the main corporate offices of Pfizer and Bristol-Myers Squibb, before heading up into Connecticut to see the West Haven headquarters of the German Bayer conglomerate—which incorporates the former Miles Laboratories—and then on to Pfizer's main research center in Groton.

That's over half of the world's major drug companies within a tank of gas of one another.

The rest of the drug industry was more spread out. In the United States, the other major research and manufacturing firms had created their own company towns: Abbott Laboratories in North Chicago; Searle in nearby Skokie, Illinois; Upjohn in Kalamazoo; Eli Lilly in Indianapolis; Marion Merrell Dow in St. Louis; the American base of the British-owned Burroughs Wellcome in Research Triangle Park, North Carolina.

In Europe, the major drug centers were in London (corporate home of Burroughs Wellcome, Glaxo, Pharmacia and Zeneca), Basel, Switzerland (home of Ciba-Geigy, Sandoz and Roche), Berlin (home of Hoechst), and Frankfurt (home of the Bayer AG Group). Japan had a large local drug industry, but it was still considered another world to the rest of the drug business, and little of the Japanese takeover fervor that seized the entertainment and auto industries in the 1980s ever reached pharmaceuticals. Japan had more than fifteen hundred pharmaceutical manufacturers, but most of them were tiny, and few had merged to grow larger because in the country's corporate culture, such deals are done only as a last resort. The major Western players made strategic alliances with the Japanese firms—like the one between Daiichi and Ortho that brought Floxin to America—but the ownership of industries, and the decision-making power, largely remained in the United States and Europe.

From a manufacturing and distribution perspective, the drug industry looked a little different. I once spent an illuminating afternoon talking with a veteran drug company executive about how the industry views the world and the servicing of various countries. "The first thing you have to remember," he said, "is that the big companies are not American or German or Canadian—they are *countries unto themselves.*"

He explained that until the early 1970s, no matter where a company was based or where a drug had been discovered, "if you wanted to sell in a country, you had to manufacture in that country." With the rise of regional trade agreements, it became possible in the 1970s and 1980s to centralize manufacturing for different regions: for example, in Mexico for all the Spanish-speaking countries in Central and South America, and in Singapore or the Philippines for Indonesia and Malaysia. But the economic dream of moving manufacturing to wherever in the world it was cheapest didn't come true overnight: it took years of mergers and improvements in computerization and international communication. Many American-sold products were still made in Puerto Rico, because of the tax advantage, or New Jersey, but plenty of the manufacturing was moving overseas.

The executive said that many of these manufacturing trends held true for most major industries and were no more or less troubling than changes in, say, the auto industry. But he was increasingly concerned about one little-discussed aspect of international drug manufacturing, known by the innocuous name "transfer pricing." He said that transfer pricing was the cornerstone of pharmaceutical price-gouging.

"Many of the big companies manufacture their own chemicals in their own chemical plants," he explained. "Then they sell the chemicals to themselves at high markups." When consumers and legislators complain about prices, "the companies point to the costs of raw materials. 'Why, the active raw material in this pill costs us eighty cents,' they'll say. But they *bought it from themselves,* and they *manufactured* that price. When a European company selling in America brings the raw materials in at some great multiple of what they actually cost, they can lower their taxes. It's a major profit center. It's legal, yeah, but it's mostly a way of getting profits out of a country."

How much cheaper would drugs be without transfer pricing? "A *lot* cheaper," he said. "Look, it's not that it shouldn't be done at all. The question is whether it is overdone. Is it extravagant greed in the extreme? I think you'd find that the answer is yes."

I had picked an interesting time to try to see the big picture of the drug world, because it simply refused to stay in focus. Business was lousy in 1995, and another round of merger mania was sweeping the industry.

The global effort to contain health care costs had finally caught up with pharmaceutical sales. After a decade of double-digit growth in global drug sales and little outside pressure to contain prices, the industry now faced only 5 percent sales growth and increasing price competition. And regardless of how hard the industry was working to highlight its contribution to scientific research, few new drugs were coming down the pipeline that might reinvigorate sales.

"I was having dinner with a major drug manufacturer . . . and this guy scared me a little," recalled one prominent pharmacy executive. "He said, 'You know . . . when you get right down to it, we've pretty much cured everything we're going to cure for the next five to seven years. Nobody has a huge pipeline of stuff coming out.' "

To maintain the high profit margins investors had come to expect, companies were suddenly merging and acquiring like there was no tomorrow. In 1994 Swiss-based Roche paid $5.3 billion for the California biotech firm Syntex, and Ciba-Geigy spent $2 billion to buy half of another California biotech firm, Chiron. Buying small promising biotech companies, which only developed drugs and didn't have their own distribution systems, was a new way of getting fresh products into the pipeline. The same year, the generic world rumbled when American Home Products spent $10 billion to buy out American Cyanamid. This merger would lead to more than 11,000 jobs being cut, a type of layoff that was suddenly becoming commonplace in the industry.

Then in early 1995 came the deal that was the Time-Warner of drugs: London-based Glaxo, Europe's largest drug company, executed a $14 billion hostile takeover of its biggest U.K. competitor, Wellcome PC, including its American arm, Burroughs Wellcome. The newly combined Glaxo Wellcome dethroned New Jersey–based Merck as the world's largest drug company. This may have just been dollars and cents to Wall Street, but within the industry both the merger and the dethroning had greater significance: they heralded that the world of legal drugs would be leaner and probably meaner. Both Wellcome and Merck were companies that stood for something creditable in the industry. They had reputations as the most ethical of the ethical drug firms, the most medically oriented and the most committed to research and drug safety. Until 1986, when it went public, Wellcome had actually been owned by a nonprofit trust. Merck had dethroned IBM as *Fortune* magazine's "most admired company" for being as scientifically correct as a hugely profitable drug firm can afford to be.

Glaxo, on the other hand, was a big, take-no-prisoners, promotion-oriented, "modern" drug company. The newly combined Glaxo Wellcome would go on to lay off 7,500 workers and reinvent pharmaceutical hardball worldwide. Some longtime Wellcome detail men were more than ready to look for other jobs because they couldn't bear what they perceived to be the new owner's kamikaze attitude. Besides massive cost-cutting, the new drug behemoth even figured out a way to turn a minor slipup by the FDA into a windfall of nearly $2 billion in free money. In Washington this money would become vilified as *extra* excess profits.

Facing an end to its lucrative patent on its best-selling ulcer medicine Zantac (ranitidine), with annual sales of $2.1 billion, Glaxo-Wellcome discovered a curious loophole in the recently signed General Agreement on Tariffs and Trade (GATT), which sets standards for international commerce. In 1995 GATT, which had been painstakingly negotiated for years, set a new international term for patents: instead of the U.S. standard of seventeen years from the date a patent was approved, the world would agree to the European standard of twenty years from the date the patent application was filed.

This change had already made generic manufacturers unhappy because they believed it would ultimately take longer for name-brand drugs to go off patent, but they had already lost that political fight. Then in its wake came a new fight, when a Glaxo lawyer discovered that the FDA had inexplicably forgotten to amend the Food, Drug and Cosmetics Act to ensure that currently running patents wouldn't be inadvertently lengthened by the new GATT rule. Glaxo made the FDA admit it had screwed up, miraculously giving the company an extra nineteen months on its American Zantac patent. Generic manufacturers screamed that this loophole would ultimately cost the U.S. public $1.8 billion in extra drug charges—the amount that ostensibly would be saved if all the drugs with extended patents had become lower-priced generics. The costs to the generic firms themselves, which had been building plants for years in preparation for old patent expiration dates, were equally astronomical.

While many other drug companies benefited from patent windfalls, Glaxo's Zantac extension was the single most lucrative—worth, according to estimates, over a billion dollars in unexpected revenue, found money. When legislators moved to close the loophole, Glaxo hired the best lobbyists money could buy to stop them, and it doubled contributions to its political action committee. The move earned the company the first annual "Green and Greedy" award from the senior citizens activist group the Gray Panthers—but the loophole never was closed.

The merger season continued after the Glaxo takeover of Wellcome. The U.K. firm Boots, which made the best-selling thyroid medicine Synthroid (levothyroxine) and owned a well-known pharmacy chain, was sold for

$1.4 billion to the German firm BASF AG. After deliberating for almost two years, German-based Hoechst finally bought Kansas City–based Marion Merrell Dow for $7.1 billion, creating Hoechst Marion Roussel, momentarily the world's third largest drug firm, behind Glaxo and Merck. The American generic manufacturer Ivax announced plans to merge with Hafslund Nycomed, Norway's biggest health care company, to create the world's largest generic manufacturer, and the Swedish firm Pharmacia announced a merger with Upjohn, which had been unable to find a new blockbuster drug to replace Halcion.

Besides buying each other, the once-insular drug firms were also creating scores of new strategic alliances to do research or sales cooperatively with their competitors. SmithKline Beecham reportedly had made 140 such strategic alliances, partnering on drugs or even just ideas for drugs. The companies also began buying out the very industries that had helped foster the price competition in the first place: the dreaded pharmaceutical benefits managers, or PBMs, which were increasingly being hired by large public and private health insurers to do pharmaceutical "cost containment." In late 1993 Merck bought one such firm, Medco Containment Services. SmithKline and Eli Lilly followed suit by buying PBMs of their own.

When the dust finally settled, the industry had spent a reported $100 billion to re-create itself. Tens of thousands of employees had been laid off all over the world: research programs had been dropped, detail teams decimated. Some lauded the changes as long overdue, hoping the industry would become less bureaucratic and more efficient. Perhaps the manufacturers would even come to realize that their own red tape might be partially responsible for the "drug lag" between European and U.S. approvals.

Others worried that the mergers and cutbacks would mean that postmarketing surveillance and epidemiology would become even less of a priority than they already were. I discussed this problem with former Dutch regulator Graham Dukes, whom I was finally able to meet in Washington, where he had traveled from his home in Norway for a meeting at the World Bank. Dukes turned out not to be Dutch at all but a jowly, Robert Morley-esque character—a British-born physician and lawyer who had left the drug industry for pharmaceutical public service and had used his dual expertise to become an international guru on the medical and legal issues surrounding drug-induced injury.

"Where will the conscience of a big company be found?" Dukes asked. "In a small company, it can be one person, maybe the medical director. In a big company, maybe no one will be willing to take responsibility for killing a drug that might be in difficulty, especially in a merger where the partners have three thousand miles between them. The bigger the company, the more difficult it is to be courageous."

The world of drug regulation was doing some merging itself. While the European Community already had a joint drug advisory board, the Committee for Proprietary Medicinal Products (CPMP), it finally had been able to organize an actual combined regulatory body, the European Medicines Evaluations Agency (EMEA), based in London. (Some speculated that one of the reasons the British were so tough on Halcion was that they didn't want to appear weak on drug safety while lobbying to be the home of the central office.) The individual EC countries would continue to have local regulators, but multination approvals would become much simpler.

A big push was also on for "international harmonization," a very utopian-sounding plan to create global definitions and standards for clinical drug testing. Harmonization was being driven by the so-called international "six-pack," which included the FDA, the Japanese Central Pharmaceutical Affairs Council and the new EMEA, as well as the American, Japanese and European manufacturers' groups.

This was in addition to the World Health Organization's multinational drug programs, which, like most UN initiatives that aren't backed up by troops, have varying degrees of success. Its main goals are to encourage the "rational" use of drugs through two powerful lists. The UN Consolidated List of banned or limited-use products provides rapid international transfer of new drug safety information. And the Essential Drugs List provides guidance on which medications countries absolutely need to approve in order to run their health care systems properly. (The WHO maintains its master list, of approximately two hundred medications, and encourages member countries to create their own and pressure local regulatory officials to approve only essential drugs.) The organization also does collaborative research on drug safety, pricing and delivery issues.

Even with all this new global cooperation, however, insiders knew which countries really mattered in drug safety. Over lunch at Georgetown one day, I asked Dr. Carl Peck—who, after stepping down as head of CDER, had spent a year on sabbatical in the Netherlands before setting up shop in Ray Woosley's department—to name the countries that made his list. He said the United States, the U.K., Germany, Canada, Australia, Sweden and the Netherlands. The last four were included

not because they have the biggest drug markets but because they are
known for having unusually creative or aggressive regulatory and academic communities in close contact with doctors and patients.

Conspicuously absent from Peck's list was Japan, which has the highest per-capita drug consumption in the world, but many peculiarities. In
Japan many physicians are still called *kusushi*—"drug-men"—and personally sell to patients all the many, many drugs they prescribe. Several
Japanese governments have tried to stop this practice. Doctors were
prohibited from selling drugs during the Meiji era (1868–1912), but
there weren't enough Western-trained physicians to keep the prohibition
in place. After World War II, Occupation authorities ordered legislation
to be drafted to formally separate the prescribing and selling of drugs;
the law was passed in 1956, but it still has enough loopholes for the
kusushi tradition to persist. The Japanese also haven't entirely incorporated the idea of "informed consent" into their drug-taking or drug-
testing. Doctors are still believed to "know best," and patients are rarely
given information about their own medical care, to the point, for example, of not being told they have cancer. Clinical trials by Japanese drug
companies are often done outside Japan because of this societal resistance to informed consent.

"The whole drug and therapeutic scene is unique in Japan," Peck
said. "It's the highest drug-taking country in the world. A *huge* market.
But it has a tradition of giving very low doses of drugs, because safety is
paramount, above efficacy. And it's so shameful to a company or a doctor if they ever injure a patient [that reactions go unreported]. . . . So,
no, Japan would not be in there."

I later asked Graham Dukes, who brings a more European perspective than Peck, to compare the various regulatory systems. He had written a short book on the subject when he served as regional officer for
pharmaceuticals and drug utilization for the World Health Organization.
"Some of the Northern European agencies have done extremely well,"
he said. "What I would call the Swedish-Dutch approach is a willingness
to bend the rules a little bit if common sense dictates, a willingness to
listen to the drug companies. What I've seen of the U.S. approach is that
they sometimes stumble over very tiny formal defects in New Drug Applications, which causes unnecessary delays—not very imaginative. Although I would put Britain among the countries that do pretty well, it
has an old boys' club that works for the companies—some of that 'Oh,
they're nice old fellows, they can't be all that wrong.'

"Australia and Canada I put together, because they both have relatively small systems with very sensible approaches. I was struck by the fact that Canada was keeping to the same standards as the FDA with about one-twentieth of the people. Australia has become too bureaucratic—demanding tests lasting seven to ten years in dogs and monkeys, and by that time they're very old dogs and monkeys, and you tend to get abnormal findings. They are sometimes too rigid. They've kept a lot of stuff off the market, which causes problems in other countries, but they certainly have succeeded in protecting their public.

"I have great admiration for Norway, where I now live, because until recently they had something called the 'need clause,' which industry loathed. They said, 'Why do we need twenty-four antirheumatic drugs?' And they didn't approve drugs that weren't needed. Unfortunately, because Norway has had to adopt a closer association with the EC, they had to drop the 'need clause.' "

While Dukes supported some regulatory consolidation, he was concerned that such moves might affect critical thinking about medications. "There's a lot to be said for having a lot of different agencies around the world," he explained. "I'm not entirely happy about regionalization efforts. The bigger an agency gets, the more frightened it gets about making mistakes. The political and tactical factors play a bigger role. I think that the truth around a drug emerges because things happen differently in different countries. They look over their shoulders all the time—'Let's see what happens after *they* withdraw it,' people will say. I'm not sure it's bad to have these variables."

Dukes brought more of a social policy perspective than his American counterparts, as did many of the other international drug experts I was meeting by phone, over the Internet (many in response to that message posted on E-Drug) and in person at conferences. When I spoke to them or read their work, I was reminded that much of my research on drugs had concerned the problems of people like myself, patients in industrialized countries with medical insurance or decent public health programs. But there is, of course, a whole other drug world out there. It's a world of starving babies and impoverished adults whose beleaguered doctors take it for granted that the wealthiest quarter of the planet's population will get nearly 80 percent of all the medicine.

In 1938 a hundred American children dying from a liquid antibiotic made with poisonous diethylene glycol changed the face of drug regulation in the industrialized world. In 1992, when the same poison was found in a cold remedy implicated in the deaths from unexplained kidney failure of thousands of children in Bangladesh, it was an obscure problem in some far-off land.

How does the relationship between the pharmaceutical haves and have-nots affect health care? My theory is that it all comes down to the politics of diarrhea.

A woman in my office came to tell me about her recent Caribbean island vacation that had been ruined by Floxin. She was prescribed the drug prophylactically to ward off traveler's diarrhea. This practice has become amazingly common, using increasingly stronger antibiotics, even though the Centers for Disease Control and the AMA, among others, all say it should *never be done*. Antibiotics cannot be counted on to prevent diarrhea, and many of them can actually cause diarrhea as a side effect. And every time you waste a course of an antibiotic on something you *don't* have, you increase the risk that it won't work for you when you actually need it. Besides the personal risk, whenever bacteria become resistant to an antimicrobial, the world moves one step closer to being ravaged by microorganisms.

And at a more practical level, a drug-induced rash and shooting arm pains from drug-induced neuralgia—as this woman said she experienced—tend to detract from the romance of breezy island nights.

Somewhere on that island a malnourished child was probably being improperly treated for an actual case of severe diarrhea. A common problem is that treatment gets focused on stopping the diarrhea with medications—many of which don't really do anything—instead of hydrating the patient to replace the liquids and nutrients that have been lost from the body. According to the WHO, 4 million children a year die from diarrhea; it is one of the leading causes of illness and death in less-developed nations. The organization has campaigned to get patients to use an inexpensive "oral rehydration" solution (of water, salt, sugar, potassium and baking soda) instead of manufactured products. International health care advocates have campaigned loudly against combination antidiarrhea medicines that include antibiotics.

From this example, it is easy to see how gastrointestinal distress can be extremely politicized. Diarrhea can be a class struggle, and its treatment often causes the lines between medical advice and metaphor to become blurry. It is no coincidence that the entire international health consumer movement was reinvented in the early 1980s by the crusade against an antidiarrhea drug. In fact, it was the same drug that Diane's neuro-ophthalmologist had told us about, clioquinol, the halogenated hydroxyquinoline that had caused the epidemic of subacute myelo-optic neuropathy, SMON, in the 1950s and 1960s.

One of the many people who had been politicized by clioquinol, it turned out, was Rizwan Ahmad, the medical student who had posted the letter about my research on E-Drug. He had sent me an E-mail that he was returning from Pakistan, so we arranged to meet.

Before our interview could begin, Ahmad excused himself to recite his afternoon prayers, seated on the living room floor of the house that he and two other single Pakistani men were renting outside Washington. Ahmad is one of the skinniest healthy people I ever met, and his face is dominated by a heavy Lincolnesque beard, dark glasses and a pronounced mole on his cheek. He is in his late thirties. But he remembers well being a medical student in his early twenties in Pakistan and discovering the fledgling world of drug advocacy through a book called *Prescription for Death: The Drugging of the Third World,* which he read about in the international edition of *Time* magazine. The book was one of San Francisco writer Milton Silverman's follow-ups to his controversial book *Pills, Profits and Politics*; this one dealt with drug problems in less-developed nations and it detailed the way that drugs considered unsafe in one country were sold freely in other countries, regardless of the efforts of the World Health Organization.

Through the book, Ahmad discovered the names of the people who would be his medicinal heroes—and eventually his peers. In the United States there was Silverman, his wife Mia Lydecker, his other collaborator Philip Lee, and, of course, Sidney Wolfe. In the U.K. there was Dr. Andrew Herxheimer, the prolific clinical pharmacologist who edited the British *Drug and Therapeutics Bulletin,* and Charles Medawar, who dispensed drug policy analysis as the founder and director of Social Audit. In Malaysia there was Dr. Kumariah Balasubramaniam, the pharmaceutical adviser to the International Organization of Consumers Unions (IOCU), based in Penang. In Australia there was Dr. Peter Mansfield, head of the international physicians' group Medical Lobby for Appropriate Marketing (MaLAM).

In Sweden there was Dr. Olle Hansson, a crusading neurologist and pediatrician in his late forties who had become galvanized by clioquinol and the efforts to get its largest manufacturer, Ciba-Geigy, to stop making it. When the Japanese convened the 1979 Kyoto International Conference Against Drug-Induced Sufferings, a watershed meeting where drug experts from all over the world first met, Hansson was asked to speak on behalf of the medical consumer and gave a powerful talk calling for a "new pharmaceutical order." His efforts had also led directly to the formation of the international consumer group Health Action International (HAI) in 1981.

Unfortunately, by the time Ahmad found out about Hansson's work, the Swedish physician was dying of cancer. While the two never met, Ahmad was later the recipient of the Olle Hansson award, which is given each year on Olle Hansson Day (May 23, the anniversary of his death at age forty-nine) by the IOCU. He won the award for the kind of consumer activities that Silverman's book inspired him to do. Ahmad began by writing letters to his country's newspapers about drugs that were banned elsewhere but were still being used in Pakistan. After a physician responded to one of his letters very dismissively, Ahmad wrote a lengthy reply, loaded with information from his new international contacts, which the newspaper ran over a full page. Only weeks later, clioquinol was banned by the government in Pakistan. By 1990 Ahmad had written a very Sidney Wolfe–ish book called *Bitter Facts About Drugs,* a guide to nearly two thousand "ineffective, unsafe, or limited use drugs widely sold in Pakistan," which was published by the HAI.

By the time the book was published, Ahmad had already decided to come and study clinical pharmacology at Georgetown under Ray Woosley and Dave Flockhart. But he was also interested in learning pharmacoepidemiology; he understood that Brian Strom, who was known for training many international students, had studied clin-pharm before epidemiology. Ahmad also hoped to work for Sidney Wolfe at Public Citizen and David Kessler at the FDA. He managed to carry out almost his entire ambitious agenda over the course of a few years. (In fact, I had reason to believe that during his FDA stint, he had been partly responsible for piquing the agency's interest in Floxin reactions.) But his career hadn't turned out exactly the way he planned. After finishing at Georgetown, he had trouble finding full-time work. He did some teaching and research at Georgetown University Hospital and was working part-time for the United States Pharmacopeia—which has been setting medicine standards for more than 175 years and, more recently, had expanded into unbiased information services for professionals and patients. But he was generally finding that his reputation as a drug consumer advocate did not help him in the country he had once viewed as the land of pharmaco-opportunity. He wondered aloud whether the time he had spent working for Wolfe had ruined any chances he had for full-time employment in the drug establishment that Wolfe regularly targeted. He was feeling rather discouraged.

Like many discouraged Americans, he was spending more time than ever on the computer. He had become one of the moderators of the E-Drug list, doing pharmacological good works largely for free over the Internet.

As I was leaving Ahmad's house, I asked where I might find a copy of his out-of-print book. He gave me one and kindly autographed it for me. I read it on the way back to Philadelphia, and then put it with my growing collection of consumer advocacy writings on drugs. There are mountains of them, few of which ever get seen by actual consumers, including a steady stream of books published by the HAI and the IOCU and self-published books by advocacy-oriented physicians. This is the essential reading in the world of Essential Drugs, and much of it is extremely critical of the pharmaceutical industry, in ways that even I sometimes find to be overkill: not because of the points made—these writers often cite the same situations and sources I do—but because of the moral of their drug stories.

Beneath the surface of many medicinal crusades is the notion that killing one drug will somehow put a stake in the heart of the drug business, slaying the monster and saving the global village. In the re-telling, these crusades often don't seem to be about medicine at all. They seem to be about capitalism. They often mask, and not very well, a baseline hatred of capitalism. Looking at them closely reminds you that there are still plenty of countries that are not committed to solving eco-nomic problems in Western capitalistic ways. Many of these countries don't even want to recognize the system of patents that allows the cre-ation of brand-name drugs. They want the right to nationalize drug manufacturing so that all medicines will be generic and cheap, and given the sorry states of their health care systems, who can blame them? The occasional donation of large batches of expired medicines from major pharmaceutical companies—a common practice, for which the firms get a tax write-off—does not assuage the resentment of the medical have-nots. As the WHO has pointed out, "There is an inherent conflict of interest between the legitimate business goals of manufacturers and the social, medical and economic needs of providers and the public to select and use drugs in the most rational way."

In reading the more compelling advocacy writing, it's interesting to see how far the authors will go to make their points. Are they trying to improve drug usage, or are they implicitly saying that drugs are all bad, a plot to steal your money and destroy your health? When they describe the myriad problems with psychiatric drugs, are they suggesting we could take them more effectively, or are they really saying we would be better off without them? It's a fine line, but outside North America and Western Europe, it gets crossed more often, and blatantly antimedical, anticorporate feelings are not held at bay. One of the few exceptions is the literature from Australia, where medical consumer groups appear more integrated into the fabric of the national health system so they don't have as much of an "outsider" mentality.

I got into a discussion about this one afternoon with Dr. Andrew Herxheimer, who was a close friend of Olle Hansson's and has been involved for decades in the drug problems of the developed and less-developed countries. We met during a conference exploring the emerging science of placebo effects.

Herxheimer has long observed the bipolar struggle in drug advocacy, and he believes that the international critiques have grown more constructive. "In the first years, advocates were focusing on individual nasty drugs and really campaigning on those," he said. "Now they're more focused on the rational uses of drugs and supporting WHO. They still focus on standards of promotion and pursue the companies like Nestlé with this whole baby milk business. It's still enormously important and long-lived, this whole issue of promoting unhealthy practices and products, bribing professionals to be silent. It takes a lot of energy and commitment to counter that.

"But it's no longer a 'them and us' mentality in drugs. We all have the same drug problems, they just come in different forms in different countries. And we have to deal with what's happening in our own countries. Industry wants to be left alone to do what it wants. They say, 'It's up to the developing countries. We abide by the laws in those countries, and we're not doing anything wrong.' So instead of campaigning on one drug, you have to teach regulators in developing countries how to deal with that. The problem is that there's pressure everywhere for less regulation. But where regulation still hardly exists, it must increase."

Like many of his colleagues, Herxheimer has exchanged some of his essential-drug rhetoric for the relatively new language of the "evidence-based medicine" movement, which is popular in Europe and is slowly catching on in America. Its proponents believe that medical treatments—drug or otherwise—need to be reevaluated based on *all* the available trial evidence, not just the handful of key studies used to get the approvals of government agencies or the endorsements of major journals. The key studies tend to be overwhelmingly positive: a report in the *Annals of Internal Medicine* found that 98 percent of articles based on drug company–sponsored studies reported outcomes favoring the drug of interest; of the articles without direct company support, 79 percent still spoke well of the studied drug. It makes more sense, of course, to examine the breadth of the clinical data on each treatment: the good news, the bad news and even all the boring studies that, alone, provide hardly any news.

"It sounds pretty straightforward, right?" asked Frank Davidoff, editor of the *Annals of Internal Medicine.* "Systematic and conscientious application of the best published evidence to the specific patient at hand. That sounds like the way things ought to be done. But it's not the way people have done things."

In Europe and the United States, *evidence-based medicine* is sometimes a euphemism for managed care, and any procedure that isn't cost effective can be decried as not evidence-based. But the movement itself has the much loftier goal of doing complete, frequently updated meta-analyses of all available clinical data on each treatment. Herxheimer is actively involved in the Cochrane Collaboration, which is the world's largest evidence-based medicine effort and has been compared, in its scope and vision, to the Human Genome Project. Based at Oxford University, it is the offspring of a thirteen-year project that systematically reviewed all randomized clinical trials concerning pregnancy and childbirth. Besides searching journals back to 1950, the researchers wrote to 42,000 obstetricians seeking unpublished trial data, turning up 3,500 previously unknown trials: the results changed several notions about pregnancy care. The Cochrane Collaboration itself began as a program of the British National Health Service in 1992 and was expanded to an international collaboration the next year, with centers all over the world.

Herxheimer believes the biggest impediment to this evidence-based research is the scientific secrecy of the drug companies and, by default, the secrets kept by the regulatory authorities. Because of this secrecy, drug safety advocates now often talk about making the process of drug development and regulation more "transparent," so more trial results would be made available to researchers after a drug is approved. With greater "transparency," your doctor might have a way of reviewing *everything known* about a compound before you put it in your mouth. And when the drug companies boast that more than 40 million patients have already taken a drug in Europe and Asia, your doctor might actually have some idea what really happened to those patients.

Listening to Herxheimer discuss the future glories of evidence-based medicine and transparency, I couldn't help but think about lost pieces of pharmaceutical evidence. I was reminded of a moving conversation I once had with a pharmacologist who had worked at several major drug companies conducting animal studies. He told me about a new psychiatric drug, heading toward FDA approval, that he had tested on monkeys before it was given to humans. It had performed well, "with no nasty effects," on every test. And then, "out of the blue," he recalled, "I killed a monkey at a moderate dose. It died about five minutes after we gave it the drug."

What did that mean?

"Well, it's possible the drug has, in one in a hundred cases, a sudden toxic effect," he said. "The other possibility is that we injected the drug into the monkey's lungs by mistake instead of its gut. We autopsied the monkey, and we couldn't really tell."

He stopped for a moment and held his hands over his eyes. "That one monkey has always troubled me," he said.

Shouldn't this have been reported?

"Well, I know our monkey never got reported," he said, rubbing his forehead. "A lot of work that's done preclinically [before human testing] is never reported. It just sits in notebooks. The FDA doesn't care. They have certain fixed procedures, and what gets reported to them is the results of formal safety testing. But it's more informal in the labs. . . . Now, look, many monkeys were tested, at fairly high doses, when the drug was turned over to the testing people, and nothing like that happened again. So maybe it was a fluke. Nevertheless, the point still stands that adverse events that happen preclinically often do not get reported to the FDA."

I would later spend an eye-opening evening with a group of human drug research subjects, or "guinea pigs" as they prefer to be called, who lay their able bodies on the line (for $200 a day) to safety-test drugs at clinical research centers in and around Philadelphia. They were brought together by the editor of the underground 'zine *Guinea Pig Zero*. Young, white "healthy normal" men of medium weight and build—most of them between lives—they had all the usual gripes one would expect about such work, everything from painful blood draws to baseline dehumanization. But more troubling was what they had to say about the information collected, or *not* collected, in the trials themselves.

Scott, a twenty-five-year-old who moved from Minnesota to Philadelphia in part because it was such a Pharm Belt mecca for guinea pigs, was appalled at the casual way test results were elicited from subjects. "It's unscientific to the point of being buffoonery, sometimes," he said. "It reminds me of an eighth-grade science experiment: here are the variables, keep it simple and clean, and these are the results you need to get a good grade. And to get things to work out, if you have to kind of flub some things, that's okay.

"For example, I was in a study for a sleeping pill. Before it started, they brought us all together, and the doctor came out and talked to us. She said, 'This is the second time we've tried this pill in humans. It's very safe. Now if you look right here in the protocol [the detailed description of the trial given to the subjects], it says some people in the first trial were seeing things.' And *then* she said, 'But these people, they hadn't been honest with us about whether they'd had mental problems before in their lives. So if you don't have psychological problems, you won't be seeing anything.' I found out later that three-quarters of the study participants had seen things. But what she's doing, you see, is implanting the idea in your head that if you're seeing things, it means you have psychological problems. . . . It's such a simplistic and mechanical way these doctors look at health. And from the beginning they're guiding how you're going to respond to the study and how they're going to report it."

Jamie, also in his mid-twenties, saw other biases as well. "First of all," he explained, "if you're a person who does drug studies, you are generally someone who is fairly resistant to drugs and don't feel the bad effects of them very easily. If you did have strong reactions, the lab would stop wanting to use you—and that happens—or you would decide you didn't want to do studies."

But Jamie has also seen some of his reactions not get reported. "If you tell them you're a little tired or have a headache," he said, "unless you tell them several times, they often don't write it down. I've looked in my book [the diary kept on each patient], and they didn't write it down.

"Look, you've got a researcher who wants to pass a drug through the study, and you have a volunteer who wants to be in the study and wants to get into other studies in the future. And I'll tell you, I've been given hints about being a good guinea pig. The nurse comes up and asks, 'You're not suffering any side effects, are you?' and she'll be shaking her head no. 'You're not feeling headachy or anything like that, are you?' and she'll be shaking her head no. 'Okay, so you're feeling fine?' and she's nodding yes."

Scott said he thought they wouldn't overlook a massive problem, but "they're willing to sweep little problems under the bed. It's not as scientific as it's presented to the public. I think it could be more scientific, but they'd have to remove certain external factors. Like the greed motive."

CHAPTER 16

Nice to Know

Just when it seemed like Diane had found some balance between her medications and her life, she had a major setback—set off by what initially appeared to be a smart drug switch. She had been taking an older neuroleptic, Trilafon, when she found the unrelenting visual distortions especially annoying. The drug didn't make the visuals go away, but as she explained with a sardonic shrug, "On Trilafon—who cares?" But her doctor was concerned about the drug's ongoing risk of causing tardive dyskinesia (TD), so he suggested she try the brand-new medication Risperdal, which was being heavily promoted by J&J.

Risperdal was the first new antipsychotic introduced since Clozaril, and it was believed to share Clozaril's very low risk of TD. But because the drug did not carry Clozaril's danger of causing life-threatening agranulocytosis, it had no black box or blood tests, so it was becoming the first antipsychotic ever to be full-out promoted in the modern way. Just as Prozac and its promotion had helped make the treatment of depression seem less scary, the campaign for Risperdal would be the first big-budget assault on the skewed mass perceptions of psychotic symptoms.

But such strong promotional campaigns also make the decision to try a new product a little easier than perhaps it should be. Risperdal was a very new, very powerful drug. It was exactly the kind of medication that Diane's Floxin experience might have made her reluctant to try, right down to the fact that it was made by a division of the same company.

As it went, her Risperdal trial was a huge disappointment. She couldn't tolerate the side effects. Risperdal wreaked havoc with her hormonal system, halting her period and inhibiting her libido. It also caused akathesia: a pathological, nerve-wracking restlessness and inability to sit still. Her experiences were all the more unbearable because some came while we were away on a long business trip to California and Hawaii. Being so far from home, I was even more concerned when she decided to stop taking the drug, as her doctor had said she could if the side effects became too intense. Although she decreased the dose gradually, as she was supposed to, I realized that this was the first time Diane had actually decided she'd rather risk a manic-depressive episode than take a medication. She was still on a mood stabilizer, but I feared that she was putting herself at too great a risk.

My fears, unfortunately, were justified, because she was sent plummeting into a severe depression that it would take her months to climb back out of. (Ironically, Dr. Miller would later come to believe that Risperdal, while useful in other illnesses, shouldn't be used for manic-depression because it made some patients manic.) So we were caught in what is sometimes called the "prescribing cascade," taking drugs to counter the effects of other drugs. It was all the more infuriating because we were supposed to know better than this. How much did you have to know before you could get it right?

Diane's experience got me interested in the hormonal and sexual side effects of drugs. After asking around to see who knew about the subject, I was steered to Dr. Theresa Crenshaw, a physician who was becoming one of the world's few authorities on these hormonal side effects. She was writing the first-ever textbook on what she called "sexual pharmacology."

According to her, Diane's experience was all too typical. One in four sexual problems are believed to be caused by medication. Conversely, Crenshaw told me, "sexual dysfunction and weight gain are the two greatest reasons why a patient will abandon a drug regimen, sometimes resulting in death. But in general, medicine still disregards sexual side effects."

Crenshaw runs a private practice in San Diego, California, specializing in sexual medicine and relationship therapy. Much of her writing seems directed at the *Cosmo* audience and is somewhat touchy-feely: her work on a sexual pharmacology text seemed like a labor of medical love, as well as a deliberate bid to be taken more seriously. Still, I found her credible on the subject of sexual pharmacology, and her gripes about the nonstudy and regulation of sexual side effects struck a chord.

"I would say the industry and the FDA are somewhere between

unaware and negligent," she explained. "The studies needed to get a drug approved by the FDA have absolutely no requirements during Phase I, II and III to assess sexual side effects at all. When they specifically ask patients, 'Are you having side effects,' sometimes sexual dysfunction is there, sometimes not. Sometimes this is very important. Prozac, for example, would *never* have escaped if they had asked routine questions about sexual side effects. Prozac is an example of complete negligence."

Because it had become politically incorrect to mention any negative side effects to Prozac, word had not yet spread that the drug, like many of the SSRIs, caused significant sexual dysfunction in many patients, both female and male. In fact, so many patients had lost their ability to achieve orgasm while taking the drugs that SSRIs were being seen by sex therapists like Crenshaw as a way of treating premature ejaculation. The only downside for the men was that their drug-maintained erections often lasted so long that they *never* climaxed.

Crenshaw was frustrated at how few patients knew about the sex problems of Prozac. "The book *Listening to Prozac* barely mentioned sexual effects," she lamented. "How hard could he have been listening to his patients? It's one of the most pronounced adverse effects of the drug." She was also concerned that managed care pressures on drug selection meant too many decisions would be made not on sexual safety profiles but on cost. "In some cases, for twice as much money, you can have an orgasm," she explained. "There are newer, cleaner drugs. But these are more expensive, and they're often not offered because the physician is being cost-conscious. So here you can end up with people who don't connect sexual dysfunction to the drug. They can end up dissolving relationships. Or equally traumatic, they're in chronic relationship turmoil."

She had no doubt that women would suffer more than men for "bad sexual pharmacology. . . . We're all uncomfortable with aspects of sex, and most mature physicians got their training when it wasn't even discussed," Crenshaw told me. "The only mention I recall from medical school was 'dyspareunia is better than apareunia.' That is, painful intercourse is better than no intercourse—or more to the point, painful intercourse for the woman is better than no intercourse for the man!"

Pharmacological gender bias, though, is much bigger than anorgasmia. It can affect every aspect of a woman's life. In November 1995 I went to suburban Washington for a two-day conference on gender and drug development, organized by the FDA's Office of Women's Health, to hear what the agency was going to do to remedy the situation.

I had long been convinced that when it came to drugs and drug reactions, women had every right to feel—well, doomed. But it was still stunning to hear exactly *how* and *why* women feel doomed. And it was shocking to realize that, even with some of the best scientific minds in the world concentrating on the problem, nobody was really going to do much about it.

That much was painfully clear during the brief preliminary remarks delivered by representatives from various constituencies. These began with an enthusiastic call to arms from David Kessler, followed by a presentation by the head of the Office of Women's Health, another from CDER and yet another from the NIH.

Then the designated representative from industry rose to address the crowded Doubletree Hotel ballroom. Dr. Janice Bush, vice president for regulatory affairs at Janssen, broke the ice with a joke about a woman reading a headstone in a cemetery.

" 'Here lies Elizabeth Matthews, pharmaceutical executive and compassionate person,' " the woman read. Then she thought for a second. "Good heavens," she said, "they had to put two people in the same spot."

There were polite titters from the crowd. But when Dr. Bush proceeded with her remarks, the room grew chilly.

"There is information which is *nice* to know," she declared, "and information which is *needed* to know." Not only did she sound patronizing and dismissive, she was using the dreaded n-word, *nice,* anathema to thinking women.

And she kept saying it over and over. Data on how the menstrual cycle affects the drugs women take might be "nice to have," she said, but it's not "needed." If the FDA were to say that the menstrual cycle was "critical in evaluation of data, *no drugs will ever be developed.*"

It sounded as if she believed that everything this two-day conference had been called to discuss was merely "nice to know." She didn't even pretend that industry was interested. The best she could muster in conclusion was a rousing pronouncement that "improvements in any area are always desired. . . . I hope we can improve our dialogue with the FDA."

During the break, I ran into Dr. Ana Szarfman, the FDA medical officer who had approved Floxin. She was very friendly—asking about Diane's health and my work—but she was still seething over Dr. Bush's "nice to know" speech.

"Can you *believe* what that woman said?" she asked, gesturing toward the podium. "This is what we have to deal with *every day.*"

Why are women doomed—to have more drug reactions and more drug-induced deaths and generally to be victimized by a system that presumes to be helping them? Well, little is known about female pharmacology. And for most of our lives, it basically has been against the law to learn much of anything new.

Since the early 1960s, there has been such a sincere, almost obsessive desire to avoid another thalidomide that the science of testing drugs on women, especially women of child-bearing age, has been largely still-born. The fear of a drug's ability to cause birth defects—its teratogen-icity—has been so high that nearly all questions concerning the pharmacology of women have been deemed unanswerable. While this fear existed from 1962 on, it didn't become law until 1977, when the FDA issued guidelines that all but banned "women of child-bearing potential" from participating in Phase I and early Phase II clinical trials. Those trials determine the standard doses to be evaluated during the rest of a drug's development. They also establish the baseline of its toxicity. By law, those studies have been populated only by men.

So it's hardly surprising that the 1977 guidelines—under which many of the medicines we take today were developed—produce drugs that are often less than female-friendly. The standard doses are often too high: one of the patients invited to address the conference, a nurse-midwife in her early fifties with a heart condition, gave a vivid description of how she shaves off part of her nitroglycerin tablets. The side effects specific to women are generally unknown. Worse, even when data on female patients exists, they aren't routinely made available as separate information. Consequently, drug study results are rarely analyzed in a way that would be especially useful to women.

Those 1977 guidelines stayed in place for sixteen years. New rules were issued in 1993 that technically overturned the ban on testing women in clinical trials. But the new guidelines were so ambiguous that one of the main goals of this conference was to figure out what they actually meant. The reason for the confusion was that the old rules hadn't been tossed out because the FDA and industry had finally come to their senses and realized that women were being hurt by the rules. In fact, industry had become comfortably accustomed to the old guidelines, especially as the relationship between patient and drug-seller grew more litigious. From a legal point of view, it was much safer to label every

drug with a boldfaced warning against taking it during pregnancy than
to take the chance that a birth defect could be linked to a product
during testing.

To get industry to take female pharmacology as seriously as it should,
the FDA would have to make this issue a huge priority and force a
paradigm shift with massive scientific, economic and legal consequences.
The agency would need to do more than lift the ban: it would have to
mandate true gender equality in testing. But everyone at the gender
conference knew that the guidelines had not been rewritten to force such
a dramatic change in thinking. Veteran FDA-watchers knew that David
Kessler had already decided that his reign would be remembered for two
other paradigm shifts: regulating tobacco and accelerating the approval
process, especially for AIDS drugs. Any doubts about his priorities were
made clear when he finished his opening remarks for the gender conference. Instead of sticking around to participate, he dashed off to spend
the day at the pivotal AIDS drugs advisory committee meeting being
held nearby.

While many forces contributed to the 1993 rule changes that provoked
the gender conference, it was clear that women with AIDS—some of the
most disenfranchised patients in all of medicine—had ultimately made
the difference. Their Joan of ARC was Terry McGovern, a perpetually
leery sparkplug of an attorney who was the executive director of the
HIV Law Project, based in Manhattan. McGovern had not set out to
force the FDA to rethink the entire subject of female pharmacology. All
she wanted was to make sure that women with HIV had the same access
to experimental treatments as their male counterparts. But to do that,
she had to take on the entire issue, which appeared to have been all but
abandoned by more mainstream women's health groups.

McGovern had made a name for herself in AIDS advocacy in 1990,
when she sued the U.S. government, claiming that the Social Security
definition of AIDS discriminated against women, who often found themselves unable to qualify for disability despite symptoms identical to those
that qualified men. In late 1992 she filed a citizen's petition demanding
that the 1977 FDA guidelines be abolished so women with AIDS could
get into experimental drug trials.

During her opening talk at the gender conference, McGovern explained that she became interested in the FDA when a woman with
AIDS and cervical cancer complained to her that she couldn't get into a
trial for a new Hoffmann-LaRoche drug because they insisted she wear

an IUD or be surgically sterilized to assure compliance with FDA rules. Regardless of whether or not the patient was heterosexually active, the FDA guideline required proof of aggressive birth control. Even with such proof, younger women were very paternalistically dissuaded from drug trials.

"The point is, there is a deep mistrust of women in the drug development system," McGovern complained. "And the result is women taking drugs and not being told about their side effects, and women being denied experimental treatments."

The 1993 FDA gender rule changes we were here to discuss had been put into place largely to respond to McGovern's petition to allow women access to all clinical trials. But she felt it was no more than lip service.

"This guideline doesn't really require *anything,*" she said. "The guideline has no actual teeth: it's not a regulation, it has no power of law. It also lets drug companies off the hook if they don't want to do these studies. There are no requirements regarding inclusion of women. They don't *have to* collect additional data.

"I've looked at hundreds of HIV-positive women who experienced terrible side effects from approved AIDS drugs. At the same time, they want to know if their increased cervical problems are from the side effects or the HIV. They're scared, and nobody can answer their questions. It's not about information that would be *nice to have,*" she said, shooting a glance over at Dr. Bush. "It's about telling women how to use drugs. I want women to be told what these drugs do. There are so many unanswered questions about quality, peace of mind and trust."

Listening to McGovern speak was my first recognition of how much insight AIDS activists had into the problems of the entire drug delivery system. I was impressed but also saddened. It was too bad that much of what they had learned was being used only for people with AIDS, when it could benefit so many people with other diseases. Terry McGovern, by her actions on behalf of several thousand women infected with HIV, had, almost by accident, helped all women who took medications. But in general the efforts of AIDS activists did not spill over into the general population: they were developing their own rules for AIDS, which were exceptions to the rules for everybody else. Instead of lobbying to reform the whole system, they had succeeded in pushing the FDA to create a wholly separate accelerated-approval process for AIDS drugs. The HIV fast track even had its own advisory committee.

At the FDA, the AIDS activists had been the squeakiest wheels in history. Maybe they had taken all the oil.

.   .   .

The gender conference was interesting both because of the provocative ideas being discussed and because I now felt I knew a lot of these people and often even understood what they were talking about. Dave Flockhart and Ray Woosley from Georgetown were there. Before his talk, Dave gave me his new business card, which had his E-mail address of the moment. Flockhart gave a very technical talk about differences in liver clearance between men and women. Woosley's speech was more dramatic. "It is a very sobering thought that we have overlooked this for so long," he said, "and it scares me to think about what else we've missed out there."

After the day's talks, Flockhart and Woosley smuggled me into the speakers' cocktail party, where I finally got a chance to meet some of the people I knew only by phone (or from poring over transcripts of advisory committee meetings). There was a fairly small cast of characters at the red-hot center of most FDA drug issues, including Mac Lumpkin, whom I had gotten to know pretty well from the Floxin experience; and Dr. Roger Williams, a compact man with a sort of ex-military quality to his clipped voice, whom I had interviewed long-distance. Williams was the agency's point man on the controversy surrounding the experimental antihepatitis drug FIAU, which had killed all those test subjects at the NIH in 1993. The agency and the NIH were still fighting over the lessons to be learned from that fiasco. I was especially interested in it, because I knew Williams was pushing for a proposed agency rule change that would dramatically broaden the reporting and analysis of drug reactions during clinical trials.

The rule would force drug companies to submit various types of "worst-case scenario" analyses of drug reactions during clinical trials, along with the usual rosy analyses they currently turn in. This new additional analysis would presume that all serious ADRs and deaths *had been* caused by the study drug. The company would also have to submit more comprehensive data on drug reactions that didn't meet the definition of "serious," and a final clinical safety report on patients who discontinued the trial. It seemed like a perfectly logical, scientifically airtight response to the discovery of a "delayed drug toxicity" to FIAU—appearing, in some cases, months after the patient stopped taking the experimental drug. Unfortunately, the plan was drowning in the whirlpool of deregulation. "It was proposed ten days before the Republicans came into office," one top FDA official would lament at a conference. "The climate changed . . . and the comments received against the proposal could be measured in linear feet." The new rules were put "on hold."

After Williams, I talked to Bob Temple, who had played a pivotal role in so many of the controversies I had been following (and was the star of Paul Leber's Halcion diary entries). For years, Temple has been the most familiar FDA figure down in the regulatory trenches. A human drug computer clothed in the gray slacks and blue blazer of a conservative doctor, Temple came out of the same group of young NIH researchers in the early 1970s that spawned Sidney Wolfe. The two reportedly had argued a lot when they were colleagues, and as they grew up together into their jobs, the argument came to impact all of medicine. While Wolfe sees smoke and generally assumes fire, Temple believes that a randomized, double-blind trial is needed before flames can be proven. Some top drug safety experts feel Temple is among a powerful handful of FDA officials who don't put enough stock in epidemiology, even when it is the only available way to analyze a certain problem. Since Temple is often the last guy a drug has to win over if it is to be approved, Wolfe is often the most relentless and powerful second-guesser of his decisions.

Temple is one of the great FDA characters. Depending on who you speak to, he is either the head wonk or the rabbi of CDER. Whenever anything goes wrong at the agency, he is viewed either as the problem or the solution—sometimes both. Even his detractors are amazed by his mental agility. Temple can swallow drug applications with his eyes and regurgitate their most minute details. Because of his amazing long-term recall and sheer longevity, he has become a keeper of the agency's institutional memory. Perhaps one reason the FDA has been so absurdly slow in fully computerizing its operations is that with Temple around, it sometimes doesn't seem necessary.

One of the most provocative people I met at the gender conference was Dr. Jean Hamilton. The former head of the Women's Health Program at Duke, Hamilton had just moved to Philadelphia to run a new program at the Medical College of Pennsylvania, which was the birthplace of women's medical education in the United States. A woman on a mission, Hamilton peppered her speech with pronouncements that women use more medications than men, suffer more adverse reactions than men, and are generally the recipients of more polypharmacy for chronic illness than men—so what was the FDA going to do about it? Although she was well known as a women's health advocate—and dressed the part, with long flowing skirts, dangly earrings and short-cropped gray hair—Hamilton's specialty was psychopharmacology, and some of the examples she gave were alarming.

She had studied menstrual effects on antidepressants and mood stabilizers, which were apparently quite significant, even though, in all the time that Diane had been taking psychotropic drugs, nobody had ever mentioned the *possibility* that her doses might have to be adjusted depending on the time of the month. Hamilton presented slides of a case of manic-depressive illness where a woman taking lithium always had breakthrough symptoms when she was premenstrual. After monitoring her blood-lithium levels, the researchers were able to determine that when she was premenstrual, she needed nearly twice as much lithium to maintain a therapeutic level of the drug. In fact, the dose she needed would have been toxic for her at any other time of the month. Hamilton also showed interesting data about how taking birth control pills changes the way women's bodies metabolize antidepressants.

When I later interviewed Hamilton at length, she explained that she had fallen into her role, which she saw as being a Ralph Nader of female pharmacology, by accident. It was primarily because premenstrual syndrome (PMS) became the "disease of the year" just as the depressive disorders lab she was working in at the NIH was looking for a new, fundable population to study.

"When doing background work for studies on the menstrual cycle," she said, "I ran across basic science data showing there were sex differences in the way drugs acted in the brain. Sex hormones had large effects on the neurotransmitter system. In rodents, you got a fifty percent difference in the cycle. In other systems, you could get a twenty percent variation. When I took this data in to my lab chief, his response was, 'Oh yeah, that's interesting. It looks like there's a sex difference in animals. It couldn't be in *people,* of course, because if there were a difference, we'd already know about it.' "

At that, she laughed out loud. "I later worked for a guy who made a comment that some people are so expert, they don't even *need* data."

Hamilton was outraged at how little progress had been made since her realization in the early 1980s that nobody was studying women's pharmacology, even though women were the ones taking most of the pills. "If you get out the bible textbook on pharmacology and look in the index on the effects of sex, or if you look at the different handbooks, there's *no mention* of using lower doses on women," she said. "In medical training, the one place you learn about individualizing doses is in pediatrics, and in the eighties there was some education about dosages for geriatrics—it's a huge blind spot. People just don't put two and two together."

Hamilton had come to this subject because of feminism. But she realized that the problem of overdosing women was part of something pharmacologically much bigger: generic dosing. That means giving everyone the same pill regardless of size, body weight, age, sex, race or physical condition.

In clinical pharmacology the female, the elderly, the prepubescent and the non-Caucasian are referred to by the catch-all euphemism "special populations," which is ludicrous considering that in many cases, the "special populations" far outnumber the "regular" populations. A general rule of thumb is that a special population is "special" not because it's in the minority but because nobody knows very much about its pharmacological uniqueness. And there is, apparently, no good financial reason to find out. "One-dose-fits-all is convenient only for the pharmaceutical companies," Dr. Jean-Louis Steimer, a tall, needle-thin French pharmacologist from Hoffmann-LaRoche, told the gender conference. "It is considered a marketing disadvantage to a company to have differential doses."

While many drugs are available in several dosages, even if your physician bothers to correctly determine that a higher or lower one is best for you, they are still standardized in a way that patients are not. Ironically, back when relatively little was known about the science of drug activity, doses were individually measured for patients by the apothecary. Today, as our understanding of pharmacokinetics and pharmacodynamics has increased to make much more exact dosing possible, pills are more standardized than ever. Many drugs come with directions about how to adjust for body weight, but unless a patient is severely ill or grossly heavy or thin, standard doses are often used first, then adjusted based on patient complaints. Apparently it even happens in hospitals, where many drugs are administered by IV in personalized dosages. I once heard a hospital drug utilization expert decry the failure of doctors to determine dose by patient body weight. "It's appalling," he said. "I mean, if only hospitals could *charge* for weighing, it would be done every time."

Drug companies blame this deplorable economic reality on lazy doctors, who will always choose the drug and dose that requires the least work for *them*. Physicians blame it on greedy drug companies that are more interested in streamlining their product offerings than in pharmacodynamics. Regardless of who is to blame, the truth is that physicians and drug companies are looking for drugs to be, as they say in computer-ese, "user friendly."

Unfortunately, they forget who the real users are. It's not them, it's *us*.

If women have it bad, children may have it worse. Women are at least considered a valuable market for pharmaceutical sales. Children generally are not. Even though it was the plight of children that sparked the two major revisions of drug law in this century—the kids who died from elixir sulfanilamide in 1937 and the thalidomide-deformed babies in the early 1960s—adult drug users have been the major beneficiaries of their suffering. For decades, pediatricians have been banging their heads against the wall trying to draw attention to the medication problems of the young. Their rallying cry has been "children are not just small adults." But hardly anyone has listened. As a result, pediatricians have been forced to do much of their prescribing off-label, or to rely on the few companies that do bother to apply for pediatric indications. According to one pediatric pharmacologist, almost none of the drugs used to treat premature babies for a variety of life-threatening conditions have been approved for use in children.

In 1979 the FDA made its first attempt to remedy the situation by publishing new regulations that would encourage manufacturers to conduct studies for specific pediatric indications. According to Dr. Sanford Cohen of the American Academy of Pediatrics, the effect of this rule change was not "more adequately labeled drugs" but more labels that say " 'the drug's safety and effectiveness in children have not been established.' Eighty percent of the prescription drugs currently marketed in the United States are labeled with such disclaimers."

One such drug was Abbott's antibiotic Biaxin (which became quite successful, having benefited greatly from the extra attention of former Omniflox sales reps). Close friends of ours, both psychologists, had a three-year-old daughter whose life had been turned upside down by the drug, which their pediatrician had prescribed for a sinus infection. After her second day on the medication, the child developed persistent diarrhea. Her mother stopped giving her the drug after the fourth day, but the diarrhea didn't stop. The pediatrician said it was "nothing," but after blood appeared in the child's stool, they went to a specialist at Children's Hospital. She was diagnosed with "C Dif," short for *clostridium difficile,* a bacterium in the intestine that an overly strong antibiotic can destroy, leading to drug-induced colitis. It was a grueling four months and many visits to the GI specialist before the little girl was well again. I added the story to my growing litany of drug-reaction true confessions.

In 1994, with a pediatrician running the agency, the FDA had taken another pass at the pediatric drug problem, urged on this time by a growing confederation of patient groups, everyone from representatives of pediatric AIDS and cancer patients to the Virginia-based Mothers of Asthmatics. The agency published new rules, but they had the same problems as the new rules for women. While they encouraged companies to test more drugs on children and be more aggressive about analyzing the data they had already collected on adults to draw more label-worthy conclusions about pediatric uses, they didn't make the companies do anything. So many companies didn't. During 1995, the first year the FDA rules encouraged additional pediatric labeling, the agency approved twenty-five new drugs. Only three had pediatric labeling. The sponsors of nine others claimed that pediatric studies were in the works, while the sponsors of the rest said no such studies were planned because the drugs weren't likely to be used for children—even though pediatric pharmacology experts felt otherwise. The FDA, however, would not actually mandate any changes. New rules that allowed and encouraged more testing on women and children were one thing. New rules that would force the issue, and might increase the amount of money companies had to spend on testing before approval—just to get information that was "nice to know"—took more political clout than the agency cared to expend on the issue at that time.

This didn't mean that pediatricians were completely making it up as they went along. There was considerable exchange of ideas on off-label uses, and there were forums for opinions to reach consensus. In 1994 the National Institute of Child Health and Human Development had created a network of five pediatric pharmacology centers to do drug research on children, with new and old drugs. But much of pediatric drug use was still based on standards that had been thrown out for adults twenty years ago, when randomized clinical trials replaced anecdotal studies and the testimonials of leading experts. And the kinds of therapeutic fine points that arise only after the basic safety and efficacy research is done—such as, how drugs used in growing children might affect their development—were subjects mostly for speculation.

While the problems of pediatric medication were age-old, they were being exacerbated by a new societal twist: single-parent families and kids in day care. Over lunch at a medical conference, a nurse from Minneapolis and a physician from Pittsburgh laid out a theory of how harried parents made the situation worse. Every mom, they said, wants an antibiotic for her kid, even if it won't help and may even hurt. "It takes me twenty minutes to explain to a mom why she shouldn't want antibiotics for her child and how they won't work," the doctor explained. "At the end of twenty minutes, with charts and articles, she'll still want the drug, and she'll go to another doc if she can't have it." While responsible doctors have long engaged in a fruitless effort to persuade their adult patients not to use antibiotics for problems the drugs won't resolve, the new wrinkle, the nurse said, was that bed rest and any other treatment *except* drugs had been all but legislated out of existence by day care. "For those to be an option, you have to take a day off work," she explained. "That's one more reason to demand an antibiotic."

Besides the problems with prescription medications, concern was also growing about the widespread misuse of over-the-counter drugs for children. *JAMA* had recently reported that over half of a representative group of three-year-olds had been given an OTC medicine during a thirty-day period. A related study said that poison control centers were receiving more than 130,000 reports a year about children under five being inadvertently overdosed with pain relievers, cough and cold products or gastrointestinal preparations. When it came to medicine, their well-meaning parents simply didn't know what they were doing.

In the summer of 1997 the White House would finally announce its intention to step in and force the drug companies to do more research on pediatric drug uses—by requiring the FDA to establish new testing guidelines. The rule would cover new drugs that either represented a significant advance in pediatric care or would be taken by more than 100,000 children a year, but the tests wouldn't be required before the drugs' approval in adults. As for existing drugs, if they were shown to be needed by children but were not being used because of the shortage of data, the FDA could compel the company to do new pediatric tests—although possibly only for safety. Given the fact that the last such sweeping change in policy—the 1962 passage of the new efficacy standard—took over fifteen years to implement, pediatric experts were hopeful, but not holding their breath.

If women have it rough and children have it rougher, women who want to have children are the "special population" that feels least special. They suffer because little is known about the specific pharmacology of pregnancy. But they also suffer because the illnesses they were successfully treating with drugs before conception are usually allowed to run unchecked for three, six or nine months in the name of safety for the fetus. Almost nothing is known about how *that* might affect the fetus.

In the drug business, information about drugs and pregnancy often isn't even "nice to know." At an FDA symposium on the subject, the chairman of UCLA's ob/gyn department said pregnant women faced "an attitude of therapeutic nihilism." Nowhere is that problem more visible than in the standard use-in-pregnancy warnings found on drug labels that purport to rate the risk of a medicine's teratogenicity. Since the 1970s the FDA and other regulatory authorities have employed a system of rating teratogenic risks either A, B, C, D or, for the most dangerous drugs, X. But drug companies are not required to give their drugs a use-in-pregnancy rating, and most drugs have not been given one by their manufacturers, leaving women with no guidance at all. Of the drugs that do carry ratings, many of their grades have been determined primarily by results of animal trials only, even though animals aren't necessarily reliable predictors of human birth defects. According to a *New England Journal of Medicine* editorial, of the twelve hundred products known to cause birth defects in animals, only thirty are known to do the same in humans. ("A" drugs have been proven not to cause defects in animals and humans. "X" drugs definitely cause defects in both, and the other rankings fall somewhere in between. See pages 393–95 for a complete description.)

In 1994 the Teratology Society, which publishes the top journal in the field, issued a harsh statement about the FDA rating system, declaring that it is "inappropriate" to be used as the "basis for decisions regarding the continuation and termination of pregnancy in women who have received medications." The statement lamented that most medications, nearly 70 percent, were classified as category C only because it was the "default assignment," which the society believed was "misleading to many practitioners who consider this rating to indicate some degree of risk rather than just a lack of information." ("C" drugs generally have not been effectively tested for teratogenicity in humans or animals, and the smattering of animal and human results haven't been troubling enough to completely dissuade use in pregnancy.) The society was recommending a complete overhaul of all pregnancy warnings—a recommendation that has so far been ignored—and pronounced the "usual labeling statement" about weighing the risks and benefit of drugs during pregnancy to be "useless."

Diane and I were learning about all these useless warnings firsthand because, to our mutual surprise, we were contemplating having a child.

The discussions had begun in the late summer during a drive home from the country, where we had spent the day with our nieces, Emma and Anna, who were then three and one and a half years old. While many of our friends have children, we had never bonded as quickly and intensely with them as we had with these two enchanting little girls. They were like poster children for having children.

The issue of kids had been off the table since Diane was Floxed. I had been ambivalent about being a father even before that, although, like those few of our peers who were still "child free," we had been wrestling with the notion for years. But since the births of our nieces, and then our two nephews, Jake and Eli, I was reconsidering. These feelings needed to be teased out, but the person I normally did that kind of teasing with was Diane, and I was afraid that anything I said to her about babies would be the wrong thing.

Suddenly, she turned the tables on me. As we motored down the turnpike, she said she was worried that I wanted a baby more than I had expressed, and that if the issue was simply pocket-vetoed by the passing of time and opportunity, we might regret it. She proposed that we should give it a try. Her only condition was that I promise never to say to others that we were "trying." It was a term she disliked, because she felt it invited family and friends to become too involved, rooting for a result.

Our official statement was to be: we were "not not-trying."

Her proposal took me completely by surprise. It made me tearful, especially since her courage came at a time when steadiness was so hard to maintain and a pregnancy would involve many risks. While I was sure I would eventually accept her proposal, I had to think about it, and of course, we had to talk to her doctors about it.

Apparently Diane had already been discussing it with her doctor, because it affected some looming decisions about the next step in her medical care. Both were pleased with her antidepressant, Wellbutrin, but the mood stabilizer she had been taking for the past two years, Tegretol, seemed to have lost its effectiveness. Her doctor wanted her either to take more Tegretol (the drug cannibalizes itself in the system, so the dose periodically needs to be increased) or switch to the NAMI wonder drug, Clozaril. The antipsychotic had been used almost exclusively for schizophrenia but was now being tried off-label for treatment-resistant bipolar disorder. In fact, some believed that it would eventually prove more effective for manic-depressive illness than for schizophrenia and might even work as a "monotherapy"—one drug taking the place of several.

This prospect was especially appealing because, like Diane, many people with manic-depressive illness find themselves burdened with scores of different medications at any given time: mood stabilizers, antidepressants, antipsychotics and sleeping agents, as well as other drugs just to combat side effects.

We had stayed in contact with Kay Jamison after I wrote about her, and we had also gotten to know her husband, Dr. Richard Wyatt, a prominent NIH clinical researcher who is a leading authority on antipsychotic drugs. So we were able to get some of the world's best advice about the medication switch. Jamison and Wyatt were among the growing group of doctors who believed strongly in Clozaril's potential as a mood stabilizer. It was wonderful to be able to talk with them about the pros and cons. Their encouragement made Diane's decision a little easier, but by no means *easy,* because the drug was still associated mostly with schizophrenia treatment. In a way, the stigma was scarier to Diane than the weekly blood testing to screen for Clozaril's worst side effect, agranulocytosis, the potentially fatal blood disorder.

Clozaril also had a slightly better teratogenicity profile than her current mood stabilizer. Tegretol was in pregnancy category C and had been associated with some serious congenital malformations, including spina bifida, not only in animal studies but also in humans. Clozaril was category B, meaning it had not been associated with any fetal malformations but also hadn't been well tested. I'm not sure most doctors would have taken the difference between B and C that seriously. But to Diane, who had little information to go on, it helped.

She decided to go on Clozaril. While it made her sleepy and caused her to gain weight, it seemed to have an immediate positive impact, and she was amazed at how quickly she was able to discontinue her other drugs. She also found that the standard dose was much higher than she needed. A "baby dose" of 100 milligrams a day proved to be enough. It was the best medication news we had had in years. But of course, it was hard to know how the "baby dose" and a baby might coexist. While she had chosen the drug largely because it seemed more prudent if she got pregnant, we still hadn't actually done anything that might, well, cause her to get pregnant. The idea was still too nerve-wracking. We needed help putting our choices into perspective.

The first time I saw Gideon Koren, one of the world's experts on what *isn't* known about pregnant women and drugs, he was on a roll, and his thick French-Canadian accent made him sound especially outraged. "I cannot think of another group that is so often orphaned by drug therapy," he declared to a large assembly of clinical pharmacologists, including many from industry who he thought just *didn't get it*. "Look at all the results presented today: ten men, fifteen men, men, men, men, men *men,* as if women don't *exist!*"

Koren wasn't trying to denigrate the other "special population" problems on the afternoon's conference agenda: liver enzyme functions unique to African Americans, an age-related side effect of an antirejection drug, a metabolic change in AIDS patients caused by an antimycobacterial drug. He just thought pregnant women deserved more attention and weren't getting it. Koren was the head of clinical pharmacology at Toronto's Hospital for Sick Children. But he was also the founder of Motherisk, the world's most comprehensive drug information service for pregnant women. The program had been in existence since 1985, yet hardly anyone outside of Canada knew about it.

Many hospitals offer referral services that simply rehash standard drug company pregnancy warnings. But Motherisk is different. Motherisk does its own aggressive research, even seeking out pregnant women who have taken drugs by mistake to follow the result. It has counseled more than 125,000 women, family members and health professionals, following up on so many of the pregnancies that it can rightly claim ownership of the largest prospective database of teratogenicity information in the world. Motherisk even studies women's placentas in the laboratory, re-creating the womb using a technique called "placenta perfusion" to see how drugs affect the placenta itself and which drugs get through to the fetus. Koren and his colleagues aren't satisfied to shrug their shoulders over the information nobody has. They try to get it themselves because they doubt anyone else will. They cleverly combine the tools of clinical pharmacology and those of epidemiology.

"Every drug we take can be measured in a baby," he said. "But now every medicine is treated as if all drugs are the new thalidomide. For example, 10 percent of women need an antidepressant during pregnancy but are told, 'It's the new thalidomide.' This causes the *women* huge damage.

"Companies say there is no way to do this research. Now Motherisk came and showed them there is a model. Maybe now the orphaned population will come to the agencies and demand these studies. The companies shouldn't be able to say, 'We'll collect any cases that call us.' They should contract for this the same way they contract for rat studies. Imagine a company coming to the FDA and saying, 'Oh, we can't do this rat study because there's nobody to do it.'"

Motherisk exists at the intersection of the legal-drug world and the real world. Consider Accutane (isotretinoin), the Roche drug for severe acne that is so X-rated for pregnant women that Koren calls it "the worst teratogen on the market today." Accutane is interesting because it was approved by the FDA in 1982 with the knowledge that it was teratogenic, and it has always been labeled that way, although there have been some disputes about the strength of that label warning and the company's candor about the defects that led to it. But Koren still questions whether a strong label warning can solve the problem.

"The regulatory agencies believe that by labeling the drug properly, women will read it and won't get pregnant," he said. "But *half of all pregnancies aren't planned and thirty percent of adults are functionally illiterate.* You can write what you want: they can't read it. This caused a major standoff at FDA. People came to say this stuff should be removed from the market, but there was also a large group of dermatologists supporting it. The result is that Accutane is the first drug in the history of medicine for which a woman has to sign a consent to read the warning and then agrees to use two sorts of contraception.

"I can tell you, the women may sign the consent, but many just take it anyway."

Koren explained that when he started Motherisk, he thought its purpose would be to protect mothers, but now it seems equally involved in protecting babies from unnecessary abortions. Women, he found, were severely overestimating the risks associated with drugs and underestimating the risks of everything else associated with their pregnancy.

"In Athens, after Chernobyl, half of the pregnant women terminated their pregnancies because doctors told them they had a hundred percent assurance of birth defects," Koren said. "This was misinformation . . . but it's indicative of the problem of many physicians telling women, 'Don't take any risk,' when what they really mean is 'Don't make *me* take any risk.' "

The new gospel of teratology is to "make sure you weigh the risk of *not* treating the mother." But it is difficult to persuade physicians and patients to do that. They must first accept the fact that even without medication, there is a 2 to 3 percent risk of birth defects. Then they must be convinced that there is a way to get good, solid numbers to establish the risk of the untreated condition, for both the mother and the fetus.

"At least fifteen to twenty percent of women who are pregnant are being treated for a serious condition," Koren told me. "And more women than ever are being diagnosed with chronic illness. There have been estimates that major depression affects ten percent of women. Many need treatment, and if they aren't treated, they will be very sick and try to commit suicide. Their ability to care for a child will be poor. Yet doctors are hesitant to treat them."

Koren's group would soon publish a breakthrough study that would change the way women with depression were treated. Its most newsworthy finding, which Koren had already been discussing at conferences, was that taking Prozac or several of the older tricyclic antidepressants didn't appear to increase the risk of birth defects. When the results were eventually published in 1997 in *The New England Journal of Medicine,* they would begin to alter the way many psychiatrists and general practitioners approached the treatment of depression. Because of Prozac's place in the psychiatric drug pantheon as the Pill of mental health, the study would also be seen as a windfall for its manufacturer, Eli Lilly. Koren found that ironic because Lilly hadn't been very interested in participating in the research and Prozac had only been added as a control drug. The study had primarily been funded by Ciba-Geigy to test one of its older tricyclic antidepressants.

Regardless of who paid and who benefited, the study was a landmark for pregnant women and for Motherisk. "Now, because of this study," Koren crowed, "psychiatrists and other health providers can tell women all over the world, 'Your baby has the same chance of being normal and going to college as the baby of a woman who was not treated.' . . . Of course, you won't find that information in the product monograph. Because of the medical and legal issues, they don't want to label it for this use."

Even after listening to Koren and calling the Motherisk hotline to get the most up-to-date information on Clozaril—there was, of course, very little, but they did recommend Prozac—we were still left hanging. Our only consolation was knowing that everyone else was in the same dilemma. We were particularly struck by our ongoing discussions with Richard Wyatt. When Diane started on Clozaril, he said that if she found she was pregnant, she should probably stop taking the drug immediately. He even wondered about whether she should stop right away *in case* she got pregnant. Several months later, when it was clear she was having a good result on a very low dose, he wondered aloud if she shouldn't just stay on the drug even *after* she became pregnant. Wyatt was not Diane's doctor, just a very knowledgeable friend. But he had done a lengthy, informal consult with Dr. Miller, and his shifting opinion mattered to us. We guessed he might have been influenced by the handful of new anecdotal reports of women who had taken Clozaril, at much higher doses, and delivered normal children. But we knew he wasn't sure.

Diane decided she would stay on the drug unless she knew she was pregnant, then would probably go off it—at least for the first three months. That's what many women on medication were being told to do. She also decided that fertility drugs would not be an option for her. We had seen too many friends suffer through harsh side effects from them, including one couple who were pushed to the brink of divorce by the wife's severe drug reactions.

From there, we decided to let nature take its course. Regardless of what happened, Diane's proposal about pregnancy was, in and of itself, one of the most important steps in our marriage. It was, in many ways, her declaration that her illness would not keep us from moving forward, wherever forward turned out to be.

CHAPTER 17

Facing Up to

Retin-A

I had been fascinated by Retin-A since my earliest blemished days. I was thirteen when the drug came on the market in 1971 as the first industrial-strength acne medicine, and I vividly recall discussing it with my very menacing dermatologist. He dissuaded me from trying it, sticking with his own regime of injections of antibiotics, low-oil diets and painful in-office blackhead removal. So it wasn't until summer camp, where kids from cities large and small came together for a month to compare zit treatments, that I first met people who used the stuff. (I also met kids who used this otherworldly green mint julep cream before bed, the smell of which I can still conjure in my mind's nose to this day.)

Because the medicine worked by burning off a layer of skin, Retin-A people had a sunburny glow that made them appear either in pain or perpetually embarrassed. I remember thinking they were crazy to use something so harsh for pimples. It was like getting chemotherapy for hiccups.

Twenty-five years later, I found myself fascinated by Retin-A for a completely different reason. Its manufacturer, Ortho—the company that made Floxin—had pleaded guilty to appalling criminal charges from the U.S. Justice Department. The company admitted to *shredding* thousands of documents requested by the FDA. The documents concerned the marketing of Retin-A, which the agency believed Ortho had been illegally promoting for its more lucrative off-label use as a prescription wrinkle cream. As part of a plea agreement, the company was also paying $7.5 million to settle the ten criminal counts of obstruction of justice and reimburse the costs of investigation and prosecution.

It was one of the largest penalties ever levied for an FDA-related criminal case, and it made a nice sound bite for the agency and the Justice Department. *The Wall Street Journal* called it "humbling," and although the company was denying it, the *Journal* also suggested that the document destruction had effectively prevented the government from finishing its eight-year investigation of the promotional practices of Ortho and its parent company, Johnson & Johnson. But veteran pharmaceutical and legal analysts knew that the penalty was barely a slap on the hand. Various tongue-clickers estimated that $7.5 million represented only a few weeks' sales of Retin-A, or about four *hours* of J&J's total annual sales.

When the company's plea was first announced in January 1995, I started doing what an old editor of mine called "saving string" on the case. The Justice Department issued a provocative sentencing memorandum in March—laying out some of what the grand jury investigation had discovered—but the gory details of the crimes were supposed to come out in the fall, when the government would try what it believed to be a slam-dunk case against the former Ortho vice president accused of actually ordering the shredding.

But the pharmaceutical executive was found not guilty, even though the Retin-A product director he had allegedly ordered to do it had testified against him. It was a stunning reversal of fortunes for the Justice Department and the FDA.

Then, a month after the acquittal, the FDA made a powerfully ironic announcement. After all that, the agency was approving Retin-A for the treatment of wrinkles—in the form of Johnson & Johnson's new, gentler version of the drug, to be called Renova. The first prescription-only medicine for wrinkles, Renova was projected to capture 20 percent of the billion-dollar wrinkle care market in the first year alone.

A big chunk of that money would go to my alma mater, the University of Pennsylvania, which had fought a controversial federal court battle with J&J over the patent rights to Renova. Penn had claimed ownership because Retin-A was discovered in the 1960s by one of its professors, Dr. Albert Kligman, one of the few truly larger-than-life characters in the drug industry. Kligman was an eccentric dermatologist whom many considered a groundbreaking genius and others, he frankly admitted, "tell me I'm a neo-Nazi."

Retin-A had been developed as part of a massive drug-testing operation that Kligman ran at North Philadelphia's Holmesburg prison during the 1960s. The prison tests, primarily on African-American inmates, were shut down by congressional pressure in the early 1970s. But there were some who still compared Holmesburg to the controversial Tuskegee experiments, in which African-American test subjects weren't told that their syphilis was being left untreated for decades, in order to see how they fared. The Tuskegee experiments were back in the news again, being blamed for the general reluctance of African Americans to get involved in clinical drug trials or even to take newly approved drug treatments. They also were the reason some of them believed that AIDS was a government plot.

Several days after the FDA approved Renova, I was given Kligman's private phone number by a colleague. While he is hardly press-shy, having given literally hundreds of interviews lauding his drug (and himself), I knew Kligman had never really spoken frankly about the checkered past of Retin-A. But perhaps he thought it was time to do it. He quickly invited me to interview him at his house at the Jersey shore.

The date we chose turned out to be the opening day of the great blizzard of 1996. But much to my wife's distress and my subject's surprise, I drove through the blinding snow anyway. In many ways, Albert Kligman was the closest thing the legal-drug world had to the Ghost of Christmas Past. He was about to turn eighty, and I had learned long ago that you never let octogenarians reschedule.

The living room of Kligman's Long Beach Island home is so jam-packed with Oriental art that it brings to mind another outspoken Philadelphia physician who made millions on a controversial drug: Dr. Albert Barnes, whose renowned art collection had just returned to its Main Line home after a world tour. Kligman has wavy white hair, hands that are still animated despite losing a pinky to sclerosis, and skin that looks too smooth for a man of seventy-nine. But its smoothness, while a remarkable testimonial to his daily use of Retin-A, is not entirely aesthetically pleasing. Instead of looking younger, his face looks as if the wrinkles that should be there have been harshly erased—along with a layer of skin.

His demeanor is somewhat rougher. "I'm a distempered man," he said, stretching his scratchy voice. "My wife calls me a loudmouth. I am a vivid teacher. I receive all kinds of awards for teaching, and I do that by overstating the case. I am a fucking loudmouth, and I am occasionally going to say something attackable."

In the early 1950s Kligman was a cocky Penn dermatologist with some psychoanalytic training, so he knew exactly what he was talking about when he came to the then-radical conclusion that treating skin conditions as psychological was "bullshit. . . . I would see a case with psoriasis and write five pages of psychoanalytic bullshit about it: the unresolved conflicts with his wife . . . case of eczema, hadn't resolved his transference reaction," he explained.

Kligman's breakthrough was to focus on acne and treat it not as a psychological manifestation or even a normal physiological condition but as a disease. He started doing biopsies of zits rather than just bursting them for a fee like his colleagues. And he started experimenting with different compounds that might prevent pimples in the first place.

One thing he tried was vitamin A, which he started giving patients orally. "They were very high doses. I damn near killed people [before] I could see a real benefit," he recalled matter-of-factly. "Every one of them got sick. Their acne got better, but their hair fell out. A few of them said, 'Okay, I'm willing to be sick: keep pouring that poison into me. I'd rather lose my hair than have pimples.'

"This is one of the reasons doctors got away with abusive treatments. . . . By that time I had learned that patients are unreliable and what they think is worthless. . . . I have a doctrine: don't believe your patients . . . because it's too easy to prescribe a drug that is ineffective or harmful but the feedback is [positive]."

He eventually started using vitamin A on the skin instead. It didn't work. So he experimented with its active metabolite, retinoic acid. Retinoic acid *did* work, but not for the reason Kligman thought it would. He initially believed that vitamin A acid would eliminate pimples by slowing the normal process by which skin cells slough off. He later came to think that it instead *normalizes* that process and prevents cells from coming together to make a pimple in the first place.

Kligman realized his future wasn't in treating patients full time. He was an inventor, a teacher, a proselytizer and a damn colorful guy who, in his free time, became a world authority on mushrooms. He also had a real gift for getting research grants. In fact, he may have been too good at it. By the mid-1960s three companies he was directing were reportedly testing nearly two hundred drugs for thirty-three different pharmaceutical firms. An FDA source told me that in his heyday, Kligman was doing "a large percentage of all the new drug studies *in the country*."

He was also doing tests for the U.S. government, for the army and, it would later be disclosed, for the CIA. While some of his research was undertaken at Penn, most of it was being done on the captive audience at Holmesburg prison. Some inmates were tested on cell block H, while others were taken to aluminum trailers, equipped with padded cells, that were parked on the prison grounds.

In 1965 *JAMA* published a landmark study Kligman had done on the controversial drug DMSO (dimethyl sulfoxide), which was then being hailed as a rub-on remedy for all sorts of problems, from joint pain to athlete's foot. (An industrial solvent, DMSO came to be associated with the testimonials of professional athletes, who used it and described the peculiar sensation of smearing it on their limbs and immediately tasting it in their mouths; it was narrowly approved in 1978 for the treatment of interstitial cystitis.) It was through the DMSO study that Kligman's operation came to the attention of Frances Kelsey at the FDA. Kelsey's Cops found the size and scope of Kligman's research operations a little troubling, so they requested the raw data on his DMSO study, rather than just the summaries normally submitted to the agency. What Kelsey discovered was shocking. One of the three groups of prisoners upon whom the drug had reportedly been tested had never existed. Those who had been tested had been given the drug for only sixteen weeks, rather than the twenty to twenty-six weeks Kligman's research stated. Instead of testing against a placebo or a control drug, Kligman's researchers had given the comparison subjects other drugs that he was being paid to test.

In July 1966 Kligman became only the second doctor in FDA history to be banned from doing human research on new drugs. His exploits even made *Time* magazine. Thirty years later, the subject was still a raw one for him.

"Look, when you work in a prison, you have to depend on prisoners," Kligman told me. "I became the victim of a fantastic scam. There was a man at Holmesburg who was a check-passer: people who write bad checks have an irreversible disease. I would say, 'Get me ten people who have dandruff' . . . and I would write a check at the end of each month to pay these ten people. I didn't know that half of these people weren't paid anything. I didn't have the faintest idea. He was the perfect con man.

"The FDA came in, and correctly, they proved that in some of the things I had published about DMSO . . . at least half of the subjects were nonexistent. It's similar to a physician billing Medicare for services never rendered. Frances Kelsey was just very good at that [type of investigation]—although her objections to the sale of thalidomide were irrational. That's the lady who has received lots of prizes, which shows that the government doesn't have the *faintest idea*. She had no evidence it was harmful."

Kligman was similarly disdainful of the way Kelsey had treated his DMSO situation. "Instead of banning me and causing me enormous pain, saying, 'This guy's a neocriminal,' they could have just come and said, 'There are discrepancies here,' and we would have done an internal investigation," Kligman said. "Instead, they came down with this heavy bureaucratic hand. . . . You want to know why people join the militia? Because they think the government is evil . . . and sometimes, the way the government acts, you can understand that."

Only a month after his myriad corporate sponsors were informed of Kligman's status, he was reinstated after quickly cleaning up his operation. Kligman told me that he thought the head of Penn's dermatology department had lobbied in his defense. But it may have also had something to do with the fact that Dr. Luther Terry, who was the vice president of medical affairs at Penn at the time, had just recently finished his term as U.S. surgeon general.

Sometimes the best science results from having friends in high places.

But while the FDA was placated on DMSO, Kligman couldn't escape the broader controversy surrounding his prison experiments. While both the agency and some of his clients had complained of sloppy work, other investigators would later become more alarmed by the *kind* of studies Kligman was doing. For example, he tested the active ingredients in nerve gas and other chemical weapons on prisoners, to determine for the army "the minimum effective dose needed to mentally disable fifty percent of a given population." When Dioxin became a big environmental issue, it turned out that Kligman had tested that on prisoners, too.

Perhaps the most chilling work Kligman did on prisoners, however, was tests to see if skin could be artificially hardened to increase its resistance to chemical weapons. "Experimental Accommodation in Humans" was the name of one 1967 study.

Some of the tests involved painting compounds on small areas of skin, everything from coal tar to hydrochloric acid. But other trials were more extreme. Kligman's reports describe coating the entire forearms of test subjects with, among other things: turpentine ("would be very suitable were it not for the development of contact sensitization in about half the subjects . . . [some] quite severe"), undiluted ethylene glycol monomethyl ether ("three of three test subjects exhibited psychotic reactions . . . within two weeks and had to be hospitalized") and benzene. Several subjects had their arms kept experimentally hardened *for a year*.

This process of burning off a layer of skin to try and create a better one is an extreme application of the basic idea behind Retin-A.

Kligman's report to the Defense Department on "Experimental Accommodation in Humans" also notes racial differences in the reactions of test subjects. "There can be no question that the Negro is more resistant to irritation," he wrote. "The greater refractoriness of Negro skin is not attributable to observational difficulties, it is genuine."

Kligman believes it was race issues that led to the controversy surrounding his work, which peaked when he was criticized in 1973 by Edward Kennedy and was evicted from his research facilities at Holmesburg the following year. "It was the do-gooders," Kligman railed. "You know, I was a liberal once. I was a *Communist,* but with age you can learn some things, and it's possible to change your mind. . . . Here's what they were saying to me: 'White society is racist, and we force blacks into ghettos into circumstances in which they commit crimes, to provide subjects for *people like you, Dr. Kligman!*' . . . I said, 'I can't *believe* this. Are you aware we are studying *shampoos and athlete's foot?* We're *paying* them. We're developing ways to show that treatments work. It's a useful social thing. They were telling me I'm a neo-Nazi. So they kicked us out."

I asked if he had any regrets about any of the prison experiments. "Any of the things we did, I would do them again today," he insisted, "provided there was a review by intelligent people. . . . I am saying those were carefully conducted experiments, at way below the levels that would have any effect [on the subjects], and given the state of the cold war, I think I would do them again . . . [even] the nerve gases. . . . I think everything in a sufficient dilution becomes nontoxic, just as everything in sufficient dose is toxic. And there is no drug that can't be diluted to a point [of safety]. You can play that game any way you like.

"Retin-A came out of those experiments, and the risks are close to zero. You have to decide what you're prepared to do. The people who [ordered those tests] were rational, reasonable people. It was part of the defense strategy. And I must say, I'm one of those people who say 'God Bless America.' Because in another country I might be in jail or prohibited permanently from doing this kind of work."

Retin-A ended up at Johnson & Johnson's Ortho dermatological division even though, according to Kligman, most of the research had been done with vitamin A provided free by Hoffmann-LaRoche. "I gave a little talk there and said, 'This stuff is interesting. It works on acne. We ought to link up,' " he recalled. "They didn't have the slightest interest. On the way back from my talk, I drove past Johnson & Johnson [in New Brunswick] and stopped to see a friend there. I said, 'I just came from those schmucks up there. Are *you* interested?' He said, 'Let's do it.' "

The drug came onto the market in 1971 as a treatment for severe

acne, and Kligman became an international evangelizer for a revolutionary approach to skin care: to have the world take pimples more seriously
by medicalizing zit removal. He was becoming a giant in his field,
authoring one of the standard textbooks, inventing lab procedures and
training heads of dermatology departments around the world.

He saw a big future for Retin-A as much more than an acne cream. "I
have plans for a crash attack on the rejuvenation of the fading broads of
the world," he wrote in 1971 to J&J's director of marketing. "I am damn
serious. We are sitting on a golden egg!" But for many years Retin-A
sales were, in Kligman's opinion, "lousy," rising from $4 million annu-
ally in the mid-1970s to just over $30 million in the mid-1980s. Then in
1986 Kligman published his first study about Retin-A and wrinkles. But
he didn't call them "wrinkles," because wrinkles aren't really a medical
illness. So the "disease state" he and his colleagues worked with to
create a wrinkle medicine rather than just another skin cream was in the
general vicinity of "sun damage."

Kligman studied Retin-A and sun damage at Penn, as did a team at
the University of Michigan led by Dr. John Voorhees, who had a million-
dollar research grant from Ortho. In January 1988, Voorhees published a
paper in *JAMA* about his promising preliminary findings on wrinkles in
thirty patients. Ortho hired a public relations firm called The Softness
Group (which was never accused of wrongdoing) to put on a lavish press
conference at the Rainbow Room in Manhattan's Rockefeller Center to
publicize the January 1988 *JAMA* study. The conference, attended by
more than sixty journalists, was followed by a "satellite media tour" to
allow those journalists who couldn't make it to New York access to
Voorhees. The entire effort was remarkably successful. In the quarter
before that press conference, Retin-A sales in the United States had
averaged $154,000 a day. In the quarter after the conference, they were
at $1,452,000 a day, nearly a tenfold increase. Before the conference, off-
label sales accounted for 6 percent of Retin-A receipts. In the year after
the publicity, it was 65 percent.

The FDA quickly began investigating Ortho, and Retin-A turned into
the first agency test case of the boundaries of propriety under the long-
standing rules about promotion of off-label uses—the same subject that
the Washington Legal Foundation would carry into deregulatory combat
several years later. While peer-reviewed articles in prestigious journals
like *JAMA* are how medical scientists are supposed to communicate with
one another about off-label uses of approved drugs, the FDA's rule is
that marketing departments of pharmaceutical firms are not allowed to
nudge that scientific communication along. Ortho was supposed to be

focusing its attention and expenditures on the studies needed to show that the off-label use had provable efficacy so it could file a New Drug Application and get a new FDA approval to add wrinkle treatment to the label. But the agency was concerned that Ortho had no real intention of seriously trying to get Retin-A approved for wrinkles—which would be especially tricky because the company would have to convince an FDA advisory committee that "sun damage" was an illness. With the newly sophisticated science of public relations, it might be easier and cheaper for Ortho just to fan the flames of consumer demand through the media.

Ortho believed that the wording of the statute was ambiguous enough that what it had done was legal. When the FDA accused it of crossing the fuzzy line of propriety, the company used a rather inventive defense. According to a Justice Department chronology (which Ortho has disputed), the company claimed that when hiring its PR firms, it used the same guidelines the FDA had created for the funding of clinical studies and symposia: that publications had to be owned independently of the drug company, and the company could have no control of the editorial content.

Ortho was therefore claiming that it had hired a publicist *over which it exercised no editorial control.*

The FDA's initial investigation of Ortho did not bear fruit. Then the media stepped in to pick up the slack. Both *60 Minutes* and *Money* magazine investigated the promotion of Retin-A. And then Representative Ted Weiss started pressuring the newly appointed David Kessler. But Ortho officials appeared unconcerned. According to the *New Jersey Law Journal,* Ortho employees "made a videotape of themselves joking about the queries from both the FDA and Congress." In 1989 the company fearlessly filed a New Drug Application for Renova.

In the middle of all this, however, the FDA investigation was fueled by an outside source: a badly timed civil lawsuit between Kligman, Johnson & Johnson and the University of Pennsylvania.

One of the feel-good selling points in the Retin-A story was that Kligman always said he wasn't making a cent off his discovery; he had donated his 3 percent royalty to the dermatology department at Penn, which had received more than $10 million by now. The actual deal was that in the late 1960s, before anyone knew that Retin-A was worth anything, Penn had agreed to let Kligman keep the patent rights and license them himself as long as he agreed to donate the proceeds to the university, which might otherwise have a claim on anything he invented while on faculty.

Before studying Retin-A again for wrinkles, Kligman had prudently filed for a new patent for the compound as a wrinkle cream, and he made a new deal with J&J to sell them exclusive rights to the patent, which was awarded in 1986 (after being turned down twice). He hadn't discussed this new patent with Penn, because the original Retin-A patent—and their deal—didn't expire until 1990, and there was no assurance that the compound would ever be approved for wrinkles. But by the time Retin-A sales began to skyrocket in 1988, the university had an aggressive outside firm administering all its patents for a 35 percent commission. The firm started asking lots of questions about Kligman and decided to sue, claiming that the university deserved to own the new patent for Renova outright. Penn, which was about to part ways with its patent manager and bring the work in-house, was initially reluctant to join the action but finally did.

The discovery process of the lawsuit threw off provocative internal documents that the FDA probably never would have known to ask about. The agency's investigators were desperately trying to figure out if J&J had innocently overpublicized its early findings about wrinkles or had a master plan never to bother getting approval for the new use. The company's cause was not helped when an internal memo surfaced during discovery that quoted Kligman telling Ortho's director of dermatology research that the process of getting a new wrinkle approval would be "lengthy, complicated and likely to fail."

That memo (which Ortho later described as a "speculative conversation" and not company policy) became one of the key reasons that the FDA turned the Retin-A case over to the Justice Department in December 1990, setting off a grand jury investigation. It was one of the first decisions David Kessler made after being appointed.

On January 2, 1991, FDA investigators, emboldened by their new commissioner, did something they almost never do: they showed up unannounced at the homes of two Ortho executives after work hours, and they asked very tough questions. Little was said to the investigators, but quite a few phone calls were made that night between Ortho executives and employees.

The next morning, Ortho employees undertook a mass destruction of the documents relating to the promotion of Retin-A. While shredding records, some employees jokingly referred to each other as "Fawn Hall," invoking the name of the secretary who destroyed Oliver North's Iran-contra documents. By noon that same day, J&J was informed by the U.S.

Attorney's Office that its Ortho division was the focus of a criminal investigation. At 4:43 P.M. a subpoena was faxed to the general counsel's office at J&J. It requested, among other things, all the documents that had just been secretly destroyed.

Three months later, as the grand jury investigation continued, Ortho withdrew its New Drug Application for Renova and appeared to concentrate its energies on getting its relationship with the FDA back on track. Within a year, however, the company had apparently decided that the worst was over; the company optimistically resubmitted its application for Renova in September 1991, and in the late winter of 1992 the FDA posted a notice in the Federal Register that the drug would be discussed at an upcoming advisory committee meeting. Suddenly, the legal wrangling over the new patent evaporated, and within weeks J&J quietly settled its legal problems with Penn, which received most but not all of Kligman's future patent revenues on Renova. (All the revealing documents from the case were then sent away to the federal court depository in the far reaches of Northeast Philadelphia, which is where I found them.)

In April 1992 the FDA advisory committee decided that Renova was "approvable," although with a great many caveats. The committee was unusually candid about its worry that the medication would be misused or overused, and it was harsh in its labeling requirements. Mac Lumpkin would later tell me it was one of the most cautionary labels he had ever seen in all his years at the FDA: they would actually force J&J to print "RENOVA DOES NOT ELIMINATE WRINKLES" on the wrinkle cream's package insert. J&J wanted the drug approved for "repairing" photodamaged skin but got only the vaguer "mitigation, palliation"—FDA-talk for "it does *something*, but not what you're hoping for"—and only for fine wrinkles, brown spots and surface roughness.

Nonetheless, the advisory committee did rule that the drug was "approvable" for some version of its newly patented use. The company was asked to do some studies to see if the drug caused cancer or birth defects in animals, or if its use actually increased the sun's ability to damage skin. Then the wait for approval was on.

In the meantime, J&J pursued what one legal analyst called a "wrinkle-free strategy." The Ortho product director who actually supervised the Retin-A document destruction, Carol Hebestreit, neglected to mention anything about it during her June 1992 grand jury testimony. She offered instead what she later agreed was "the company agenda" that no one had done anything wrong. It was only after another Ortho employee told company lawyers months later that he planned to tell the grand jury about the shredding that J&J decided to let federal prosecutors in on the secret, which it finally did in December 1992.

From that point on, the company's legal strategy was clear: J&J would attempt to plead to charges that it had obstructed justice by destroying the documents related to an FDA investigation in exchange for an end to the investigation itself. By doing so, the company could save itself a huge amount of money. If J&J had been forced to plead guilty to the FDA violations being investigated—rather than the obstruction charges alone—the company would have faced a maximum penalty of double the gain derived from its illegal activities. According to an analysis in the *New Jersey Law Journal,* that fine could have been $1 *billion.* So if the company could make a deal to plead only to the document destruction, it could agree to pay one of the highest penalties ever levied in an FDA action, pay its legal fees and still theoretically save itself more than $950 million. It was a bargain, but it took over two years to hammer the bargain out.

All that while, Renova was "approvable" but unapproved. The FDA had asked for some teratogenicity trials in animals, one of which appeared to show that rats treated with high doses of Renova were having babies with more birth defects than those on placebo. The company argued that this was because the rats were actually licking the drug off their bodies; ingested, it was far more toxic. The FDA made the company do the tests again, this time with the rats wearing collars. The drug passed, but it remained unapproved—even at a time when the FDA was desperate to speed up approval times to respond to congressional pressure. Many assumed it would never be approved.

"As far as I knew," Kligman told me, "Ortho had given up on it being approved in this millennium."

Then the government lost its case against Lester Riley, the former head of Ortho's dermatology division. At issue wasn't whether the documents had been shredded but whether Riley had ordered the action. His position was that his overzealous aide and his secretary had misinterpreted his instructions on that fateful morning. He couldn't understand why they had destroyed all the Retin-A documents—even though, according to his secretary's court testimony, he had said, "Now would be a good time to clean out the files."

In December 1995, nearly eight years after the Rainbow Room press conference, five years after the FDA had turned the Retin-A case over to the Justice Department, three and a half years after Renova had been deemed "approvable" and less than a month after Lester Riley was acquitted, J&J received a letter that its new drug would be approved for sale. It's not unusual for there to be a desk-cleaning flurry of approvals right at the end of the year—and the FDA knew it would be facing another vicious round of congressional hearings in 1996, during which every lagging approval would be thrown in its face—but the sequence of events was too ironic to ignore.

As soon as I heard about the approval, I called Mac Lumpkin. What did this say about the FDA approval process? Was Renova approved only because the government had lost and it was now politically expedient? Was the FDA saying that J&J had been right all along, and the agency and the press had overreacted? Or had the company simply worn the agency down, outlasting any outrage over the way Retin-A had been promoted?

Lumpkin chose his words carefully. He said the timing was serendipitous, the studies and paperwork just happened to have been nearing completion at the time of the trial. Just as companies were supposed to keep a strict separation between medical and marketing efforts, "there is a very real wall between the New Drug side and the Compliance element," he said. "We were to proceed with our jobs and answer the efficacy and safety questions. As far as legal things, we had no idea what was going on. We see stuff in the press, but in reality no one ever called and said, 'Hold up on this approval.' It was all very coincidental."

He did concede, however, that the timing was "interesting."

CHAPTER 18

Self-Medication

N ow that Retin-A was finally going to be legally promotable as a wrinkle treatment, in the form of Renova, it became interesting for a completely different reason. Although it was a prescription drug, it was going to be advertised directly to the consumer—or in FDA parlance, DTC—in print ads in newspapers and magazines, and perhaps on television as well. J&J was going to compete head-up with cosmetics manufacturers who were already repositioning their products to fill the growing demand for more scientific-sounding skin care, prompting the *New York Times* business section to identify a "novel trend: beauty ads with some basis in fact."

There had been, in the previous year, a dramatic growth in direct-to-consumer advertising of prescription drugs in the United States. Drug companies would spend nearly $600 million in DTC advertising in 1996, twice as much as they had in 1995 and nearly ten times more than they had in 1991. In fact, 1996 was the first year in history that drug companies spent more money advertising to patients than they did to doctors. Although there was talk of loosening international standards, DTC advertising was still banned in most other major medicine markets and was expressly forbidden by the World Health Organization's Ethical Criteria for Medicinal Drug Promotion. Frankly, many American consumers were surprised to find out that it was perfectly legal in the United States, because until recently it hadn't been done very much. At one time, the major drug houses had referred to themselves as "ethical" largely because they didn't advertise to the public like the patent medicine manufacturers. Now their ads were fattening mass-market publications the same way they had always filled professional journals and the handful of general interest magazines for physicians. These new DTC ads were employing a message of "Ask your doctor," which really meant "Tell your doctor to write you a prescription, or you'll find a doctor who *will*." Physicians were taking the implicit threat very seriously; according to one 1995 survey, 99 percent of doctors said they would prescribe or consider prescribing a drug after being "asked" by a patient.

At the same time, pharmaceutical companies were pushing to have their prescription drugs switched to over-the-counter products—often at the same prescription dose—at an unprecedented rate. Since 1986, the FDA had approved only thirty-three prescription-to-OTC switches: six of those came in 1995 and another seven in 1996, which would prove to be the biggest year for switches in FDA history. Some of them were being made partly because the drugs were facing the end of their patent protection, and the patent holders felt they could better compete with generic manufacturers in the wide-open OTC market than in the more controlled prescription market. Once a drug is switched, of course, almost all the advertising goes directly to the consumer. OTC advertising was on the rise as well.

The DTC and OTC trends, however, were part of something much larger than advertising sales. They represented a revolution in what is referred to as "self-medication." It was unclear if the drug companies were responding to public opinion or trying to manufacture it, but the result of their actions was a change in the balance of power between doctor and patient, and a change in the notion of what a drug is supposed to be.

I first got to talking about this with Albert Kligman. After spending several hours recounting his role in the Retin-A saga and watching the snow drift up against his curved glass living room wall overlooking the bay, he got going on the changing roles of physicians, patients and pills in modern health care.

"In the first two decades I practiced, we were goddamned heroes," he declared. "We were stopping polio and syphilis, conquering acute infectious disease. Now everything has changed. We have an older population. People don't die of polio and meningitis; they now live long enough to get cancer and hypertension and depression and any number of day-to-day troublesome things. So now the population has turned against us. Despite our technology, despite all our *stuff,* people don't like us . . . because we're dealing with chronic conditions for which we don't have immediate and long-term treatments.

"I came into medicine when a doctor was a fucking saint: a father, a lovely man, a helper. Now most people think medical people are greedy, avaricious, you get a hustle act and out you go."

Kligman saw DTC advertising as one more indication that the medical world had gone to hell. "Look at *Time* magazine!" he croaked. "You'll see full-page ads for drugs telling you to go see your doctor. They're selling drugs via the consumer—I remember when the consumer was the *doctor*! I think this is potentially dangerous. Patients can't tell if the ad they're reading has any merit, and whether the drug has been judged against ten other drugs, or what chronic problems there are with the drug. . . .

"I think it's time to stop people from advertising directly to the public. Holding symposia is one thing . . . just saying, 'Here's the drug— let the doctors figure out if it's worth anything.' But when it comes to advertising Prozac in *Ladies' Home Journal,* that crosses the line. Selling drugs directly to the consumer is *not* a good idea."

Ironically, it was an idea that Kligman may have had a hand in nurturing. While hawking Retin-A in the early 1970s, he began pontificating about a blurring of the line between pharmaceuticals and cosmetics. At that time—before the great corporate consolidations of the 1980s and 1990s—most prescription drugs were still sold by companies that were primarily in the drug business or in the drug and chemical businesses. Johnson & Johnson was one of the few that primarily sold shampoo and baby products; it acquired its very marketing-oriented drug divisions only later.

So it made sense that, as J&J's consultant, Kligman would begin preaching the gospel of a new class of products that he called "cosmeceuticals."

"The first time I used that term," Kligman remembered, "I was talking to the manufacturers of cosmetics at their annual meeting. I took them to task. I said, 'You pretend your products are only cosmetics, that they don't affect the skin, only because you don't want the FDA on you. . . . Most things sold as cosmetics are cosmeceuticals. Stop kidding yourself.' . . .

"There's a lot of puffery. People need hope, and they think it's gonna help their skin. . . . [Cosmeceuticals] shouldn't be regulated as drugs. If Leonard Lauder can decide he has to have a new moisturizer that's an alphahydroxy acid—which is mainly bullshit—I don't want him to have to pay a million bucks [for FDA approval] to put it out. . . . The law should be rewritten."

The law was never rewritten. Over the course of time and commerce, however, Kligman's idea mutated into something quite different. In the early 1970s there were few over-the-counter drugs besides basic pain relievers and cold remedies. There were hardly any generic drugs. When Kligman talked about "cosmeceuticals" back then, he was mostly talking about zit creams and wrinkle removers. It was unimaginable that twenty years later companies would be trying to figure out how to market nearly *all* prescription drugs as if they were face creams.

By 1997 almost any drug that could be made into a pill or an ointment was effectively being marketed as a cosmeceutical. About the only old-fashioned "medical drugs" left were cancer chemotherapy agents and intravenous antibiotics and painkillers. Patients were being encouraged to self-medicate with over-the-counter drugs as a form of medical empowerment, no matter how ill suited they might be for the task of taking care of themselves. And prescription drug ads were, as one top pharmacy executive pointed out to me, "turning consumers into detail men. What else does this sound like to you? 'Jeez, doc, I saw this ad . . .'"

American consumers could hardly ignore the new flood of ads for prescription drugs in their newspapers and magazines. But they were given little in the way of media explication of the trend. Journalists were usually willing to flog drug-related issues for easy headlines, but on this topic there was too much at stake.

Drug company advertising was not just the biggest growth area for the print media. It was one of the *only* growth areas in that industry, which was otherwise facing an erosion of both its advertising base and its readership. These were the very publications that had been cringing for several years at the prospect of a ban on cigarette advertising—and the lost revenues it would entail. They were so worried about offending tobacco advertisers that they had a quiet practice of warning them ahead of time when an antitobacco story was going to appear, so the ads could be pulled. (That courtesy was later extended to big fashion and automobile advertisers as well, and magazine editors were soon wondering where it would all end.) If magazine publishers were angry with David Kessler for trying to ban tobacco advertising, they could also thank the FDA because for years its archaic rules on DTC promotion of prescription drugs had the effect of funneling most of new legal-drug advertising money into print rather than television. Through 1996 magazines and newspapers were capturing almost 90 percent of all the drug ad spending.

The longtime FDA rules hadn't prohibited TV advertising: they were just much harder to navigate for broadcast. For DTC advertising, as for advertising in medical journals, companies still had the choice of doing either a full-fledged ad that actually recommended a therapy—and had to be accompanied by a "major statement" about the drug's safety profile and a "brief summary" of its indications and side effects—or doing a "reminder" ad that simply reinforced the brand name of the product. In a magazine or newspaper format, companies could do either type of ad, because they could always buy space for the "brief summary." In fact, magazine publishers were especially pleased that it was nearly impossible to create a good-looking, informative drug ad on a single page. The "brief summary" of the package insert material—which was neither brief nor much of a useful summary but, printed in the most diminutive type the FDA would allow, was an eyesore whether you tried to read it or not—needed its own page or part of a page. Unlike the disclaimers on cigarette ads, it wasn't inconspicuous enough to be shoved into a corner of an otherwise appealing display.

But there was no logical place to put a brief summary on a TV ad. So for years almost all television ads for prescription drugs had been "reminders": by FDA standards, no different from pens or notepads. Pharmacia & Upjohn was one of the first companies that tried putting a "brief summary" on TV, in its ads for its injectable contraceptive Depo-Provera; half of the two-minute spots were taken up with screen after screen of side-effect listings. But most TV ads were "reminders," and because of the extreme limitations of the format, the DTC broadcast ads often seemed peculiar, as if no official language had yet been developed for such communication. Consumers were left shaking their heads wondering, "What did I just see?" or "What does it do?" Scary sneezing faces were shown among otherworldly fields of flowers, or computer-generated windsurfers rode fields of wheat, all with a constant, Big Brotherish voice droning, "Ask your doctor, ask your doctor." The ads were, for the most part, kind of creepy.

There had always been something kind of creepy about DTC advertising. In the early 1980s, after a small uproar about the mass promotion of prescription ibuprofen, the FDA held a symposium on DTC advertising, after which the agency placed a two-year moratorium on the ads to study their impact. In 1985 the ban was lifted, and new rules requiring the "brief summary" were put into place. After that point, every new

DTC ad campaign—and for years, there were only a handful—spawned controversy. In 1995 the FDA held another symposium on the future of DTC. I spoke to one of the agency organizers, Dr. Nancy Ostrove, who said the remarkable thing about the second symposium was how similar the discussions were to the first one. After more than ten years, almost no progress had been made, although the agency was considering the possibility of making new rules just for television.

The dilemma of DTC advertising was similar to many other dilemmas in drug regulation: it hinged on the issue of freedom versus protection, the public's right to choose versus the public's right to safety. But the decision the FDA now faced was mostly about money, market share and the ability to freely assail one's competitor in the media. So many people stood to make so much easy money in so many different ways—all in the name of "patient education"—if the ads were deregulated. But if the regulations stood, nobody stood to make an extra penny, even if loosening them turned out to be bad medicine.

In August 1997 the FDA would finally announce new rules that opened the floodgates for prescription drug advertising on TV. It turned out that the regulations had always provided for an alternative to the "brief summary"—something called an "adequate provision of dissemination of approved package labeling." This "adequate provision" ostensibly referred to getting out the printed warnings separately from the actual television ad; but this had never been done because the FDA never said what it would consider "adequate." Not defining it had been one subtle way of keeping the lid on TV advertising.

While the FDA was still several years away from actually writing new DTC regulations, it decided in the interim to finally define the "adequate provision" as a mention of a toll-free number where consumers could ask for the label information, a concurrent mass-market print campaign where they could read the "brief summary," a World Wide Web site where they could access the label information, and broadcast assurance that you could "ask your doctor" or pharmacist for more information. These were only small technical changes, but they would quickly have industry analysts predicting that pharmaceutical ad budgets would more than double over the next two years. And, almost overnight, prescription drug ads on television began looking and sounding like the ads for everything else.

Regardless of specific rule changes about TV advertising of prescription drugs, the larger issues involved in selling through patients instead of through doctors really haven't changed much. The line between prescription and over-the-counter drugs has been growing fainter for years anyway, and internationally it is sometimes nonexistent. Many drugs that are available only by prescription in the United States are available over the counter in Europe, Japan, South America and even Mexico (to which many Americans make regular legal-drug runs). More important than whether the ads are DTC is the problem of how to balance the public's new right to self-medicate with its proven ineptness at self-medication.

The term *self-medication* is an interesting one, because it has two very different meanings. It has most recently been used to refer to the buying of OTC drugs, "asking your doctor" about new prescription drug treatments and generally "taking charge" of your pill-taking life. But it has traditionally been employed to refer to the use of alcohol and illicit drugs to self-treat undiagnosed symptoms, usually of mental disorders. Such self-treatment sometimes masks the symptoms of an illness, and worse, addiction to the drugs used to self-medicate can become a bigger problem than the original illness. This is one of the dangers inherent in legal "drug-seeking behavior."

Dutch drug regulator Ronald Meyboom once gave me a rousing lecture on this subject. He believes there is no such thing as true self-medication: food can be taken by normal people, he says, and driving can be done by normal people, but drugs, no matter how idiot-proof, are too often misused to be given to the public.

"In self-medication, people are being told to use drugs with little benefit that have rare but substantial risks," he said. "People say, 'Even crossing the street has a certain danger.' But when you cross the street, perhaps you know you take a risk, but you also know that you'll get to the other side. In nine out of ten cases with self-medication, there's no need for it. They're not getting to the other side. They just do it because the nurse said so, or the woman next door, or Granny.

"In your country [the United States], for ten or more years there has been a planned propaganda campaign by the pharmaceutical companies to train . . . people that living healthy is your own responsibility, which means to take the right vitamins and pills. It's a whole machine to teach people that taking drugs is part of natural healthy behavior. I once heard a paper with slides of examples from these advertisements. In my view, they were immoral."

When I spoke to drug safety experts about this problem, they criticized the drug industry from several different approaches. Some bemoaned the way drug company marketing encourages too much medicalization or "disease-ization," requiring diagnoses to be fixed and certain. Over dinner at a conference, the head of quality care for a small hospital in Michigan told me about "diagnosis-state management," which he said is "something the drug companies are investing in very heavily, because it cements a drug-related intervention for each step of all illnesses." In this brave new medicalized world, any given diagnosis requires a particular medication; any doctor who describes a constellation of symptoms as a mere "syndrome," in which the underlying disease isn't known, simply isn't trying hard enough as a diagnostician. "In this type of nonsyndromal thinking," he lamented, "there's no place for a nondrug phase."

At the same time, these drug safety experts also bemoaned the way prescription drugs themselves were being consciously "unmedicalized" by direct-to-consumer advertising. DTC ads could give the impression that prescription drugs were safer than they really were—the unreadable "brief summaries" communicated almost nothing about their individual safety profiles or what made them different from each other.

This was especially ironic since in the over-the-counter market, which was historically rather unmedical, everyone was suddenly talking about side effects.

In March 1996 the makers of the top two products in the $2.7 billion over-the-counter painkiller market, Tylenol (acetaminophen) and Advil (ibuprofen), started an ad war over side effects. The war began on television, but when the major networks refused to run the ads anymore because they were scaring consumers, the companies switched over to print. Because both drugs are over-the-counter, the ads did not come under the FDA's direct regulatory control. OTC drugs are considered no different from cosmetics or any other commercial product, and their ads are regulated by the Federal Trade Commission, which gives advertisers much more leeway than the FDA. (The FTC does sometimes consult about medical claims with the FDA, which still regulates OTC safety.)

But this ad war caught the attention of the veteran drug watchers. Some had participated as expert witnesses in the legal case that had spawned the ads. Others were just appalled on general principle.

The legal case was that of Antonio Benedi, a former scheduler for President George Bush. In February 1993, on the Sunday night before he was to start a new job at a computer firm, Benedi, a thirty-seven-year-old accustomed to having two to three glasses of wine with dinner, came down with a flu he suspected he had caught from his kids. He took two

Extra-Strength Tylenol tablets and went to bed, continuing the dosage every six hours, as suggested on the label, for three continuous days. He did not drink any wine while taking the medication. On the third day he fell into a coma and was hospitalized with liver failure. He was saved only by a last-minute liver transplant. (*The New England Journal of Medicine* would later report that overdoses of the active ingredient in Tylenol were the leading cause of acute liver failure at one large hospital, noting that heavy drinkers were especially at risk.)

Benedi sued McNeil Laboratories, the Johnson & Johnson subsidiary that markets Tylenol. In the fall of 1994 he was awarded over $8 million by a Virginia jury, in large part because the drug label didn't mention any danger from social drinking (although there was some debate at the trial about what constituted "social" drinking). The case made some local headlines, then disappeared. The appeal came up in the fall of 1995. J&J lost again. It paid the verdict, and after legal fees, Benedi got about $5 million.

At the same time, McNeil began an attack campaign against Advil, which is made by the American Home Products subsidiary Whitehall-Robins Healthcare. McNeil's ads warned people who have ulcers or take blood pressure–lowering medicines that ibuprofen could be dangerous. It was one of the first times that a company overtly did what drug reps had been doing for years—selling their drug by flailing away at the labeled safety profile of a competing product.

McNeil had just reinvented "side-effect slinging." Whitehall-Robins quickly slung back. Naturally, it attacked the side effect that had formed the basis of the Benedi case—and was now on the Tylenol label. In February 1996 the company began running ads warning those who drank regularly to consult their doctors before taking Tylenol. On March 14, six days after the networks said they would no longer run pharmaceutical attack ads, Benedi took out a full-page ad in *The Washington Times*—the weak sister to his local *Washington Post* but, with his disability and mounting medical bills, all he could afford—and wrote an open letter to the public describing his case and warning about the dangers of Tylenol and alcohol. He said he was annoyed that Tylenol was still using its advertising slogan: "the safest type of pain reliever you can buy."

The anti-Tylenol letter caused only a minor stir until Whitehall-Robins received permission from Benedi to reprint it as a full-page ad in *The New York Times*. The ad ran only with the company's relatively generic-sounding name and without any mention that it was the manufacturer of Advil. The ad later appeared in major newspapers across the country.

A McNeil spokesman called the campaign "a new low." The whole episode, of course, was a new low. The reality was that the FDA had been trying to get the makers of *all* the major pain relievers to put alcohol warnings on their products for years. But nobody was going to take out an ad to tell the public *that.* Besides, the story of two drug behemoths battling it out over an obscure side effect was considered more compelling than the side effect itself, so the FDA's actual cautionary message got buried deep in the news stories and never reached most consumers.

The companies had all resisted the relabeling, as companies invariably do. They hold out as long as they can because they know themselves too well: they realize that as soon as something is on the label, a competitor will consider it fair game for counter-detail. McNeil had voluntarily relabeled Tylenol for potential alcohol problems in 1994, a year too late to avoid losing the Benedi case but several years before its competitors, which chose the normal route of buying time by negotiating as long as possible with the FDA. Ironically, by putting the alcohol issue on the label, McNeil probably made it easier for Whitehall-Robins to justify using it in an attack ad.

Eventually the battle fizzled out, but it laid the groundwork for the new generation of more medical-sounding OTC ads. Even as the painkiller warfare receded, companies were already planning their next big OTC confrontation: the battle of the drugs formerly known as ulcer treatments. They included Zantac 75 (the Glaxo drug being marketed in an OTC version by Warner-Lambert), Tagamet HB (from SmithKline Beecham) and Pepcid AC (the Merck drug being comarketed for OTC use with Johnson & Johnson). They were going to sling label language as well.

In a unique set of circumstances, the three drugs were set to come over the counter almost simultaneously. Not only were they all going off-patent after amazing careers as some of the best-selling name-brand drugs in history, but to a large degree they were being reinvented as medicines. Ulcers were no longer believed to be caused by stomach acid, which these medicines treated, but couldn't cure. Ulcers were now thought to be caused by a bacterium called *Helicobacter pylori,* and many physicians believed that antibiotics and a shorter course of antacid treatments could actually cure them.

To replace the revenues destroyed by all those cured ulcers, manufacturers had to recast their chronic ulcer medications as industrial-strength heartburn treatments. But over-the-counter antacids were only a $1 billion-a-year market. So on the theory that it was better to sell a pound of prevention than an ounce of cure, consumers were now urged to buy the drugs and take them *before* eating foods that might give them heartburn. This wasn't just preventive medicine; this was "treat the illness whether you have it or not." This TV ad war would become a battle over minute differences in the labeling language—specifically, over how long before ingesting a potentially sickness-inducing meal a patient was supposed to take the capsulated antidote.

I found these new OTC ads particularly fascinating because antacids were among the very few medications I actually used with any regularity. In the time since Diane had been Floxed, I had never had the need to take a single prescription drug. The only products I used were Rolaids and ibuprofen, which I had been taking religiously for years for my recurring back pain. To prevent inflammation, a conditioning trainer had convinced me always to take ibuprofen *before* I worked out. I had no idea if it was helping, but it had become a routine. For years, I bought name-brand Advil, primarily because I loved what is called the "mouth feel" of the red-brown pills, which was similar to that of M&Ms. But then I got spoiled. A friend whose sister worked for Whitehall-Robins gave me a Baggie filled with free Advils. Then they really *were* like candy. But once the Baggie was empty, I had a hard time paying retail for the pills anymore, and I switched to the far less orally gratifying generic brand. Probably because they were cheaper, I upped my regular dose to two. Nothing ever went wrong, so I assumed that was a safe dose.

When I saw this blitz of antacid advertising, I wondered what it would take to make me change my minor anti-inflammatory drug habit. But I probably wouldn't have given it much more thought if I hadn't been elbowed in the jaw during my regular Sunday morning half-court basketball game. When I went to my internist to make sure I was all right, we discussed whether she should give me anything extra for the pain. I told her I was already taking two ibuprofen almost every day. She was incredulous. She had been my doctor for four years, and I had never mentioned it before. "Taking that much ibuprofen is not such a great idea," she said.

Perhaps because I had been writing so much about drugs, she assumed I knew better. She guessed that taking the pills daily had made sense to me because so much media attention had been given to the idea of taking a low-dose aspirin tablet daily to prevent heart problems. She was in favor of daily aspirin for her patients—especially someone like me, with a family history of heart problems—but she pointed out, "Steve, you do realize that aspirin and ibuprofen aren't the same thing."

I did, of course, but she was probably right about how I had come to self-diagnose my need for daily ibuprofen. It was an interesting insight into how people self-medicate, based on some peculiar combination of habit, information half-communicated by the media and sometimes just forgetting to ask our doctors if our half-baked medical assessments are correct before consuming over-the-counter drugs in doses once allowed only by prescription. I felt stupid.

After the conversation I spoke to my younger brother, who also has recurring back pain and picked up the ibuprofen habit from me. I asked him how many he usually took.

"Oh, you know," he said, "a handful."

Nowhere had the problems of self-medication been more clear than in the diet pill business. From a public health standpoint, it was the ultimate "ask your doctor" nightmare and a stunning reminder of the downside of the freedom American doctors have to prescribe whatever they want to whoever asks for it.

For years, the world's strip-malls were increasingly populated by weight-loss "centers" that sold whatever foods, vitamin supplements and quasi-medicinal products went along with the diet plan *du jour*. But as new weight-loss medicines became popular just as managed care was squeezing physicians into new lines of work, many diet centers quickly hired doctors and added prescriptions to their product lines. In some cases, doctors opened their own competing weight-loss centers. They all sold the same things: hope and access to diet pills which, in time, became one and the same. In this case, hope was a prescription for "fen-phen."

In 1979 a clin-pharm professor at the University of Rochester, Dr. Michael Weintraub, got the idea of combining two older diet drugs so long out of vogue that they weren't even mentioned in most of the mass-market pill books; the very name of their drug class, "anorectics," had itself become politically incorrect. One was the amphetamine-like fenfluramine, a Schedule IV controlled substance (drugs with addiction potential are classified, in descending order of risk, from I to V) that had been sold as Pondimin for years by the A.H. Robins company but would later be marketed by Wyeth-Ayerst, its sister company under the American Home Products umbrella. The other was the non-amphetamine appetite suppressant phentermine, which was sold under several names by several companies but was best known as SmithKline Beecham's product Fastin. Weintraub studied the combined drugs in 121 obese patients, mostly women, and the average study patient of over 200 pounds successfully dropped thirty of them. This result proved to be more interesting to him than to the major medical journals, so the paper ended up being published in July 1992 in the leading journal for drug experts, *Clinical Pharmacology and Therapeutics.*

Regardless of its low-profile publication, word of the study spread quickly in a community with an insatiable appetite for quick-fix solutions and a deep need for diet pills to be safer than they ever really turn out to be. By 1995 fen-phen fever was sweeping the world of American weight-loss products. Diet chains like the Philadelphia-based Nutri/Systems began offering fen-phen prescriptions as a way to halt the precipitious drop-off in their business, which they blamed, in part, on dieters who felt they needed to choose between diet drugs and prepackaged meal plans.

Weintraub was horrified: his study almost singlehandedly created what began to be called "the pill mills." Never in the modern history of medicine had a prescription medication been so brazenly offered as a commodity. And because fen-phen was an off-label prescription with no direct drug-company advertising—the weight-loss centers and doctors did all the hawking themselves—the FDA, where Weintraub later came to work, was nearly powerless to do anything about the pill mills. While several states, notably Tennessee and Florida, tried to thwart fen-phen sales with local regulations, sales continued to skyrocket; from 1992 to 1995 Pondimin sales rose 3,000 percent. And soon a so-called "herbal fen-phen" that purported to do the same thing "naturally" appeared in health-food stores as well.

In the meantime a small biotech company in Massachusetts, Interneuron, was seeking approval for a new drug that had the potential to be a fully patented, FDA-sanctioned combination of fen and phen in one pill: dexfenfluramine. Since 1990, it had been marketed outside the U.S. by Serview, the French company that had created the compound. The drug was to be sold under the brand name Redux, using the marketing muscle of Interneuron's eventual partner Wyeth-Ayerst. Redux quickly ran into regulatory roadblocks. It was being proposed as a drug for treating clinically defined obesity, which had its own health risks against which the benefits of the drug would be weighed. But many feared that, once approved, it would primarily be prescribed, like fen-phen, to all the people who *thought* they were obese because they felt fat. It would be the ultimate cosmetic pharmacology: diet pills dispensed the way nose jobs were performed.

There was growing public debate about whether that outcome was, actually, such a terrible thing. Nose jobs had become acceptable. And, as the population grew fatter, there was more support for a redefinition of obesity that would make diet pill use defensible for the merely chunky. Obesity was in the midst of being redefined as a medical condition rather than the state of one's weight. Fighting it was becoming part of preventive medicine. And, even though fen-phen had never been studied for long-term use, it was being prescribed that way, and the developers of Redux wanted their drug to be approved for such extended use. In September of 1995, an FDA advisory committee initially voted against approving the drug at all, but after an impassioned speech by one of its members, the committee changed its mind, narrowly recommending approval by one vote.

The drug was approved in the spring of 1996—the first new prescription obesity treatment in twenty years—and diet pills made the cover of *Time* magazine. Redux was then endorsed in an editorial in *The New England Journal of Medicine,* but its authors were quickly criticized for allegedly failing to completely disclose their consulting ties to the drug's manufacturer. But neither the conflict-of-interest controversy nor another article in the same issue about cases of lung-scarring blamed on fen-phen had any impact on the rapidly inflating diet pill market. In the coming year, over two million prescriptions would be written for Redux, along with eighteen million for the combined components of fen-phen. Several companies announced they were developing new diet drugs to respond to inflating demand and societal acceptance.

Eventually, however, the diet drug market would pop. In the summer of 1997, a major journal article from the Mayo Clinic would indict fen-phen in a series of twenty-four cases of drug-induced heart valve damage. And, one year after its glowing endorsement of Redux and pharmaceutical treatments for obesity, *The New England Journal* would call for a moratorium on diet drug use "for cosmetic purposes" and a reconsideration of the logic of approving Redux in the first place. Sales of Redux and fen-phen quickly dropped 40 percent. Then the FDA received reports of 291 more patients, mostly women on fen-phen, with damaged aortic or mitral valves. The next day, fenfluramine and Redux would be removed from the market—the largest and most public new drug withdrawal since Omniflox in 1992. Ray Woosley and Brian Strom would try to use the media attention to gain support for an independent national Center for Drug Surveillance that would study such medication disasters in the way the National Transportation Safety Board looked into airplane crashes. But much of the news coverage would focus on the patients who wanted the diet drugs regardless of their safety. Since their physicians had been largely ignoring the label warnings on the drugs for years, they didn't quite understand why all of a sudden everyone was being so picky about a few hundred heart valves.

CHAPTER 19

Spin Control

Betsy Lehman would have done a great story about her case if she had lived to write about it. A health columnist at *The Boston Globe,* Lehman was killed by the chemotherapy agent being used to combat her breast cancer at the renowned Dana-Farber Cancer Institute. In December 1994 Lehman, thirty-nine, was accidentally given a quadruple dose of a drug that was already used at near-toxic levels to fight tumors. During a review of her case after she died, the mistake was missed and wasn't discovered until two months later by an assistant data manager checking up on clinical trial projects.

Her case brought national headlines and a massive lawsuit against Dana-Farber, which was settled fairly quietly. It is always interesting, however, to see what reactions a case like Betsy Lehman's inspires in the mass culture—how the public decides which lessons to learn from a disaster, and who steps up to teach the lessons. Once the public is scared, many different things can result from its fear. As an investigative reporter, I have dealt with such media issues for years, and I often find myself speaking to bereaved families about how a tragic loss might be framed by the media, what "larger story" their cooperation would allow me to tell.

At Dana-Farber, Lehman's case eventually inspired a new pharmacy computer setup, more supervision of junior doctors and, most radical, a new system for paying closer attention to patient complaints about side effects. Lehman apparently had suffered immediate complications from her overdose—becoming swollen, with abnormal blood tests and EKGs—but the symptoms were shrugged off as a normal reaction to a strong experimental treatment. In the aftermath, however, it was the subject of rectifying hospital medication errors, and not listening to the patient in a new way, that got the most public attention. Lehman's case inspired a conference in Boston in January 1996 that attacked the drug safety problem from a novel perspective: it focused on preventing hospital medication errors. By this time I was attending any symposium that might even vaguely touch on the issues surrounding Diane's drug reaction—trolling for sources, ideas, perhaps even tidbits about her specific case. I got a notice about the conference from the medical writer who had been Floxed and periodically faxes me interesting drug-related journal articles, and I hurriedly booked a flight to Boston.

The subject of preventing medication errors didn't sound much different from what I had been researching. But when I got to the conference, I realized it was. The conference focused less on inadequate drug knowledge and communication problems than on hospital system errors. And the symposium was directed less at doctors than at hospital administrators, with much of it couched in the language of management consulting rather than medicine. Sponsored by the nonprofit Institute for Healthcare Improvement as part of its "Breakthrough Series" on reducing costs and improving outcomes, the conference was chock-full of what were called "change concepts: great ideas ready for use." It was hosted by Dr. Lucian Leape, a self-described "unfrocked pediatric surgeon" with grand bushy eyebrows who had settled into a late-career role as a Harvard-based health policy expert.

Leape ran through the hospital error numbers that his and other studies had determined. Approximately 1.3 million Americans a year are injured by hospital treatment, 180,000 of them die and 69 percent of those injuries are from errors that can be found in hospital records if someone looks hard enough. Medication errors are the highest single category, accounting for nearly 20 percent of all treatment injuries—or looked at another way, 7 percent of all hospital patients experience serious error with their medications (although not every error results in an injury). Using a systems approach, however, Leape was quick to compare these figures to other fields.

"Unlike the surgeon, the airline pilot will die with his passengers," he noted, contrasting the number of people who die from their medical treatment to "the equivalent of three jumbo-jet crashes every two days." Leape posed the example of a five-hundred-bed hospital with 24,000 patients a year and an average medication use of ten drugs per patient. Assuming that each doctor made errors only 1 percent of the time (which was probably generous) and that each pharmacist and nurse, being more careful about drugs, made errors only 0.1 percent of the time, he calculated there would be more than eight thousand medication errors each year. "We have to do better than that, more like 99.9 percent efficiency," he said. "If other industries had the error rate of hospitals, we would have, in the United States, eighty-four unsafe landings a day. Every hour there would be sixteen thousand lost letters and thirty-two thousand bank check errors."

The problem, he said, is that "the medical model doesn't focus on systems but on individuals. It's never 'What went wrong?' but always 'Who is to blame?' "

Although a lot of interesting ideas about systems approaches to medication errors were bandied about—one expert raised a good number of "hmmms" by positing that "safety is the difference between what we can do and what we are doing"—the conference sometimes seemed like nothing more than theories searching for practical applications. Only one speaker at the conference could honestly say he was already doing something about the problem. That was Michael Cohen, who was introduced by Leape as "a single voice in the wilderness." For years he had been America's one-man medication error detection system.

Cohen is a squirrely, driven man with a perfectly round face and a black comb-over. He has been collecting reports of medication and device errors—at first almost as a hobby—since the early 1970s. He started noticing medication errors as a young pharmacist at Temple University Hospital in Philadelphia. The errors were often caused by unreadable doctors' orders, confusing product labels or improper IV connections. Cohen would hear about the errors mostly from nurses and pharmacists, because "doctors barely ever talked to pharmacists," and he eventually began doing a little column for a nursing journal. In 1980 he had his first major run-in with a manufacturer, who tried to get him fired for calling attention to a new IV system's peculiar tendency to fall out of patients' arms, causing a deadly air embolism.

Over the years Cohen collected more errors—always reported to him anonymously—and eventually set up his own little nonprofit organization, which he called the Institute for Safe Medication Practices (ISMP). Once based in his house, the ISMP is now run out of a small office in Warminster, Pennsylvania, just south of the middle of nowhere. Since 1989, managing it has been Cohen's main job; for years, his wife was the Institute's sole employee. He does it because someone has to, and amazingly enough, for years he was the only person in the world doing it.

Unlike many consumer advocates, he delights in finding *solvable* problems. His greatest joy seems to come from convincing a large drug or
device company to change a label or alter an IV connection so that fewer
bad things will happen to good sick people. He recently turned over the
medication-error reporting part of his company to the United States
Pharmacopeia (USP), to add to its information services. But his quest
continues and, via computer, is now worldwide.

Still, Cohen and the ISMP are largely unknown to physicians. What
he does is mostly appreciated by pharmacists and nurses, who are the
ones who almost invariably get blamed for medication errors, even ones
they didn't actually cause. Cohen said he was seeing more reports of
errors that he blamed on all the pressures caused by hospital downsizing.
He told me that a big part of the problem is "temp" nurses and pharmacists, who are brought in from agencies to fill in for fired full-time employees and are unable to get up to speed on the idiosyncrasies of a
hospital's procedures. This issue is a ticking time bomb, he believes,
because other pressures are also conspiring to dramatically increase hospital medication use. For example, managed care is forcing all but the
sickest patients out of hospitals, which means that inpatients are sicker
than ever and are more likely to require more medications.

Cohen was one of the least alarmist people I had met in my alarming
quest for information about drugs and drug safety. He called attention to
himself and his cause with a lot of the same scary stories others used, but
I recognized in him the difference between a crusading physician and a
crusading pharmacist. He didn't have the charisma of a Sid Wolfe or
even a Ray Woosley, and he brought to his task the pharmacist's lack of
surprise when doctors, nurses and patients proved themselves clueless
on the subject of medicines. He reminded me that pharmacists are the
bartenders of medicine: they've seen it all, and they're hardly ever
shocked.

Perhaps because of his less strident disposition, he scared me even
more than the others did. But I didn't realize the extent of my fear until
days later, when I ended up in the same emergency room where I had
brought Diane when she was Floxed.

It was a Saturday night, and I was getting ready to go to Florida to
cover a clinical pharmacology convention, when I started feeling shaky.
Within hours my fever soared to 104. I called my doctor, who told me to
go to the hospital. After an exam and a chest X-ray, I was diagnosed
with walking pneumonia and assured that if Tylenol and an IV antibiotic
brought down my fever, then I could go home with some pills. Since the

ER was packed, I lay on my back on a gurney lined up next to the front desk. When I asked which antibiotic would be prescribed for me to take home, the ER doctor said, "Biaxin."

Despite my febrile confusion, I managed to ask: "Is that clarithromycin, the Abbott drug?"

He regarded me more carefully before admitting that he didn't know, then instructed the tech behind the desk to check. Then he turned back to me, clearly puzzled if not a little defensive, and asked, "Why would you want to know that?"

"You don't want to know," I groaned. "Right now, *I* don't want to know what I know."

With an IV of saline and then Rocephin (ceftriaxone) dripping slowly into my veins, I couldn't help but remember Mike Cohen's hospital horror stories of patients mistakenly hooked up to potassium chloride, an agent used for capital punishment. I must have made Diane check the names on the IV bags a dozen times as I waited for the medicine to bring relief. But even with her assurance, I was still looking at the dripping fluid, thinking: *Please don't hurt me.*

Sure, I was semidelirious from the fever. But my fear of a drug reaction, I knew all too well, was justifiable.

An hour later, my temperature returned to normal and I felt well enough to go home.

Thank God for drugs—sometimes.

Two days later, I was well enough to fly to Florida to watch some of the country's top clinical pharmacologists act like kids at a science fair, standing next to their posters waiting for someone to ask them about their projects. At scientific conferences research that isn't far enough along to merit a whole lecture is presented during breaks at "poster sessions," where scientists pin up a bulletin board's worth of data and chat about it with whoever wanders by between finger food and coffee. Hundreds of posters are presented, and aisles and aisles of clinical observations await appreciation, analysis or in the case of failed experiments, pity. Some posters are presented to float a new idea, others to quietly lay claim to some patentable insight. Wandering down the aisles, I overheard snippets of clinical pharmacology gossip: "In the meantime, the drug is killing tens of thousands of people" or "Now, about those 120-day reports . . ." When someone referred to the "halcyon days," it took a second before I realized he was talking about the drug Halcion.

The poster sessions were rather overwhelming, reminding me just how much there is to know and not know about the drugs we take. Ray Woosley and Dave Flockhart had encouraged me to come to the convention to meet people and get a feeling for the world of clinical pharmacology. The feeling I got was that I was drowning in a sea of scientific observations, any one of which might be a good reason to use a certain drug—or not use it.

While much of the clinical pharmacology convention was taken up with discussing individual side effects, there were also provocative talks about big-picture problems. Brian Strom, who I had interviewed earlier in Philadelphia about FDA-related issues, gave a talk on his work trying to improve drug utilization at the Hospital of the University of Pennsylvania (HUP). In the late 1980s the Joint Commission on Accreditation of Healthcare Organizations (JCAHO), the body that licenses American hospitals, started leaning on facilities to put systems in place to improve usage and monitor drug reactions. Strom recalled that in 1989 the hospital was proud that it had reported only four drug reactions the entire previous year—until the JCAHO informed HUP that four reports in a year was not a good thing because it couldn't possibly be accurate. (Penn wasn't alone: according to the JCAHO executive who spoke after Strom, the annual number should have been about three thousand, and from most places "we were having one-hundred-thirty, ten, twenty-seven. . . .")

Strom was part of the team that devised the hospital's new automated drug utilization system. Like many hospitals, HUP has a system that allows a doctor to type in a prescription order and get instant recommendations on dosage, drug interactions and alternative therapies right onscreen. But physicians regularly disregard the advice of the computers. "It tells you that you prescribed wrong," he said. "The problem is, the doctor knows it's wrong and knows there is enormous bad use of drugs, but does it anyway. . . . The need is there and the technology is there. We just need to generate some *willpower*."

Later in the conference I heard a very futuristic talk by Stephen Spielberg—that's Dr. Stephen Spielberg, the clinical pharmacologist—who had left his post at the highly regarded Adverse Drug Reaction Clinic in Toronto and crossed what someone at the conference referred to as "the Berlin Wall between academia and industry, which has become quite porous." He was currently a top drug safety researcher at Merck, which gave his pronouncements greater weight in industry. He spoke about the almost Star Trekkian possibilities of what he jokingly called "clinical adverse-reaction-ology" and discussed a great and glorious future in which there would be ways to screen for very obscure risk factors before patients were given medicines. He was echoing comments I had heard others make about futuristic prescreening technology. Ray Woosley had told me that he was consulting on a project with Hewlett-Packard in which they were inventing a machine that would take a drop or two of your blood and in as little as five or ten minutes, automatically subdivide and test it for sensitivity to medicines by screening various genetic markers that might affect pharmacokinetics and pharmacodynamics. (The GeneArray scanner would come on the market in 1997 at a price of $92,683.)

Spielberg did admit that some current methods of predicting, say, liver toxicity, were ridiculously expensive and "won't work anyway." But he was crystal clear on one point that I suspected many others from industry needed to hear more loudly. "You know," he said, "we just can't hide behind 'Oh, it's too hard to do' anymore."

While I was in Florida, I went to meet with Barbara Taylor, whose daughter had died from the most famous drug reaction—or *reported* drug reaction—in recent history. Certainly it was the first ADR to make the cover of *People* magazine. Taylor's teenage daughter Krissy, a sweet country girl who had seemed poised to join her famous older sister Niki in a professional modeling career, had now been dead for almost nine months. Her cause of death had been the subject of endless gossipy speculation in the U.S. and British press. Barbara—who is blonde and round-faced, like a Floridian version of actress Ellen Burstyn—knew that the rumors of illegal drug use were ludicrous. But she had to admit that on any given day she could be swayed to believe any one of a half-dozen reasons why her seventeen-year-old daughter had been taken from her.

Krissy's death had initially been blamed on an inhaler of an over-the-counter asthma medication, Primatene Mist. The suggestion alone had set off a panic about the inhalers, especially in central Florida, where the Taylor family lives. The panic was a combination of basic knee-jerk hysteria, egged on by extensive media coverage and lingering questions that certain pharmacologists had had for some time about Primatene inhalers. Concern was growing that an easy-to-use inhaler shooting pure epinephrine on demand was a self-medication nightmare waiting to happen. (Epinephrine is a very potent drug; Primatene pills, which also treat asthma, contain another drug altogether, theophylline.) An FDA advisory committee had recently discussed whether to categorize the Primatene inhaler, which some consider an outdated approach to asthma care, as a prescription drug, in order to limit its use. Cardiac specialists had been worrying about Primatene triggering sudden heartbeat abnormalities—which was the scenario first leaked to the press in July 1995, when Krissy was found facedown and unconscious in the living room of her home and couldn't be revived by paramedics.

After the initial media deluge, the family had decided not to share any more details with the public until they had an authoritative diagnosis. While the family waited for test results, Barbara started worrying that somebody from the drug company would spy on her because of the threat Krissy's story posed to its product. The investigation was made more difficult because, as Barbara quickly surmised, every new theory came with a potential legal action and a potential social cause to which the Taylor name could be attached. If the cause had been the Primatene Mist, then they could lobby to get the drug off the market and call more attention to the problem of adverse drug reactions, maybe even fund a Krissy Taylor ADR Research Center. If the cause was undiagnosed asthma, Krissy could become a posthumous poster child for that. A doctor from Johns Hopkins had already approached Barbara about setting up a facility for the treatment of childhood asthma, of which he, of course, would be the director. Krissy's heart was examined and reexamined for a possible congenital defect. If the cause lay there (as was eventually decided), then Krissy's tale could be used to popularize the problem of undiagnosed heart problems.

When I asked to interview Taylor, it was my hope that she would let me follow along in the investigation. But because I was writing a book about drugs and drug reactions, she was wary of my motives, assuming I was interested only in exploring the Primatene theory. Unfortunately, I couldn't convince her otherwise. She did, however, agree to meet with me once to discuss the possibility of such a project.

Over dinner, Barbara said something very interesting. One of her biggest disappointments, she confessed, was something she heard from the medical examiner, who had been talking to an out-of-town journalist about Krissy's cause of death. The journalist kept asking if the case involved illegal drugs. When the examiner finally convinced him the answer was no, the journalist replied that he was "no longer interested in the story" and left.

I found this anecdote particularly revealing. It said a lot about the peculiar relationship people have to drugs, legal and illegal, and I thought about it again when several other celebrity drug reaction stories hit the news. I heard that *Vanity Fair* was working on two prescription drug–

related book excerpts. One was from actress Claire Bloom's *Leaving a Doll's House,* about her years living with novelist Philip Roth, in which she revealed her belief that much of Roth's cruel behavior could be traced to his use of Halcion and Xanax.

The other excerpt was from *A Mother's Story,* a mini-memoir by socialite Gloria Vanderbilt, who disclosed new information about the 1988 suicide of her twenty-four-year-old son Carter Cooper. As Vanderbilt had tried to talk him down off the terrace wall of her fourteenth-floor apartment on Manhattan's Upper East Side, Carter had yelled "Fuck you!" and jumped, clinging momentarily by his fingertips before letting go.

Vanderbilt was convinced that her son had experienced a psychotic reaction to a prescription asthma medication and that "the respiratory inhaler was the key to the demon that took Carter's life." She did not discount the salient facts that Carter had just broken up with his girl-friend, moved back home and begun seeing a cognitive therapist. But she was more swayed by what she said was her own doctor's theory, that the inhaler had blown him over the edge. She recalled that the day before he died, Carter suddenly had chills and was acting strangely, asking her at one point, "Mom, am I blinking?" When she asked if he was "taking anything"—meaning illicit drugs—he said no, and post-mortem blood tests apparently confirmed that.

But he had been taking something that a new doctor had prescribed for his allergies and asthma. Vanderbilt was a little cagey about what it was exactly. I got a copy of the uncorrected page proofs of the book. On one page she referred to "medications for asthma like theophylline," but later on she mentioned a specific brand-name inhaler of albuterol, which is also a bronchodilator but, in fact, is in a different class from theophylline. In the finished book, however, only the "medications . . . like theophylline" reference remains, apparently because *Vanity Fair*'s law-yers excised the drug name from the excerpt and the book publisher, Knopf, followed their lead. Either way, Vanderbilt had read up on bronchodilators in the *PDR* and ended up writing what is undoubtedly the only high-society memoir that quotes from the *Journal of Allergy and Clinical Immunology.*

While Vanderbilt's *A Mother's Story* is a curious book in both form and content, I was taken aback by the sort of "yeah, *right*" tongue-clicking that surrounded its publication. It was the same kind of attitude that had surrounded Krissy Taylor's death: a collective expression of disappointment, because a catastrophic health problem caused by an adverse reaction to a legal drug simply *wasn't a good enough story.* It wasn't sexy enough. It had insufficient psychological intrigue. Somehow the reader felt cheated if a victim died from a legal drug.

I had noticed a similar phenomenon while covering mental health stories over the years. As mental health care grew more medical and less Freudian and psychological, the public seemed to resist biochemical explanations for dramatic or crisis situations. As mental illness became more treatable with medications, I found that editors were less interested in assigning stories about it. Medicalization somehow had made the human condition less compelling.

Even prescription drug addiction somehow wasn't a good enough story. An admission of legal-drug addiction had come to be seen as the new "big lie," a sort of celebrity plea-bargain to a lesser offense. When musician Kurt Cobain was still alive, for instance, his last few drug relapses—as well as those of his wife, Courtney Love—were blamed on prescription drugs, not on the heroin he had already admitted using. Only after he shot himself was it okay to cop to the higher offense of illicit drug use.

Interestingly, while many celebrities had publicly admitted to having "problems" with prescription drugs, the only arena where drug safety seemed to be discussed seriously was professional sports. A whole host of athletes have opened up about their difficulties with legal drugs, most prominently Green Bay Packers quarterback Brett Favre, the National Football League's MVP, who very publicly went into rehab to kick his dependence on Vicodin (hydrocodone with acetaminophen), a narcotic painkiller. Favre later explained that as his addiction grew, he got more pills by using leftover prescriptions from his teammates. In fact, the sports pages had become the best place in the newspaper to read about the perils of pharmacotherapy. According to published reports, it was common for players to trade pharmaceutical sales reps tickets to games, or access to locker rooms or after-game parties, in exchange for samples of narcotic painkillers.

One morning in the spring of 1996, I opened *The New York Times* and saw a peculiar full-page ad having something to do with retired financier Jack Dreyfus spending $80 million to expose a "flaw in our system of bringing prescription medicines to the public." The ad, which also appeared in *The Wall Street Journal,* was for a book Dreyfus had written called *The Lion of Wall Street,* but the ad copy also said that the book included within its pages another book Dreyfus had written, *A Remarkable Medicine Has Been Overlooked.* I had heard of this one. A copy of the slim gray volume stood on one of my many drug bookshelves; I had picked it up at a used book store that I regularly checked out for obscure works on pharmaceuticals, but I had never actually gotten around to reading it. What unfolded from the book, and from clips I called up about Dreyfus, was an oddly fascinating portrait of a man who had gone on his own drug quest after an unexpectedly *good* reaction to a medication. In the process, he became the Don Quixote of Dilantin.

In the 1950s and 1960s Dreyfus had made a fortune as the portfolio manager of the Dreyfus Fund, one of the first popular, heavily advertised mutual funds. He spent his free time playing tennis and bridge and breeding horses. But as a pet cause, he also got involved in medical advocacy.

Dreyfus had suffered a severe bout of depression in the late 1950s and was briefly hospitalized. At that time the breakthrough antidepressant Tofranil was just coming into common use in psychiatric hospitals. But Dreyfus had other ideas. He came up with a crude "body chemistry" theory of his own. He decided that his depression had something to do with electrical currents in his body, and he asked his doctor to give him Dilantin, the leading medicine used to treat seizures. Several days later, he reported to his doctor that he was well, requiring no further treatment.

This event could easily have turned Jack Dreyfus into a zealot for the biological treatment of psychiatric illness, especially anticonvulsants for mood disorders. He would have been ten or twenty years ahead of his time, and the combination of his money and his willingness to go public about his depression at the absolute height of his fame—in 1966 he was profiled in *Life* magazine—might have prevented the suffering of millions and hastened the modern era of psychiatry. Or he could have become a zealot for off-label drug use; he might have championed the free speech issues surrounding the dissemination of off-label prescribing information and lobbied for changes in FDA promotion rules.

Instead, Dreyfus became obsessed with Dilantin itself. He recommended it to his housekeeper and then his tennis partner in Miami, both of whom believed it cured their depression. Eventually he went on a mission to turn on the entire world. Over the years Dreyfus became convinced that Dilantin had more uses than aspirin. He grew incensed that the medical establishment saw the drug only as it was labeled, as an anticonvulsant. He couldn't understand why the FDA or the drug's manufacturer, Parke-Davis (and later Warner-Lambert), wouldn't do anything about this. It wasn't enough that it was perfectly legal for any doctor to prescribe the drug for depression. He wanted to convince them to *do* it.

Because he was Jack Dreyfus, he could get appointments with the heads of the Department of Health, Education and Welfare, the FDA, and Parke-Davis—even presidents of the United States. They all agreed to "look into it." Because he was Jack Dreyfus, he could also fund his own scientific studies when the drug company wasn't interested. Soon he was giving a million dollars a year to the Dreyfus Medical Foundation, the sole mission of which was to legitimize the off-label uses of Dilantin. When *Life* magazine said it would do a follow-up story on him and Dilantin only if there was a big medical conference to peg it to, he paid to set up a conference.

Dreyfus was absolutely right about some of the things he said about the FDA and the drug business. I knew exactly how he felt when he first realized how the pharmaceutical industry really works. But he didn't really want to fix the system. He just wanted everyone to try Dilantin. Its nonuse was, in his words, "a catastrophe." He felt that if the FDA refused to list his evidence of the drug's ability to treat everything from arrhythmias and diabetes to hiccups and stuttering on the label, the least it could do was list under its indications that it was a "stabilizer of bioelectrical activity."

In the late 1960s Dreyfus retired before he turned fifty and devoted himself full time to his quest. The Dreyfus Medical Foundation spent millions sending scientific papers on Dilantin to every prescribing doctor in America. Eventually Dreyfus decided to write a book about his experiences with the drug, and he hired superagent Mort Janklow, who got him a deal with Simon and Schuster. But since the foundation gave the publisher a $2 million grant—ostensibly to keep the hardcover price down to $9.95—many saw Dreyfus's 1981 *A Remarkable Medicine Has Been Overlooked* as the largest vanity publication in history. He surely penned it himself, because it is far too weird to have been ghostwritten. It begins with an open letter to then-President Reagan, followed by a rambling account of how Dreyfus had discovered the drug and his jet-setting adventures trying to popularize it. The rest of the book includes hundreds of pages of medical literature on Dilantin, which he calls "the most broadly useful drug in our pharmacopoeia."

Despite an advertising blitz unheard of in the publishing business—full-page ads in magazines and in several different sections of major newspapers—most of the 50,000 hardbacks were returned, and the paperback publication the next year, which had its own $1.5 million advertising budget, didn't do much better. In 1988 Dreyfus self-published a slightly updated hardcover edition of the book, which was mailed to every prescribing physician in America, with an updated version of the medical literature on the drug. At my local used book store, there were eight copies on the shelf.

In late 1995, at the age of eighty-two, Dreyfus had the book republished again. This time he added some more non-Dilantin biographical material, but *Kirkus Reviews* still dismissed it as "a plug for phenytoin masquerading as autobiography." Several months later, Dreyfus took out those new full-page ads in the *Times* and *Journal*.

I had to admire his persistence. But I also had to wonder how much drug safety that $80 million would have bought if it had been invested in Ray Woosley's program to create CERTs—independent Centers for Education and Research in Therapeutics—or simply given to the FDA to fund research that drug companies wouldn't support.

While I was exploring how drug safety situations had played out in the media, I had to take a harder look at the impact of my stories about Diane, Floxin and the FDA. I was certain that, among those who had read or heard about the pieces, some thought Diane and me brave and others thought us foolish, dangerously stirring up fear and outrage where none was justified. I had, over the years, met and spoken to both types of people. I was still being contacted by many people—patients, family members, doctors, lawyers—who had just found out about the article. The initial flurry of attention over my magazine stories and national television appearances with Diane was already several years behind us, but I still received several calls a month, usually at my office at *Philadelphia* magazine.

Some calls were from people who, after experiencing reactions to a quinolone, searched the literature as I had and came up with my name. Others had found me through transcripts of *Oprah*. There was a Pulitzer Prize–winning reporter at one of America's top daily newspapers, who reported having panic attacks that began while he was taking Floxin for prostatitis and which he was unable to control long after he had stopped the drug. There was a psychologist from Kent, England, who reported having persistent visual distortions since taking Cipro. There was a psychiatrist from the Midwest who reported losing his clinical privileges after experiencing seizures and psychotic reactions while taking Floxin. There was a Virginia housewife who reported having various CNS effects and neuropathy after taking Floxin; she had found Dave Flockhart through my story in the *Post* and even ended up appearing along with Sidney Wolfe on *The Phil Donahue Show,* where they discussed, among other drug safety topics, adverse reactions to quinolones. (That woman ordered a personalized license plate—"FLOXED"—for her car, but she had so many fender-benders because of her visual problems that her family decided the plate was cursed and made her remove it. I have it on my office wall.) There were several middle-aged men whose fathers had become suicidal while taking Floxin.

Other calls were from people I'd been hearing from since the very beginning, either because they or their parent or their spouse were suffering in the aftermath of a reported quinolone reaction. Many of them hadn't gotten much better. A few were pursuing legal action, with varying degrees of success. But most of them wanted to know how Diane was doing and whether my research had uncovered any miracle cures for whatever ailed them. More than anything, they were looking for a sympathetic ear, because even if they hadn't yet exhausted their medical options, they had clearly exhausted their doctors.

Ironically, a lot of my time on the phone was spent trying to convince them to "ask their doctors" about medications. Some of them wanted to know how different Floxies had been treated. Others had doctors who had already told them what pills they should be trying, but they were refusing to take them. Many were so spooked by their experience—the reaction itself, or perhaps a doctor or two telling them that it couldn't be a drug reaction—that they were distrustful of taking any medication at all. Others, however, seemed to have been made more fearful about pills by what I had said in print or on TV.

Even though I understood how little information patients generally have about the drugs they take, I was surprised at how little appreciation they had for the downside risk of not taking a new medication, or of stopping one they were already taking. My goal had never been to encourage people to stop taking drugs; my hope was that the work I was doing would help them start taking their drugs more seriously.

I would talk to Diane about the calls from the Floxies and my concerns over the effects of what we had done. She had had similar conversations with friends who had stopped taking their medications at the slightest hint of a problem—because of "what happened to you." We had, by this point, developed a fairly advanced perspective on drug-taking. We knew how to research drugs and take all reasonable precautions before swallowing them. And we had learned a lot about how to discuss drugs with our doctors and pharmacists. But it wasn't easy to share that perspective with others who hadn't been through what we had over four years.

Moreover, Diane felt our attitudes on the subject of drug reactions still differed. She believed that I hadn't yet forgiven drugs for having side effects. Diane had forgiven them long ago, because she didn't really have any choice. To continue treatment after her Floxin experience and all the lesser reactions she'd had since, required a certain informed surrender to the known risks. Since I wasn't taking the drugs, it was easier for me to focus on the flawed system by which risks become *known.*

At the same time, she appreciated the investigative work I was doing and was alarmed by much of what I had uncovered and documented. She knew there were times when my inability to forgive drugs their side effects was probably the only thing that kept me going.

A lot of these issues were on my mind in the fall of 1996, when I went to Amsterdam for the annual convention of the International Society for Pharmacoepidemiology. I was there because Jerry Avorn and Brian Strom had urged me to go. But I was also intrigued by the main subject of the conference—a day-long analysis of a panic that had been set off in the U.K., Europe and Australia over potential side effects of the popular new low-dose birth control pill. The panic began in mid-1995, but its consequences didn't manifest themselves until—well, at least nine months later, when the British birth rate began to rise because women had been scared off using any birth control at all.

In the days leading up to the convention's main event, I had some interesting experiences. During the opening reception I sat in the bar trying to communicate with two Russian pharmacoepidemiologists as we all drank very good Dutch beer. They were trying in vain to translate into English each other's observations on the changes in the drug business since the fall of the Soviet regime. I had been told that there was a very large black market for medicines in Russia, but they were explaining that the latest news was the arrival of American drug companies in the former Soviet Union. When one of the men went on a long rant in Russian, I turned to his comrade for a translation.

"He say, 'Big corruption—now, *white* market!' " he laughed, taking another gulp. We were speaking the international language of drug company distrust.

During the next few days I listened to lectures that took me, literally, around the world of pill-taking. I heard a talk about drug usage in

China, which, according to expert Dr. Guiqing Wang, has 5 million serious drug reactions and 190,000 drug-induced deaths each year. Wang also lamented that there was no "concrete regulation" of China's 3,400 drug manufacturers, "so most don't think they have any responsibility to report drug reactions."

I heard an expert on Indonesian midwives, Aryanti Radyowiyati, explain their appalling misuse of antibiotics. Since midwives are allowed to give up to three drugs, she said, patients always get three. If there are two different treatments for diarrhea, they get them both. Midwives usually give antibiotics prophylactically because they are allowed to charge more for their services if they do, and they prefer to give injections rather than the same dose in pills because they are convinced the injections work better. Indonesian children are given antibiotics "if their parents are believed to be unable to take care of them," she explained, and midwives generally believe that "only stupid people need drugs that are correctly labeled."

I heard a Spanish expert, Dr. Francisco Abajo, give a social history of Clozaril, which has been on the market in Spain longer than almost anywhere else. Abajo raised the very provocative question of how many people who should be using the drug *weren't,* simply because of the inconvenience and expense (which Diane could certainly vouch for) of the blood testing to monitor for agranulocytosis. He believed that in Spain there were close to 80,000 treatment-resistant patients who needed the drug, but 75,000 of them had never been able to try it. Ironically, Spanish studies showed that the rate of the severe blood side effect was "lower than expected." (In the summer of 1997 the FDA would announce that Clozaril patients could reduce blood testing to twice monthly after the first six months.)

I also came away with a few pharmaco-epi cocktail party tidbits. Did you know, for example, that the French rate of psychotropic drug use is two to five times higher than that of any other Western country? (While Americans apparently take more antidepressants, the French lead the pack because of their heavy use of short- and long-term benzodiazepines.)

Before the actual day-long seminar on the low-dose birth control pill, I had lunch with John Urquhart, and we talked about media perceptions of drug-related risks. While I had spoken previously with the bearish pharmaco-guru about compliance issues, I'd never heard his rap on risk. It is the subject for which he is probably best known, ever since his 1984 book *Risk Watch* (written with German collaborator Kurt Heilmann) raised provocative real-world questions about the arcane problems of responding to drug crises and questioned commonly held beliefs about the incidence of adverse drug reactions. Urquhart's guesstimates are almost always used as the low end of the incidence range, although he has also been a strong advocate for taking the impact of each reaction much more seriously.

One of the more sobering examples in his and Heilmann's work is a comparison of the risks averted by taking or not taking medications. They determined that if you stopped taking drugs altogether, eliminating the risk of drug-induced harm would increase your life expectancy by only thirty-seven minutes; but simultaneously, you would decrease your life expectancy by *fifteen years* because of all the untreated illness. The two authors were part of a landmark conference in 1987—organized by William Inman, the former British regulator who became the world's first professor of pharmacoepidemiology and devised the English yellow-card system for collecting adverse reaction reports—that was very critical of the media for its portrayals of drug risks.

Urquhart believes that the public is unable to tell small risks from large, and he blames the media for that. He sees a structural bias in journalism toward exaggerating adversities that pose small risks; this bias is exacerbated by the fact that bad news outsells good news and pessimistic forecasts outnumber optimistic ones. He also blames "victim-oriented reporting" for milking the entertainment value out of victims' plights without helping the audience to deduce "whether the latest misfortune is a big risk or a small one." (I didn't ask if he thought I was guilty of any of these.)

Urquhart believes the public needs more context. "Look," he told me, "we register about twenty-five new agents a year, and we basically have an adverse reaction 'hoo-hoo' about once every two years. So one in forty drugs comes in and has enough of a surprise to make a hoo-hoo. And the hoo-hoo, depending on how abrupt the newsbreak, is dealt with either by relabeling or by kicking the drug off the market. In retrospect, most things kicked off have been a mistake, and they would have been better dealt with by labeling. We're supposed to be balancing risk and benefit, and if you throw the drug off the market, the benefits are gone.

"If you're in this field, the question you're always confronted with is, 'Did the product bring this problem to the patients, or did the patients bring this problem to the product?' "

The low-dose birth control pill was a perfect example of what Urquhart had been complaining about. The Pill will always be unique in the legal-drug world because it was, as one drug expert noted, "the first prophylactic drug for *well* people." Because of what it does, it is always going to attract controversy, and certain political and religious groups actually root for it to have safety problems. In 1995 the mass panic arose in the U.K. over the side effects of a newer low-dose birth control pill, which had smaller amounts of both the hormones estrogen and progesterone. Since the introduction of the Pill in the 1960s, it has been linked to an increased risk of thrombosis—blood clots—in certain women. These third-generation low-dose pills, the most popular of which was Schering's Femodene, were supposed to be safer for women at risk for thrombosis than previous versions. But in October 1995 several epidemiological studies showed that the low-dose pill was actually causing twice as many blood clots as the older pill: twenty out of 100,000 patients instead of ten. This finding made front-page news in the British tabloids, especially after the government's Medicines Control Agency urged women to stop taking the new low-dose pill and return to the older version. (The German government authorities—who often take their regulatory cues from the United States and the U.K.—went a step further and banned the drug for women under thirty who had never taken it.)

Public health officials were initially quite proud of themselves for quickly identifying a new public health problem. Then they realized they had inadvertently caused an even bigger one: the stories about the low-dose pill were scaring many women off birth control altogether. In the months after the announcement, the British national abortion rate, which had been steadily falling, instead increased by 11 percent. Some five thousand extra abortions in Britain were blamed on the pill scare. Later, the British birth rate shot up: some hospital maternity wards were reporting up to 25 percent more babies than usual.

At the day-long seminar I attended, the pharmacoepidemiologists spent a whole afternoon teasing out and restyling the numbers on the new pill. The epidemiologists considered novel interpretations: perhaps the number of thrombosis cases had notched up because more at-risk people had decided to try the supposedly less-risky pill.

During the day there was much flogging of the media, which had been on the story well before the government's action—mostly covering individual cases of adverse reaction lawsuits against manufacturers—then helped turn it into a juggernaut after the MCA pronouncement confirmed the journalists' worst fears. But by day's end, it was clear that the scientists were willing to admit that the low-dose pill affair was as much a reflection on them as it had been on the media and the pill itself.

The experts hadn't been as clear and cautious as they should have been. Only days after the government announcement, for example, the Canadian epidemiologist whose work formed the basis of the warning flew to London for three hours just to tell the media in person that he was outraged by "the misuse of five years of my life's work" and to accuse the MCA of creating an "epidemic of anxiety."

Harvard's Jerry Avorn, who had just been elected president of the International Society for Pharmacoepidemiology, did his best to sum up the morals of the story. Pharmacoepidemiologists are supposed to be multidisciplinary marvels who weigh all the different variables, balancing questions that can be tested clinically and those that can be addressed only with mathematical models. There is something very utopian about the way they view the drug world, as if every force of nature could be assigned a value and figured into the equation.

"Are we going to start weighing the nonuse of drugs because of what the epidemiologist said?" he asked, only half-joking. "Were we surprised about what happened with these birth control pills because we *just assumed nobody would read our papers?*"

Still confused about the role of the media in the drug world, I took a trip—a sort of pilgrimage, actually—to meet Morton Mintz, the *Washington Post* reporter who had first broken the thalidomide story in 1962. Now in his seventies, he lives with his wife in a comfortable home in Chevy Chase and still occasionally weighs in with a freelance piece about some FDA-related subject. Mintz greeted me warmly, and we retired to the kitchen to talk and drink coffee. He wore a bow tie, a freshly pressed shirt and khaki pants, and two pairs of glasses for his tired eyes: one on his face, another, for reading, dangling around his neck. While he looked more like a retired economics professor than a feisty muckraker, he still had the burn.

After the thalidomide story fell into his lap, Mintz wrote investigative pieces and books on FDA-related subjects for fifteen years. In 1977 he was reassigned, grudgingly, to cover the Supreme Court. He believed he was reassigned because some *Post* colleagues thought he had become obsessed with the Pill and its possible links to breast cancer. He was later brought back to Bob Woodward's investigative team and did a series on the Dalkon Shield intrauterine device, which had been withdrawn under pressure in the United States and then dumped overseas.

Mintz didn't come out and say so, but he insinuated that the *Post* felt his writing had become—or had *remained*—too brazenly anticorporate even for the antiestablishment paper of record in the financially forgiving 1980s. Like the drug companies he was covering, Mintz often seemed more interested in exposing profits than pills. He later resigned from the *Post,* a move he would come to regret because freelancing, even for an award-winning reporter, is a lot harder than it looks.

We spoke for hours, and then he invited me up to his private office and asked if there was anything in his drug library I'd like to see. As we pored through his collection, he glanced at his watch, told me he had a lunch appointment that would take only an hour and kindly offered to let me stay and rifle his file cabinets unchaperoned.

Some of his files went all the way back to the early 1960s, including yellowed clips of his original thalidomide stories. Some were very recent and showed he was still on top of current FDA-related issues. He even had my story from the *Post* magazine. What amazed me, besides the sheer volume of articles, was the repetition. With other media following his lead, Mintz had done the same story over and over again, not because he didn't have a fresh eye—he did—but because drug world scandals repeat themselves in such a stale way. Was that the media's fault, or were we just covering a world so fundamentally unable to address its gross problems that it did nothing but continually cry wolf?

"Nothing changes in industry," Mintz said, without a hint that something *should* have changed because of his many influential articles and books. "What that means, of course, is that there are fundamental forces at work here, forces that make themselves felt regardless of what anyone does." I nodded knowingly.

Later, as we shared drug war stories, Mintz said with a sigh: "You are naive the same way I am naive."

I wasn't quite sure how to take that.

CHAPTER 20

Attack of the

Killer Formularies

During a big family dinner, my uncle asked me if I could explain something troubling that had just happened with his heart medicine. He had received a notice that he was being switched from the calcium channel blocker he had been taking for years for high blood pressure, Procardia XL (nifedipine), to another, newer drug, Norvasc (amlodipine), made by the same company. He was told that his doctor had already approved the switch, and that it was being made because of something called a "formulary." He didn't know what a formulary was, but he thought it sounded rather ominous.

Before taking the new drug, my uncle made a few calls. He spoke to a nurse in his physician's office, who said the switch had been made as a "cost-cutting measure." He then spoke to his physician, who said he had approved the switch because the new medication was a "better drug." My uncle thought the whole thing was a little weird.

I told him that it might be weird, but it wasn't unusual. He had just experienced "therapeutic substitution," one of the thorniest new phenomena in the legal-drug world. A pharmaceutical benefits manager (PBM) had looked at my uncle's case and decided that another drug would be "better" than the one his doctor had been prescribing.

But "better" could mean any number of things. It could mean, as the doctor had said, that the drug actually worked better—or longer, or with fewer side effects. Although, you could reasonably wonder, if the doctor really thought the drug was so much better, why hadn't he initiated the change himself?

"Better" could also mean, as the nurse said, that the drug was cheaper, either because its retail price was lower or because its manufacturer had made a special volume deal with the PBM. That deal would be made not just to get my uncle to switch, but to make sure that every patient the PBM covered for these drugs got switched. The drug company executive who cut such a deal was doing the work of thousands of detail men.

My uncle's therapeutic substitution was done through Medco Containment Services. Its specialty is lowering pharmaceutical costs to public and private health insurers by offering patients the opportunity to order their chronic-use drugs in larger quantities by mail instead of fussing with pharmacy visits. Other PBMs work by directly managing reimbursements for drugs purchased at pharmacies, trying to control both the retail price and the fee the pharmacist charges for filling the prescription (which is figured into the retail and reimbursement prices). But they all profit the same way: by pocketing a percentage of the money the health insurer saves off regular retail prices. The drug companies all had to make deals with the PBMs to remain competitive.

Medco is one of the largest PBMs in the world, and it had been drawing fire ever since being purchased by Merck in 1993—not only for squeezing profits from drugstores but for switching a disproportionate number of its customers to Merck drugs. Seventeen states had recently forced Merck/Medco into a $1.9 million settlement, in yet another legal assault led by the bold Minnesota attorney general's office. Besides the payment, Medco had to agree to fully disclose Merck's ownership to all doctors being called to switch prescriptions and distribute millions of brochures to patients about how to challenge switches.

But the substitutions did not abate—they just came with a better disclaimer—and Medco was hardly the only company making them. Such substitutions were being done every day at retail pharmacies all over the country. In some situations the PBM hired by a patient's health insurance company pushed the issue and contacted the doctor. (By this time, SmithKline and Lilly both owned PBMs, and other drug companies had purchased shares in such firms as well.)

In other situations, the pharmacists themselves initiated the switches by calling physicians—because pharmaceutical manufacturers had made deals directly with the pharmacy. The drug companies offered pharmacies elaborate rebate programs to get patients switched by actually calling the prescribing physicians directly, and the competition between rebate programs was fierce. To push its new, heavily advertised allergy medicine Flonase (fluticasone), for example, Glaxo Wellcome promised some pharmacies a 2 percent cash rebate if they switched 27 percent of their allergy customers to the drug. If they could get 34 percent of their customers on the drug, the rebate jumped to 8 percent.

One consumer advocate called such incentives "pharmaceutical payola," echoing the practices of record companies who, in the 1950s, paid off disk jockeys to buy chart-topping hits.

I explained to my uncle that most of the complaints about therapeutic substitution had been financial; outrage was growing at the market manipulation that made individual detail visits to doctors offices seem almost benign. But to me, there was also a much more interesting medical issue, to which very few people were paying attention.

I knew that the FDA had a large Office of Generic Drugs that made sure that each generic was "bioequivalent" to its name-brand drug. The science of bioequivalence—whether two drugs are therapeutically identical—had grown more complex as more was learned about "bioavailability." Two pills may contain the same amount of an active ingredient, but differences in their formulation can make the ingredient either less or more "available" to the body once it is delivered via the bloodstream. There are some complex ongoing controversies—part scientific, part economic—about whether it is even possible to make bioequivalent copies of certain medications. The best-selling hormone replacement therapy Premarin, for example, is made from animal estrogens that its manufacturer, Wyeth-Ayerst, claims cannot be synthesized. The equivalency issue is so complex that the Office of Generic Drugs issues a monthly report called "The Orange Book," containing each generic's therapeutic rating.

If regulating generic bioequivalence was hard, I imagined that figuring out if two entirely different drug products were substitutable would be nearly impossible. As I watched Diane zero in on the right medications for her, I had seen the vast differences in the way drugs in an identical therapeutic class act when they are in one individual's body. So I called the FDA, asking which department was in charge of deciding what drugs, be they name-brand or generic, could be safely substituted for entirely different drugs.

The answer is: No department at the FDA regulates therapeutic substitution. Regulators approve and analyze drugs only one at a time. Therapeutic substitutions are done by a higher authority than the FDA.

The formulary.

There was a time when the word *formulary* wasn't that ominous at all. It was nothing more than a list of drugs, a pharmaceutical menu. Hospitals have always had their own formularies, so doctors could know what drugs the facility was stocking. Many health insurers have always had formularies as well: the national health insurance systems of entire countries, state Medicare and Medicaid boards, private health maintenance organizations, even self-insured companies. For many years, such formularies were largely driven by the prescribing needs of physicians. If a hospital doctor wanted to try a new drug on a patient, it was easily added to the formulary.

But as health care costs rose, imposing restrictions on formularies came to be seen as a way to control drug prices: offer shorter menus at better prices. No longer were formularies driven by physicians' needs; instead, private and public health insurers created their own formularies to restrict what they would reimburse, or they adopted the strict formularies of a PBM. Of the tens of thousands of available drugs, some tight formularies list fewer than one hundred.

The formulary committees that choose what is on these lists are now powerful enough to make decisions that regulators can't—and doctors won't. They decide which drug treatments are "preferred" and which aren't. These decisions are based partly on clinical studies and partly on drug company salesmanship. But the FDA does not yet regulate the claims made behind closed doors to get drugs onto formularies.

If a drug is not listed on an insurer's formulary, it is very hard for a physician affiliated with the insurer to write a reimbursable prescription for it. If a drug is listed on the formulary but is not marked "preferred," it is only a matter of time before the doctor will be called to ask if the patient can be switched. It is the doctor's decision, but physicians know the long-term consequences of fighting cost-containers. If they fight at all, they pick their battles.

Even in countries with national health insurance, some physicians treat certain patients outside the confines of a formulary. And in the United States there are still unaffiliated doctors with private-pay patients. But for most patients, the impact of formularies is already large and is growing exponentially.

Some experts complain that restrictive formularies prevent patients from getting the newest, best drugs, which are also invariably the most expensive. Others complain that doctors are being relentlessly second-guessed and relieved of their responsibilities as caregivers, and that clinical pharmacology has been reduced to analyzing the pharmacodynamics of prescribing rebates.

A third group thinks that, considering how dim-witted some doctors' prescribing habits are, managed drug care is, on balance, the best thing that has ever happened to patients.

In a way, they are all right. I had been told that if Diane's gynecologist had prescribed Floxin for her uncomplicated urinary tract infection through an HMO with a tight formulary, the prescription would likely have been questioned, if not refused—not because of safety concerns but because quinolones are considered far too expensive to use before cheaper antibiotics have failed to work. A physician friend loaned me a purloined copy of a 1994 formulary from the California-based Kaiser Permanente HMO. Kaiser is notorious for having one of the most powerful and restrictive formularies in the country. The book's appendix had a special section on Cipro—the only quinolone in the formulary that year—which took great pains to dissuade doctors from using it unless absolutely necessary. An Australian physician I was in touch with, David Henry, told me that because of the quinolones' "restricted benefit" status in that country's formulary, he would have needed "prior approval" from the national health service to prescribe Floxin in Diane's case.

But the same kind of tight formulary might also have refused to pay for some of Diane's more expensive medications. Mental health care professionals have been particularly distressed that some cost-containment companies limit their choices of the newer SSRI antidepressants, even though it is clear that, especially among female patients, the drugs are in no way interchangeable.

"This is a basic misunderstanding of medicine," growled Dr. Leroy Schwartz, a Princeton-based physician and health policy advocate who was way ahead of the curve on therapeutic substitution, writing about it years before most physicians saw it coming. "We are dealing with the elderly, women, infants, minority groups, people on different medications, people with different illnesses. These drugs are simply not interchangeable. There is no evidence that one works the same way as another in a particular patient. This needs congressional oversight!"

But he had to know that, in this political climate, a congressional oversight committee was more likely to *ban* the FDA from getting involved with therapeutic substitution at all than to empower the agency to regulate the practice. (In early 1998, the FDA announced it would try to at least regulate the promotional materials used to encourage drug switches by those PBMs that were owned by or had special financial ties with pharmaceutical firms.)

.   .   .

The tension in the world of drug dispensing wasn't helped by the fact that most of America's drugstores were suing most of the world's top pharmaceutical manufacturers. In retaliation, the drug companies joined the Federal Trade Commission in suing to stop the biggest drugstore chain merger in history. At the center of the storm was a guy I had grown up with in Harrisburg, who also just happened to have recently assumed control of the massive Rite Aid pharmacy chain, which his father had founded. I went to interview him over lunch at Rite Aid's big black corporate headquarters, just across the river from the Pennsylvania state capitol building.

While waiting for his chance to run the company, Martin Grass had earned the deep-sunk, sad eyes that made him look much older than forty-three. He survived a bitter sibling squabble that sent his younger brother off to buy a competing chain in Indiana, then a painful 1989 criminal prosecution that typified the increasing acrimony in this once-gentlemanly industry. In one of the first of many mergers and unfriendly takeovers in America's chain drugstore business, Rite Aid was swallowing the Ohio-based Peoples Drug Store chain whole. A member of the state pharmacy board, who also worked for Peoples, tried to foil the takeover by accusing Grass of bribing him. The charges were dismissed, and his accuser later apologized as part of a civil settlement.

Today, of course, pharmacy takeover targets realize that resistance is futile.

Unlike his father, who has always been somewhat restrained with the press, Martin Grass is surprisingly candid and quotable, beginning with the subject of the pharmaceutical industry itself. "They've always hidden under the cloak of 'We're these great research and development houses, and without us there would be no medication,' " he said. "I think they're full of shit. . . . The fact that they're manufacturing quote/unquote 'life-saving drugs' has given them a certain holier-than-thou attitude."

Grass took a bite of his sandwich. "Listen," he said, "I'm somebody who takes pharmaceuticals. I'm on Synthroid for my thyroid, and I want to make sure there's enough of a profit motive so that companies will invest capital for new and improved drugs. You can say that drug manufacturer profits are obscene, but nobody wants a weak pharmaceutical industry."

The class action suit that the pharmacies brought against the manufacturers was filed in 1993, but it had its roots several years earlier, when Grass began investigating the slowly emerging phenomenon of pharmaceutical benefits management. He started asking questions about a little mail-order company hardly anyone had ever heard of called Medco.

The fiscal stability of the pharmaceutical industry was built on the tacit understanding that nobody competed on price for brand-name drugs. It had always been one price for everybody. Then Grass heard that Medco was getting a discount. When he asked about it, some manufacturers swore it wasn't true. Others admitted that it was true but claimed that the mail-order business wasn't direct competition for drugstores.

"You know, these guys botched it," Grass told me. "They had a great deal going with this one-price-for-everybody thing, if you ask me. Walgreens [a large chain] was paying what a guy with two stores in Northeast Philly was paying for drugs. They never should have opened this Pandora's box of mail order. If they had stuck with 'You want our product? This is the price,' their margins would have been even higher, and everything would have been more gentlemanly. I think now, if the truth be known, they probably wish there was none of this therapeutic substitution."

The mail-order business grew precisely because it was cheaper. "I went around the country talking to people about drugs," Grass recalled, "and I never ran into anybody who said they switched to mail order because it was a wonderful convenience. They had beat us on price." It was all part of a sea change in drug pricing in which many of the new large buyers of drugs—HMOs and hospital groups—got volume discounts unavailable to retail stores.

Martin Grass's company was once considered the ruination of the retail pharmacy business, forcing down the profit margins of family-owned drugstores to the point where they could no longer compete. Now he was trying to recast himself as a drugstore hero by taking on the pharmaceutical industry. In 1993 Grass's father made a presentation at the board meeting of the National Association of Chain Drugstores to lay out his plan to sue the drug companies for price-fixing on behalf of his 2,700-plus stores. He asked if anyone wanted to join him as a co-plaintiff. Eventually 40,000 retail pharmacies filed suit.

In the meantime, Rite Aid hedged its bets. Martin Grass created his own PBM, called Eagle Managed Care. Its selling point was that it was the only pharmaceutical benefits manager that wasn't owned by one of the drug companies it was supposed to be managing.

A year later, after being crowned chairman and CEO, Grass made his first major play as boss by announcing that Rite Aid would become the world's largest drugstore chain by buying out one of its top competitors, the two-thousand-store Revco chain, for $1.8 billion. The move was bound to raise an eyebrow among antitrust regulators because so many stores were involved, some competing for identical markets. Then a border skirmish in the Rite Aid–Medco war made the Federal Trade Commission's eyes pop wide open.

In Maryland Rite Aid organized a drugstore boycott of Merck/Medco—which had a contract to contain pharmaceutical benefits for state employees—to protest its reimbursement rates, which the pharmacies felt were too low. In retaliation, Medco sued Rite Aid and the other pharmacies, and the state launched a probe into possible collusion among the drugstore owners. This Maryland probe didn't help the status of Grass's merger deal with the FTC. Nor did Grass ingratiate himself with FTC regulators, who apparently got the impression that he really didn't think the government would stop his merger with Revco. The FTC wanted Rite Aid to divest itself of nearly seven hundred stores to assure that no markets were left without local competition; Grass eventually offered to divest the company of 340 stores, but his offer came only after the antitrust review period was extended seven times.

To add to the confusion, the negotiations between Rite Aid and the FTC came just as a federal judge in Chicago was reviewing a proposed settlement of the price-fixing suit brought by the pharmacies against the drug companies. Unwilling to settle cheap, Rite Aid and several other chains had opted out of the class action to pursue individual claims. But lawyers for the remaining class members had tentatively agreed to cave in and accept $409 million for their troubles. The presiding judge, however, threw the settlement out because it did not include any mention that the drug companies would actually change their pricing policies. In effect, the drug companies were just paying the stores to go away. (The companies eventually agreed to change the pricing policies and pay a $351 million settlement.)

Three weeks after the judge threw out the class action settlement, the FTC announced it would file lawsuits to prevent Rite Aid from buying Revco. Grass told the *Cleveland Plain Dealer* that he believed the White House was pulling strings on behalf of the drug companies, which "feared bargaining with a bigger drugstore chain."

While he was stunned that the FTC's action had torpedoed his big deal, Grass looked at the situation as a businessman. "This might have all been because it was an election year," he mused. "A lot of people think that because Revco is based in Ohio, which was considered a pivotal state in the election, the corporate changes and the store closings in Ohio could have lost jobs and had an impact.

"All I know is, our company has never really been involved in national elections. I looked at this FTC thing and just felt, 'Hey, this was not decided by the merits of the law.' So we made contributions to both sides, through a PAC [political action committee]. Because you know, you gotta have political support for these deals. Unfortunately, that's one of the bad things about getting so big. We used to be able to ignore national politics. But no more."

Nobody in the legal-drug world could afford to ignore national politics anymore. Several FDA-overhaul bills were looming in the House of Representatives, and a big one in the Senate, sponsored by outgoing Kansas Republican Nancy Kassebaum, who was intent on leaving her mark on American health care before stepping down. Capitol Hill was turning into a drug-regulation debating society.

I watched the whole thing with fascination and horror. It was amazing to be able to turn on CNN and C-SPAN and see many of the people I had been interviewing and reading for several years trotting out their stump speeches for the camera and the public record. Little of what they had to say was new, but the sheer volume of historical debate about drug regulation being dumped into the public record was staggering. The usual suspects from the FDA, drug industry trade groups, academia and consumer advocacy and medical charity organizations gave speech after speech for or against the various bills. The endless hearings mirrored the FDA regulatory process itself, relentless in both importance and tedium.

A great deal was at stake. During the previous congressional session following the 1994 midterm elections, the Gingrich-driven hearings had tried to cripple the FDA with a strategic strike aimed at the Washington Legal Foundation's favorite target: the off-label promotion controversy. (Just to stick it to Kessler, the Republican-controlled House had also rejected the agency's $67 million appropriation request for a new FDA building.) This time, it was an all-weapons assault on the FDA's very reason for being. Using all the age-old criticisms, even the ones that Kessler could prove he had actually addressed pretty successfully, the FDA's enemies now wanted to effectively relieve the agency of its power to be the world's last word on drug safety and efficacy. Much of the discussion centered on passing laws to end the "drug lag," the months or years that pass during which a drug is available in countries with less restrictive approval processes but not in the United States. The FDA was defended on the "drug lag" issue by, of all people, Sidney Wolfe, normally one of its strongest critics. He offered an analysis of the number of drugs approved by various countries that later had to be withdrawn for safety reasons. From 1970 through 1992, the British had recalled twenty-three drugs, the Germans thirty and the French thirty-one; during the same period, the FDA only recalled nine drugs.

One bill said that any drug already approved in Europe should get a rubber-stamp approval by the FDA. Other bills sought to privatize much of the reviewing of drug applications. The number of clinical trials required to approve a drug would be cut, as would the total amount of data required for submission. Short deadlines were proposed that would give the agency only months to act on New Drug Applications, after which the companies would be free to get private reviews. The FDA had already set up a small pilot program to see if some of its functions could be done by agency-approved private companies. Its critics wanted the whole agency run that way.

In fact, the general tenor of the debates was, "Why can't the exception be the rule?" In 1991 the FDA had created the special "accelerated approval" track for drugs for AIDS and Alzheimer's—diseases with no known treatments and victims desperate enough to put aside the normal risk/benefit ratio. Now some manufacturers and patient groups wanted to know why there couldn't be accelerated approval for *everything*. Let the patients, not the FDA, decide what risks they wanted to take. The industry trade group, which had recently renamed itself the Pharmaceutical *Research* and Manufacturers Association (PhRMA, referred to as "pharma"), flew in 140 different patients or family members to testify that they needed the FDA to get them new drugs faster. This effort had decidedly mixed results. The industry manipulation of patients was so heavy-handed that some groups previously critical of the FDA took the agency's side in Congress.

"The Kassebaum bill had us reviewing every drug in six months," Kessler later complained to me. "Look, it takes an enormous effort to get a drug out. Sure, we've done a couple [of AIDS drugs] in forty days, but when you're running a marathon, you can only sprint *some* of the time. You sprint on the big ones. We need the ability to set priorities at the agency, to say, 'These drugs for this class of diseases deserve priority.' You then do the drug that doesn't offer the great therapeutic advance but might be important economically in, you know, a short period of time. But all drugs in six months? That's not in the *public's* interest."

FDA supporters argued strenuously that the agency had dramatically speeded up drug approvals. But this wasn't true for medical devices and food products, which the agency also regulated, and the approvals for spinal screws and food additives hadn't kept pace. Also, Kessler had already made it clear that he believed that the FDA's statutory authority could be expanded to include regulation of tobacco products. This gave more incentive than ever for the agency's enemies to try to chop away at the roots of the FDA's statutory mandate, rather than just prune the saggier branches. Not only did it add tobacco lobbyists to the antiregulatory coalition, but some FDA stalwarts, fearful of another "unfunded mandate," joined the anti-Kessler ranks because they felt the agency would implode if required to add tobacco to its workload.

One of the more prominent of these was Jim Phillips, who had been Kessler's colleague when the two worked for Orrin Hatch and later became one of the FDA commissioner's close advisers on compliance investigations. Phillips quit in a huff in July 1994 and soon after began publicly criticizing Kessler's tobacco initiative—which he believed was absurd as long as the FDA was still shirking so many of its responsibilities. Phillips was especially concerned about the agency's ability to handle inspections of foreign manufacturing facilities as more and more medicine production was moved overseas to lower prices. The overseas inspections that had been done uncovered nearly twice as many "serious manufacturing deficiencies" as in domestic plants. Phillips told *The New York Times* that the FDA foreign inspection program was "a ticking time bomb that could explode at any time." While Phillips took other potshots at Kessler that made his attack seem more personal—he referred to him as "soundbite man"—his characterization of the commissioner as obsessed with tobacco allowed him to be targeted as a shill for big business. But it would later turn out that some other top FDA officials shared some of Phillips's opinions about tobacco.

Kessler and his supporters were fighting valiantly on the Hill, but there were those who felt the FDA had already lost much of the battle. *The Washington Post* did a big piece on what it called "de facto deregulation"—previously strident agencies like the FDA pulling back on enforcement to keep from losing their statutory right to regulate at all. A new rhetoric was sneaking its way into the language of regulation, the idea that the FDA could be a "partner" with industry. The term was even used by Carl Peck, the former head of CDER, who was at Georgetown developing new models that might allow drugs to be approved with only one trial for efficacy, instead of the traditional two.

"I didn't like it when Carl Peck said, 'We're your partners in drug development,'" one former FDA department head told me. "Today, when the FDA makes an approval, the announcements are couched in this 'See, *we* have found this new drug.' That rings phony to me."

Another veteran FDA-watcher was more succinct: "Partner? That's such crap!"

As things heated up on the Hill, *The Wall Street Journal* broke a shocking drug story. For a newspaper with a well-known deregulatory stance, it was quite a commentary on what the world might be like if drug companies were left to police themselves.

In the world of clinical drug testing, the greatest fear is that a study capable of transforming clinical practice overnight will be suppressed for financial reasons. That's why the tale of Betty Dong's research on Synthroid (levothyroxine), the top-selling treatment for the increasingly widespread diagnosis of underproductive thyroid gland, sent such a shudder through the medical community. Dong, it turned out, had been quietly forced to withdraw a research paper that was about to be published in *JAMA* because her drug company sponsor, the manufacturer of Synthroid, knew that her conclusions could slash its share of the thyroid supplement market.

In 1987 Betty Dong was a drug researcher at the University of California, San Francisco (UCSF), which had one of the powerhouse clinical pharmacology programs in the country. She had already done several studies on generic and branded synthetic thyroid supplements, all of which supported the contention of the British drug company Boots that its synthetic hormone Synthroid was beyond "better" than its competitors. Boots believed that another name-brand synthetic thyroid hormone, Levoxine, and the two available generics simply were not the same medicine as Synthroid, weren't "bioequivalent." This gave Boots a lock on a very lucrative market, which would keep growing because thyroid deficiency does not go away; patients take Synthroid for life.

But Boots wanted a new study, so they gave Betty Dong $250,000 to prove the point again in twenty-four patients. Two years later, they started asking her for preliminary test-tube results. Certain that Synthroid would be triumphant, they insisted she break the study "blind" to identify which randomized drug was clearly superior. The results would be crucial for fighting the decisions by state formularies in New Jersey and Massachusetts to add Levoxine, regardless of any consensus on bioequivalence, because it was cheaper than Synthroid.

Dong refused to break the study blind, and her relationship with the company was never quite the same. But she did continue her research, and by late 1990 she knew the startling preliminary results. According to her study, the three competing thyroid products were bioequivalent to Synthroid. The 8 million Americans who took thyroid supplements every day could safely save an estimated $350 million a year by switching to the generics—that is, if they ever found out about the study. Boots immediately began to challenge Dong and the validity of her work, and for the next three years, the study's procedures were analyzed and re-analyzed by outside consultants before the results were even finalized. In January 1994 Dong sent a final draft of her manuscript to Boots. According to *The Wall Street Journal,* the company's vice president for market-ing wrote on a copy of her cover letter "must review harshly" and "begin to get our ducks in order with the salesforce." The company spent an-other year trying to convince Dong to change her paper, especially its conclusion that patients could safely switch from Synthroid, or to do another study. They hired a private investigator who petitioned UCSF for financial information about Dong and looked into whether someone at the school had leaked the study to the manufacturers of Levoxine.

When Dong still wouldn't back down and her paper was just about to appear in *JAMA,* Boots invoked an obscure clause in the research con-tract that said she needed the company's written permission to publish the results. It was a hardball move, but it was a hardball time for the company: Boots was in negotiations to be sold to the German conglom-erate BASF AG for $1.4 billion, and the market stability of Synthroid was clearly a cornerstone of that purchase price. Since Dong had signed the research contract on behalf of UCSF—and never checked with a lawyer, who might have told her that the clause violated the school's research policies—she consulted an aide to the university's new attorney about what to do. She was told to back down, abide by the clause and pull the article. Disgusted, she did.

Four months later, in April 1995, the Boots sale went through and Synthroid was absorbed by the new owner's U.S. pharmaceutical arm, Knoll. Dong was hoping that she still might be able to publish her study until she saw the June 1995 issue of the peer-reviewed *American Journal of Therapeutics,* which carried a sixteen-page evisceration of her still-unpublished study. Its lead author was Dr. Gilbert Mayor, an editor of the journal who just also happened to have been the drug company's medical services director. Mayor had been one of the firm's leading internal critics of Dong's work since 1990.

In the spring of 1996, more than a year after she pulled her *JAMA* paper and vowed never to do drug company research again, Betty Dong got her story to *The Wall Street Journal.* It ran the story in the marquee position—front page, right-hand column—on a fateful Thursday in

April, right in the middle of the House and Senate debates on streamlining the FDA.

The story would lead to much soul-searching in the world of clinical drug research, especially since it came on the heels of a *New England Journal of Medicine* article by a leading cancer researcher detailing four instances he knew about that involved promising research being squelched by corporate secrecy demands. The FDA would eventually pressure Knoll to release the Synthroid study. *JAMA* would eventually publish it, two years late, placed amid a package of powerful commentaries about the dangers of suppressing studies. In response to the *JAMA* coverage, editors of other journals would wonder publicly about the cumulative lost impact of the many studies that never got published, positive, negative or just tediously inconclusive.

The FDA's Dr. Mary Pendergast would admit publicly what most insiders already knew. Whether it was because of contracts like Betty Dong's or for other reasons, she said, it was "fair to say that . . . the data set the FDA sees is often not consistent with the far rosier picture portrayed in the published scientific literature . . . [and] from our perspective . . . there is a discordance between the full news about a new therapy and that which is published in the scientific literature in many cases."

Eventually, an $8.5 billion class action suit would be filed against Synthroid's manufacturer on behalf of thyroid patients. The company would initially call the suit "unfounded" and "grotesquely excessive," but would later begin settlement negotiations.

With all this turmoil in the worlds of drug dispensing and regulation, Georgetown's Ray Woosley knew that his proposed CERT program had never been more necessary—or more politically doomed. His lobbying efforts on behalf of independent drug research and education centers had gone nowhere. He testified to Congress during the FDA hearing, but he recognized that his role there was primarily to do damage control, keeping the agency from being completely defanged, rather than take bold steps forward. For the moment, he would have to satisfy himself with teaching the public about medication safety one drug at a time.

Ever since his involvement with the discovery of arrhythmias caused by interactions with the nonsedating antihistamine Seldane back in the early 1990s, Woosley and his clin-pharm group at Georgetown had been following what doctors, pharmacists and patients were actually doing with that information. Was anybody reading that black box, the one that had been warning since 1992 about Seldane's potentially fatal interaction with erythromycin and several other drugs? They thought not, suspecting that patients were still being prescribed Seldane together with those drugs—sometimes by the same doctor, sometimes by two separate doctors who didn't know of each other's prescriptions. The last best defense against such potentially dangerous prescriptions was supposed to be the pharmacist, who presumably would notice that the unwitting consumer was being put at risk unnecessarily, and either warn the patient or call the doctor. If the actual pharmacist didn't notice, most major pharmacies had computerized screening programs that were supposed to notice for them.

As a test, the Georgetown team sent one of their clinical pharmacology fellows to fifty pharmacies in the Washington, D.C., area, armed with prescriptions for Seldane and erythromycin. All but two of the pharmacies used computer screening programs.

One-third of the pharmacists, sixteen out of fifty, filled the prescriptions together, without a word of caution to the "patient." Before leaving these sixteen pharmacies, the undercover Georgetown clin-pharm fellow gave the pharmacists one last chance by specifically asking if the two drugs should be taken together.

The majority of these pharmacists said there was no problem taking the drugs together.

The 1995 study appeared as a letter in *JAMA,* after which *U.S. News & World Report* gave Woosley funding to repeat it nationally in 245 pharmacies in seven major cities with several different dangerous drug combinations. In the meantime, another study appeared in *JAMA* that focused the blame back on prescribing doctors. Using a database of computerized pharmacy claims from a large New England health insurer, the researchers found that many patients were still receiving Seldane and erythromycin prescriptions together. While the rate of such overlapping prescriptions had been cut by 57 percent since the black box had been added, more than 2 percent of all the patients getting Seldane were also still getting erythromycin.

In a subtle bit of side-effect slinging, this last study was funded by Schering, the drug company that manufactured Seldane's archrival, Claritin (loratadine). In fact, the black box on Seldane had played out interestingly in the marketplace. In response to it, Seldane's manufacturer, which had since been bought out by the German firm Hoechst, partnered with a small Massachusetts company, Sepracor, one of several new biotech firms that specialized in isolating the parts of a molecule that cause specific adverse reactions and rebuilding safer versions of drugs. Sepracor was working on more than a dozen drugs that either had high-profile side effects or were just nearing the end of their patent protection and might be reinvented. The firm was able to patent a new use for a metabolite of Seldane, fexofenadine, and licensed it to Hoechst Marion Roussel, which convinced the FDA to approve it as a nonsedating antihistamine without a black box. The new drug would be sold under the name Allegra. Hoechst assumed the approval meant it would now have two nonsedating antihistamines to fight Claritin. Instead, the FDA soon began asking why Seldane should be on the market at all.

As Seldane's fate was being discussed in Washington, Woosley's 1996 study for *U.S. News* confirmed and broadened his earlier findings. Reporters were sent out with three paired prescriptions for drugs that, for a variety of reasons, shouldn't be taken together. Once again, many pharmacists filled all the prescriptions without comment. The pairing with the most serious labeled contraindication was filled one-third of the time with no verbal caution of any sort. The pairing of a birth control pill with an antibiotic that can render it ineffective was filled by more than three-fourths of pharmacists with no caution. And only three out of sixty-one pharmacists flagged a possible interaction between two high blood pressure medicines. Independent drugstores failed to warn more often than chains, and stores in lower-income areas failed to warn more often than their upper-income counterparts.

While the research had begun as a way to make a point about drug interactions and physician prescribing habits, it was now also a strong commentary on drugstores. When pharmacists were later interviewed about the errors, they were quick to blame the harsher realities of life behind the white counter. "This place is a sweatshop," said a druggist in a Denver Kmart pharmacy while counting out pills. A freshman pharmacist in Columbus said she failed to warn about the black box interaction because "I'm new . . . I never dispensed a drug in my life."

None of this came as a complete surprise to me, because Diane and I had noticed it at our own pharmacy. When she first had her drug reaction, we relied heavily on the advice and counsel of the two pharmacists at our local drugstore, Ann McParlin and Kristen Burt. The store was part of a big national chain, but the pharmacists themselves were local and very involved. They knew us and we knew them; when Ann came back from maternity leave, we weren't the only customers asking to see baby pictures. But four years later, Ann and Kristen were long gone. So were their replacements, with whom we had tried diligently to bond, especially when Diane was first started on Clozaril, which is a pain in the neck to dispense because of the paperwork nightmare created by the weekly blood tests.

Now the place seemed to have a revolving door of pharmacists, assistants and trainees. They always asked if we had any questions about our prescriptions. But they asked the way employees at fast-food chains ask if you want fries with that.

As for Seldane, the FDA would announce in January 1997 that it planned to withdraw approval for the Hoechst Marion Roussel antihistamine. The agency decided that the recent approval of Allegra—which had the same active metabolite—sufficiently altered Seldane's risk/benefit ratio to make it unacceptable. During the thirty-day comment period (except for emergency drug withdrawals, FDA rulings are usually issued conditional to a comment period), Schering, the makers of Claritin, would take out full-page attack ads in several national newspapers—and just to rub Hoechst's face in it, the company's American hometown *Kansas City Star.* Hoechst would convince a hometown judge to grant a temporary restraining order on the ads and go on to sue Schering for false advertising. (The case was later settled.)

From that point on, Hoechst would focus its efforts on holding off the FDA's final judgment—which it did for almost a year—while switching Seldane users to Allegra before any more of them switched to Claritin. In the interim, the FDA would put new label warnings on Seldane—including one that finally urged patients not to take the drug with grapefruit juice, as Dave Flockhart had first discovered. (*The Oprah Winfrey Show* ended up scooping the FDA on this warning by approximately four years.) Lost in this whole scramble was the fact that Seldane and Allegra were not identical, only similar. When the 1997 allergy season began, a guy I play basketball with would lament the virtual unavailability of Seldane, which he had used successfully, without side effects, for years.

"I took Allegra, and it didn't do anything," he said. "Neither did Claritin. I don't get it. Why can't I just take Seldane?"

CHAPTER 21

The Race to

the Cocktail

The last thing I expected at this late date was a drug story with a happy ending. And then suddenly a magazine assignment offered me the chance to be airlifted into a world that had just been radically changed by a new pill.

Actually, it was three new pills, the product of a decade-long, multibillion-dollar race pitting all the top drug companies against AIDS and each other—probably the most time, money and scientific manpower ever focused on a single medicinal target. Merck, Abbott and Roche, three companies whose corporate personalities couldn't have been more different, had crossed the finish line together.

My editor's initial interest in the AIDS drug race had come from a personal experience. A member of the magazine staff had AIDS and had been pulled out of what appeared to all to be his death spiral by this new drug treatment. Someone suggested the magazine do portraits of the doctors responsible for the pills, which led to the notion of an article and a photo essay. I soon found myself driving up the Northeast Extension of the Pennsylvania Turnpike on a blustery fall afternoon to visit the sprawling suburban Philadelphia research campus of Merck.

I was coming not as the unwelcome outsider I had grown accustomed to being, but as an invited guest. After four years, I was finally interested in a story that industry actually wanted told, a story in which the drug companies were not only the good guys, but maybe even *great* guys, leaders of science. It was also a chance for me to explore the part of the drug business I understood the least, because it is usually so shrouded in mystery and corporate platitudes: the big science and high drama of drug discovery and development.

But more important, it was the first time in four years I could ask whatever questions I wanted, and somebody at a drug company would actually try to answer them.

"You want to see it?" Dr. Emilio Emini asked. He was offering to show me the enzyme on which he had bet ten years of his virology career and a billion dollars of his company's money. Rising from his desk, Emini, who is tall, dark and hairy—and a little too big for his surprisingly small office at Merck—reached over into a folder and handed me a single photographic slide. I held it up toward the window, trying to catch the light of a dreary day.

The enzyme popped bright blue off the slide's black background. It was the HIV protease, which had suddenly become the single most important molecule in all of AIDS. The drugs that were built to stop this enzyme from working, the protease inhibitors, had dramatically changed nearly every aspect of AIDS treatment. The fastest-approved drugs in FDA history, they were being swallowed by nearly half of the Americans on antivirals for HIV after only six months on the market. It was one of the quickest treatment changeovers in modern medical history.

Protease inhibitors provided the kick for a new multidrug regimen known as the "cocktail." Because this potent combination forced the virus in the blood down to undetectable levels in many patients, AIDS researchers were beginning to talk about the disease as a manageable chronic illness instead of a death warrant. Some patients had already experienced such an astonishing reversal of symptoms that they had begun asking the complicated questions of newly leased life, such as, "How do I pay for twenty thousand dollars a year in drugs if I go *off* disability?" and "Do I like my caregiver enough to stay with him if I'm *not* going to die?" The companies that bought life insurance policies from AIDS patients for cash and then settled with insurers after their deaths were starting to close down because the old actuarial tables appeared moot.

This little blue enzyme had turned the AIDS world upside down—or actually, rightside up.

At first glance, the HIV protease (pronounced "PRO-tee-ace") looks like a schematic drawing of a bug's head, with two pincers protecting the mouth cavity. Those pincers are the key to what the protease does. When HIV is reproducing itself, it grows strands of proteins, which the protease helps birth by chemically biting them off. A protease inhibitor is like a rock that gets jammed into the bug's open mouth, preventing the pincers from working and, ultimately, HIV from replicating.

Others have described the protease as looking like two fists, knuckle to knuckle, thumbs peaked at the top. I asked Emini for his interpretation of this molecular Rorschach. At first, he gave a typical scientist's answer. "To me, it just looks like protease," he said. Then he sighed reflectively. "I guess I've heard people say it looks like a Pac-Man—although nobody knows what a Pac-Man is anymore."

When Merck scientists first made this molecular portrait, people still knew what a Pac-Man was. That was back in late 1988, which was also the last time Emini saw Dr. Irving Sigal, the brilliant young molecular biologist who convinced him, and Merck, that the protease would be HIV's glass jaw. Sigal had been the soul of Merck's protease program. If not for him, Emini's otherwise spare office probably would not be adorned with a sleek black promotional clock for Crixivan (indinavir), the top-selling protease inhibitor, which at the moment Merck couldn't make quickly enough to keep up with demand.

A wiry, vigorous thirty-five-year-old who crammed his leisure time with scuba diving, long-distance running and playing the sax, Sigal had been whipping his team to finish "solving" the protease when he had to fly to London to give a talk. Sigal hated to travel without his wife, Cathy, a Merck engineer whom he sometimes called three times a day. After the lecture Sigal was supposed to stay over one more night. Instead, he called Cathy that evening from the airport and said he had been able to snag a seat on the red-eye.

For years that flight, rather than the protease molecule, was Irving Sigal's legacy. It was Pan Am flight 103, which was destroyed by a terrorist bomb over Lockerbie, Scotland. When the structure of the HIV protease was published in the distinguished British journal *Nature* two months later—and the coordinates deposited in a data bank so all scientists could use them—the news of Sigal's death was included as an unusual humanizing footnote on the title page.

When I finished talking to Emini, two people from Merck's huge public relations staff came to escort me to my next interview, with one of the company's top chemists. It took about ten minutes of brisk walking, mostly outdoors, to get to the conference room where he was waiting for us. As we passed building after building, I couldn't help but be a little awestruck by the sheer mass of the enterprise. And this wasn't even Merck's main headquarters. It was just the satellite research facility.

The most prominent buildings were, of course, the most modern. Closest to the highway, they were also the buildings that looked most out

of place in this location, which was once rural but now had some suburban development nearby, along with a school and an elaborate miniature
golf course. Behind the recent buildings were ones that had been "modern" in decades past, as well as the jury-rigged structures of scientific
enterprise, the biohazard trailers, which have a way of becoming temporarily permanent. At what was once the center of the maze, but was now
hidden by the efforts of a succession of architects, stood an old red brick
building with the company's earlier name etched in concrete: Merck
Sharp & Dohme. The etching was clearly newer than the building itself.
New Jersey–based Merck had merged with Philadelphia-based Sharp &
Dohme in the early 1950s, and this had been S&D's original research
center.

I had heard a lot about Merck over the years. Before I even started
writing about drugs, I knew it as a fixture in greater Philadelphia. I knew
of many local Merck families, in which several generations had worked
for the company. Later, I came to understand Merck's place in its own
industry; the firm views itself as the United States of the legal-drug
world, paternalistically looming over the rest of the industry. It was no
longer the world's largest drug company. In fact, it had recently slipped
to third, behind not only Glaxo Wellcome but the newly formed Novartis, the product of a $27 billion Swiss merger between Sandoz and its
crosstown Basel rival Ciba-Geigy. But in the drug business, Merck remained synonymous with a certain pharmaceutical high-mindedness,
and being described as "very Merck" was still quite a compliment.

The Race to the Cocktail had begun on March 28, 1986, the day a team
from Roche's academic research center published an article in *Science*
that drew the first big theoretical bull's-eye on the HIV protease, suggesting that the recently discovered molecule, one of the three enzymes
the retrovirus needed in order to replicate, might be a good place to
attack. The idea immediately attracted widespread attention, because
this new drug "target" was one that the industry had experience shooting at. Roche, Merck, Abbott and many other companies were blowing
millions trying to develop a drug that lowered blood pressure by dis-
abling renin, an enzyme remarkably similar in structure to the HIV protease. The renin-inhibitor programs looked as though they were going to
end the way most drug company research ends: with squat, no drug
worth marketing. But without those renin programs, the companies
might not have bothered to start HIV protease programs from scratch.

Almost every drug company scientist and executive I spoke to mentioned the impact of renin. But when I asked what actually had finally gone wrong with renin inhibitors, almost everyone was a little vague. Only Abbott's John Leonard, a former NIH virologist who looks harmless enough but talks tough, would come right out and say what happened. "We realized we would not be able to make them cheaply enough," he explained matter-of-factly. "They could have been a major medical advance, but they also needed to be competitive with other drugs' prices."

Quite a few brand-name drugs that controlled blood pressure fairly well were already on the market, several of which were about to come out in generic form. "The antihypertension market was reasonably well satisfied," Leonard explained, "and to have a drug that would need to be more expensive, it would need to offer a *huge* incremental improvement."

But the AIDS market was different. "With AIDS," he said, "everybody is dying."

In 1986 many drug companies were setting up AIDS divisions. The horror of the disease was coming into full focus just as the industry was having a banner year for profits and a malaise in scientific direction. "There were rumblings in certain corners of the business," recalled Merck CFO Judy Lewent, the highest-ranking woman in the pharmaceutical industry. "People were wondering, why do we even invest in research in the pharmaceutical industry? What's left to do? People looked at antibiotics and vaccines and had a sense that the major scourges of the world had been conquered. Then along comes this unfortunate situation." There was another spur as well. In addition to the normal challenges of drug development, AIDS offered industry the chance to attempt "Nobel-laureate-caliber work, which we don't get to think about all too often."

At the time, though, inhibiting protease was *not* considered the most promising new path toward that AIDS therapy Nobel. AZT (zidovudine), a failed anticancer compound extracted from salmon sperm, was being rebirthed by the National Institutes of Health and Burroughs Wellcome, which was rushing it toward FDA approval. So an AZT me-too was the top priority of every company's AIDS program. AZT attempted to stop HIV infection a different way. HIV reproduces by invading human cells, CD4 lymphocytes, with three enzymes that act in sequence: protease, integrase and reverse transcriptase. AZT attempted to inhibit the action of reverse transcriptase; there was also believed to be a second way to accomplish the same mission. Inhibiting protease was a long-shot third.

.   .   .

How do you look for a new drug to develop? At the beginning of the AIDS drug race, this was *the* raging question in the pharmaceutical industry. Merck's Irving Sigal had wanted to use the search for protease inhibitors to test a radical new theory about how drugs could be discovered.

Traditionally, drugs that weren't tripped over by independent inventors, like Retin-A, were found by laborious drug company screening. That's how Sigal's father, Max, had done things as director of research at Eli Lilly. Drug company scientists create biological tests, called assays, for a given drug activity: say, stopping HIV from replicating. Then they take thousands of compounds found in nature—mostly those soil samples lugged back from around the world and placed in a "library"—as well as every compound the company has ever synthesized in its own lab, and screen them all with the assay. It's like trying thousands of keys in a lock. If one of the compounds seems to work, they then try to figure out how it can be refined and mass-produced. Learning how and why it actually works is something of a luxury and is usually beyond the current abilities of medicinal science anyway.

While such screening was always going to be part of pharmaceutical research, the next wave in drug development involved finding and mapping a precise medicinal target, the keyhole rather than the key, and then designing molecules from scratch on the computer that might open it or lock it (or, in this case, break off in it). This was referred to as "rational" drug design, as if the old way were somehow *not* rational. Like much of what the computer revolution promised, the benefits of rational drug design were still theoretical: no marketed drug had ever been designed entirely rationally. But younger scientists like Irving Sigal believed strongly in the approach. It was more scientific than the monkey work of screening, more interesting, more like the academic research they had left for the security of drug company jobs.

Because of the renin experience, protease inhibitors were a logical choice to become the first marketed drugs ever designed "rationally." If that happened, there would also be a certain personal irony within Merck. The renin project was run by Joshua Boger, Sigal's archrival for young hotshot status in enzyme inhibition, which was the company's research specialty.

For both types of reverse transcriptase inhibitors and for protease inhibitors, Merck did the kind of expansive, expensive research program for which the company is legendary. Teams of scientists were put on traditional drug screening *and* rational drug design. Other teams were assigned to address certain basic science questions they couldn't wait for others to answer, questions that were crucial to rational design.

Somebody, for example, had to prove that inhibiting protease really did stop the virus from replicating, because at that point it was no more than a promising theory. To do that experiment, Merck needed both a preliminary protease-inhibiting compound that worked at least to some degree and a large amount of HIV refined from human blood to make the assays. Somebody else had to map the atomic structure of the HIV protease, so that when the researchers were fine-tuning their drug, they would know the exact size and shape of the protease's "mouth" and could design their "rock" accordingly. To make that map, the first task was to crystallize the virus itself, which is extremely delicate work performed by some of the true artists of the drug business, the crystallographers. The process requires vast quantities of refined HIV protease. Once crystals were made, X rays could be shot through them so a molecular road map of their atoms could be made.

But the main work was done "at the bench," as medicinal chemists say. After inhibitor molecules were chosen—and the best ones at Merck all came from rational design—they had to be physically synthesized in a test tube. Because these molecules are very complex to create, each one required over twenty individual steps, more than twice as many as the usual drug "candidate." While a chemist might be working on two or three molecules at a time, each one took a couple of weeks to finish, and endless minute variations were tried on each candidate. Then the protease-inhibiting compounds were transferred from regular test tubes to miniaturized ones mounted in blocks of ninety-six for mass testing with HIV protease assays. The assays are clear to the naked eye, but when fluorescent light is shot through them, they turn blue if the protease in them has been inhibited, yellow if it has not. The tests were repeated with hundreds of compounds.

By its nature, it is a slow process. After years of design, synthesis, testing and molecular renovation, a compound *might* be ready to feed to a rat. Or several rats. "For every compound we evaluated, we used, I would suppose, five to six rats," one protease researcher told me. "We evaluated a couple hundred, so that's at least a thousand rats. You also use dogs and monkeys to do the same kinds of experiments, but you can reuse the dogs over and over. With a rat—well, with the amount of blood you can get out of a rat, by the time you're done, they aren't in very good shape."

Merck planned to take its time, believing it was better to be best than first. Roche, however, wanted to be first. At its Welwyn, England, research lab, it ran a tightly focused research program, entirely "rational" but in a more modest, more typically "industry" way. Where Merck would test thousands of compounds, Roche would test hundreds. Merck wanted a *good* drug. At Roche the team knew to stop experimenting at "good enough."

Creating a protease inhibitor that was merely good enough was, of course, no small feat. It was simply a smaller feat, or a different feat, than what Merck had in mind. And speed had its own premium. If protease inhibitors actually worked, many people were likely to die during the time lag between good enough and good.

The two companies would toil away for over a year before Abbott Laboratories joined them in the protease race. Abbott's John Leonard was hesitant to devote much time or money to protease inhibitors. The company was starting late, and its last AIDS drug had been blown out of the water in a patent dispute with Bristol-Myers Squibb. So in 1988 Abbott decided to do its best with a very modest expenditure. The firm devoted a grand total of four people to the protease project, compared with forty at Roche and perhaps four hundred at Merck. It quickly cast itself as a David against the pharmaceutical Goliaths.

The protease race started heating up later that year, when Merck published the first conclusive proof that inhibiting protease really did kill HIV—in a test tube, anyway—by preventing it from replicating. In the fall of 1988 Irving Sigal was given an audience with Merck's senior executives and board in Rahway, New Jersey, to present even more exciting news. His team was rushing against a group at the NIH to be the first to publish the crystal structure of the protease.

Normally, when a drug company makes such a scientific breakthrough in its lab, it keeps the results as quiet as possible for as long as possible, to stay ahead of the competition. It releases the information only after it has successfully patented the compound it made using that information. This was Roche's approach. After its 1986 *Science* article, the company kept its protease research to itself. If Roche scientists "solved" the protease structure first—and they would later make statements suggesting they did—they had no intention of revealing it.

Merck, however, was committed to publishing whatever it found out along the way about the basic chemistry of HIV. This kind of magnanimity allowed Merck to feel as scientifically correct as a hugely profitable company can afford to be. It also positioned Merck's stock to compete not only with traditional drug companies but with the new biotech firms.

These new companies raised money through what are called "story stocks," public offerings snatched up not because of a company's balance sheet but because of a convincing "story" about its future balance sheets.

But a new scientific discovery does wonders for any stock's story, because it can be spun to show that a company is ahead or winning in some kind of race. Solving the protease first was likely to create big news for Merck in *The Wall Street Journal* and make investors feel very smart about owning its stock.

At this heady moment, however, Merck was nearly pushed out of the protease business altogether. Sigal died in the plane crash on December 20, 1988. Several days later, Josh Boger, the company's other bright young star in enzyme inhibition, announced he was leaving to start his own firm in Boston, a pharmaceutical micro-brewery called Vertex. He was soon joined by several major players from Merck's "first team" in basic science. It was probably the most painful basic science defection that "Mother Merck," as employees sometimes referred to the company, had ever experienced. These blows cost its program at least a year.

In the meantime, Roche became the first to test its protease inhibitor—known internally as RO318959, later to be called Invirase (saquinavir)—in animals in late 1989. Invirase passed those tests, and the next spring the company also became the first to cross the most important threshold in all of drug development: the moment when a drug is first given to a brave human being.

Merck, still struggling to recover from its setbacks, was finally just getting its first protease inhibitor into animals. But it didn't take long for the drug to crash.

"This is not going to work," the toxicologist said when he brought Emini the news about the eight dying dogs.

"Ah, *shit!*" Emini groaned. The rats weren't doing any better. Merck's drug had a nasty habit of shutting off bile flow to the liver. Emini felt that if the animal test results were that severe, it was "unethical" to even attempt the study on humans.

"So there went four years," he told me with a shrug.

Spencer Cox, already a veteran of HIV activism at twenty-eight, was describing the turning point in AIDS drug advocacy. In 1991 ACT UP, the seminal AIDS activism organization founded four years earlier by Larry Kramer, was rocked when most of the members of its "treatment and data committee" quit. They reorganized as TAG, the Treatment Action Group.

"ACT UP was really falling apart, and the last straw," he said, grinning through his goatee, "was some project to send dental dams to lesbians in El Salvador. . . . So we spun it off, thinking it would be a similar organization. But instead of just pulling a giant condom over the home of [conservative Senator] Jesse Helms, we would go more in the direction of a think tank."

TAG also wanted to go in the direction of more professionalism, which meant salaries rather than the strict volunteerism of ACT UP. To raise the money, TAG members went to the same place everyone else in the medical world goes: to the drug companies. They accepted a million-dollar donation from Burroughs Wellcome, the very company that had been the focus of so much of their guerrilla activism because it manufactured AZT. ACT UP had done many outrageous things, including a barricade of the FDA building to prevent the "bureaucratic butchers" from getting in. But it was best known in the legal-drug world for the fall morning in 1989 when its members smuggled a banner into the VIP balcony of the New York Stock Exchange and unfurled it just before the opening bell. The banner said something more shocking than any message about AIDS, death or even sex could.

It read, simply, "Sell Wellcome."

That was the day the drug companies realized that the activists knew where they lived—or at least where they banked. But it took the activists far longer to infiltrate the scientific side of the drug business. Because there they couldn't just yell, they had to read: documents, long, dull, impenetrable documents. They had to figure out which government agency was responsible for which research, and which butchering bureaucrat was in charge. They had to learn the language of pharmaceuticals and do more than simply take sides in ongoing debates in industry or academia. They had to add something to the discussion. Two TAG members, for example, set out to analyze every single AIDS-related grant being funded by twenty-four different institutes of the NIH. Based on their report, Congress would eventually restructure all government-funded AIDS research.

The treatment advocates—and besides TAG, there were major players from the New York–based Gay Men's Health Crisis and the California-based Project Inform, among others—also had to develop a more productive way to both hate and love the drug companies. "Every drug company has its story," Cox said. "They get up in the morning because they care about the patients, blah blah, but they would still cut anybody's throat to make a buck. It's not that they aren't caring. There are people in industry I really like. But I always keep in mind their job is to return to investors. That's not my job. My job is to make sure the treatments are safe and effective."

To do that job, the treatment advocates had to understand the family dynamic of the drug business, and the different personalities of the companies. "The Merck people are much more interested in the science than other companies, but they're also really good bullshitters," said Cox. "Everybody hates Abbott: they get a D in 'works well with others,' maybe an F. But they are honest. When Abbott wants me to fuck off, they tell me to fuck off. When Merck wants me to fuck off, they say they feel my pain."

I laughed out loud when Cox said that. He was funny and charming and he knew it. But he also knew almost as much about AIDS drugs as the people who made or approved them. He had started out just as I had, a curious layperson trying to navigate the confusing world of legal drugs. The difference was, he had access to a small army of angry patients who would publicly protest to the bitter end even the slightest injustice he uncovered.

I was experiencing a very common phenomenon in any field associated with medicine: AIDS envy. The AIDS activists have been so much more effective at raising funds and public awareness than anyone else that you often hear people grumbling jealously at their remarkable success. People will whisper that it's because they're primarily young, single gay men with no other commitments. But the truth is that they're just better at this than everyone else: more effective, more driven. If not smarter, then at least better informed.

As I listened to Cox, I couldn't help but wonder what this kind of energy and insight would do if it were directed at the treatments for other diseases as well. I had always wondered what the world would be like for patients if they were truly informed about the pills they took and unflinching in their pressure on drug companies, drug regulators, doctors and pharmacists to do better jobs. Cox lived in a pharmacologist's utopia: a world where the development of drugs is heavily influenced by the people who actually have to take them. I asked him if he realized that what he had learned about AIDS drugs was very relevant to other drugs.

Cox seemed not to understand what I was talking about. To him, this wasn't about drugs. It was about AIDS.

Then the alarm on his digital wristwatch went off. Still talking, he rose from the small dining room table and walked into his tiny kitchen, where he began removing large bottles of pills from the closet shelves as well as the refrigerator.

"It's four-thirty, I have to take my drugs," he said. "They cost about six hundred dollars a month, and that's just my primary HIV drugs. I'm an insurance company's worst nightmare."

Nearly two years after TAG was formed, Spencer Cox experienced an activist's worst nightmare. In the summer of 1993 at the International AIDS Conference in Berlin, researchers discussed the controversial results of the largest trial ever done on AZT, the gold standard for AIDS treatment. The study showed that AZT alone—which for years had been used by *every* AIDS patient taking antivirals and was still used by the majority of them—didn't increase life expectancy even one day. In fact, slightly more of the placebo group lived longer.

As far as new drugs went, the protease inhibitor research described in Berlin was mostly about how the compounds that Merck and Abbott were developing *hadn't* worked so far. Recalling his company's humbling exposure at the Berlin conference, Abbott's John Leonard said, "I felt so sorry for the guy having to present *that* embarrassing story." But he was also feeling a little sorry for himself. After spending "about seventy-five million bucks," he had already watched several promising protease inhibitors fail in development, and he was about to kill another.

It was the most disillusioning moment in AIDS treatment history. "I remember talking to scientists in Berlin," Cox recalled, "and having them say, 'The way this virus functions, we may never be able to treat it.' There were treatments we had fought for, and we were asking ourselves, 'Are we doing any good?' It was looking very frighteningly like the answer was no. A lot of activists said, 'I can't do this anymore. It's too depressing.' "

Author Andrew Sullivan, who was then the editor of *The New Republic,* found out he was HIV positive during that summer of dread. "The massive media hype about hopelessness was just horrible," he told me. But he clung to the idea that as long as drug research continued, he could "get on one slowly sinking ship, and by the time it was under the water, another would be there."

By December 1993 the FDA's David Kessler was announcing the formation of a National Task Force on AIDS Drug Development. It was widely viewed as his concession that all efforts to develop AIDS drugs had failed. That included the "accelerated approval" process for which the activists had fought so hard.

．　　　．　　　．

By this point, Merck already knew it would not win the protease race, but it didn't care. Emilio Emini had so little respect for the Roche drug that, as far as he was concerned, it was "still just us against the virus." Everybody knew the Roche drug had low "bioavailability," meaning that although the drug did its job well on HIV cells in the lab, it couldn't be kept "available" in the bloodstream long enough to perform the same tasks in the body. The liver quickly skimmed the drug out of the blood.

When Roche had committed to its compound back in 1989, it believed that bioavailability would always be an unsolvable problem for any protease inhibitor. But with an extra three years of medicinal science, Merck had been able to dramatically improve bioavailability. In fact, even though he had no good news in time for Berlin, Emini had finally found an inhibitor he liked, L-735,524, eventually to be called Crixivan, which was getting excellent results in animals and in humans. In December 1993, at the First National Conference on Human Retroviruses and Related Infections in Washington, Merck made its first presentations on the drug, giddily announcing that three patients in the Crixivan trial had seen the virus in their bodies driven down to undetectable levels.

The only problem was, even as the test results were being announced, the virus in two of the patients was already mutating around the drug, building up resistance to it. Merck just didn't know it yet.

Late one freezing cold January afternoon, the company found out. Molecular biologist Jon Condra, one of the few Merck employees who had been brave or stupid enough to make it in to work through the drifting snow, was scanning computer analyses of the viral RNA from the subjects in the protease trial. There are ninety-nine amino acid positions on each RNA strand, and a mutation—a change in the normal enzyme structure that the drug expects to find when it comes in to attack—can start at any one of them. The computer notices any such change, and it announces the bad news by replacing a hyphen with a code.

Condra's tired eyes caught a blue "V82T" on the screen. "Oh hell, it finally happened," he said to himself. The mutation was at position 82, which was right where their "rock" fit into the protease's "mouth." Condra called Emilio Emini at home and told him to log into the company's computer system right away. Emini was horrified.

The mutation was just part of the bad news. That same day, Emini learned that a revolutionary new test had detected HIV in Merck's so-called "undetectable" patients. Until that time, HIV-infected blood had been tested for p24, a viral protein believed to be the best-available "surrogate marker" for the actual viral level. With the new test, it was possible to measure the actual viral RNA itself, or what would come to be referred to as "viral load." In most of their patients, viral load was rebounding.

The Merck protease inhibitor looked doomed. The only hope was one man in Protocol 010, a study at Thomas Jefferson University Hospital in Philadelphia, who was still "undetectable" even after the new viral load tests. He was a law student in his early forties known to them only as Patient 142. Since Emini couldn't bring him up to be interrogated and probed, they peppered 142's physician with questions about him. And whenever his blood was retested, everyone checked the computer for the results.

"We just kept looking at this guy," Emini told me. "He was the only patient keeping the hope alive. This is the guy who kept us from just throwing our hands in the air."

Patient 142 was on the higher of the two doses they were trying. So instead of dropping the drug, Merck took the risk of starting a new trial with everyone at much higher doses.

They also began another trial combining their drug with AZT and other antivirals. Although combination therapies historically were more common in virology than in other areas of drug treatment—and about 19 percent of AIDS patients were already using AZT and the related new Roche antiviral ddC (dideoxycytidine) together—this was still a radical move. Protease inhibitors had been developed to blow all the other AIDS drugs out of the water. Drug companies don't normally spend hundreds of millions of dollars to develop really expensive drugs that work only when taken with the really expensive products of their main competitors.

But the AIDS virus was forcing drug companies to do lots of things they wouldn't normally do. With mounting pressure from the company's finance side to kill its protease inhibitor, Merck had to give Crixivan one last chance.

In the meantime Abbott had been quietly testing a new inhibitor of its own in Europe. In early 1994 the company decided to bring some of the compound—ABT-538, which would become Norvir (ritonavir)—back to the United States for testing. It was time to hand the drug over to Abbott's secret weapon in the protease race: David Ho, the research virologist who ran what many considered the "Manhattan Project" of AIDS, the Aaron Diamond AIDS Research Center in New York.

·　　·　　·

I went to see Ho at the Diamond Center, a shiny little basic science lab—from its DNA-emblazoned rug by the elevators to its high-design wood and stainless steel door treatments—in an otherwise dilapidated public health building at First Avenue and Twenty-sixth Street. A casually serious, baby-faced Taiwanese-American with preppy clothes under his lab coat, Ho had developed a reputation at both Harvard and UCLA for doing research that challenged popular notions about the early years of being infected with HIV. To him, the idea of a period of "dormancy" was counterintuitive, wishful thinking, and he focused much of his attention on newly infected patients who were otherwise healthy. In 1991 he had been called in to treat the ultimate patient of this type, Earvin "Magic" Johnson, whose doctor in L.A. chose Ho to manage the case.

Ho hooked up with Abbott that same year after a chance meeting in a long airport checkout line with the lead chemist working on the company's protease inhibitor. When Abbott finally had a compound that seemed to work, Ho was very eager to test it. He was interested in the drug's activity, of course. But what truly fascinated him was what the drug and the new viral load tests were telling him about AIDS.

"Week after week we'd see the virus go down so dramatically," he recalled. "We realized it should go down, but not by *that* magnitude. Why does the virus go down *so much*? I'm just sitting, staring at the data. And it's telling me that the virus is replicating at a tremendous clip and the body is removing it at a tremendous clip."

With this information Ho realized he might be able to finally prove his long-held, sparsely shared view of what AIDS really was. It wasn't a viral time bomb. From the minute it got into the blood, it was a goddamned Roman candle.

"It *explodes* in the first weeks," he said excitedly, "but this is brought under control spontaneously when the person starts their immune reaction to HIV. It could *look like* the patient is holding his own. But what is really occurring is that the virus is just *cranking,* just churning out tens of billions of particles a day. The patient feels nothing, because the initial battle line is drawn, and it's stable for a long time, with high casualties on each side." Full-blown AIDS was the end of the war, not the beginning.

Ho's enthusiasm was contagious. As he told me the story, I found myself getting caught up in just how visionary drug research could be if it was done by people who actually *had* vision and were allowed to use it to address big questions. So much time and money were expended on endless years diddling the molecules of another me-too antibiotic.

He was so excited, he recalled, that he would wake up in the middle of the night with ideas about how he could prove his points better. Showing how rapidly the AIDS virus replicated and died in the body—about half of it turned over every two days—was going to be the observation of a career. Even though he knew he should keep quiet, Ho could hardly contain himself around his colleagues. Then, several weeks after the breakthrough, he found himself in Seattle for a conference, and he went out to dinner with a group of the world's top AIDS researchers, including oncologist George Shaw—codirector of the country's largest AIDS research program, at the University of Alabama at Birmingham—and virologist Dani Bolognesi from Duke.

"Dani sat there, and we were just talking about science," Ho recalled. "And he asked a question: 'I wonder how fast the virus is turning over.' George and I simultaneously gave the answer. And it was *the same answer.*

"And then we just looked at each other."

Shaw *knew.* The moment couldn't have been more pregnant. After all, AIDS research had been forever discolored by an epic clash over who deserved credit for the discovery of HIV. Nobody knew that better than Shaw, who had been doing a postdoctoral with Dr. Robert Gallo in 1985 when the virus hit the fan.

Now Shaw and Ho were watching medical history about to repeat itself. Shaw's group had made pretty much the same observations as Ho's, at the same time and in a similar number of patients. The only difference was that Shaw had tried not only the Abbott drug but the Merck drug and even nevirapine, a potent experimental antiviral from Connecticut-based Boehringer Ingelheim that worked more like AZT (and would later be marketed as Viramune). Both men knew full well how to race to publication. The new custom among young, science-media savvy researchers was to play the major journals, *Science* and *Nature,* off each other in order to publish even a week ahead of the competition. Then they could spend the next year fighting over bragging rights and trolling for Nobels.

Instead, Shaw and Ho spared the AIDS world and agreed to submit both their papers, simultaneously, to *Nature.*

In the meantime, they would look for the next opportunity to present some of the exciting data, which would suggest a dramatic change in the way to treat AIDS patients. There was only one problem: the drug companies owned the data, and Abbott, in particular, didn't want them to release it. Neither Abbott nor Merck had committed to actually marketing its protease inhibitor. The "go/no-go" decision still hadn't been made. A "go" would mean immediately doubling the hundreds of millions the companies had already sunk into Norvir and Crixivan by commissioning large clinical trials.

Ho and Shaw wanted to present the data at an upcoming conference in Florida. The day before the conference began, Abbott was still saying no.

That evening, Ho and Dr. Michael Saag, Shaw's top clinical researcher at Alabama, had dinner with the Abbott top brass, who had flown down from Chicago. The executives explained that they still hadn't made their decision yet. A "go" would mean "taking a big pile of money" and pouring it into those larger clinical trials, Ho recalled, "and if they didn't give it the green light right away, it was going to be 'no-go' for a while. . . . We were trying to convince them to just go for it." They succeeded. By the end of the dinner, Ho and Saag were told that Abbott would "green-light" the drug and give permission for the researchers to present the data.

The next day, the entire AIDS epidemic changed because of the drug industry. It is an awesome power when used for good.

CHAPTER 22

Checkered Flag

Nobody at the FDA had ever seen a development plan like the one Abbott delivered in the fall of 1994. "They're *crazy*," FDA medical officer Dr. Jeff Murray said when he got his first look at the astonishingly aggressive new schedule for Norvir. "There's *no way* this can be done."

When the people at Merck heard that Abbott planned to cram what would normally be several years of clinical testing into less than a year—basically squashing all three phases of FDA approval into one—they also agreed it was crazy. Except that they knew it could be done. And if they weren't willing to do it too, Abbott was going to leave Merck in its dust. Emilio Emini was always quick to take a swipe at the Abbott drug, then and now: "It is intolerable to take," he told me. "You can go out and ask." But he knew his Crixivan would go from a very smug second to a painfully distant third unless the company did something entirely unMerck-like and rushed into wide-scale testing.

The protease race was shifting into an overdrive higher than anyone in the drug business ever experienced.

As the Shaw and Ho papers were appearing back to back in the January 12, 1995, issue of *Nature,* Merck CEO Raymond Gilmartin countered Abbott by approving the first huge clinical trial for Crixivan: 4,800 patients in eleven countries. By the end of the month, at the Washington Retrovirus Conference, it was clear to anyone paying attention to the field that the protease inhibitors could become the first AIDS drugs that actually *worked.*

Unfortunately, hardly anyone could get them. One group of underground activists began gathering technical information and money to manufacture some Crixivan of their own. The AIDS Project Los Angeles newsletter was soon reporting what the underground price might be: $10,000 a year.

At the end of February, the National Task Force on AIDS Drug Development held its long-awaited meeting on protease inhibitors. David Kessler had to personally twist Abbott's corporate arm to get the company to show up along with its competitors and share what, for any other drug being reviewed by the FDA, would be considered absolutely secret, proprietary information. The activists, the researchers and the competition got an opportunity to publicly grill the firms about the most minute aspects of their research plans.

Much of the pressure concerned "compassionate use" programs that would get the drug to people who otherwise wouldn't live to see it approved. The FDA has always allowed drug companies to give investigational new drugs (INDs) to physicians not involved in clinical trials for patients with emergency needs; during the 1970s beta-blockers were distributed to some heart patients before approval. But "compassionate use" came of age with AZT in 1986, when more than four thousand patients not enrolled in trials got the drug before approval. The next year, the FDA instituted new "Treatment IND" guidelines for all drugs, and thereafter AIDS activists learned exactly how to push the "compassionate use" button. Roche had such a program, but Abbott and Merck did not, insisiting it was costing them millions just to make enough of their compounds to conduct their clinical trials.

Moreover, Merck still wasn't entirely sure it was going to market Crixivan at all. Even though the higher dose worked much better, the company was still reluctant to rush ahead with the kind of highly speculative commitment that Abbott had made. To stay competitive, Merck finally made another "very un-Merck" decision to invest millions in retrofitting plants to manufacture Crixivan, just so the company would be ready if it decided to apply for fast FDA approval. But that decision still hadn't been made.

By early summer the activists were frantically trying to get drugs for compassionate use. They were also keeping friends abreast of every opening in every clinical trial, each one of which had its own rules about how sick the patients had to be and what other drugs they could be taking. Andrew Sullivan was unable to get into the trial: he was told he wasn't sick enough. At the Aaron Diamond Center, David Ho decided he didn't want to take the risk of using experimental drugs on Magic Johnson, who was already doing well enough on a combination of antivirals.

Greg Louganis's doctor got him into the trial for the Abbott protease inhibitor. By this time, the retired Olympic diver had been taking medication for his HIV infection for over seven years, and his coming-out autobiography had been on the best-seller lists for months. He started taking the Abbott drug during his book tour. The side effects were immediate and literally gut-wrenching. "A half hour after I took it," he recalled, "I was either flat on my back with no energy, or on the toilet." Even though he got constant encouragement from friends like activists Larry Kramer and Mary Fisher, he wasn't sure he could continue taking the drug, especially after the side effects forced him to postpone a book signing in Denver.

Although he felt like hell, the drug was working wonders on his viral load levels, so he felt trapped. "It messes with your self-esteem," he told me. "I felt I should be able to be stronger. I always said I didn't want HIV management to be my second occupation. And here my quality of life was being *consumed* by my HIV drug."

In July 1995 David Ho had an editorial in *The New England Journal of Medicine* that declared a new standard of care for HIV infection. His team had been combing New York hospitals to find patients who knew, for whatever reason, that they had *just* been infected. Based on his observations of a dozen such patients, as well as many other studies—all reconfirming his belief that the virus never let up from the moment it entered the body—Ho declared it was "time to hit HIV early and hit it hard." If Ho's proclamation was correct, AIDS might be turned into a manageable illness. Either way, he had just dramatically increased the size of the $1 billion antiviral AIDS drug market (which, by drug company standards, still wasn't very profitable), because patients would now take the drugs from the moment they tested positive, instead of waiting months or years until their viral loads reached certain thresholds or they developed symptoms of full-blown AIDS.

Merck held a lottery to choose eleven hundred AIDS patients for "compassionate use" supplies of Crixivan. More than eleven *thousand* people signed up for the spots. Several weeks later, Roche submitted its New Drug Application to the FDA for accelerated approval of its drug Invirase. David Kessler decided to send a signal to Merck and Abbott that he wanted to see *their* protease applications on his desk, too. He chose a *Nightline* appearance with Larry Kramer as the forum. Kessler went on the show and "basically came as close to saying these drugs are safe and effective as I could," he told me. "I almost sent them the approval letter [over the air]. I figured that was the best incentive. I wanted them to know we were ready, and there should be nothing holding them back."

At the same time Abbott was meeting quietly with Roche to discuss an odd pharmacological plot twist. They had accidentally discovered that the Abbott drug made the Roche drug more bioavailable—Norvir actually blocked the body from dumping Invirase out through the liver. Roche, distrustful of a competitor claiming to have "raised Invirase from the dead"—when they didn't think it *was* dead—had initially blown off Abbott's inquiries about the interaction, which might allow the two companies to team up against Merck. To pressure Roche, Abbott filed for a patent on the idea of using the drugs together, then submitted a "late-breaker" paper to the next big scientific meeting to publicly announce the promising interaction. Finally, Roche agreed to negotiate a deal to study the drugs together. In the last lap of the race, it would be the collaborations between competitors that would make the difference in creating the most potent cocktails.

Abbott's Norvir was approved on March 1, 1996; Merck's Crixivan on March 14. Without identifying which protease inhibitor he chose for Magic Johnson, David Ho acknowledged that he did wait for these later approvals before starting him on one. Andrew Sullivan chose a cocktail with both the Abbott and Roche inhibitors, swallowing twenty-three pills a day—including Ritalin (methylphenidate) to combat drug-related sedation—at three separate forced feedings. Besides suffering severe side effects, which influenced his May 1996 decision to resign from *The New Republic* and "come out" with his HIV status, he had nightmares of walking down the street haunted by "this huge noise of rattling pills." But his excellent viral load numbers, which he obsessively charted on his computer, made it worthwhile.

Greg Louganis refused to put up with the side effects and quit the Abbott clinical trial. Ironically, when the Abbott drug was approved, he was asked to give a pep talk to the company's sales reps. Instead, he lectured them about what it was *really* like to take their drug, and he urged them to keep in mind, during their "struggle for the almighty dollar . . . [that] not every drug is for every person." He joined another cocktail trial with the antiviral nevirapine instead of a protease inhibitor. But after several months he discovered—by having his pills analyzed—that he was in the group taking the placebo. Dejected, he briefly eschewed all meds and started treating his HIV infection again only after a dramatic scene at a promotional appearance for the paperback of his book.

"This kid, who was diagnosed the same time I was, asked me how I stayed motivated to take my meds," he said. "I just started crying. I said, 'I don't deal with it well, especially not right now.' " Shortly thereafter, Louganis stopped drinking, stopped smoking and went on the Crixivan/ nevirapine cocktail.

The Protease 500 was over. And the victory lap was soon sullied by price, supply and all the other mundane realities of scientific commerce. In July 1996 the AIDS Conference in Vancouver became the "coming out" party for the data that had been presented, or predicted, in Washington. *Science* magazine went on about how well all the "new guard" scientists got along. But behind the scenes, people were clucking their tongues about scientists "overpromising" what the protease inhibitors could actually do, and complaining about who got the most individual press for this highly collaborative effort. Months before he was named *Time*'s 1996 "Man of the Year," David Ho was already feeling the heat.

Regardless of all the histrionic "AIDS cure" stories, nobody knew what an "undetectable" viral load in the blood really meant or how long it would last. The virus might still be lurking in lymph or brain tissue, but how much of their bodies could test patients be expected to donate to science while they were still alive? By the normal standards of drug development, these medications were still experimental. Those taking them were part of an ongoing science project.

Part of the project was to see if activist AIDS patients would be compliant, because protease inhibitors are some of the least forgiving drugs ever marketed. If you take them improperly—even if you miss only a few doses—the drugs can actually make the virus in your body less treatable than it was before you started, creating resistance that will render the entire therapeutic class useless for you. Some AIDS patients were being refused protease inhibitors because they were considered too unreliable to keep to the very rigorous dosing schedule. Terry McGovern and other activists for women with AIDS believed a disproportionate number of patients were considered "unreliable" simply because they were women.

Of course, some of the people who took their pills religiously didn't get the miraculous viral load results. The press painted this group of protease underachievers as a comparatively small minority, of perhaps 20 percent of AIDS patients on the cocktail. This was a rather industry-friendly way of perceiving the problem, since many Americans with AIDS, and the vast majority of the 22 million HIV-infected patients in the world, were unlikely to get their hands on the very expensive protease inhibitors to see if the drugs worked for them, too. The drugs were being sold at prices ranging from $5,000 to $8,000 a year. The price was so high that just after protease inhibitors were approved, President Clinton ordered a $52 million grant to help patients pay for them. The money wasn't going to last very long.

Yet it was becoming harder and harder to guard one's optimism about the drugs. The creation of protease inhibitors was clearly the proudest achievement in years for the research-based pharmaceutical manufacturers. It was also a marquee event for the FDA, primarily because of the sheer speed of the approvals. When I talked to Kessler about the drugs, he was effusive. "Five years from bench to bedside—that's historic," he said. "I think this could be the beginning of a whole new era for all drug development, not just AIDS drugs."

Equally possible, however, was that the protease experience, like most aspects of AIDS treatment, would be the exception that proved all the rules. Less than a year after protease inhibitors were approved, for example, it became clear that many doctors were prescribing the antivirals improperly and haphazardly—wrong combinations, wrong doses—and putting patients at high risk for resistance and adverse reactions. The federal government expressed its shock and dismay, immediately impaneling experts and issuing tough guidelines that told doctors exactly how they were to use the drugs.

For decades, antibiotics have been prescribed just as improperly and haphazardly, along with anti-inflammatories, antidepressants, antihistamines, antifungals . . . the list goes on. There has been no government shock, dismay or tough guidelines about them.

At the end of the day, Bob Hattoy sat in his office at the Department of the Interior, wondering if he could learn to love again. "I'm willing to enter into this relationship having been burned in the past," he told me. "It's a very intimate thing, you know. And you're very leery: 'No, it won't be like that this time, no, this time it will be supportive, it will make you better.'"

Hattoy, the White House liaison to the department and highest-ranking member of the Clinton administration who is open about being gay and having AIDS, was not talking about a new man in his life. He was talking about protease inhibitors. "It's like you have to make love to the drug," he said. "And all you really want to know is, *is it safe?*"

Among his friends, Hattoy was one of the last to consider taking a protease inhibitor. In early 1996, when he was sitting on the task force that convinced the president to assist patients who couldn't afford the new drugs, he was still deeply ambivalent about taking them. When Clinton asked whether Hattoy was taking the protease inhibitors himself, he told him, "No, I'm not sick enough yet." He knew that was only half true.

During the 1992 presidential campaign, Hattoy had almost died of AIDS-related lymphoma. After successful chemotherapy, he avoided all medicines, including antivirals. But in the summer of 1996 he found himself feeling weaker. He went to the doctor, got his first-ever viral load test and was prescribed AZT and the antiviral 3TC (lamivudine). For the first time since he had tested positive back in 1989, he actually took the antiviral drugs on time, every day, believing they might actually do something.

He realized he had been "busy saving the world and not taking care of myself, which happens to activists. I became a little grandiose, a little egocentric, but being a visible person with AIDS, I've been bombarded with every treatment activist, every scientist, every peach pit and crystal therapy. When I first heard of protease inhibitors, I just thought, 'Great, great, one more thing that eventually is not going to work.' "

So he waited and watched as some people were seemingly brought back to life by the drugs, and others still died taking them. Viral load testing was new, but its results had a familiar ring. "It's still a bunch of guys sitting around comparing who's bigger," he joked. "We've just become viral-load-size queens."

In the late fall of 1996 Bob Hattoy had decided to take his first protease inhibitor. He just hadn't gotten around to it yet. "Many of us had already decided we'd live for a while and there wouldn't be a cure," he told me. "We made some decisions and some changes based on that. To decide, 'My god, the protease inhibitors might *not* be a betrayal, and we might *live* for a long time—' well, that profoundly changes how you view yourself."

He sighed. "It's just so hard to intellectually embrace science again and psychologically embrace life. It's a leap of faith." Several months later, he would take the leap.

In November of 1996, just after Bill Clinton's reelection, David Kessler announced his resignation as commissioner of the FDA. I had been pretty sure Kessler was going to quit, because when I had interviewed him just before the election and asked about his future, he didn't even bother to be cagey. He noted that six years was a long time to be in the job, and he pointed out that his team had accomplished a lot of what it set out to do. Without saying so, he said he was going.

Kessler was named head of Yale's School of Medicine, and in February 1997 he left the FDA, temporarily replaced by one of his deputy commissioners while a search went on for a replacement from outside the agency. Ray Woosley from Georgetown made the short list of people to be interviewed for the job, even though he was a registered Republican.

The end of the Kessler era seemed like a good point for me to stop and take a deep breath. I knew what Kessler meant when he talked of having done the job long enough. It had been almost five years since I made my first contacts with people at the FDA about Diane's drug reaction. Perhaps it was time for me to think about winding down my quest. I began checking in with some of the people I had met along the way.

I called George Praeger in FDA Compliance, to see what had happened with his Omniflox investigation. Almost a year after I first met him, Praeger had called with an odd request: he wanted to know if he could borrow my copy of a deposition that the FDA's Mike Blum had given. I asked him why he didn't just order one from the court reporter like everybody else. He said he could, but that would cost about $500 (which is what it cost me), and he didn't think he could get the expenditure approved. I felt odd handing it over to save the government $500, but I wanted Compliance to decide whether Abbott had broken the law. I also suggested there were other depositions and discovery materials he should look at. He made it clear that if I didn't give them to Compliance myself, nobody was ever going to go look for them. He also warned that the statute of limitations on any possible prosecution was five years and could run out before the material got published in my book. I told him I'd think about it.

A year later, with the statute of limitations looming, I called Praeger again to ask where his investigation was. He said he was still waiting to see the other materials. So I sent him the Weisberg deposition and even highlighted the parts I wanted Compliance to comment on. Again I heard nothing. When I checked in one last time, Praeger didn't call back for weeks. Just after the statute of limitations passed, he left me a voicemail saying he'd been busy and hadn't gotten around to reading the deposition. We talked several more times, and I urged him to look at the material so his new boss wouldn't see it for the first time in my book. He promised he'd get back to me. I'm still waiting.

Then I called Philadelphia attorney Steve Sheller, to see what had happened to the Stacy Phillips lawsuit. I hadn't spoken to Stacy herself in years. But her husband had called me once from Florida with a decidedly mixed report about her health, and the best I had ever heard from others was that she was doing "pretty good." The only consolation was that Ortho had decided to settle Stacy's lawsuit just before the trial date. Over the years, I had spoken to Floxies all over the country who were suing or thinking of suing, but this was the first I had heard of an actual Floxin settlement.

Sheller refused to comment on the financial details of Stacy's confidential arrangement with Ortho. But he did say he thought Ortho settled because Stacy had been given Floxin and Motrin together (and never had any previous reactions to the pain reliever). The interaction with Motrin and other NSAIDs wasn't on the Floxin label when Stacy took the antibiotic—which makes for a strong "failure to warn" case—but it has been there since late 1992. It's such a quiet caution, however, that in all my years of discussing quinolone safety with experts, I have *never* heard anyone mention it as a potential problem. When Sheller brought it up as a key to his case, I rushed back to re-read the label.

But the failure to warn, itself, probably wouldn't have been enough to win. (I later learned from another source that she got a six-figure settlement, a decent amount in such a case, but still a pittance compared to the scope of her suffering and loss.) Stacy got something for her troubles primarily because her own doctor testified for her, stating in a deposition that if he had known of the possible dangers of an interaction between the two drugs, he never would have prescribed them for her. Sheller said it was unusual in a case like this to get such strong, supportive deposition testimony from the treating physician.

"Usually the drug companies get to the docs," he said.

After calling several other sources, I ended up chatting on the phone with Mac Lumpkin, who, five years after first encouraging me backstage at *Good Morning America,* seemed like an old friend in a high place.

He expressed the same sense of relief I had heard from others that the FDA had survived the legislative attacks of 1996. There were a lot of theories about how the FDA had dodged the bullets of legislative overhaul. Senator Nancy Kassebaum's decision not to run for reelection, combined with the three separate bills her legislation had had to compete with in the House, had eventually undercut the deregulatory momentum. The Democratic victory in November appeared to be a referendum on the previous election's antiregulatory referendum, so perhaps America was not enamored of Newt Gingrich and his FDA-busting rhetoric after all.

Inside the FDA they preferred to think that once the core issues of drug regulation had really been debated in front of the American people, many had realized the whole attack was about business and not medicine. The public was growing rebellious about health businessmen who were now telling patients and doctors what was "for their own good."

One top FDA official admitted to me that in 1997, without the "lightning rod" of David Kessler, the deregulation debate was going much differently at various FDA-related hearings. "It was interesting in the House and Senate," he explained. "We said the same things David said last year, in terms of agency performance, speed of approval, etc. People sort of took umbrage when David said these things. This year the same people were nodding their heads in agreement."

This year there was also more at stake. Inside the agency, Lumpkin said, people were watching the legislative tussles with special fascination and fear because there was no way to completely dodge the bullet this time: some new FDA-related bill had to be signed into law. The Prescription Drug User Fee Act (PDUFA) was up for renewal after its successful five-year trial run, and getting it passed was the key to keeping FDA fiscally solvent; without that six-figure application fee for each new drug (the price of which was going up to $250,000), the FDA was just another underfunded federal agency with a shrinking budget. But antiregulatory forces had been able to attach to the PDUFA renewal various chunks of the myriad FDA reform bills. And the drug industry, heading into its second straight banner year after massive consolidation, was feeling flush.

The combined Food and Drug Administration Modernization Act of 1997 was ultimately a watered-down version of some of the harshest FDA-bashing proposals, but it was still the first major agency reform bill in twenty years. It surrendered much of the agency's ability to control the dissemination of journal articles about off-label uses for drugs—like the one that set off the fen-phen craze—and some were already predicting that even more rampant abuses in off-label prescribing would be the next growing problem in drug safety. It also loosened agency control over several aspects of medical device regulation, and put into law several previous rule changes, like the one that allowed some drugs to be approved with only one well-controlled study.

The new act did ease some patient access to the experimental drugs, and it did take a stab at improving drug research on children (although there was plenty of wiggle room in the new statute). And buried deep in the fine print was a bone thrown to the clin-pharm community. Ray Woosley called me one day from the Newark airport to make sure I had noticed it. "They finally authorized funding a CERT," he said excitedly. "Did you see it in the bill?" I quickly had the legislation downloaded from the FDA web site and, lo and behold, there it was: Section 409 of the new bill amended Title IX of the Public Health Service Act with a new Section 905, in which subsection (e) authorized funds for a pilot program of the Centers for Education and Research on Therapeutics: $2 million the first year, and $3 million a year through 2002. Ironically, Woosley would have to compete with other universities to snag the first center, which he had originally proposed, for his department at Georgetown. And the money was a fraction of the FDA's previous budget for extramural research. But Woosley was thrilled that his legislative quest had made an impact.

(While he had me on the phone, Woosley asked if I remembered the date of the advisory committee meeting at which I had spoken. A friend of his at the FDA had just experienced a troubling CNS reaction to a quinolone—panic attacks, the whole nine yards—and was trying to gather more information without drawing any attention.)

Lumpkin and I discussed why the new FDA bill directed no new money for postmarketing surveillance. He said the agency had fought harder this time to get the drug companies to allow some of the $36 million in new PDUFA money to be used for that purpose as well as speeding up approval. But industry wouldn't budge. Everybody claimed they wanted a system that was less onerous before approval and more responsive after approval, but all they really wanted was to see their money spent on faster approvals. If the citizenry was so interested in increased drug safety, it could pay for it out of its own pockets. So far, it had paid little. Five years after its debut, the much ballyhooed MedWatch program for gathering adverse drug reactions had a budget of only $140,000 and it had only four employees. Although MedWatch statistics were later analyzed by some 48 other employees in different departments, the frontline monitoring and "signal" generation for the entire nation was handled by fewer people than the FDA had in its overburdened press office. Dr.

Janet Woodcock, Lumpkin's boss, had recently admitted that she was "real unhappy" with the system.

Several years before, the agency had apparently coughed up $3.5 million to begin a complete computerization of the spontaneous ADR reporting system, which Lumpkin conceded was still "pretty much like a library card catalog." They were hoping the system might be operational sometime in fiscal 1998. Maybe by then, the endless talks about international harmonization of drug regulation would be nearing completion and the major players would finally be as globally well connected as the drug companies had been for years. Then for the first time perhaps drug regulators could be, he hoped, "a little more proactive about drug reactions, not just waiting for a signal but doing more active surveillance."

It was going to be "a whole new postmarketing surveillance world with this new 'airs system,' " Lumpkin said enthusiastically. I interrupted him to ask what he meant by "airs."

"Oh, it's AERS, A-E-R-S, Adverse Event Reporting System," he explained. "That's what the whole new computer system is called."

AERS, I thought. Ayres. Ayres is Diane's surname. Well, at least we had left some small mark on the world of drug safety.

I told Lumpkin I was discouraged because I had recently received from Ortho a retrospective of Floxin labels from 1992, when Diane first took that one pill, through 1997. The only difference was that some time in 1996, three years after the advisory committee meeting, the paragraph on CNS side effects in the Warnings section had been nudged up from sixth to third and a rather vague line about neurological side effects had been added to the Information for Patients.

The advisory committee had recommended that the paragraph be *first,* ahead of the standard boilerplate language about how the drug hadn't been tested on children, adolescents or pregnant women, and another passage about how giving sixteen times the normal dosage to rats increased the incidence of rodent osteochondrosis. The committee also recommended that there should be a boldfaced line about seizures, so the first impression a doctor got when looking at the Floxin warnings was that it had unusually strong CNS side effects. And they wanted the language about using the drugs in patients with known or suspected CNS disorders to be stronger than the standard "use with caution."

None of these things had been done. None of them were going to be done.

Quinolone sales continued to improve: from $842 million in the U.S.

alone in 1992 to well over $1 billion by 1997—roughly one-seventh of all American antibiotic revenues. And Ortho had recently released a new quinolone, Levaquin (levofloxacin). I first heard about it from a microbiologist who had run quinolone development programs for two different drug companies and had since left industry. He called because he was preparing to be the expert witness for a Floxie who was suing Ortho. His understanding was that Levaquin had been developed as a less neurotoxic version of Floxin, and the company would allow it to quietly displace Floxin without ever conceding the first drug's CNS problems. But when I compared the label warnings on the two drugs, they were identical.

"So, Mac, what did it all mean?" I wanted to know. "Was *anything* accomplished?"

Lumpkin disagreed that little progress had been made. "People do not look at quinolones as they do, say, penicillins anymore," he said. "We now know they have very interesting side effects, some of which are class-specific, some drug-specific, and we've made a real effort to tease out which are bad actors for CNS, which are bad actors for Achilles tendon rupture. I think we've been able to communicate some of this stuff, and the health care practitioner is putting it into the equation.

"Whether it has gotten into the equation to the degree I would like, well, that will always be debatable. There's no scientific way to know that. But I do believe that people now think about quinolones differently than other oral antimicrobials."

But, Mac, this is not what the advisory committee said was needed.

"Steve," he said with a slight sigh, "you know as well as anyone that once drugs are approved we're on a very different negotiating status with the companies. I know these things are incredibly frustrating to you as they are to me. . . . Is this the most optimal? In the postmarketing world, the way it's set up you don't get optimal. If this was something *absolutely critical* and there was no other way to get the message across, we push and push. But [we were convinced] that the warning about the lack of safety and efficacy data for children and pregnant women is the most important to the broadest group of people. And putting the neurological language into the Information for Patients section can get it into the conversation. The physician is supposed to talk to the patient about those things. And then the patient can ask, 'Doctor, this is an antibiotic for urinary tract infections and it can cause *seizures*? Why are you giving it to me instead of ampicillin?' "

Before heading off to a meeting, he asked, as he always does, how Diane was doing.

"Really good," I told him. "I think she finally found the right medication. Actually, we're trying to have a baby. I have no idea if we'll succeed, and I'm not really sure it matters. The fact that we reached the point where life goes on is more than I ever thought I could hope for."

EPILOGUE

For over four years, I had been taking care of my wife. Even after her condition improved and she probably didn't need to be taken care of any more than I did, my role as caretaker, protector, was clear to me. I would still catch myself watching her instead of looking at her, waiting for the next problem to emerge or fearing that the last problem would return.

Diane kept telling me that it was time for me to stop treating her like a patient, time to stop thinking I could control her life and thereby minimize her suffering. "I didn't die, you know," she would say. I heard her, but I'm not sure I listened.

My father always told Diane and me that we worked too much. That was easy for him to say, in semiretirement from a job he'd grown tired of, while we were in our prime years doing work we really loved. But he was right that drawing the line between vocation and life had always been difficult for us. And as I was writing the drug book, it had become all too intertwined: Diane's life, or at least the particulars of her health care, had become part of my job.

Then the phone rang.

Dad called on a Thursday evening to tell me that his chronic stomachache was something else, something worse. An ultrasound had revealed a mass. Two days later, he was diagnosed with Stage IV colon cancer, spread to his liver, pancreas, stomach lining, everywhere. Most of it was inoperable. At age sixty-one, he was given, at best, a year or two to live.

He accepted this news more gracefully and philosophically than any of us did. Reminding us that he had almost died at twenty-nine from a heart attack, and again in his forties before bypass surgery, he claimed he knew he had been living on borrowed time for decades. It had been a good life, he said, filled with the love of his family and friends, world travel and three-jetty walks on the beach.

He reassured us that he had no regrets. And then he said that this was the story he was sticking with. Somehow, he did.

After years of examining the world of legal drugs, I couldn't believe how unprepared, how absolutely ineffectual I felt watching my father struggle with the medicines that were supposed to either prolong or sustain the quality of his life.

He was put on 5FU (fluorouracil), which has been the gold standard treatment for colon cancer for over twenty years. It was given intravenously, five days in a row, an hour a day, followed by three weeks off. I expected the experience to seem completely different from anything Diane and I had seen in the world of pharmacy-dispensed drugs. In fact, it reminded me that all drug treatments are, technically, chemotherapy. The arbitrary line between "medicine" and "chemo" was drawn at a much earlier time in pharmaceutical history, when strong drugs were available only by injection.

My father's experience with the chemo resembled nothing so much as a typical drug reaction for which his doctor could have prepared him but simply didn't, perhaps hoping to spare him somehow. We were told, for example, that 5FU was one of the "easier" chemotherapies: that it didn't make patients very nauseated or cause them to lose their hair. For some reason, we actually believed this. So when he became severely nauseated and his hair started falling out, we all felt a little betrayed.

A week after his chemo, he developed painful mouth sores. I had, by this time, joined an Internet group for colon cancer patients and their families, so I posted a query about the sores. "Didn't they give him ice chips to put in his mouth during the chemo?" many people asked. Apparently this simple trick almost always prevents the sores. The next time he got chemo, I asked the oncologist about ice chips; he ordered them, and my dad never got the sores again.

I had expected the chemo to be unforgiving. But the surprise was that his other drugs, the prescription medicines used to treat common symptoms such as pain, diarrhea and nausea, quickly became a problem. They turned into the props in an overwrought family drama. My father had been a fairly compliant patient his entire life, but after his diagnosis he turned into an erratic, irascible pill-taker. The choice of whether or not to take the next dose of Ativan or Darvocet seemed like the only real choice he had left.

So even when he was in distress, he was maddeningly inconsistent in his willingness to treat his symptoms. He was supposed to take pain medication every four hours. Sometimes he would. Other times, regardless of the level of pain, he seemed intent on playing some kind of mind game over the very *idea* of the drug. For one thing, his painkiller was a narcotic, and taking narcotics was a sign of weakness to him. But he also had issues with the person who generally brought him his medicines—my mother. She needed him to take the drugs as much for herself as for him, so that she could feel she was doing *something* to help him. His suffering was as much her heartbreak as his. But he resented feeling like a child around someone who had been, until recently, his equal.

I found my father's attitude toward pills strange because he seemed so reasonable about everything else. I spoke to him daily by phone and drove from Philadelphia to Harrisburg to see him whenever I could, which was often. He and I spent a lot of rich time together, fishing, buying flowers at the farmer's market, talking for hours about subjects deep and shallow—everything from life after death to his recollections of being a chain-store toy buyer the year the Barbie doll debuted. His attitude about his illness was inspiring. His attitude about his pills, however, was just plain bitter. When I tried to talk to him about his treatment, he would stare at me stone-faced until I dropped the subject.

Behind his back, my mother and I were becoming obsessive about his drug regimen. Every late or missed pill affected us personally. Considering how pharmacologically fastidious we were trying to be, it was almost comical how cavalier his doctors sometimes were about his medication. I realized very quickly the impact of the medical generation gap between my parents and me. People from their generation like to be told precisely what to do by their physicians. Especially when it comes to medications, they aren't really interested in becoming well-informed consumers. They don't want personal empowerment; they want omnipotent and omnipresent doctors.

Over the course of his illness, my father had been given two different painkillers, one by the oncologist, another by his longtime general practitioner. At one point he was refusing to swallow either of them, and after watching him sit on his living room recliner for hours wincing against the pain, I finally just said, "Dad, you know, drugs work much better when you take them." He chuckled because it was the kind of folksy advice he liked to give to clients, but then we realized we really didn't know which one he should take. I was able to persuade him to call his oncologist and ask. When he finally got her on the phone, she told him it didn't really matter—whatever *he* wanted.

My father's doctor is a very pleasant person, and I'm sure she thought she was doing him a favor by giving him a choice. But instead she only added to my father's frustration and confusion. She reinforced his suspicion that, when it came to drugs, the doctors were just making it all up as they went along. So why shouldn't he?

Several weeks later, a nurse claimed that one of my father's doctors apparently *had* made up a drug dosage. Dad was being switched from a painkilling pill to an increased dose delivered by a combination of liquid and a transdermal patch. But within hours of the changeover, he was in more pain than ever. A nurse visiting my parents' house was baffled until she looked at the liquid dose: it had been computed improperly, so my father was actually now getting less painkiller than previously. She even took out a chart to show me.

"Don't get me started on doctors . . ." she grumbled, shaking her head. The recomputed dosage relieved his pain in minutes.

As these events unfolded, I seemed to be confronting again almost every wrong I had set out to right in my quest to investigate drug safety. I knew every pitfall to avoid—as did my father, who had been reading a rough draft of my manuscript because I feared he wouldn't live to see it published. Yet we fell into every pit anyway.

Even though I had learned so much, knowledge seemed to be failing me. Information was not making my father stronger or healthier. Understanding what was wrong with the system was not helping us beat it. At best, it gave me the proper jargon to describe my frustrations and failures.

I began to consider the shortcomings of consumer education. It is, of course, incredibly important. But being an educated consumer does not make you a doctor or even "almost a doctor." And it can be counterproductive, as my father occasionally cautioned me, to "think you know too much." Consumer education is supposed to be the *last* line of defense. It is becoming the first line only by default, because the people we pay to be the first line of defense are too often inconsistent or unreliable. Consumers may be getting better at being consumers. But it is the people who make the pills, regulate the pills, prescribe the pills and dispense the pills who must be better at *their* jobs—even though they are under more time and economic constraints than ever—before care will really improve.

One afternoon my brother and I were sitting at my dad's bedside. The quality of his days could be measured by the firmness of his voice, and on that day he spoke with such clarity and authority that we used the opportunity to nudge him into making some business decisions he had been putting off. The funny thing about my father was that while he fully accepted that he was dying, he couldn't deal with the idea of retirement. So his personal financial affairs were in order, and he was bonding with his family, but his business dangled by a thread. In fifteen minutes he made a year's worth of "final" decisions, many of them too late, about what should be done with the firms he had spent his lifetime building. I wrote down his wishes on a blue envelope left over from a get-well card.

When he finished, he was both relieved and shaken. My brother and I rose and walked to either side of his bed. He grabbed our hands with more strength than I thought he had left in him and, with a look of sheer panic, said what he had avoided saying for all these months.

"I want more *time*," he cried.

At that moment, I wanted to forget everything I knew about his illness and about drugs. I wanted to be a happy, hopeful idiot again so I could believe that medicine could save him or at least buy him that time. I had just read somewhere that the original Latin word for *drug* had three meanings: remedy, poison and magical charm. I wanted to believe in the magic.

As my father's illness rapidly progressed, I noticed something changing between Diane and me. For the first time since she had been Floxed, I didn't feel as though I had to take care of her. Quite the opposite. Now she was taking care of me.

At first I didn't trust the feeling. The frustration of living with someone with manic-depressive illness is that almost any mood you grow accustomed to will eventually cycle away. It will undoubtedly come back another day, but as soon as you realize you're trying to hold on to a good mood, it's gone.

But this newfound feeling seemed to be surviving the cycles. I asked Diane what was different. Was it just the passage of time, greater insight into her illness, a natural abatement of symptoms?

No, she said, it was the drug. Clozaril was stabilizing her moods. It didn't eliminate all of her symptoms, but it allowed her to surf them instead of being dragged down by every big wave.

One pill.

There we were, in the midst of an anguishing family crisis, and I could see that largely because of one pill—not an antidote, but an effective treatment—Diane was able to experience this emotional event in real time. I had spent so many nights and mornings watching her cry, for no other reason than that the mood thermostat in her brain was broken. So for her to feel appropriate sorrow and just grieve for my father seemed like a small miracle. For us to be able to face this heart-wrenching loss truly together was my sole consolation.

I remember the exact moment that I realized Diane's emergency—our emergency—was over. It was late Saturday evening, and the family was huddled around my father's bed. He had only hours left to live, but he was still talking, sometimes incoherently, then lucid for a moment. Ironically, he seemed to make the most sense when he was due for his next dose of morphine, as if the pain brought clarity. We decided to ask that his painkiller be given sooner, even though it might mean depriving ourselves of some extra last words.

As we waited for the next dose to take effect, my father looked up and said, "I'm going to die." Diane burst into tears. So did I, but not only because of what was happening to my father. I was also struck by the realization that I had never seen my wife cry in front of other people. At that instant I felt more connected to her than I had ever thought was possible.

My father died at 6:16 the next morning. I had been holding his hand, and when he was gone, I used it to wipe my tears.

Then I went to my wife, as if for the first time, and we began to take care of each other again.

AFTERWORD

S everal days before the hardcover edition of *Bitter Pills* was published in April of 1998, a science writer friend called to say that the *Journal of the American Medical Association* was about to release a stunning study on medication safety. Researchers would be identifying adverse drug reactions as the fourth leading cause of death in America, based on their new estimate of the number of hospitalized patients who die from ADRs—approximately 106,000 a year in the U.S. alone. The study would estimate that more than 2.2 million Americans had serious but nonfatal adverse drug reactions. And the research included only reactions to drugs that had been given error-free: properly prescribed by doctors and properly dispensed by pharmacists.

The new issue of *JAMA* would also feature a ringing editorial on the problem of adverse drug reactions. Together, they would represent the loudest shout about drug safety issues in the general medical literature in years, maybe decades.

The science writer knew all this because even *JAMA* has detail men. The journal's studies are released to the media by publicists five days before their Wednesday publication date, allowing journalists to prepare laudatory stories and maximize buzz. The material is embargoed until Tuesday evening at five o'clock eastern time, insuring that any juicy research can headline the national evening news. So, the Monday that *Bitter Pills* was published, we already knew that a stampede of drug safety coverage was heading right at us.

The *JAMA* study was published on Wednesday, April 15, a landmark day in the history of medicine for several reasons: that same tax-day morning, a little blue diamond-shaped pill called Viagra (sildenafil) first went on sale. After that day, it was clear that the risk/benefit ratio was never going to be the same again. (Maybe April 15th should be proclaimed a national drug holiday, Risk-Benefit Day, devoted to medicine education.) The erectile dysfunction drug from Pfizer immediately became the most popular new medicine in pharmaceutical history and its financial, social and sexual implications received unprecedented media attention. Viagra got more ink and air time each day than the entire process of FDA reform had received over the previous three years. In a mad dash for *any* new angle on the story, the media picked up on whatever drug safety issues it could find, as long as they could be spun into a story that included the words *Viagra, penis* and *erection*. So, the medication became a way of talking about everything from the horror of pill-mills, which were quickly set up so all the now-unemployed phen-fen docs could go into the Viagra prescription business, to the possible perils of "lifestyle" pharmacology.

Then adverse reaction reports started coming in on the drug. It caused temporary blue vision in many patients, but in a chosen few—most with a history of heart troubles—Viagra was associated with a more permanent, somewhat Victorian reaction: death after sex. With this news, the *JAMA* study coverage and the Viagra stories converged. Drug safety experts were deluged with interview requests. The phones at the Georgetown pharmacology department were ringing off the hook.

The first news was that the agency had sixteen reports of patients who had died while taking Viagra after the drug was approved, and there were eight cases of deaths during clinical trials. Some had fallen victim to a prominently labeled interaction with the angina treatment nitroglycerine, and others had died for less clear reasons involving the heart; but neither Pfizer nor the FDA was blaming Viagra as the primary cause. I started looking over the Viagra material released by the agency so I could prepare intelligent answers to the questions that were coming up in the press and TV interviews for the book. Everyone wanted to know what the growing death toll of people who had taken Viagra meant about the safety of the drug.

I did my best to explain why this was a hard question to answer, and I recognized in these reporters the same incredulity I had experienced when I first found out how Phase IV worked—and didn't work. I also did my best to explain that Viagra's safety would be judged by a different standard than other drugs that had been in the news. Viagra was a true breakthrough medication, the first and, so far, the only pill that effectively treated organic erectile dysfunction (via a mechanism so novel that the underlying science would win the 1998 Nobel Prize in medicine). Its problems, no matter how severe they might turn out to be, would most likely always be remedied through labeling, unlike a me-too antihistamine or pain reliever that could be removed from the market without severely limiting the choices for physicians and patients.

Even before the book was officially published, Diane and I had started hearing from many new Floxies, as well as their family members, physicians and lawyers. We had appeared on *Dateline* on publication day, and when I checked my E-mail after the segment aired, there were already several dozen messages from people who had seen the show and needed help. Because Dave Flockhart was also featured on *Dateline*, he was deluged with E-mails and phone calls from patients and physicians. He assisted as many people as he could, and some of his patients—including the woman who had sent me her "Floxed" license plate—began an informal phone and E-mail support group for ADR victims.

I was asked to do an op-ed piece for *The New York Times* on the *JAMA* study, drug safety and the failures of postmarketing surveillance. Not long after it appeared, I received an E-mail from Dr. Jack Chow, who advises Senator Arlen Specter on medical policy issues for the Senate Appropriations subcommittee on health. Chow said the senator had seen the *Times* op-ed and was thinking of holding a hearing on "the prescription drug reaction issue." He wanted to know if I would consider testifying.

In his E-mail, Chow pointed out that the subcommittee on health did not handle appropriations for the FDA. It covered only the U.S. Public Health Service. "For us to hold a hearing on the topic," he wrote, "may mean asserting a broader scope of authority than what is covered by FDA."

Chow's words had a profound impact on me. He had seen something in the *JAMA* article, and even in my op-ed piece about it, that I hadn't clearly observed myself. *This is a public health problem. The FDA can't solve it because the FDA is a regulatory agency, not a public health agency. The FDA is not allowed to look at the big picture of public health. Someone else in the government has to do it.*

I called Chow to talk about how hearings could shift the focus of the drug safety debate away from FDA regulatory controls and toward solutions that could improve public health, perhaps even knock adverse drug reactions out of the top four causes of death in the U.S. Of course, the FDA would do a better job if it actually had a boss. At the time, David Kessler's job had yet to be filled after eighteen months. But we agreed that this public health problem was bigger than the FDA.

Not long after my conversation with Chow, I read in the paper that

Senator Specter had been taken to a hospital in center city Philadelphia with chest pains and was facing open-heart surgery. He was in the hospital much longer than originally predicted, and when he was discharged, he looked fragile and shaky. Chow told me that Specter's staff was protective of him in his weakened condition and couldn't push for him to take on any additional duties. For the time being, the hearings were off.

Still, my discussions with Jack Chow stayed with me. I shared them with Ray Woosley and several others. Woosley had actually been up to see Chow, hoping to convince Senator Specter to support funding for the Centers for Education and Research on Therapeutics (CERT). It turned out that just because the sweeping FDA Modernization Act of 1997 "authorized" funding for the pilot program didn't mean the money would actually be appropriated. CERTs are a good idea, and I hope Woosley's lobbying efforts succeed. But we need more. We need one central figure, someone whose job it is to focus solely on the public health issues surrounding medications.

We need a Legal Drug Czar. We need someone *empowered* to be the public health conscience of the legal drug world. Someone who can declare war against adverse drug reactions and enlist the support of physicians, pharmaceutical companies, regulators and pharmacists, instead of pitting them all against each other.

Why can't we have a czar for a drug war that might actually be winnable?

The average shelf life for a public outcry over adverse drug reactions in the United States is a few days, a week or two at the most. The outcry that began on April 15, 1998—Risk-Benefit Day—lasted for much longer, and people in the drug safety world watched it with amazement, the way financiers gape at an unexpected bull market, and wondered how the media's attention was kept riveted for so long. My theory was that the *JAMA* article and Viagra craze had come at a time when people were still digesting the whole fen-phen disaster of the previous fall. The public was also generally disoriented about medication because of the deluge of new TV ads for prescription drugs. While many consumers said they liked the TV ads, surveys also showed that more than 60 percent of consumers felt that they "confuse people about the risks and benefits of drugs." With some ads, the majority of viewers couldn't figure out what condition the drugs were meant to treat.

Regardless of the reason, the drug safety issue continued to be in the news. On May 20, *JAMA* ran another strong piece, a detailed commentary called "Time to Act on Drug Safety." It eviscerated the FDA's MED-Watch system, calling it a "drug safety program without reliable data."

Then on June 8, the FDA announced that the Roche calcium-channel blocker Posicor (mibefradil), which treated angina and hypertension, was being withdrawn from the market because of dangerous interactions with more than 25 different medications. The withdrawal of the drug was especially tricky because it was dangerous for patients to stop taking the drug abruptly. Two weeks after Posicor was withdrawn, the FDA announced that the Wyeth-Ayerst arthritis medication Duract (bromfenac sodium) was being taken off the market because of severe liver failure in patients who used it for extended periods of time. Duract, a nonsteroidal anti-inflammatory analgesic, had been approved to be used for no more than ten days, but doctors kept prescribing it for longer periods, even after the FDA had put a black box on the drug.

Both Duract and Posicor had been on the market for less than a year, and both had been approved after David Kessler left the agency and an acting director had been filling in. News stories noted that Posicor marked the fifth drug withdrawn by the FDA in less than a year, even though in the previous ten years, the agency had banned only six drugs. Fear was high. I heard some drug safety experts worrying aloud about the specter of "another thalidomide," even as thalidomide itself was finally being approved for limited use in Hansen's disease (leprosy).

In early July, Oprah aired a new show on adverse drug reactions, with a new cast of experts and patients. That same month, the FDA approved the first-ever celebrity endorsement for a TV prescription drug ad: former *Good Morning America* coanchor Joan Lunden hawking the antihistamine Claritin. I later called the agency's point person on such decisions, Nancy Ostrove, to ask her how such ads could possibly be approved. Hasn't the entire mission of the FDA since the late 1950s been to force the industry to rely on hard science rather than paid testimonials? "There's nothing in the regulations that prohibits any of this," she said, a little defensively. "Whether we *like* it or not is irrelevant. The question is: is it legal?" I had some other questions. Was there a clinical trial to see if Joan Lunden had a good result with the drug? Did an FDA medical officer verify that she hadn't experienced any adverse reactions? "We asked the manufacturer if she was taking the drug," she explained. "They said she was."

In August, drug safety fell off the national radar screen, just like every other national and international policy issue, when the whole country stopped working to gawk at the spectacle of the Monica Lewinsky affair. So there was little room in the newspaper for the first major reactions to the FDA Modernization Act of 1997, which had been signed into law but would take years to actually implement. The analyses came from the so-called CDER Stakeholders, academic, industry and nonprofit groups that would be affected by the new statutes, and were presented at a meeting on August 17—the day of President Clinton's grand jury testimony. Many of the damning critiques of the new FDA act were written by the very experts whom the media had been clamoring to hear from only months before. (Dave Flockhart wrote one in his capacity as chair of the government affairs committee of the American Society for Clinical Pharmacology and Therapeutics.) The critiques raised crucial issues about the very structure of our drug approval system and its postapproval monitoring. These were the real, *enduring* public health issues, much more important than a side effect of blue vision with a Viagra erection. But this time nobody was paying attention.

As for Diane and me . . . well, we're moving on with our lives. Just before *Bitter Pills* came out, Diane found out that a small literary press would publish one of her novels. This encouraging news provided a distraction from the sometimes overwhelming interviews she did for my book. The TV crews and print reporters we welcomed into our home were mostly kind and respectful of Diane. Her greatest dread was that they would portray her as a hopeless or bitter victim. It was important to her that they convey she had long since recovered from the ADR itself. Of course, she will take medication to treat her manic depression for the rest of her life, but, she is, at the least, a *very* informed consumer.

Even Ortho finally acknowledged her. When *Dateline* gave the company the opportunity to respond to the book, the doctor who spoke for Ortho actually appeared somewhat sympathetic and, while admitting no liability, didn't try to deny or minimize the reality of Diane's medical crisis. "What happened to Diane Ayres is very unfortunate," he said. "I wouldn't want it to happen to anybody . . . to my patients, to a family member, anybody."

People magazine had been preparing a story on the book and on us, and they finally ran it around Labor Day. The article captured something that most of the other coverage had missed. A journalist friend of ours who called after reading the article put it best.

"See," she said, "they just saw the whole thing as a love story." She admitted that she had skimmed much of the technical information in the book to get to the stuff about our relationship. "It's just a love story, right? A pharmaceutical love story."

Actually, that's what I always thought it was.

APPENDIX

Bitter Pills: The Antidotes

How are we supposed to personally navigate the world of bitter pills? It isn't easy. If it makes you feel better, it isn't any easier for the people who work in the field. They are, I can attest, just as likely as anyone to be scared to death by stories about new side effects or become transfixed by reports of new wonder drugs that will cure anything and everything.

Looking for some practical guidance, late one morning I picked up a couple of hoagies from a Philly lunch truck and went to Penn to speak once again with Dr. Brian Strom, one of my most helpful sources in this project because his considerable expertise in both clinical pharmacology and epidemiology means he's not only a multidisciplined thinker but I got to hang out with him at twice as many conferences. He's also a very user-friendly doc who cares about the way individual patients are affected by drugs. We talked about how patients could be smart consumers of drugs without becoming completely paranoid.

I told him that I wanted his help in addressing three basic problems: how to read a drug package insert, how to make your doctor write smarter prescriptions and how to avoid adverse drug reactions. He laughed and said he wasn't sure patients should learn how to read drug package inserts, because they were really written for doctors and lawyers (although not necessarily in that order). There were several information sources he preferred to drug labels, especially the annual consumers' guide published by the nonprofit United States Pharmacopeia, which he had helped produce. But I convinced him that, for some patients, the insert was all they had. And for better or worse, it's the government's official last word.

Besides advice from Strom, these appendixes include information from government documents and from several hundred books and articles that I have read or skimmed over the years. They also incorporate questions raised during interviews with various drug experts around the world, beginning with Dr. David Flockhart at Georgetown University Hospital, my first pharmacological reality check, and his boss, Dr. Raymond Woosley. In addition, I have tried to address the concerns of some of the hundreds of patients who have called and written us since my original article on Diane's drug reaction. Thus, while Drs. Strom, Flockhart and Woosley were the ones I bugged the most over the years with these questions, the advice is ultimately my own, and it should be used, like anything you can get over-the-counter, with caution.

HOW TO READ A DRUG PACKAGE INSERT

First, you have to get your hands on one, which isn't always easy. Your pharmacy should have a current package insert for any drug dispensed; if it doesn't, ask the pharmacist to get you one. Package inserts are not the same as the abbreviated safety information printouts, often very helpful, that many larger pharmacies offer with your prescription: make sure the pharmacist knows you want both. (Note: Since the printed material on inserts is referred to by the FDA as "labeling" information, "package insert" and "label" are used interchangeably. Neither refers to the label affixed to your pill bottle.)

Some patients know to look in the *PDR*, which is a compendium of package inserts provided by pharmaceutical companies. What we often forget about the *PDR* is that older editions often have outdated label information, and because of printing schedules, even the newest edition can easily be a revise behind. Many package insert revises are minor, but not all. Check at the very end of the package insert or the *PDR* entry to see when it was last updated.

Package insert styles vary from company to company. You can usually tell which companies view them as a useful exercise and which do them grudgingly because they're forced to. But inserts do generally conform to a basic eleven-point format mandated by the FDA since 1979. Since the print is usually as small as the statute will allow, use a magnifying glass if you need to.

Begin with your drug's **Name:** note both its brand name and its generic name. You can then generally skip the **Description,** as well as the section on **Clinical Pharmacology** (unless you are very curious about how much of the drug will end up in your urine). Go directly to **Indica-**

tions, which is the diagnosis or diagnoses that the drug has been formally approved to treat. This is a basic piece of information that consumers often don't know. However, just because you have been given a drug doesn't mean that you have been diagnosed with one of the illnesses listed under Indications. Bear in mind that a drug can be prescribed for various reasons other than the FDA-approved indications, and many drugs have well-established secondary off-label uses.

If a drug is being prescribed to you for something other than the FDA-labeled indications, you should feel free to ask your doctor why. But make sure you ask in a noncombative way and with the understanding that off-label uses are not only perfectly acceptable but are sometimes more beneficial than the labeled uses. Just say, "I saw this on the label, and can you explain it?" You may learn something and in the process, if you teach the physician something, all the better. You can also ask your pharmacist to ask your doctor.

Next are **Contraindications.** These contain the strongest warnings about reasons the drug should *not* be used because the risk clearly outweighs any possible benefit. More often than not, the contraindications consist only of known hypersensitivities to the drug itself or to other drugs in its "therapeutic class" (for example, not just "antibiotics," but "*quinolone* antibiotics"). Therefore, in order for you to read the contraindications properly, you need to know the class of the drug as well as any experience you might have had in the past with that specific drug class. (The class can usually be discerned from the contraindication language itself, although if you're not sure, ask your pharmacist.) Contraindications can be general, or specific to your age, sex or disease state or even to other medications you are taking, either by prescription or over the counter.

Keep in mind that there are some circumstances in which any label caution, even a contraindication, might be reasonably disregarded by your doctor. For example, you may have already tried and failed all the other less risky treatments for an illness that requires treatment. On the other hand, you should never simply assume that your doctor has put a great deal of thought into this kind of a risk/benefit assessment. It is equally possible that he or she forgot about the contraindication, forgot about your previous hypersensitivity to a drug in the same class or forgot the drug was in the same class. Again, it never hurts to ask.

The next two sections, **Warnings** and **Precautions,** are meant to be the meat of the label for both doctors and patients. They are supposed to provide as much useful information as possible to assist in handicapping the risk/benefit ratio for the drug in any given situation. They are also a legal minefield, since many product liability cases involve "failure to warn." Therefore, some of the language of these cautionary guidelines is meant to be more preventive for the drug company than the patient. The decision whether to place this information in Warnings or in Precautions is often subject to drug company idiosyncrasies or legal strategies—as well as FDA advisory committee mandates—so the two sections are best read and digested together. Warnings, by statute, are supposed to be "serious adverse reactions and potential safety hazards," while Precautions are there to help doctors and patients exercise "special care."

The strongest warnings are not actually in the Warnings section. They appear in what is called a **black box,** which is usually placed at the very top of the insert. Technically, a black box warning (which most drugs do not have) is slightly less absolute than a contraindication, but it often has an equal if not stronger impact because of its prominent placement. As with contraindications, there are circumstances in which black box warnings may be reasonably disregarded by your doctor, after a careful assessment of the possible risks and benefits. However, even though the addition of a black box to an insert is often heralded by letters to physicians and coverage in the professional and lay press, don't assume that the news got to *your* doctor. If you are being told to take something that contradicts the caution in the black box, ask your doctor why this is so.

While Warnings can be about anything and appear in any order, there are more formal rules for Precautions. The **General** precautions and the **Information for Patients** tend to be two versions of the same information, one for your doctor, the other for you. Basically, Information for Patients is supposed to list everything your doctor or pharmacist should have told you before letting you take the drug, in order to prevent any of the problems listed elsewhere on the label. After that, often, comes **Laboratory Tests,** a section that tells the doctor which tests are recommended to assure that the drug is at the proper therapeutic level in your bloodstream. Some tests may also be recommended to check the functioning of organs or body systems that are occasionally affected adversely by certain drugs. Many drugs do not require any lab tests at all. On the other hand, some doctors can be lax about ordering those tests that *are* required or recommended, assuming they will be able to "tell" if there's a problem (or presuming that you will "tell" them). If your doctor does not order these tests at the recommended intervals, ask about it.

The **Drug Interactions** section lists the known interactions of the drug with other drugs and will sometimes also note whether any commonly predicted interactions have been experimentally ruled out. To read this section properly, you must know the generic name and the therapeutic class of all medicines, both prescription and over-the-counter, that you are taking, because the interactions are never listed by brand name. Your doctor, of course, must also have the same information about *all* the medicines you take, both prescription and over-the-counter. Remember that interactions are not all equally predictable or equally dangerous. Some are listed to keep patients from having certain drugs together in their system *at all*; others are listed to keep patients from swallowing two drugs together; others are listed to let the doctor know about possible changes in laboratory findings that the patient would never actually feel. (If your doctor should need more information, these interaction listings generally refer to specific studies or case reports available from the drug company.) Either way, if you are prescribed drugs together that have a listed interaction, you may wish to ask your doctor about it.

If you are neither pregnant nor a woman, skip ahead to **Adverse Reactions,** unless you're the parent of a small child, in which case stop just before that at **Pediatric Use.**

If you are pregnant or are considering getting pregnant, the **Carcinogenesis, Mutagenesis, Impairment of Fertility** section refers only to animal study results in these areas. If there is evidence that the drug causes such problems in humans, that information goes in the Warnings section.

Move on to the **Pregnancy** precaution, which begins with a letter grade, A, B, C, D or X. Category A drugs have been clinically tested in pregnant women and have failed to show a risk to the fetus even if taken during the first trimester (which is considered a more vulnerable period for drug-related birth defects than the second and third trimesters); they have also failed to cause birth defects in animals. Category B drugs either failed to show a risk in animals and haven't been tested on humans, or failed to show a risk in human tests but did show some birth defects in animals. (Animal tests for birth defects are not directly predictive of human birth defects.)

Most drugs that carry a rating are category C—in part because it is the default rating for drugs about which little is known but also because, presumably, the benefits of using the drug may acceptably outweigh the risks. Technically, C drugs either haven't been tested in animals or humans or have been shown to have an adverse effect on the fetus in animals but haven't yet been tested in humans. Category D drugs have shown evidence of human fetal risk based on individual cases reported during testing or postmarketing, although the potential benefits—in a serious or life-threatening situation—might still outweigh the risks.

Category X drugs are absolutely contraindicated for pregnant women because the risks to the fetus clearly outweigh any possible benefits to the mother. (Teratology experts are lobbying for an end to these categories—except the X—and a more narrative approach to explaining what is known about pregnancy risks. For an excellent, free consultation on pregnancy risks for the drugs you are taking or thinking of taking, call the Motherisk service in Toronto, 416-813-6780.)

Also listed in this section are **Nonteratogenic Effects,** which are nonpermanent problems the drug can cause the fetus or newborn infant, including such conditions as withdrawal symptoms and hypoglycemia.

The **Labor and Delivery** section is for drugs that have a recognized use during labor or delivery, regardless of whether it is an FDA-approved use, and it describes anecdotally what effect they have. The **Nursing Mothers** section explains what is known about whether the drug is excreted in human breast milk and whether it has been associated with serious adverse reactions in infants. If human data are available, you are told either to use the drug with caution while nursing or, if it has more serious risks, to choose between nursing or taking the drug. The same two warnings are used in cases where there are no human data.

Pediatric Use is usually the section where the label says "safety and effectiveness in children has not been established." This doesn't mean the drug can't or shouldn't be used in children. It just means that the drug company has not submitted studies for specific pediatric indications or dosages for FDA approval. Sometimes this section echoes cautions in the Warnings section about not using the drug in children under certain ages.

Adverse Reactions is the section that your doctor would rather you didn't read, because it often leads people to overreact. The drug company is legally required to list every adverse reaction to its drug ever reported in this section and to attempt to quantify the risks involved, but the lists often do little but frighten patients. The rules are a little vague on whether the severity of a reaction or its frequency is more important, and the companies are given considerable leeway in how they present the litany of reported reactions. For these reasons, it is almost impossible to compare drugs on the basis of their Adverse Reactions sections. In theory, at least, a drug's individual safety profile is supposed to be determined by which reactions graduate from this catchall section to Warnings or Precautions.

Reactions from preapproval clinical trials are listed first, beginning with reactions seen in more than one percent of the test subjects. Next come the "less than one percent" reactions, usually broken down by body systems. This is followed by a separate list of adverse reactions that were reported after the drug was on the market but *not* prior to approval.

Ultimately, the Adverse Reactions section is useful chiefly for one thing. If you are given a new drug and experience what appears to be an adverse reaction and your doctor says, "That's impossible" or "I never heard of this drug doing that," you can check and see if the reaction is listed. If it is listed, it doesn't prove that it is the same reaction you had, but it can move the conversation to a more constructive exchange. If you have a serious reaction or one that isn't listed, you or your doctor should be reporting it to FDA's MedWatch system (see the form on page 416).

A **Drug Abuse and Dependence** section appears only if the drug is considered a "controlled substance," because of its potential for abuse or dependence, by the Drug Enforcement Administration (DEA). These drugs, which include amphetamines, narcotic painkillers and some benzodiazepines, are rated by the DEA for abusability on a five-point scale, with "Schedule I" drugs being the most dangerous. The Abuse section includes the type of abuse, adverse reactions caused by the abuse and descriptions of susceptible patients. The Dependence section describes both physical and psychological dependence, the quantities needed to cause dependence and the adverse effects of chronic abuse and withdrawal.

Overdosage describes the symptoms of an overdose of the drug, possible treatments and the amount of a drug likely to be life-threatening.

The sections on **Dosage and Administration** and **How Supplied** contain information primarily for your doctor. But if you believe you are being given more or less than the "usual dose," you might want to ask your doctor why. The How Supplied section may give you a clue to the best values in prescribing costs. (For example, sometimes a dose that is twice as strong is not twice as expensive. If the higher-dose pill can be cut in half, you can save money.)

At the bottom of the label, companies have the option of adding **Animal Pharmacology,** results of specific **Clinical Studies** and relevant **References.**

There are, of course, dozens of reference books geared to consumers that offer more accessible versions of the information on FDA-approved drug labeling. They include big, thick lay guides by the United States Pharmacopeia and the American Medical Association; substantial, non-confrontational general-audience books like *The Essential Guide to Prescription Drugs* and *The Pill Book*; substantial, confrontational general-audience books like *The People's Pharmacy* series and Public Citizen's *Worst Pills, Best Pills*; and many lesser books masquerading as substantial. There are several things I have noticed about these books over the years.

First, they do not all contain the same information, and the subtle variations in individual entries can either allay or augment fears about specific medications in a way that is more subjective than most readers will realize. Some of these books are simply more party-line-oriented than others. Others appear to update certain drugs more aggressively than they do others. And when they update, they may or may not be persuaded by certain new reports, or they simply may not be as interested in certain kinds of reactions as you are.

Second, these books are not updated as quickly as you would like them to be, and even editions stamped with the current year may be a year or several years behind on the entry for the drug you are about to take. If you are taking a relatively new drug, it is especially important to consult the most up-to-date edition of the most aggressive resources you can find. (You should not assume that information on the Internet is more up-to-date simply because you got it via a newfangled delivery system. Much of the reference information about drugs on the Internet is completely undiscerning, boiled-down package-insert material from two years ago.)

Third, it is important to use all these resources as a guide to conversations with your doctor or pharmacist and not as an excuse to stop taking a medication because it seems too scary. One of the scariest things you can do is stop a medication without telling your doctor.

HOW TO MAKE YOUR DOCTOR WRITE SMARTER PRESCRIPTIONS

1. Treat every doctor's office visit as an opportunity for a drug consultation. It is not unreasonable for you to bring *every* drug you are currently taking—prescription, over-the-counter and naturopathic remedies—with you to these office visits. Just throw the pill containers in a bag. Your doctor probably has a better chance of figuring out just who is treating you for what—and *with* what—by looking through that bag than he does by any other way. Senior citizens have been encouraged to do this for years; there's no reason why everyone shouldn't benefit from this basic, sound practice, too.

Besides seeing what other doctors are giving you, this practice also gives your physician an opportunity to assess all the over-the-counter medications you decided to give yourself. If you're like most people, you may not be doing an ideal job of self-medication. You may also be self-treating a problem that you never bothered to share with your physician.

2. Give your doctor a complete history of your medication use. The best doctors work from a careful patient history. You cannot give such a history if you don't *know* the information about your past treatment, especially your past medication use. It is important to keep track of precisely which medications you have taken safely over the years and which ones have given you problems. It is not enough, for example, to tell your doctor you once had a bad reaction to an antibiotic: the doctor needs to know the name of the antibiotic and, preferably, the dose. (Some reactions are dose-related, and over the years companies change some standard doses to prevent reactions.) If you do not provide this information to your doctor, you cannot assume he or she will get it in some other way.

On page 418 you will find a form to begin your "medication diary." Start by writing down all the medications—prescription and over-the-counter—that you currently use, then try to reconstruct your past medication history. (Old pill bottles in the medicine cabinet will help; when you're finished copying the labels, throw them out because saving old pill bottles is a rotten idea.) For each drug, write down the brand and generic names, the symptom treated, the dosage and any side effects (or noneffects). If you have been told you had a problem as a child, try to verify if your memory of it is accurate so you don't provide misinformation that could mistakenly eliminate therapeutic options. (An improper or overblown recollection of a childhood reaction to penicillin, for example, could cause a physician to improperly dismiss an entire range of antibiotic choices.)

Whenever you are given a new drug, add it to your medication diary.

3. Ask questions, even if you're afraid they seem dumb. Bring a pen and paper to write down the answers. Don't let your visit end with the doctor handing you prescriptions and showing you to the door. If you don't feel comfortable asking your doctor questions, get a new attitude or a new doctor.

4. Ask what each new prescription is for. If it isn't written on the prescription, ask the doctor to add it, so it will go on the label, or to tell you so you can write it down yourself. (If you feel self-conscious having the diagnosis typed onto the container label, write it on yourself when you get home.) If you can't read something on the prescription, ask what it says. (Doctors' handwriting is notoriously illegible.) Ask how the drug is to be taken and what to do if you miss a dose. Be sure you understand at what intervals your doctor wants you to take a drug: for example, do you have to get up in the middle of the night to take that third or fourth daily dose, or can you take it during normal waking hours?

5. If you have never taken the drug before, ask if it is new on the market or old. If it is very new (especially if you are being given samples), you might want to ask why your doctor prefers it to whatever he or she had been using previously for the same problem, and how many patients he or she has personally tried on the drug.

If a medication has been on the market for less than a year, be particularly wary because its side-effect profile cannot possibly be well known yet. Unless the new drug is in some way a true breakthrough medicine—the first to effectively treat a certain condition, or the first of a new class that represents an indisputable therapeutic advance—it might be safer to wait until after its first year on the market.

6. If you are being switched to a new drug for a condition your doctor has treated successfully in the past with something else, be especially curious. There are many forces these days that pressure doctors to switch drug treatments for nonmedical reasons. A switch from a brand-name drug to a generic is generally done for reasons of cost only. A switch from one brand-name drug to another can be done for sound therapeutic reasons, or because your health insurer's pharmaceutical benefits manager (PBM) made a more attractive arrangement with a competing drug company. Doctors won't always volunteer information on why a switch was made, but asking a question or two might help you assess the situation. A bold question, but one well worth asking, is whether the doctor would still prefer the new drug being prescribed if you were willing to pay for it out of your own pocket rather than being reimbursed by your insurer. (Some switches are done via telephone rather than during an office visit; if you have questions about your switch, call your doctor.)

7. Always tell your doctor about suspected drug reactions. This will not only assure that the information gets entered into your chart, it will also provide an opportunity to discuss the suspected reaction with your doctor. Make sure you do it in a noncombative way, because it is human for the doctor to feel defensive when accused of giving you a drug that hurt you. Besides, there are always many possible explanations for symptoms other than a drug reaction. However, if you have a new symptom and it began just after you started taking a new drug, you should always assume initially that the drug might be the cause and follow through with your doctor. Together, you should be able to agree on whether you had a drug reaction. If it was serious—which means it caused or lengthened a hospitalization or caused permanent impairment or damage—it should be reported to FDA's MedWatch program (1-800-332-1088; also see pages 416–7 for an adverse reaction reporting form).

8. Use your pharmacist as your advocate with your doctor. See below.

HOW TO MAKE YOUR PHARMACIST
FILL SMARTER PRESCRIPTIONS

1. Buy all your medicines, prescription as well as over-the-counter, from the same pharmacy. If you have an emergency prescription filled elsewhere, bring the bottle to your regular pharmacy the next time you go there and ask that the information be entered into your computer file. When buying over-the-counter medications, pay for them at the pharmacy counter rather than the front checkout so the pharmacy staff is aware of every medicine you're taking.

2. Get to know the head pharmacist and the regular staff at that pharmacy. They could save your life. If your pharmacy has frequent staff changes—many are under harsher financial pressures than ever—take the time to acquaint yourself with the new staff, or find a more stable pharmacy.

3. Ask your pharmacist any question that you forgot to ask your doctor about your medications. If nobody at the pharmacy knows the answer, ask them to call your doctor. Your pharmacist is always more likely to get comprehensive answers from the prescribing physician than you.

4. Choose a pharmacy that has a computerized system to prevent drug interactions and adverse drug reactions. Providing your pharmacists with a copy of your completed "medication diary" (see page 418), to be entered into the computer system, is your best protection.

5. Try to visit your pharmacy during less crowded times of the day.
That way you will have more of chance to speak with the staff. Now that
some chain pharmacies have automated telephone prescription-refill
lines, the visit to the pharmacy may be your only chance to speak with a
human being.

**6. Ask your pharmacist if the doctor has written the prescription in a
way that makes the most medical sense.** Your doctor may be unaware
of a new dosage size or an extended-release pill that might be easier to
take and appropriate for your condition.

**7. Ask your pharmacist if the doctor has written the prescription in a
way that makes the most economic sense.** Doctors rarely have any idea
of what your drugs cost. Use your pharmacist to make sure your doctor
is writing the cheapest possible prescription that will be safe and effective for you, especially for chronic-use medications. This does not necessarily mean taking the cheapest generic version every time. First, ask if
generics exist for the drug you've been prescribed, and, if they do, find
out if one is made by a division of the same company that makes the
name brand: it might be the same exact pill at a fraction of the price.
Don't hesitate to ask what experience your pharmacist has had with the
name-brand drug and its generics. Also, if you find a generic doesn't
work as well as the branded drug or another generic, don't hesitate to
ask your pharmacist about switching back. Then make sure you or your
pharmacist talks to your doctor about rewriting the prescription. (State
laws often require pharmacies to switch you to an available generic unless the prescription specifically says "brand name only.")

With certain drugs, it is also worth comparing prices on dosage sizes
and exploring whether it may be cheaper to buy a larger dose and cut
the pill in half. But make sure you discuss any pill cutting you are considering (or are already doing) with your pharmacist. Drugstores usually sell
inexpensive pill cutters, and some tablets are even scored to make cutting them easier. However, a growing number of pills (especially buffered and time-release tablets) cannot be safely cut—capsules are an
obvious example, but also there are medications with special coatings
that need to stay intact if they are to work properly.

**8. When the prescription is filled, make sure the label on the bottle
matches what your doctor wrote.** It may take a hieroglyphics expert to
figure out exactly what your doctor wrote, but check anyway.

9. Ask specifically if a new drug you've been prescribed has any interactions with ones you are already taking. Ask this of the pharmacist even though it is something your doctor should already have checked, and your pharmacist should have double-checked. Pharmacy computer systems are supposed to flag possible drug interactions, but pharmacists can miss them, especially if they're harried and facing a long line of customers.

10. If your physician gives you a free sample of a medication, bring it to your pharmacy before taking so it can be entered into the pharmacist's computer and you can ask any additional questions you might have. The American Pharmaceutical Association, the pharmacists' national group, has been lobbying for years to get rid of free samples and replace them with free vouchers that can be redeemed at pharmacies. Until the pharmacists win their battle, this is the next best way to protect yourself from unnecessary drug reactions and interactions from samples.

HOW TO WATCH A TV DRUG AD

1. Try to determine as quickly as possible if the drug being advertised is one you are already taking. This is not always as easy as it sounds. Direct-to-consumer drug ads are a new form of communication, and many of them seem to have been badly translated from another language. Then determine if the ad campaign is offering some discount on the product. The best drug ad campaigns are those offering bargains on your preferred medication. All other drug ads are trying to get you to switch drugs for a condition you're already treating or to diagnose yourself with a new problem for which you can ask your doctor for new drugs.

2. Try to separate the drug being advertised from the "treatment message." The drug being advertised is just one more product being pushed on you. No patient should be choosing medications based on advertising campaigns, nor should any doctor. Period. The treatment message, however—that there's a new way to treat depression, for example, or migraines or high cholesterol—might have value for you. If you are already being treated for an illness, there may very well be a new class of drugs that you haven't heard about that can improve your treatment. You might also recognize symptoms of an illness in the ad that sound like something you may actually have. These are both good things to ask your doctor. But you are better off first asking the doctor about them *without* also mentioning the medication. You are likely to get a more honest assessment of your condition and the preferred treatment that way. If the doctor prescribes something different from what you saw touted on television, you might then—and only then—ask why. But approaching your doctor about an advertised drug could turn you into a detail man for a pharmaceutical company, or a self-diagnosing hypochondriac, rather than an informed patient with a health concern.

3. Disregard all the side-effect information on TV ads. Much of the information is misleading, either because it reflects only pre-approval clinical trial results or is delivered in such happy-talk patter that bad news is often made to sound like good news. The FDA requires the companies to tell you in their TV ads where to find their magazine ads and their web sites. Both of these must include complete safety information from the package insert. Then, using the guide on page 391, you can decode the insert.

4. Do not watch ads that refuse to explain what the medication actually does. These are "reminder" ads, and they only exist to etch the product name into your brain. The only health they are meant to improve is the financial health of the manufacturer. They are what remote controls were invented for.

5. If you absolutely cannot resist the temptation to directly "ask your doctor" about a drug you saw on a TV ad, try to pose the question in a way that suggests you are asking about the drug and not for it. According to recent survey results, 80 percent of the patients who ask their doctors for drugs they saw on TV get prescriptions for them. (The survey did not dare assess the appropriateness of the prescriptions.) Physicians will not necessarily be honest with you about how comfortable they are writing you an "ask your doctor" prescription. But one good indication is that in a recent survey, the majority of doctors—65 percent and rising—said that direct-to-consumer advertising should decrease or discontinue altogether.

HOW TO AVOID ADVERSE DRUG REACTIONS

1. Read the labels carefully and knowledgeably, and talk to your doctor and pharmacist before taking a new drug, including an OTC drug.

Keep a written record of all your current and past medication use to facilitate that process, and hold on to package inserts. If you add a new drug, you'll want to recheck all their drug interaction warnings. Remember, interactions are listed by a drug's generic name or its class and not by its brand name.

2. Make sure you are taking the fewest drugs possible to address your medical problems. Ask your doctor and pharmacist if any two (or three) of your medications are doing basically the same thing. Include OTC drugs when you ask this.

3. If you take multiple pills several times a day, devise a foolproof system to avoid under- or overdosing yourself. Separate them into compartmentalized containers, or write out a list and check off each dose as you take it.

4. As a precaution, never take any medication with grapefruit juice. It can inhibit many drugs from being normally metabolized through the liver, which can cause a standard dose to become an overdose.

5. Follow dosing instructions. If the drug is labeled to be taken on an empty stomach, or with food, or with plenty of fluids, then do what the label says. If you are unclear how long your stomach has to be empty, or how much food or fluid is necessary, don't be afraid to ask. If you just guess, you could guess wrong.

   If your drug has an alcohol warning on the bottle, make sure you find out if it is an absolute prohibition against mixing the drug with alcohol—because the interaction itself can be dangerous—or simply a warning that the drug will enhance the effects of alcohol. In a social situation the difference could determine whether you skip a dose of your medication (which presents its own dangers), let someone else drive home or simply skip the drink.

6. If you are taking the first dose of a new medication, try to do it at home, and plan on staying there for the next few hours, preferably with someone else around. Never take your first dose of a new medication before driving a car.

7. If you feel you are having an adverse reaction to a drug, do not take the next dose until you have spoken to your doctor. While some drug reactions come with the first pill, others are cumulative. (Some can even come after prolonged or intermittent safe use.)

8. With some pills, it may be prudent to start with a smaller dose and work your way up, although doctors will not always mention this. Many medications will require dose adjustment, or titration, up or down. You're generally better off being titrated up to the right dose than finding out the hard way that your initial dosage was too high.

This is not true of antibiotics, which must be taken full strength for the entire course of the prescription. If you are going to have an adverse reaction to an antibiotic, however, the highest risk tends to be with the first pill.

9. Drug metabolism changes with age. At milestones—especially age sixty—it is appropriate to reconsider dosages of drugs even if you have been taking them for a long time. Discuss this with your doctor.

10. Never take another person's prescription drug even if he or she appears to have the same problem you do.

11. Never take medicines in the dark. You're just asking for trouble.

DRUG INFORMATION AT YOUR FINGERTIPS: A GUIDE TO INSTANT ACCESS

There is much more information available about most prescription drugs than you could possibly want—but, too often, it's hard to find the information that you really need. One of the rare positive results of the FDA's recent reinterpretation of its direct-to-consumer advertising statutes is that drug companies have to be much more responsive to phone, fax and Internet requests for information than they ever were before. Also, many of the government and corporate web sites have been dramatically overhauled. This new guide to drug information reflects those changes.

The first information you need about any drug—whether it is new or just new to you (and your body)—is the complete, most current FDA package insert. If you are having a prescription filled, you should be able to get this from your pharmacist, along with the pharmacy's edited version of the side effects. But you should still take the next step of doing some online research or asking the drug company for more information on the drug you are about to take. My prescription is: always read *before* swallowing.

Listed below are phone, fax and Internet access information for the FDA and major manufacturers, with some tips on how to best use the services they offer. (The companies that don't include fax numbers generally won't accept faxed requests but can respond to your requests by fax.) The manufacturers' web sites vary in quality and ambitiousness; Merck and SmithKline Beecham have two of the best. And both the FDA and the industry are better at providing information about drugs that were approved (or withdrawn) in the past few years, now that they've started doing everything by computer, than they are with the thousands of older medications we take every day. The web sites all tend to have search engines—usually the word *search* with a box next to it that you can click into with the mouse—that allow you to simply type in the name of your medicine and access a list of all the places on the site where you'll find information about it. Always search the brand name as well as the generic name, because there can be variations in the way the drugs are referred to in the files being searched.

When you finish with the FDA and the manufacturer, move on to the advanced course. There are four main sources of free drug information: federal agencies in each country that regulate medications, nationwide or international organizations dedicated to health-related topics, manufacturers and manufacturers' organizations, and various web sites and services that allow you to join discussions with experts or fellow consumers.

If you want to know how the drug has fared in actual clinical practice and check on any reported problems, try running a medical literature search through an online library such as MedLine (a comprehensive medical literature database now available free of charge on the Internet). In addition, many online libraries of academic institutions offer access to services such as Lexis/Nexis and Ovid.

If you are interested in more technical reports on the drug, try the home pages of regulatory bodies in the major countries that approve drugs, or the World Health Organization. Like the FDA, most federal agencies offer computer access to self-contained search programs that allow you to search some of their literature. The FDA is slowly making more types of "public record" material available via computer. For new, hot-button drugs (e.g. Viagra), they are beginning to post medical officers' reviews of New Drug Applications and transcripts of advisory committee meetings. On highly charged political topics, such as the FDA Modernization Act of 1997, the agency even posted all the critiques of the new law from various professional groups and private citizens. This is all good news, although it does beg the question of why some pieces of "public" information are more public than others. Until that question gets answered, however, most drug-application material and minutes of FDA meetings must still be requested the old-fashioned way, on paper.

Once you have gathered as much printed information on a drug as you can handle, it makes sense to try to contact others who have used the drug or are considering it. There are several WWW sites, such as MedHealth, which have question-and-answer forums. These offer consumers "virtual options" on specific questions, often from a panel of experts who communicate through E-mail. MedHealth also has a live chat function which allows you to create a room dedicated to a particular drug-related subject and communicate with others. If you access the web through CompuServe or America Online, their health-related forums also offer forum and chatroom options.

All these services are generally broken down by illnesses rather than medications. The pharmacy-related forums are often empty while the mental health forums, for example, always have lively discussions about medications. This is just as well—you should be exploring not only the drug itself, but how the drug fits into the treatment of your particular illness. There are usually a variety of drugs available to treat an illness, depending on the severity of symptoms and the general health of the patient. It's good to know in what order the most informed, up-to-date physicians try them. For example, for mood stabilization in manic-depressive illness, my wife's physician followed the generally accepted course: first lithium, then the antiseizure meds, then the atypical antipsychotics. If we had known more about the order in which antibiotics are supposed to be used for uncomplicated UTIs, Diane would never have taken Floxin first.

Besides forums and chat rooms, you might also want to try illness-related list-servers, to which you "subscribe"; all the running posts are then sent to your E-mail address. The level of expertise in the list-servers is often a bit higher, although so is the level of illness obsession. Another way to get person-to-person support online is through what is called the Usenet: a system of virtual bulletin boards that allow you to post and receive messages with hundreds of people at the same time.

With this guide, you should be able to easily contact some of the most important organizations, agencies and companies in the legal drug world. Or, if you prefer, you can contact them over the Internet through the *Bitter Pills* page at my own web site, which can be reached at **www.bitter-pills.com** or **www.stephenfried.com.**

U.S. Food and Drug Administration
www.fda.gov/cder/
Phone: 800-532-4440

This is the page for the FDA's Center for Drug Evaluation and Research. By clicking on the drug information icon, you can choose from a number of pharmaceutical-related FDA programs. You can also get information on newly approved drugs from the Consumer Drug Information Page and access the MEDWatch site from that page. (Direct access to MEDWatch: **www.fda.gov/medwatch/index.html** or 800-FDA-1088.) Especially interesting is the Annual Adverse Drug Experience Report, which has the names of any drug which is considered to be potentially dangerous and the number of adverse reactions that have been reported.

Pharmaceutical Companies

Each industry web site has a search engine where you can type in the name of your medicine and get all of the information on the web site concerning it. Most of the sites provide package inserts for their newer drugs online, but you can also call the numbers listed below to order a copy of the package insert and any other literature published by the company.

Abbott Laboratories
www.abbott.com
Phone: 800-222-6883
Fax: 847-938-0644

Agouron Pharmaceuticals
www.agouron.com
Phone: 888-847-2237
Fax: 619-678-8266

American Home Products
www.ahp.com
Phone: 800-934-5556 (for prescription products: Wyeth-Ayerst, Im-
        munex)
        800-322-3129 (for OTC products: Whitehall-Robins, Cyana-
        mid)

Bayer
www.bayerus.com/products/index.html
Phone: 800-229-3727
Fax: 203-812-6516

Bristol-Myers Squibb
www.bms.com
Phone: 800-332-2056
Fax: 609-897-6859

Eli Lilly & Co.
www.lilly.com
Phone: 800-545-5979

Glaxo Wellcome
www.glaxowellcome.com
Phone: 800-722-9292

Hoechst Marion Roussel
www.hmri.com
Phone: 800-552-3656

Johnson & Johnson (includes access to various Ortho-McNeil and
Janssen divisions)
www.jnj.com/who_is_jnj/opsites_index.html
Phone: 800-682-6532

Merck & Co.
www.merck.com
Phone: 800-672-6372

Pfizer
www.pfizer.com
Phone: 800-438-1985

Novartis
www.novartis.com/index.html
Phone: 888-644-8585
Fax: 973-781-8265

Rhone-Poulenc Rorer
www.rpr.rpna.com
Phone: 610-454-8000

Roche
www.roche.com/pharma/Index.htm
Phone: 800-526-6367

Schering-Plough
www.sch-plough.com
Phone: 800-656-9485

GD Searle & Co.
www.searlehealthnet.com
Phone: 800-323-4204

SmithKline Beecham
www.sb.com
Phone: 215-751-4000

Solvay Pharmaceuticals/The Solvay Group
www.solvay.com
Phone: 800-241-1643

Warner-Lambert (includes Parke-Davis)
www.warner-lambert.com
Phone: 800-223-0432

Pharmaceutical Research and Manufacturers of America (PhRMA)
www.pharma.org
Phone: 202-835-3400
Fax: 202-835-3414

Regulatory Agencies in Other Countries

United Kingdom: Medicines Control Agency
www.open.gov.uk/mca/mcahome.htm

Canada: Health Canada
www.hc-sc.gc.ca/hpb-dgps/therapeut/htmleng/dpd.html

This site allows you to search for drugs approved for use in Canada (mostly the same ones available in the U.S.) and get dosage information as well as the generic name and the manufacturer. It can be helpful when researching to see if you have been prescribed a commonly used drug and dosage.

Japan: National Institute of Health Sciences (in English)
www.nihs.go.jp/

South Africa: South African Medicines Control Council
home.intekom.com/pharm

Other Useful Resources

U.S. Pharmacopeia
www.usp.org
Phone: 800-822-8772

Click on the "search" icon and you'll be linked to USP's Drug Information page, which allows you to search your drug (by generic name only) and get warnings and prescribing information. Their "Just Ask" site under the "Patients and Consumers" icon provides helpful general information about proper medication use and allows you to request their printed material (**www.usp.org/pubs/just_ask/index.htm**).

Bitter Pills Hotline: Georgetown University Medical Center Pharmacology Department
www.dml.georgetown.edu/depts/pharmacology
Phone: 202-687-2882

Since the publication of *Bitter Pills*, Dave Flockhart and the Georgetown University Medical School clin-pharm staff have been inundated with questions about ADRs and requests for consultations and physician referrals. They are very generous with their time and expertise, but they cannot treat patients over the phone and they cannot legally dispense medical advice into states where they are not licensed. For this reason, they are likely to initially refer you to a clinical pharmacologist at an academic medical center near where you live. (Keep in mind that if you've already had a drug reaction and have stopped taking the medication, you're less likely to need a clinical pharmacologist than a specialist in the type of symptoms you've been having—a psychopharmacologist or neurologist for CNS symptoms, a cardiologist for heart symptoms.)

Georgetown's Bitter Pills Hotline web site is now set to take questions primarily from physicians, and generally directs patients to the FDA. The site also provides access to Flockhart's Cytochrome P450 web site to help physicians prevent drug interactions by cross-referencing new information, updated monthly, about how different medicines are metabolized in different cytochrome P450 pathways in the liver.

Clinical Pharmacology Online
www.cponline.gsm.com

This excellent, easy-to-use site allows you to search a drug by generic or brand name and returns a page with its chemical structure, how it works and a general description of its effects on the body (including speed and course of treatment). It also includes descriptions of the drug in all its generic forms.

Department of Health and Human Services
www.os.dhhs.gov

This site has a link to the DHHS's Healthfinder site, one of the best new sites (**www.healthfinder.gov**) to provide patients with information on courses of treatment, health care professionals, and support groups in their area. You can also access online medical journals, libraries and dictionaries, and there is a section that provides specialized information for minorities, children, and the elderly.

MedHelp International
www.medhelp.org/index.htm

This is one of the best and most comprehensive sites on the Internet for medical research by consumers. It has links to medical libraries, a Q&A forum and excellent chat rooms.

Pharmaceutical Information Network
www.pharminfo.com

This site provides links to forums and discussion groups on particular infections and diseases.

U.S. Centers for Disease Control and Prevention
www.cdc.gov
Phone: 404-639-3311

This site provides information on all of the CDC's disease-oriented drug initiatives. The best way to navigate the site is to search for a particular disease or virus and then scan the pages it returns. For example, a search for the term "influenza" will bring up the CDC's flu tracking system and give relevant information about the newest developments in flu-related vaccines and treatment drugs.

World Health Organization
www.who.org

By running the term "essential drugs" in the search engine, you can bring up the WHO's Essential Drugs Monitor, which provides readers throughout the world with news about the very latest national drug policies, drug regulation programs and information about rational use of drugs. This site is especially useful for public policy and new regulation information.

U.S. National Institutes of Health
www.nih.gov

This is an excellent page for researching pharmaceuticals, since the NIH now offers a number of free research links for users, including the National Library of Medicine (**www.nlm.nih.gov/**). It is also a good site to visit when looking for national organizations for various illnesses.

MEDLINE
www.nlm.nih.gov/databases/freemedl.html

This search engine allows you to search some 250 medical journals for information about specific health topics and pharmaceuticals, as well as to access other search engines, such as AIDSLINE, HealthSTAR and TOXLINE, which provide more directed specific searches. The page includes information on how to use the system. For a more user-friendly tutorial on how to use MEDLINE, Dr. Felix's Free MEDLINE Page (**www.docnet.org.uk.drfelix**) has several easy-to-use tutorials, as well as access to other sites where MEDLINE is available at no cost and in several languages.

Institute for Safe Medication Practices
www.ismp.org

An international clearinghouse for confidential reports of medication errors, especially in hospitals.

National Center for Complementary and Alternative Medicine
altmed.od.nih.gov
Phone: 888-644-6226

This site provides information on alternate courses of treatment for various illnesses. Do not seek the therapies provided on this site without first consulting a physician.

Healthcare Communications Group
www.healthcg.com

This is one of the top providers of information on AIDS drugs.

Medicine Online
www.meds.com

This site is geared toward cancer drugs and provides information about new or alternative treatment options.

National Alliance for the Mentally Ill
www.nami.org

This site is a premier resource for mental illness information.

Publications

The New England Journal of Medicine
www.nejm.org
Phone: 800-843-6356
Fax: 781-893-0413

This site allows you to see abstracts from the current issue of the journal and search the past-issue archives. You can read only an abstract online, but you have the option of ordering the full text article over the web.

American Medical Association (includes *JAMA*)
www.ama-assn.org/public/journals/jama/jamahome.htm
Phone: 312-670-7827
Fax: 312-464-5831

The AMA provides abstracts from *JAMA*'s current issue, as well as an archive that allows you to download abstracts going back four years. You can request the full text of the article online, or by phone or fax for a small fee.

British Medical Journal
www.bmj.com

You can read the full text version of the latest journal on this site and you can search the archives by keyword and get the full text of older articles.

The Lancet
www.thelancet.com

MED**W**ATCH

THE FDA MEDICAL PRODUCTS REPORTING PROGRAM

For VOLUNTARY reporting
by health professionals of adverse
events and product problems

Page ___ of ___

Form Approved: OMB No. 0910-0291 Expires:12/31/94
See OMB statement on reverse

FDA Use Only

Triage unit
sequence #

A. Patient information

1. Patient identifier

In confidence

2. Age at time of event:

or ___

Date of birth:

3. Sex
☐ female
☐ male

4. Weight
___ lbs
or
___ kgs

B. Adverse event or product problem

1. ☐ Adverse event and/or ☐ Product problem (e.g., defects/malfunctions)

2. Outcomes attributed to adverse event (check all that apply)

☐ death ___ (mo/day/yr)
☐ life-threatening
☐ hospitalization – initial or prolonged

☐ disability
☐ congenital anomaly
☐ required intervention to prevent permanent impairment/damage
☐ other:

3. Date of event (mo/day/yr)

4. Date of this report (mo/day/yr)

5 Describe event or problem

6. Relevant tests/laboratory data, including dates

7 Other relevant history, including preexisting medical conditions (e.g., allergies, race, pregnancy, smoking and alcohol use, hepatic/renal dysfunction, etc.)

C. Suspect medication(s)

1. Name (give labeled strength & mfr/labeler, if known)
#1
#2

2. Dose, frequency & route used
#1
#2

3 Therapy dates (if unknown, give duration) from/to (or best estimate)
#1
#2

4. Diagnosis for use (indication)
#1
#2

5 Event abated after use stopped or dose reduced
#1 ☐ yes ☐ no ☐ doesn't apply
#2 ☐ yes ☐ no ☐ doesn't apply

6. Lot # (if known)
#1
#2

7. Exp. date (if known)
#1
#2

8. Event reappeared after reintroduction
#1 ☐ yes ☐ no ☐ doesn't apply
#2 ☐ yes ☐ no ☐ doesn't apply

9. NDC # (for product problems only)
— —

10 Concomitant medical products and therapy dates (exclude treatment of event)

D. Suspect medical device

1 Brand name

2. Type of device

3. Manufacturer name & address

4 Operator of device
☐ health professional
☐ lay user/patient
☐ other

5. Expiration date (mo day yr)

6.
model # ___
catalog # ___
serial # ___
lot # ___
other #

7 If implanted, give date (mo day yr)

8. If explanted, give date (mo day yr)

9. Device available for evaluation? (Do not send to FDA)
☐ yes ☐ no ☐ returned to manufacturer on ___ (mo/day/yr)

10. Concomitant medical products and therapy dates (exclude treatment of event)

E. Reporter (see confidentiality section on back)

1. Name, address & phone #

2. Health professional? ☐ yes ☐ no

3. Occupation

4 Also reported to
☐ manufacturer
☐ user facility
☐ distributor

5. If you do NOT want your identity disclosed to the manufacturer, place an " X " in this box. ☐

FDA

Mail to: MED**W**ATCH
5600 Fishers Lane
Rockville, MD 20852-9787

or FAX to:
1-800-FDA-0178

FDA Form 3500 (6/93)   Submission of a report does not constitute an admission that medical personnel or the product caused or contributed to the event.

ADVICE ABOUT VOLUNTARY REPORTING

Report experiences with:
- medications (drugs or biologics)
- medical devices (including in-vitro diagnostics)
- special nutritional products (dietary supplements, medical foods, infant formulas)
- other products regulated by FDA

Report SERIOUS adverse events. An event is serious when the patient outcome is:
- death
- life-threatening (real risk of dying)
- hospitalization (initial or prolonged)
- disability (significant, persistent or permanent)
- congenital anomaly
- required intervention to prevent permanent impairment or damage

Report even if:
- you're not certain the product caused the event
- you don't have all the details

Report product problems – quality, performance or safety concerns such as:
- suspected contamination
- questionable stability
- defective components
- poor packaging or labeling

How to report:
- just fill in the sections that apply to your report
- use section C for all products except medical devices
- attach additional blank pages if needed
- use a separate form for each patient
- report either to FDA or the manufacturer (or both)

Important numbers:
- 1-800-FDA-0178 to FAX report
- 1-800-FDA-7737 to report by modem
- 1-800-FDA-1088 for more information or to report quality problems
- 1-800-822-7967 for a VAERS form for vaccines

If your report involves a serious adverse event with a device and it occurred in a facility outside a doctor's office, that facility may be legally required to report to FDA and/or the manufacturer. Please notify the person in that facility who would handle such reporting.

Confidentiality: The patient's identity is held in strict confidence by FDA and protected to the fullest extent of the law. The reporter's identity may be shared with the manufacturer unless requested otherwise. However, FDA will not disclose the reporter's identity in response to a request from the public, pursuant to the Freedom of Information Act.

FDA Form 3500-back   **Please Use Address Provided Below – Just Fold In Thirds, Tape and Mail**

Department of Health and Human Services
Public Health Service
Food and Drug Administration
Rockville, MD 20857

Official Business
Penalty for Private Use $300

BUSINESS REPLY MAIL
FIRST CLASS MAIL   PERMIT NO. 946 ROCKVILLE, MD

MED**W**ATCH
The FDA Medical Products Reporting Program
Food and Drug Administration
5600 Fishers Lane
Rockville, MD 20852-9787

Medication Diary

For each drug in your diary, try to write down the following information:
1) Name of drug: brand and/or generic
2) Type of drug (including drug class if applicable, e.g. "quinolone antibiotic" instead of "antibiotic") and condition you're taking it for
3) Dosage: pill size, number of times (X) you take it daily
4) How taken: with/without food, time of day
5) Side effects: any you've experienced, and any reaction that correlates with these effects (e.g. "stomach upset if not taken with food")
6) Prescription or over-the-counter (OTC), name of prescribing physician

Sample: Synthroid (levothyroxine); thyroid hormone; 0.125 mg 1X; on rising, with water; none; prescription, Dr. Pratorius

Drugs you take every day:

1. _____

_____

2. _____

_____

3. _____

_____

4. _____

_____

5. _____

_____

Drugs you take periodically (including medications for allergies, pain, headache, constipation, etc.)

1. _____

_____

2. _____

_____

3. _____

_____

4. _____

_____

5. _____

_____

Drugs you have taken successfully in the past (go as far back as possible)

_____

_____

_____

_____

Drugs you have had problems taking in the past (include reason and severity of problem, e.g. stomach upset or didn't work or caused a seizure/CNS reaction)

_____

_____

_____

ACKNOWLEDGMENTS

This book grew out of my attempt to make sense of my wife's drug reaction through a series of investigative projects made possible by various editors at the magazines I have called home. It began at *Philadelphia* magazine—where I have lived for the better part of sixteen years—with editor Eliot Kaplan, who did a terrific job balancing his professional and personal interests in the story and luckily made me throw out the original lead. Many other people at *Philadelphia* helped on those pieces or just generally made daily life more interesting over these years. But I'm especially grateful to Loren Feldman, who edited the follow-ups; Bob Huber, who did thoughtful copyediting and graciously read book drafts for me; and Betsy Brecht and Frank Baseman for visual consults; as well as former staffers Tim Haas, who copyedited, draft-read and computer baby-sat me; Andrew Corsello, who did a constructively brutal job of fact-checking the original story; and Ken Newbaker, who did the original type treatments echoed in the book.

I may not have written another word about drugs after those first pieces if it hadn't been for Linton Weeks, who was then my editor at *The Washington Post Magazine.* It was his idea to take my original story about Diane and Floxin and use it to explore some of the broader concerns about drugs that Ray Woosley and Dave Flockhart were raising. He left the magazine before this hybrid article could be perfected, and his boss, Bob Thompson, ultimately showed me how to make it work. Bob was also instrumental in several other stories that helped form this book.

Wayne Lawson, my editor at *Vanity Fair,* insisted over drinks at the Algonquin that I undertake the investigation of Omniflox, during which I learned how to find the drug drama between the lines of fine print. Liza Mundy, who inherited me at the *Post Magazine,* edited the hell out of my piece on Kay Jamison and taught me a lot about covering esoteric subjects like mental health care with some bite—a lesson that helped me finish my year-long project on psychiatry at the Institute of Pennsylvania Hospital for *Philadelphia.*

All these editors and stories influenced my decision in mid-1995 to begin writing a book about drugs (as did timely pep talks from Barry Jacobs, Tom Junod, Steven Levy and Randy Rothenberg). I worked on

Bitter Pills nonstop from then on, test-driving other parts of it in magazine form first: I wrote about Retin-A and guinea pigs for *Philadelphia*; *Vanity Fair* sent me into the world of AIDS drugs (with legwork by Craig Offman), although the piece ended up in *The Washington Post Magazine* and was rebuilt thanks to detail man John Cotter; and Klara Glowczewska at *Condé Nast Traveler* sent me to the Amsterdam pharmaco-epi conference.

Besides these individual pieces, several magazine contracts kept me afloat during the time I worked on this book, as well as the time I spent away from it (and the world) while helping take care of my father: thanks to Graydon Carter at *Vanity Fair,* Ruth Whitney at *Glamour* and Herb Lipson and David Lipson at *Philadelphia.* Also, thanks to Lisa Bain, my former editor at *Glamour,* and Tracy Hill of the Press Network for their support on other stories while I wrote.

I have never worked on a project where the cooperation of sources, and their encouragement, has meant so much. Thanks to Dave Flockhart, Stacy Phillips, Ana Szarfman, Steve Sheller, Wally Kennedy, Mac Lumpkin, Ray Woosley, Sue and Kent Smith, Alice McGee, Dan Sigelman, Sid Wolfe, Mike Blum, David Graham, Kay Jamison and Richard Wyatt, Brian Strom, Jerry Avorn, Graham Dukes, Andrew Herxheimer, and Ellen t'Hoen; the press offices at the FDA, the IMS, Merck and Abbott; Diane's patient docs Michael Miller, Amy Finkelstein and Steven Galetta; Bantam's Barb Burg and Chris Artis; and all the Floxies. I'm especially indebted to the Floxed medical writer I mention early in the book, who faxed me journal articles and encouraging notes literally for years after my original piece. A book like this one grows only if your interest is continually renewed after being thoroughly exhausted. It was often her faxes, or impassioned calls and letters from her fellow Floxies, that re-piqued my curiosity.

I had terrific research assistance on this project, which has gone on for so long that some of the original interns now have better jobs than I do. Thanks to Jennifer Kornreich, Dennis Berman, Sandy Stahl, Melissa Wagenberg, Ben Brody and Sabrina Rubin (both for her research and, later, for lending me her drug-rep interview notes). But I owe the biggest thanks to the invaluable Kate Khatib, who did the lion's share of the research and fact-checking, some of it twice, and stuck with this book for nearly two years. She also did the compilation of the Web sites.

Mark Hunter and Jerry Fried read early drafts of the manuscript for me; Sarah Hultman gave us a major assist on fact-checking; the Ayres/ Organic household put me up during many Washington trips; both

Sandy Bloom and her cabin contributed greatly to our mental health (as did Isaiah's murals); the Sunday Morning Invitational basketball players and Jim Gorman helped me maintain some semblance of physical health.

Several journalists offered assistance along the way. Thomas Moore gave me a generous telephone briefing about the usual suspects of drug safety when I was starting out, and his book *Deadly Medicine* was a good resource. Dan Golden of *The Boston Globe* shared the material he had gathered for one of the first good stories about Omniflox. Joe Graedon ably straddled the line between colleague and source and was always available to answer questions. Jonathan Kaye, then of the *Daily Pennsylvanian,* shared a lot of his research on Albert Kligman, and Tim O'Brien of the *New Jersey Law Journal* was very helpful during the time we were covering J&J's problems with the Justice Department. John Schwartz at *The Washington Post* passed on some FIAU phone numbers but, more important, his FDA and science coverage was an invaluable resource, as were the regular coverage in *The New York Times* by Philip J. Hilts and Lawrence K. Altman, *The Wall Street Journal* by Elyse Tanouye and Ralph King, *U.S. News & World Report, Money,* the *Financial Times, Science* and, of course, my hometown *Philadelphia Inquirer,* where Donald Drake, Marion Uhlman and Huntly Collins have all done provocative enterprise reporting on drugs.

I met my wonderful editor at Bantam, Ann Harris, the way writers are supposed to meet wonderful editors but rarely do: she sent me a blind fan letter after reading one of my magazine pieces. I have never met a book editor with her level of intellectual and emotional engagement: I'd say she's the last of a breed, except I'm simply not sure there ever *was* anyone else like her before.

As usual, my agent, Loretta Fidel, did a great job selling this book and keeping me sane while I wrote it. Anyway, if she tired of hearing me whine about it, she never let on.

Thanks to our families, the clans Fried, Ayres, Schultz and Caplan; and any previously unacknowledged bowlers—Joel and Lisa, Kim and Moon, Ronnie and Noel, Daph and Frank, Sally and Rob, Reenie, Doug and Jill, Geoff and Meg, and Dan.

I can't say enough about my wife's bravery and honesty in letting me write about her illness, and the amazing amount of work she put into the researching and editing of this book. She informs me, however, that I have already said too much.

SELECTED BIBLIOGRAPHY

Ahmad, Syed Rizwanuddin. *Bitter Facts About Drugs*. Karuchi: HAI Pakistan, 1990.

Andreasen, Nancy C. *The Broken Brain*. New York: Harper & Row, 1984.

Barondes, Samuel H. *Molecules and Mental Illness*. New York: Scientific American Library, 1993.

Berkow, Robert, ed. *The Merck Manual of Diagnosis and Therapy*. Rahway, NJ: Merck & Co., Inc., 1992.

Breggin, Peter R. *Talking Back to Prozac*. New York: St. Martin's Press, 1994.

Burkett, Elinor. *The Gravest Show on Earth*. New York: Houghton Mifflin, 1995.

Burkholz, Herbert. *The FDA Follies*. New York: Basic Books, 1994.

Byock, Ira. *Dying Well*. New York: Riverhead, 1997.

Chetley, Andrew. *A Healthy Business?* London: Zed Books, 1990.

———. *Problem Drugs*. London: Zed Books, 1995.

Crenshaw, Theresa Larsen. *Sexual Pharmacology*. New York: Norton, 1996.

Davis, Peter, ed. *Contested Ground*. New York: Oxford University Press, 1996.

Drake, Donald, and Marian Uhlman. *Making Medicine, Making Money*. Kansas City: Andrews and McMeel, 1993.

Dreyfus, Jack. *A Remarkable Medicine Has Been Overlooked*. New York: Dreyfus Medical Foundation, 1988.

Drug Information Association. *Adverse Events*. New York: Pergamon Press, 1987.

Duesenberg, Peter H. *Inventing the AIDS Virus*. Washington: Regnery, 1996.

Dukes, Graham. *The Effects of Drug Regulation*. Lancaster: MTP Press, 1985.

———. *Responsibility for Drug-Induced Injury*. Amsterdam: Elsevier, 1988.

———. *Side Effects of Drugs Essays*. Amsterdam: Elsevier, 1990.

Fink, Paul Jay, and Alan Tasman, eds. *Stigma and Mental Illness.* Washington, DC: American Psychiatric Press, 1992.

Goodwin, Fredrick K., and Kay Redfield Jamison. *Manic-Depressive Illness.* New York: Oxford University Press, 1990.

Graedon, Joe, and Teresa Graedon. *The People's Pharmacy.* New York: St. Martin's Press, 1996.

Hamilton, Jean A., et al., eds. *Pharmacology from a Feminist Perspective.* New York: Haworth, 1995.

Hansson, Olle. *Inside Ciba-Geigy.* Penang: International Organization of Consumers Unions, 1989.

Harris, Richard. *The Real Voice.* New York: Macmillan, 1964.

Illich, Ivan. *Medical Nemesis.* New York: Pantheon, 1976.

Jamison, Kay Redfield. *Touched with Fire.* New York: Free Press, 1993.

———. *An Unquiet Mind.* New York: Knopf, 1995.

Kallet, Arthur, and F. J. Schlink. *100,000,000 Guinea Pigs.* New York: Vanguard Press, 1933.

Knightly, Phillip, Harold Evans, Elaine Potter, Marjorie Wallace. *Suffer the Children.* New York: Viking Press, 1979.

Kramer, Peter. *Listening to Prozac.* New York: Viking, 1993.

Lang, Ronald W. *The Politics of Drugs.* Westmead: Saxon House, 1974.

LaPlante, Eve. *Seized.* New York: HarperCollins, 1993.

Liebenau, Jonathan Michael. *Medical Science and Medical Industry.* Baltimore: Johns Hopkins, 1987.

Maeder, Thomas. *Adverse Reactions.* New York: William Morrow, 1994.

Mintz, Morton. *At Any Cost.* New York: Pantheon Books, 1985.

———. *By Prescription Only.* Boston: Houghton Mifflin, 1967.

———. *The Therapeutic Nightmare.* Boston: Houghton Mifflin, 1965.

Moore, Thomas. *Deadly Medicine.* New York: Simon & Schuster, 1995.

Nelson, Gary. *Pharmaceutical Company Histories.* Bismarck: Woodbine, 1983.

Physicians' Desk Reference. Medical Economics Data.

Project Inform. *The HIV Drug Book.* New York: Pocket Books, 1995.

Reekie, Duncan, and Michael Weber. *Profits, Politics and Drugs.* London: Macmillan, 1979.

Rybacki, James J., and James W. Long. *The Essential Guide to Prescription Drugs.* New York: HarperPerennial, 1997.

Shilts, Randy. *And the Band Played On.* New York: St. Martin's Press, 1987.

Silverman, Harold. *The Pill Book.* New York: Bantam, 1994.

Silverman, Milton. *Bad Medicine.* Stanford, CA: Stanford University Press, 1992.

————. *The Drugging of the Americas.* Berkeley: University of California Press, 1976.

————. *Pills, Profits & Politics.* Berkeley: University of California Press, 1974.

————. *Pills & the Public Purse.* Berkeley: University of California Press, 1981.

Soda, T., ed. *Drug-Induced Sufferings: Medical, Pharmaceutical and Legal Aspects.* Amsterdam: Excerpta Medica, 1980.

Strom, Brian L., ed. *Pharmacoepidemiology.* New York: John Wiley & Sons, 1994.

Strom, Brian L., and Giampaolo Velo, eds. *Drug Epidemiology and Post-Marketing Surveillance.* New York: Plenum, 1990.

Urquhart, John. *Risk Watch.* New York: Facts on File, 1984.

Vanderbilt, Gloria. *A Mother's Story.* New York: Knopf, 1996.

Werth, Barry. *The Billion-Dollar Molecule.* New York: Touchstone, 1994.

Wolfe, Sidney M., Christopher M. Coley, and the Public Citizen Health Research Group. *Pills That Don't Work.* New York: Farrar Straus Giroux, 1981.

Wolfe, Sidney M., Rose-Ellen Hope, and the Public Citizen Health Research Group. *Worst Pills, Best Pills.* Washington: Public Citizen, 1993.

INDEX

ABOUT THE AUTHOR

Stephen Fried is an award-winning investigative journalist and essayist. His work has appeared frequently in *Vanity Fair, The Washington Post Magazine, GQ, Glamour*, and *Philadelphia* magazine. His articles on drug safety brought him his second consecutive National Magazine Award, the highest honor in magazine journalism, and his commentary on pharmaceutical issues has appeared in *The New York Times, The Washington Post,* and *The International Herald-Tribune.*

His previous book was *Thing of Beauty: The Tragedy of Supermodel Gia*, the widely praised biography of model Gia Carangi and post-mortem on her era.

Fried lives in Philadelphia with his wife, fiction writer Diane Ayres.

(www.stephenfried.com)